Jens Müller
Julius Wiedemann (Ed.)

Essay by
R. Roger Remington

Essay by
R. Roger Remington

LOGO
MODERNISM

TASCHEN

Contents

Logo
Jens Müller

Pick up any book about logos published 50 or 60 years ago and sooner or later you will come across references to how simplicity and directness serve as a counterbalance to our "complicated world." Since time immemorial the world has been perceived as complex, and the need for simple, clear signs is nothing new. We have to realize that these and similar statements made in the mid-20th century were part of the efforts of contemporary designers to free themselves from what they saw as the mystique surrounding commercial artists. The birth of modern graphics coincided with the moment when modern graphic designers were striving to create clear-cut systems and concepts rather than to display artistic genius. Of course, the late 19th century had produced a few design pioneers, which makes it almost impossible to determine exactly when the change in the perception of graphic design occurred. However, from the 1940s onwards, what might be termed Modernism in graphic design began to take hold. Over the next two decades, as international businesses and small enterprises alike set about revamping their corporate image, Modernist graphics started to appear across the globe in every area of graphic design. Perhaps the most obvious and most enduring changes are the result of the Modernist approach to logos. Representational images made way for simple shapes. Today, the zeitgeist, trends and technical advances are leading to different solutions, the roots of which are to be found in the design parameters set in the heyday of Modernism. It is worth revisiting that era.

Ethnologists, art historians and scholars have researched the origins of signs and symbols, producing a vast body of literature. While the subject of this book is the nature and design of the Modernist logo, it is also interesting to travel further back in history and focus on some of the logo's forerunners. The historiography of design takes us back to the dawn of human history, shedding light on the cave paintings of southern France and the rock art of North America and southern Africa. Rightly so, for it was from these, humanity's earliest forms of visual expression, that script and written language were developed. Here, too, we are sure to find the roots of the modern logo. However, if we are looking for indisputable precursors of the logo, it helps to establish what the precise purpose of the medium was and continues to be, namely a label and a distinguishing mark.

Researchers have regularly found notches or grooves on pottery dating from the dawning of the advanced civilizations of Asia, Africa and the Americas [01]. These were both makers' marks and quality indicators. Chinese and Roman ceramics of somewhat later date bear even more distinctive markings that can easily be interpreted as direct forerunners of what would later become logos. So-called mason's marks have been found in tombs and other ancient structures dating back as far as 2000 BC. These abstract line graphics, each with its own specific characteristics, referred to a particular family or workshop (→ 02). From this time, it was also the custom to brand farm animals. The current meaning of the word "brand," applied to an organization's trademark, goes back to a technique developed in much earlier times. The process of creating a logo out of signs and symbols was already practiced several thousand years ago. Keepers of livestock branded them with a single initial letter, or several interwoven letters, to identify the farmer or farming community to which they belonged. In the Middle Ages it was also customary for soldiers to be branded with the monogram or emblem of their warlord (→ 03).

A monogram, as its etymology suggests, was originally a single letter with embellishments of some kind. Today what we mean by a monogram is a design based on the initials of a person's given and family name. In the days of the Holy Roman Empire this type of monogram was most commonly used in European culture by monarchs and other rulers (→ 04). It might consist of a handwritten signature or as a stamp or seal for use in official communications. These practical ways of identifying the sender of a document were later adopted by entrepreneurs and artists (→ 05). One of the best-known and most striking examples of a monogram was the "AD" used for the first time in 1498 by the artist Albrecht Dürer.

Crusades, jousting tournaments and battles for land and other possessions all helped to shape medieval society and politics. In Europe, the High Middle Ages, between the 11th and 13th centuries, coincided with the introduction of heraldic devices—images of birds and animals, such as the eagle or the lion, symbolizing power, combined with colorful motifs and insignia of supremacy such as a crown, key or scepter (→ 06). Such crests might represent estates, cities or noble families and their possessions, helping to distinguish one from another. Similarly, professional associations and other groups developed their own signs and symbols. Skilled artisans formed guilds, whose coats of arms bore emblems associated with their crafts (→ 07). A trade guild's coat of arms was not only an early version of a seal of quality. At a time of widespread illiteracy, it was also a much-needed badge of recognition for business people operating in only recently established towns and cities.

In Japan in the same historical period, *mon* ("signs" or "emblems") came into being. Based on stylized representations of plants or animals, usually monochrome and surrounded by a circle, these were first used to identify the imperial family and the families of the shoguns, or hereditary military commanders. From 1600 onwards they were adopted by people of all social classes (→ 08). Like European coats of arms, they were handed down from generation to generation in accordance with a specific set of rules. For many years, *mon* played only a minor role in everyday Japanese life but with the passage of time they came to be used as identifying marks for a family business. The famous logo of the automobile manufacturer Mitsubishi is an abstract combination of the *mon* of the two founding families.

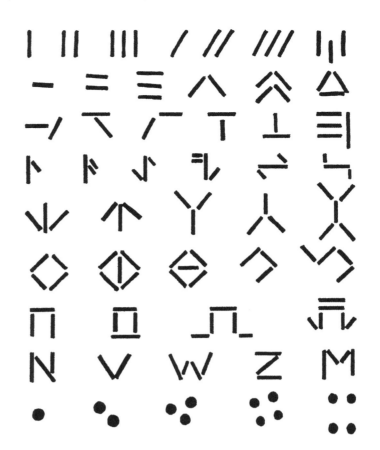

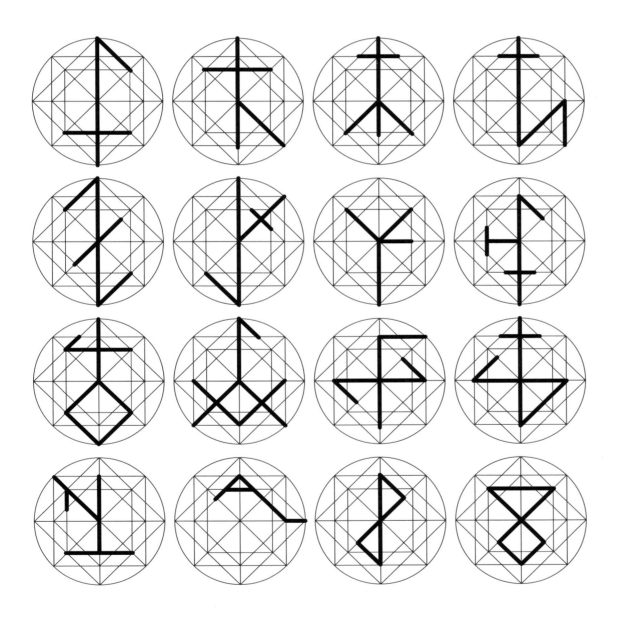

01

Makers' marks on Greek
earthenware pottery,
c. 2300 BC

Herstellerkennungen auf
griechischen Tongefäßen,
ca. 2300 v. Chr.

Marques de propriétaires
sur des poteries grecques,
vers 2300 av. J.-C.

02

Gothic mason's marks in
St Stephen's Cathedral, Vienna

Gotische Steinmetzzeichen
aus dem Wiener Stephansdom

Marques de tâcherons
gothiques, cathédrale
Saint-Étienne de Vienne

No. 5.

No. 4

No. 1

Figura 10.
Cap. 10.

No. 3.

No. 2.

03

Medieval soldiers being branded,
copper engraving, 1616
(detail)

Mittelalterliche Brandmarkung
von Soldaten; Kupferstich
aus dem Jahr 1616 (Detail)

Marquage de soldats au
fer rouge. Gravure sur
cuivre de 1616 (détail)

With industrialization in the second half of the 18th century, nearly every area of commerce underwent gradual change. Companies extended their geographic areas of operation and an entirely new class of customer emerged, as factory workers earned considerably more than their forebears. Urban development led to different consumer behavior and an increase in the supply of goods, which in turn sparked off the product market. Under these new selling conditions it was more vital than ever before to distinguish one supplier from another, whether selling food, furniture or fashion. In many cases, elements from a family coat of arms became a company's first logo. For example, in 1878, one of the founders of the German stationery manufacturer Pelikan registered his family crest, the pelican, as the company trademark and brand name. Pelikan owes its continuing international fame to that decision [→ 09]. In the 19th century, easily recognizable figure depictions like the pelican were a common form of visual imagery. Following in the tradition of trade guilds' coats of arms, a logo was always intended to create a clear, eye-catching link with the advertiser and/or its products. At this period, there were very few examples of abstract, non-representational signs. One of the earliest was the logo of the English William Bass brewery, whose products have displayed a red triangle since around 1875 [→ 10]. Revolutionary for its time, the logo was streets ahead of all the competition and even now stands out from other brewers' more traditional visual identities. An interesting historical detail: the Bass triangle was the first-ever trademark to be registered in the United Kingdom and is hence the most strongly protected.

With a few exceptions, Modernist logos only began to appear in any number in the 1920s. Influenced by the De Stijl and Bauhaus art and design movements, the still-new discipline of commercial art changed significantly at this time. Turning to abstract shapes and skilfully intermingling them with geometric forms, commercial artists created designs quite unlike the figurative images that had so far dominated their work. Oskar Schlemmer's 1922 Bauhaus logo is a perfect example of the move towards abstract graphics [→ 11]. Writing in April 1926 in *Die Form*, the magazine of the Deutsche Werkbund (German Association of Craftsmen), the designer Johannes Molzahn, a close associate of the Bauhaus group although never a member, traced the thought process of an avant-garde artist bringing a logo design to fruition. "The meaning of the brand is paramount and the form is determined only by visual and mechanical laws that are intrinsic to design. Here, as in engineering, function dictates form. In reality, the creation of a brand is not so much an artistic problem as a technical and scientific one, involving both wit and imagination. Just like a machine, an aesthetically pleasing form is no more than the result of perfect construction combined with the objective of achieving the best performance." This philosophy is immediately apparent in groundbreaking logo designs like those of Wilhelm Deffke or Karl Schulpig [→ 12]. Many of the succeeding generation of international designers, such as Paul Rand and Yusaku Kamekura, acknowledge the Bauhaus and its achievements as a major influence on their creations.

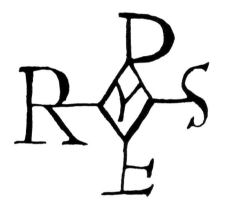

04

Monograms of Frankish and
Holy Roman/German emperors,
between 768 and 921

Monogramme fränkischer und
römisch-deutscher Herrscher
zwischen 768 und 921

Monogrammes de souverains
francs et romains germaniques
entre 768 et 921

12

Even so, it was not until the 1940s that the Modernist logo truly began to play a major role in new designs or in the reworking of existing ones. Ultimately, it was the Swiss Style typography, initially developed by 1920s avant-garde designers and later known as International Typographic Style, that helped Modernist design to achieve its final global breakthrough in the 1950s [→ 13]. Switzerland escaped much of the upheaval caused by World War II, which meant that its designers could continue to develop ideas and applications of abstract graphics, which in turn went on to inspire the new, post-war generation of designers in neighboring countries. One major contribution to the spread of the Swiss Style came from the magazine *Graphis*, founded in Zurich in 1944, and its yearbook *Graphis Annual*. The annual in particular, with its selection of Modernist graphic art from all over the world, was considered the definitive trade publication and influenced designers on every continent. In retrospect, the Swiss Style appears to have represented a finite period in the history of design which set the artistic tone, especially for such media as book jackets and posters, but which underwent partial change as new influences, such as Pop Art, began to emerge. However, its impact on the field of logo design was so radical that graphic art of the period can be seen as a genuine turning point in the history of the medium. Fundamental design parameters and methods changed, as did people's perception of the logo. Now, for the first time, as logos came into use across the board, designers were free to experiment with them.

Throughout the 1960s, as integrated corporate design systems became the norm, the logo's field of application broadened even further. The unified company image with its specific colors, typography and imagery was gradually catching on. The designer's individual method of dealing with signs and symbols was superseded by a rational, systematic approach [→ 14+15]. Until the introduction of the design manual, many companies routinely used different and often playful variations on their logos for different media of communication, such as posters, annual reports and such like. Even so, apart from barely noticeable alterations in a very few logos, these variations had little effect. Only the digital revolution in media production in the 1990s brought about real change in logo design. To begin with, few designers exploited the extra possibilities offered by digital image processing and most updates to logos were purely cosmetic. Adding a drop shadow or introducing other three-dimensional effects were among the most common. In recent years, purely 3-D logos have become increasingly popular [→ 16]. Because of their complexities of color and design, 3-D logos cannot be produced in single-color versions without losing important details of the design. The old ground rules, which made it impossible to include color or too many details because of reproduction problems, no longer apply thanks to advances in printing technology.

Today it seems that the logo gives designers greater freedom than ever before, but it also makes it more vital than ever to stick to a manageable number of basic design parameters. For this book several thousand Modernist logos—mostly dating from the 1950s to the 1980s—have been collected and formally analyzed. The three main chapters, entitled "Geometric", "Effect" and "Typographic", which in turn are divided into numerous sub-categories, take this representative selection of logos and pinpoint the most important basic forms, as well as the design possibilities they offer. Leafing through the collection, it might seem at first glance that there is nothing more to add. On closer inspection, it becomes clear that by combining the design parameters introduced in the book there is still much to discover about the process of design.

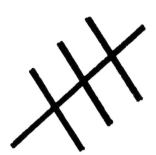

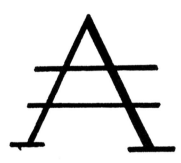

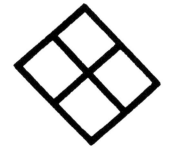

05

London coopers' monograms,
second half of the 18th century

Monogramme Londoner
Tonnenmacher (zweite Hälfte
des 18. Jahrhunderts)

Monogrammes de tonneliers
londoniens (seconde moitié
du XVIIIᵉ siècle)

15

Typical examples of family and trade guild coats of arms

Typische Darstellungen verschiedener Familien- und Zunftwappen

Représentations caractéristiques de différents blasons familiaux et corporatifs

Logo

Jens Müller

Nimmt man Publikationen über Logos zur Hand, die vor 50 oder 60 Jahren veröffentlicht worden sind, wird dort früher oder später stets auf die „komplizierte Welt" verwiesen, in der das Elementare oder Vereinfachte zum Ausgleich und zur Bewältigung dient. Die Welt wird also schon eine ganze Weile als komplex wahrgenommen und der Bedarf an einfachen und eindeutigen Zeichen ist nicht ganz neu. Man muss diese und ähnliche Ausführungen aus der Mitte des 20. Jahrhunderts heute neben anderen Aspekten als versachlichende Legitimation von Gestaltern verstehen, die sich von der mystischen Aura des Werbekünstlers befreien wollten. Denn die Geburtsstunde der modernen Grafik geht einher mit jener des modernen Grafikdesigners, der sich statt von künstlerischem Genie eher von Nüchternheit, Konzept und Systematik lenken ließ. Selbstverständlich gab es einzelne Vordenker auch vor dieser Zeit, gegen Ende des 19. Jahrhunderts, und eine Bestimmung des exakten Zeitpunktes der Veränderung des Berufsverständnisses ist kaum möglich. Dennoch ist zu erkennen, dass sich ab den 1940er-Jahren so etwas wie die Moderne im Grafikdesign durchzusetzen begann. Spätestens in den beiden folgenden Jahrzehnten sind Arbeiten neuen Stils in nahezu allen Teilen der Erde und in sämtlichen Bereichen des Grafikdesigns zu finden. Internationale Konzerne wie auch lokale Kleinunternehmen verändern ihren visuellen Auftritt. Der modernistische Ansatz hat beim Medium Logo vielleicht die deutlichsten und nachhaltigsten Veränderungen mit sich gebracht. Gegenständliche Zeichen wurden endgültig von einfachen, grafischen Formen abgelöst. Trend, Zeitgeist und technische Weiterentwicklung führen heute zwar zu veränderten Lösungen, ihre Wurzeln liegen dennoch in den Gestaltungsparametern jener Hochphase des Modernismus. Ein Blick zurück lohnt also.

Ethnologen, Kunsthistoriker und Designwissenschaftler haben die Ursprünge von Zeichen und Symbolen ausführlich erforscht und umfangreiche Literatur dazu verfasst. Auch wenn in diesem Buch das modernistische Logo und seine Gestaltungsformen im Vordergrund stehen, ist es interessant noch etwas weiter in die Geschichte zurückzugehen und den Fokus auf verschiedene Vorfahren des Mediums Logo zu lenken. Die designbezogene Geschichtsschreibung wirft ihr Licht vielfach bis in die Frühzeit der Menschheit und führt die Höhlenbilder Südfrankreichs oder Felszeichnungen in Nordamerika und Südafrika an. Zu Recht, denn aus diesen ersten visuellen Äußerungen der Menschheit entwickelten sich letztlich Schrift sowie geschriebene Sprache. Und mit Sicherheit finden sich hier auch die fundamentalen Wurzeln des heutigen Logos. Sucht man aber nach ganz eindeutigen Vorfahren, ist es zunächst hilfreich sich der bis heute unverändert zweckgebundenen Aufgabe des Mediums Logo bewusst zu werden: Kennzeichnung und Unterscheidung.

Aus der Entstehungszeit früher Hochkulturen in Asien, Afrika und Amerika datieren keramische Arbeiten, auf denen Forscher

THESE ARE THE ARMES OF ALL O

Dyers. Brewers. Letherſellers. Pewterers. Barbers-Chirurgeons. Armourers. White-Bakers. Wax-Chandlers.

OF THE HONOVRABLE CITTY OF

Curriers. Masons. Plumbers. Inholders. Founders. Embroiderers. Poulters. Cookes.

OF WHICH THE LORD MAIOR IS

Fruiterers. Scriveners. Bottle makers and Horners. Stationers. Marblers. Wooll-packers. Farriers. Paviours. Lorinors.

07

Overview of all the coats of
arms of the London trade guilds
between 1627 and 1677

Übersicht aller Wappen der
Zünfte von London zwischen
1627 und 1677

Vue d'ensemble des blasons
de toutes les corporations de
Londres entre 1627 et 1677

THER WORSHIPFVLL COMPANIES

Tallow-Chandlers. Cutlers. Girdlers. Butchers. Sadlers. Carpenters. Cordwainers. Painters

LONDON BESIDES THE TWELVE OVT

Coopers. Brick-layers and Tylers. Bowyers. Fletchers. Blacksmithes. Ioyners. Plaisterers. Weavers.

ALLWAYES CHOSEN.

Brown-bakers. Woodmongers. Vpholsters. Turners. Glasiers. Clearkes. Watermen. Apothecaries.

systematische Einkerbungen fanden [01]. Diese dienten der Markierung unterschiedlicher Hersteller und als Hinweise auf abweichende Qualitäten. Auf chinesischer und römischer Keramik etwas späteren Datums waren konkretere Kennzeichnungen von noch größerer Eindeutigkeit zu finden, die endgültig als direkte Vorläufer der späteren Markenzeichen zu interpretieren sind. Auf Grabmälern und anderen historischen Bauwerken, die bis auf 2000 v. Chr. zurückdatiert werden können, fanden sich sogenannte Steinmetzzeichen. Diese abstrakten Strichgrafiken verwiesen auf unterschiedliche Familien oder Werkstätten und hatten ihre eigene Systematik [02]. Zur gleichen Zeit war es bereits auch üblich Nutztiere mittels Brandzeichen zu markieren. Das heutige Verständnis des Begriffs „Branding" für die Kennzeichnung einer Marke geht auf diese in der Frühzeit entwickelte Technik zurück. Für das bis heute praktizierte Verfahren der Brandzeichnung wurden schon vor mehreren tausend Jahren eigene Zeichen und Symbole entwickelt. In der Nutztierhaltung wurden dazu einzelne oder verbundene Buchstaben verwendet, die für den Besitzer oder eine Farmgemeinschaft standen. In der Zeit mittelalterlicher Schlachten war es auch üblich Soldaten per Brandmarkung mit dem Signum oder Monogramm ihrer Kriegsherren zu kennzeichnen [03].

Ein solches Monogramm war, wie sich etymologisch ableiten lässt, ursprünglich ein ausgestalteter Einzelbuchstabe. Heute verstehen wir darunter vor allem die kombinierte Gestaltung von Anfangsbuchstaben eines Vor- und Nachnamens. Schon in die Zeit des Heiligen Römischen Reichs Deutscher Nation zurückdatierend, ist diese Buchstabenmarke vor allem in der europäischen Kultur ein von Herrschern und Monarchen verwendetes Zeichen [04]. Es wurde sowohl als handschriftliche Signatur wie auch in Form von Stempel oder Siegel für die administrative Kommunikation eingesetzt. Diese praktischen Absenderkennungen machten sich später auch Unternehmer und Künstler zunutze [05]. Eines der bis heute bekanntesten und markantesten Monogramme ist beispielsweise das von Albrecht Dürer 1498 erstmals verwendete „AD".

Kreuzzüge, das ritterliche Turnierwesen sowie Kämpfe um Land und andere Besitztümer bestimmten Gesellschaft und Politik des Mittelalters. Zur Zeit seiner europäischen Hochblüte zwischen dem 11. und 13. Jahrhundert entstanden die Wappen: gegenständliche Darstellungen von Kraft ausstrahlenden Tieren wie dem Adler oder dem Löwen, verbunden mit farbigen Mustern und Darstellungen von Machtinsignien wie Krone, Schlüssel oder Zepter [06]. Sie kennzeichneten Ländereien, Adelsfamilien oder Städte sowie deren Besitztümer und halfen, sich voneinander abzugrenzen. Parallel entwickelten auch nicht adelige Berufsgruppen und andere Gemeinschaften eigene Zeichen und Symbole. Handwerker schlossen sich zu Zünften zusammen und entwickelten Wappen, die gegenständlich eine visuelle Kurzform der jeweiligen Tätigkeit abbildeten [07]. Diese Zunftwappen waren nicht nur eine Art frühes Qualitätssiegel, sondern aufgrund des noch weit verbreiteten Analphabetismus eine notwendige Kennzeichnung für die Unternehmer in den noch jungen Städten.

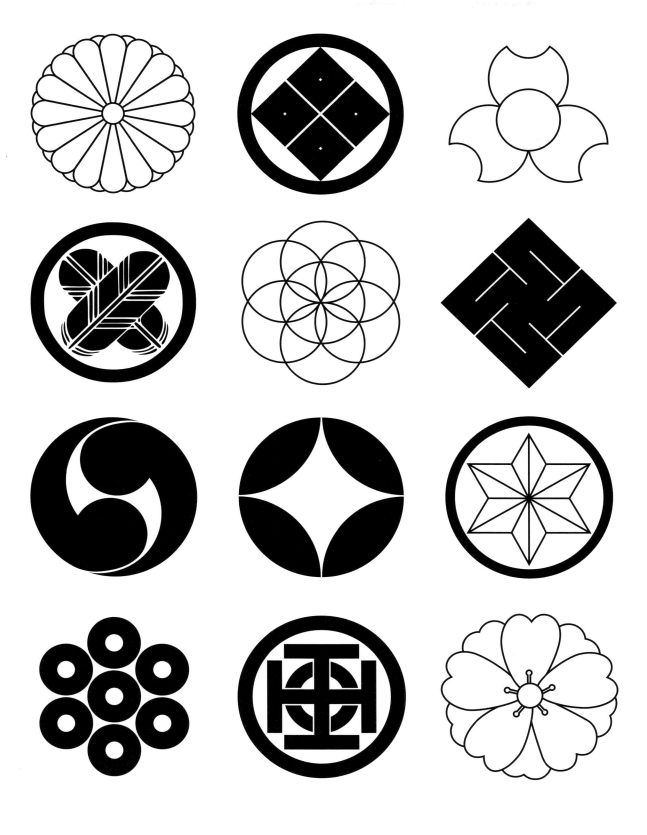

08

Examples of Japanese *mon*,
whose forerunners were
family crests dating back as
far as the 12th century

Beispiele japanischer Mon,
deren Vorläufer seit dem
12. Jahrhundert als Familien-
zeichen in Gebrauch waren

Exemples de *mon* japonais ;
leurs précurseurs étaient
utilisés comme signes familiaux
depuis le siècle

09

Development of the logo of
the stationery manufacturer
Pelikan between 1873 and
2003, which originated from
a family crest

Entwicklung des Logos des Schreibwarenherstellers Pelikan zwischen
1873 und 2003; seine Ursprünge
liegen in einem Familienwappen

Évolution du logo du fabricant
d'articles d'écriture Pelikan
entre 1873 et 2003 ; les
origines du logo remontent
à un blason familial

In Japan entstanden zeitgleich die sogenannten Mon (dt. „Zeichnung, Muster"). Basierend auf stilisierten Darstellungen von Pflanzen oder Tieren, meist einfarbig in einem umrandeten Kreis platziert, kennzeichneten sie zunächst die Kaiserfamilie und den japanischen Kriegsadel, ab 1600 schließlich auch Familien aller Stände (→ 08). Ähnlich wie die europäischen Wappen wurden sie nach bestimmten Regeln von Generation zu Generation vererbt. Im täglichen Leben spielten die Mon lange Zeit eine untergeordnete Rolle, erst im Lauf der Geschichte wurde es üblich die Symbole auch als öffentliche Kennzeichnung eines Familienunternehmens zu verwenden. So ist das bekannte Logo des Automobilherstellers Mitsubishi eine abstrahierte Kombination der Mon beider Gründerfamilien.

Mit der Industrialisierung zur zweiten Hälfte des 18. Jahrhunderts veränderten sich nach und nach fast alle Branchen. Unternehmen erweiterten ihre geografische Reichweite. Mit den im Vergleich zu ihren vorherigen Lebensumständen nun bessergestellten Fabrikarbeitern entstand eine ganz neue Käuferschicht. Die Urbanisierung führte zu einem veränderten Konsumverhalten und einem Anstieg des Angebots; eine Art Initialzündung des Produktmarkts ereignete sich. Ob Lebensmittel, Möbel oder Kleidung – Differenzierung war in der veränderten Marktsituation notwendiger als je zuvor. In vielen Fällen wurden Elemente aus Familienwappen zu ersten Markenzeichen. Der Pelikan als Wappentier der Familie des deutschen Schreibwarenherstellers wurde 1878 beispielsweise zum Logo und Markennamen des Unternehmens. Ihre internationale Bekanntheit verdankt die Marke bis heute auch dieser Entscheidung (→ 09). Figürliche Darstellungen, wie der genannte Pelikan, waren im 19. Jahrhundert eine übliche Form der Visualisierung. Aus der Tradition der Zünftewappen heraus wurde angestrebt, dass ein Logo eine deutliche und plakative Verbindung zum Unternehmer oder zum Angebot des Unternehmens herstellte. Nur vereinzelt entstanden bereits zu dieser Zeit abstrakte und nicht-gegenständliche Zeichen. Eines der ganz frühen Beispiele ist die englische Brauerei William Bass, die spätestens seit 1875 ein rotes Dreieck als Logo auf ihre Erzeugnisse druckte (→ 10). Die damals revolutionäre Kennzeichnung hob sich mehr als deutlich von der gesamten Konkurrenz ab und unterscheidet die Marke bis heute von der eher traditionell geprägten visuellen Erscheinung anderer Bierbrauer. Als interessantes Detail der Geschichte war das Bass-Dreieck das allererste überhaupt in Großbritannien angemeldete und damit geschützte Markenzeichen.

Von einigen Ausnahmen abgesehen begann die erste Phase modernistischer Logos jedoch erst in den 1920er-Jahren. Von den künstlerischen und grafischen Bewegungen um De Stijl und Bauhaus geprägt, veränderte sich die noch junge Disziplin der Gebrauchsgrafik in dieser Zeit maßgeblich. Der Griff zu abstrakten Formen und die gekonnte Kombination geometrischer Elemente führten zu neuen Lösungen, die einen extremen Gegensatz zu den bis dahin vorherrschenden gegenständlichen Ausdrucksformen darstellten. Das 1922 von Oskar Schlemmer entworfene Logo für das Bauhaus selbst ist ein ideales Exempel für den Übergang zur abstrakten Grafik (→ 11). Im April 1926 erschien in der

Werkbund-Zeitschrift *Die Form* ein Artikel des dem Bauhaus nahe-stehenden Gestalters Johannes Molzahn, worin die Gedankengänge der Avantgardisten zum modernen Logo auf den Punkt gebracht werden: „Der Markensinn ist absolut und die Form wird allein bestimmt von optisch-mechanischen Gesetzen, die die Gestalt nach sich ziehen; hier fordert Funktion eine Form in derselben Weise wie im Maschinenbau. Die Markenfrage ist in Wirklichkeit kein künstlerisches Problem zuerst, vielmehr ein technisch-wissenschaftliches und lebendig-psychisches; die ästhetische Form ist hier genau wie bei der Maschine nur das Resultat vollkommener Konstruktion, mit dem Sinn höchster Leistungs-fähigkeit." Diese Philosophie wird in Pionierarbeiten der modernen Logo-gestaltung wie etwa von Wilhelm Deffke oder Karl Schulpig unmittelbar spürbar [→ 12]. Auch zahlreiche internationale Gestalter der nächsten Generation wie Paul Rand oder Yusaku Kamekura nannten das Bauhaus und seine Errungenschaften wichtige Einflussfaktoren ihrer Arbeit.

Dennoch begann sich das modernistische Logo bei Neuentwürfen oder Überarbeitungen alter Zeichen erst im Laufe der 1940er-Jahre flächendeckend durchzusetzen. Die wiederum durch die Avantgardis-ten der 1920er-Jahre begründete Bewegung der Schweizer Typografie, später auch als „International Typographic Style" bezeichnet, verhalf der modernen Grafik schließlich ab den 1950er-Jahren endgültig zum Durchbuch – auch international [→ 13]. In der durch den Zweiten Welt-krieg weniger belasteten Schweiz konnten sich Ideen und Ansätze der abstrakten Grafik weiterentwickeln, und sie wurden nach Ende des Krieges von einer neuen Gestaltergeneration dankbar aufgenommen. Einen nicht unwesentlichen Beitrag zur Verbreitung des Schweizer Stils dürften dabei die 1944 in Zürich gegründete Zeitschrift *Graphis* und ihr Jahrbuch *Graphis Annual* geleistet haben. Vor allem das Jahrbuch mit einer Auswahl moderner Arbeiten aus aller Welt war so etwas wie das Leitmedium jener Zeit. Es erreichte und beeinflusste Gestalter auf allen Kontinenten. Bezogen auf Medien wie Buchumschläge oder Plakate stellt der Schweizer Stil rückblickend eine abgeschlossene Ära der Designgeschichte dar, die gestalterisch den Ton angab, später aber zumindest in Teilen durch neue Einflüsse – unter anderem aus der Pop Art – verändert wurde. Der Einfluss im Bereich des Logos war jedoch so einschneidend, dass man das damalige Schaffen als wirkliche Zäsur in der Entwicklung des Mediums werten kann. Grund-legende Gestaltungsparameter, die sowohl die Entwurfstechnik wie auch die Wahrnehmung von Markenzeichen verändert haben, wurden damals erstmals in voller Bandbreite angewendet und ausgelotet.

Im Laufe der 1960er-Jahre wurde das Anwendungsfeld des Logos durch integral konzipierte Corporate-Design-Systeme noch einmal erweitert. Einheitliche Unternehmensauftritte mit Normen zu Farbigkeit, Typografie, Bildsprache und anderen Elementen setzten sich zuneh-mend durch. Reglementierte Systematik und Ordnung lösten den bis-lang individuellen Umgang mit Zeichen ab [→ 14+15]. Bis zur Einführung von Design-Manuals war es in vielen Unternehmen üblich, das Logo in verschiedenen Kommunikationsmedien (Plakat, Geschäftsbericht etc.) ganz unterschiedlich und oft auch spielerisch variierend einzusetzen.

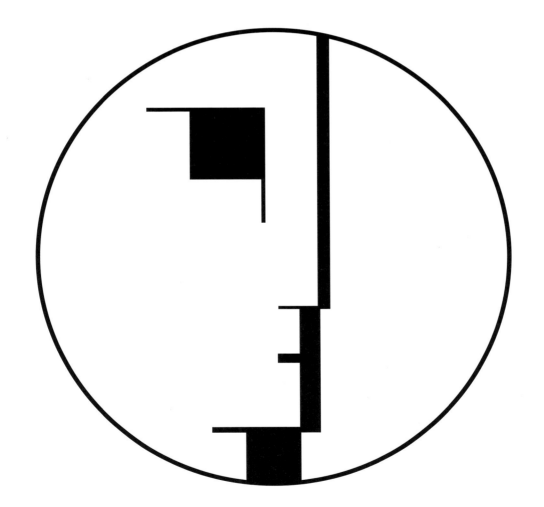

10

Logo of the English William Bass
brewery, introduced *c.* 1875

Markenzeichen der englischen
Brauerei William Bass,
entstanden ca. 1875

Marque commerciale du
brasseur anglais William Bass,
créée vers 1875

11

Logo of the Bauhaus
in Weimar, designed by
Oskar Schlemmer in 1922

Logo des Staatlichen Bauhauses
in Weimar, entworfen 1922 von
Oskar Schlemmer

Logo du Bauhaus de
Weimar, dessiné en 1922
par Oskar Schlemmer

DEGUSSA

VOX

12

Designs from the 1920s by
German logo pioneers Karl Schulpig
(left), Johannes Molzahn (center)
and Wilhelm Deffke (right)

Entwürfe der deutschen Logo-
pioniere Karl Schulpig (links),
Johannes Molzahn (Mitte) und
Wilhelm Deffke (rechts) aus den
1920-Jahren

Réalisations des pionniers
allemands du logo Karl Schulpig
(colonne de gauche), Johannes
Molzahn (colonne centrale)
et Wilhelm Deffke (colonne de
droite) datant des années 1920

In ihrem grundsätzlichen Aussehen wurden die Logos durch diese Veränderungen jedoch nur unwesentlich und in Einzelfällen beeinflusst. Erst die digitale Revolution im Bereich der Medienproduktion in den 1990er-Jahren verursachte Veränderungen in der Logoausgestaltung selbst. Erweiterte Möglichkeiten der Bildbearbeitung am Computer führten zunächst zu eher rein kosmetischen Aktualisierungen zahlreicher Zeichen. Das Hinzufügen eines Schlagschattens oder das Einfügen anderer dreidimensionaler Effekte waren die gängigen Eingriffe. In den letzten Jahren entstanden verstärkt auch rein dreidimensionale Logos [→ 16]. Aufgrund ihrer Komplexität können 3D-Logos nicht einfarbig wiedergegeben werden, ohne dabei wesentliche Gestaltungselemente zu verlieren. Alte Grundregeln, nach denen Farbigkeit oder zu viele Details aufgrund von Problemen in der Reproduzierbarkeit ausgeschlossen waren, gelten dank fortgeschrittener Drucktechnik nicht mehr.

Das Logo bietet heute also scheinbar mehr Gestaltungsfreiraum denn je. Umso notwendiger ist der Blick auf die überschaubare Anzahl grundlegender Designparameter. Für dieses Buch wurden mehrere tausend modernistische Logos – vor allem aus den 1950er- bis 1980er-Jahren – zusammengetragen und formal analysiert. Die drei Hauptkapitel „Geometrisch", „Effekt" und „Typografisch", die wiederum aus zahlreichen Subkategorien bestehen, zeigen dabei die wichtigsten Grundformen und Entwurfsmöglichkeiten auf, die in dieser repräsentativen Menge von Logos zu finden sind. Beim Durchblättern dieser Sammlung scheint es zunächst so, als wäre alles schon einmal da gewesen. Bei genauerem Hinsehen wird jedoch deutlich, dass in der Kombination der vorgestellten Gestaltungsparameter noch unlimitierte Möglichkeiten liegen, die es im Entwurfsprozess zu entdecken gilt.

Logo
Jens Müller

Lorsqu'on passe en revue les publications parues voici cinquante ou soixante ans autour du logo, on tombe tôt ou tard sur un passage évoquant ce « monde compliqué » auquel l'élémentaire et la simplification doivent servir de contrepoids et d'outils de contrôle. Le fait que le monde soit perçu comme complexe ne date donc pas d'hier, et le besoin de signes simples et intelligibles n'est pas vraiment nouveau. Tout comme d'autres aspects, cette explication et d'autres de la même veine avancées au milieu du XXe siècle doivent être comprises comme une recherche de légitimité objective de la part des designers, qui voulaient se débarrasser de l'aura mystique entourant l'artiste affichiste. De fait, la naissance du graphisme moderne est indissolublement liée à celle d'un graphiste moderne moins inspiré par le génie artistique que guidé par la sobriété, la conceptualisation et la systématique. Des précurseurs isolés ont bien sûr existé dès avant cette époque, vers la fin du XIXe siècle, ce qui rend difficile de désigner le moment précis où la conscience du métier a changé chez les professionnels. Reste qu'à partir des années 1940 on observe que quelque chose que l'on pourrait appeler la modernité commence à s'imposer dans le domaine du design graphique. Au plus tard pendant les deux décennies suivantes, des travaux représentant ce nouveau style apparaissent un peu partout dans le monde et dans tous les secteurs du graphisme. Des groupes internationaux aussi bien que de petites entreprises régionales rénovent alors leur présentation visuelle. C'est peut-être dans le domaine du logo que l'esprit moderniste a produit les changements les plus manifestes et les plus durables. Si les tendances, l'esprit du temps et les évolutions techniques conduisent aujourd'hui à des solutions divergentes, celles-ci n'en plongent pas moins leurs racines dans les paramètres créatifs de cette apogée de la modernité. Un regard rétrospectif ne peut donc être qu'enrichissant.

Les ethnologues, les historiens de l'art et les spécialistes du design ont analysé en détails les origines des signes et des symboles de l'humanité et produit une immense littérature sur ce sujet. Même si le logo moderne et ses manifestations formelles constituent l'objet principal du présent ouvrage, il n'est pas inutile de remonter un peu plus haut dans l'histoire et de mettre un coup de projecteur sur quelques ancêtres de ce média. L'historiographie du design fait souvent remonter jusqu'à l'aube de l'humanité en citant les peintures préhistoriques du sud de la France et les dessins pariétaux d'Amérique du Nord ou d'Afrique du Sud. À juste titre, car c'est à partir de ces premières manifestations visuelles de l'humanité que se sont finalement développés l'écriture et le langage écrit, et c'est aussi là qu'on trouvera les racines primordiales du logo actuel. Lorsqu'on cherche toutefois les ancêtres qui coulent de source, il s'avère utile de saisir la fonction du logo qui, aujourd'hui comme hier, ressort d'un usage utilitaire : caractérisation et démarcation.

De l'apparition des premières civilisations en Asie, en Afrique et en Amérique datent des pièces de céramique sur lesquelles les chercheurs ont trouvé les premières entailles systématiques $^{(\to\,01)}$. Celles-ci servaient

33ª Biennale Internazionale d'Arte

Venezia 18 Giugno 16 Ottobre 1966

Riduzioni ferroviarie

N. 1084/66 Esente da bollo Min. Fin. N. 37495 dell'11/3/96.
Stampa: Poligrafico G. Colombi S.p.A. - Milano-Pero - design / Bob Noorda - Unimark

13

Poster for the 33rd Venice Biennale, created by the Dutch designer Bob Noorda in 1966 for the Milan office of Unimark International

Plakat zur 33. Biennale in Venedig, entworfen 1966 vom niederländischen Gestalter Bob Noorda für das Mailänder Büro von Unimark International

Affiche de la 33ème Biennale de Venise dessinée en 1966 par le designer néerlandais Bob Noorda pour le bureau milanais d'Unimark International

à identifier différents fabricants et à signaliser des qualités divergentes. Sur les céramiques chinoises et romaines d'époques un peu plus tardives, on a trouvé des caractérisations encore plus claires qui ne laissent subsister aucun doute sur le fait qu'elles sont les précurseurs directs des futures marques commerciales. Sur des tombeaux et des édifices historiques qui peuvent être datés jusqu'à 2000 avant notre ère, on a trouvé des « marques de tâcherons ». Ces gravures linéaires abstraites renvoyaient à différents ateliers ou familles et avaient leur propre systématique [→ 02]. À la même époque, le marquage des bêtes au fer rouge est déjà une pratique courante. La compréhension de l'anglais « branding » pour désigner la caractérisation d'une marque commerciale remonte à cette technique apparue à la fin de la préhistoire. Dans le cadre de la pratique du marquage des bêtes, qui s'est conservée jusqu'à nos jours, des signes et des symboles ont été développés voici plusieurs milliers d'années. Dans le domaine de l'élevage, on utilisait des lettres isolées ou combinées représentant le propriétaire ou une communauté fermière. À l'époque des batailles médiévales, il était aussi courant de marquer les soldats du signet ou du monogramme de leur commandant [→ 03].

Comme l'indique l'étymologie du terme, le monogramme a d'abord été une lettre isolée intégralement dessinée. Aujourd'hui, le terme désigne surtout une graphie visuelle combinant les initiales d'un prénom et d'un nom de famille. Dès l'époque du Saint Empire romain germanique, ce type de sigle fut utilisé par les princes et les souverains – avant tout dans la culture européenne [→ 04]. On le trouve alors aussi bien sous forme de signature manuscrite que de cachet ou de sceau dans le cadre de communications administratives. Plus tard, les entrepreneurs et les artistes tirent à leur tour parti de ces caractérisations d'expéditeur de nature pratique [→ 05]. Un des monogrammes les plus célèbres reste à ce jour le sigle « AD » utilisé pour la première fois en 1498 par Albrecht Dürer.

Le monde des croisades, de la chevalerie et des tournois, mais aussi les conflits autour de la conquête de territoires ou d'autres biens ont déterminé la société et la politique du Moyen Âge. À l'apogée de cette période historique, entre les XIe et XIIIe siècles, apparaissent les blasons, représentations figurées d'animaux rayonnant de force comme l'aigle ou le lion, représentations associées à des motifs colorés et des insignes de pouvoir comme la couronne, les clés ou le sceptre [→ 06]. Les blasons servent à marquer des terres, à caractériser des familles nobles ou des villes ainsi que leurs propriétés, et à se démarquer les uns des autres. En même temps, des groupements professionnels appartenant au tiers état et d'autres communautés développent à leur tour leurs propres signes et symboles. Les artisans se regroupent en corporations et développent des blasons qui représentent leur activité par un raccourci figuré [→ 07]. Ces blasons corporatifs n'étaient pas seulement une sorte de label de qualité, mais aussi, dans le contexte d'un analphabétisme encore largement répandu, une caractérisation incontournable pour les entrepreneurs des jeunes métropoles.

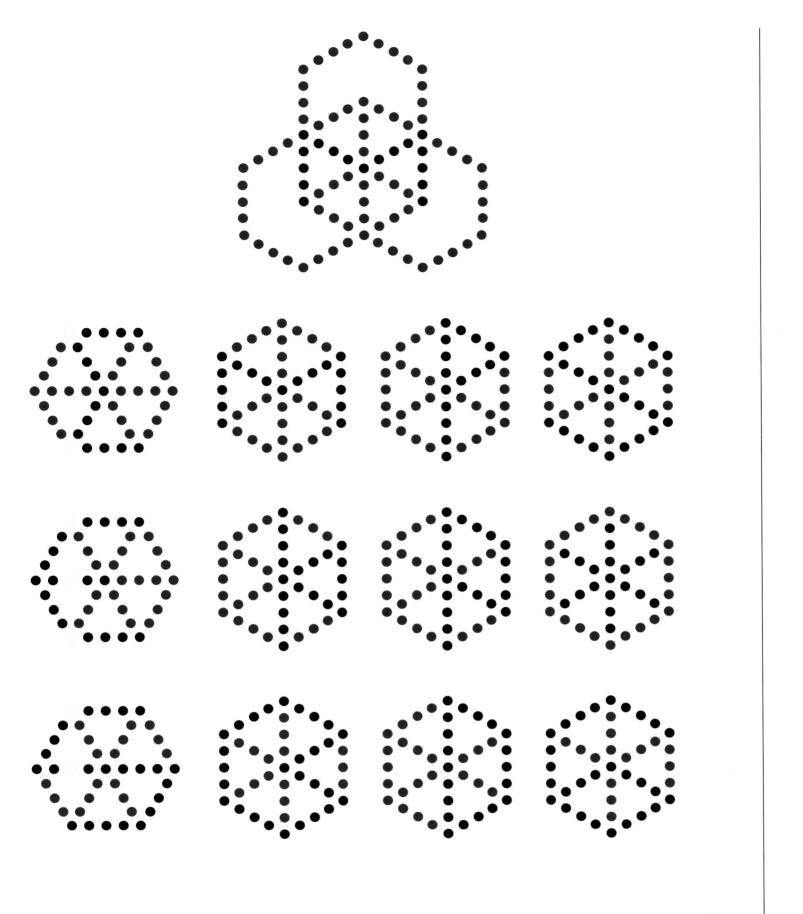

14

Design system developed by
FHK Henrion in the 1960s for
management consultancy Metra
and its international subsidiaries

In den 1960er-Jahren von FHK
Henrion entwickeltes Zeichensystem
für die Unternehmensberatung
Metra und deren internationaler
Tochterunternehmen

Système de signes développé dans
les années 1960 par FHK Henrion
pour la société de conseil Metra et
ses filiales internationales

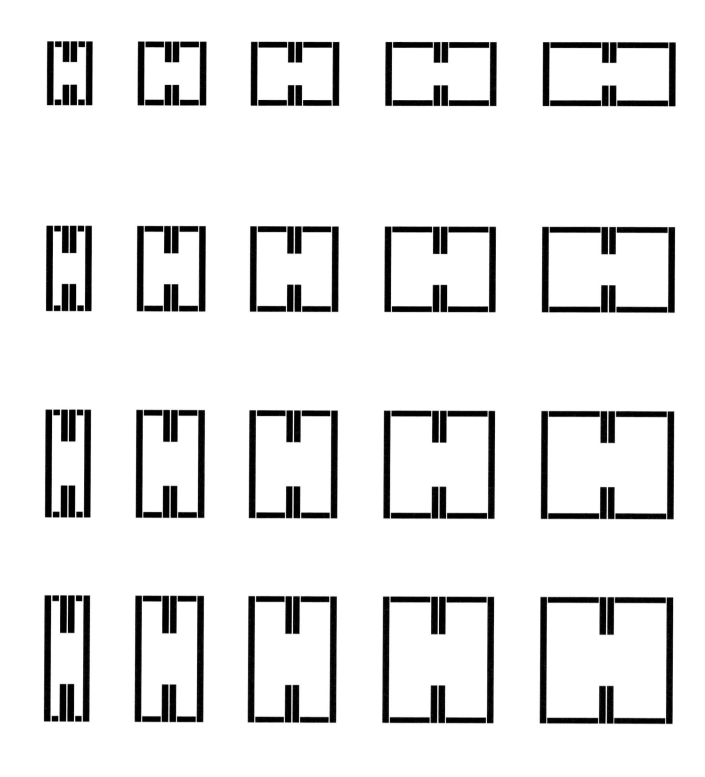

15

Karl Gerstner's 1960 modular logo system for the German furniture manufacturer Holzäpfel

Von Karl Gerstner um 1960 entwickeltes modulares Logosystem für den deutschen Möbelhersteller Holzäpfel

Système de logo modulaire développé vers 1960 par Karl Gerstner pour le fabricant allemand de meubles Holzäpfel

À la même époque, on voit apparaître au Japon les insignes héraldiques appelés *mon* (fr. dessin, motif). Créés sur la base de représentations stylisées de végétaux ou d'animaux généralement monochromes placées dans un cercle clairement cerné, les *mon* caractérisent d'abord la famille impériale et la noblesse guerrière du Japon et, pour finir, à partir de 1600, également les familles de toutes les classes de la société [→ 08]. Un peu comme les blasons en Europe, ils se transmettent de génération en génération selon des règles bien précises. Dans la vie quotidienne, il devint ensuite courant d'utiliser ce type de symboles pour la caractérisation publique d'une entreprise familiale. C'est ainsi que le célèbre logo du constructeur automobile Mitsubishi est une combinaison abstraite des *mon* des deux familles fondatrices.

Avec la révolution industrielle de la seconde moitié du XVIIIe siècle, presque toutes les branches de l'industrie évoluent peu à peu. Les entreprises étendent leur rayon d'action géographique. Avec les ouvriers d'usines, dont le statut était alors comparativement meilleur, une toute nouvelle couche d'acheteurs voit le jour. L'urbanisation croissante modifie les habitudes de consommation et entraîne une augmentation de l'offre. Il se produit ainsi une sorte de mise à feu initiale du marché des produits. Alimentaire, mobilier ou habillement – dans le cadre des nouvelles conditions du marché, il devient plus nécessaire que jamais de se démarquer. Bien souvent, les premières marques commerciales sont créées à partir d'éléments tirés de blasons familiaux. Pour citer un exemple, en 1878, le pélican, animal héraldique de la famille du fabricant d'articles d'écriture Pelikan, devint le logo et le nom de l'entreprise. C'est notamment à cette décision que cette marque doit jusqu'à aujourd'hui sa notoriété internationale [→ 09]. Au XIXe siècle, les représentations figurées comme le pélican deviennent une forme courante de représentation visuelle. Dans la tradition des blasons corporatifs, l'on cherche alors à ce qu'un logo exprime un lien clair et frappant avec l'entrepreneur ou l'offre de l'entreprise. Dès cette époque apparaissent aussi des signes abstraits et non figuratifs, mais ils sont encore l'exception. Un des tout premiers exemples en est le brasseur anglais William Bass qui, au plus tard en 1875, fit imprimer sur ses produits un triangle rouge utilisé comme logo [→ 10]. Cette caractérisation révolutionnaire se démarquait alors de manière pour le moins voyante de toute la concurrence et continue à distinguer aujourd'hui cette marque parmi les identités visuelles plutôt traditionnelles des autres brasseurs. Détail intéressant dans ce contexte, le triangle de Bass fut la toute première marque commerciale déposée – et donc protégée – enregistrée au Royaume-Uni.

À quelques exceptions près, il faut toutefois attendre les années 1920 pour voir s'ouvrir la première phase du logo moderne. À l'époque, le design graphique, discipline encore jeune, change de manière décisive sous l'influence des mouvements artistiques et graphiques de la mouvance De Stijl et du Bauhaus. L'utilisation de formes abstraites et la combinaison savante d'éléments géométriques conduisent alors à des solutions inédites qui sont en opposition maximale avec les formes d'expression figuratives jusqu'alors prédominantes. Le logo qu'Oskar Schlemmer conçoit précisément en 1922 pour le Bauhaus illustre parfaitement cette transition vers le graphisme abstrait [→ 11]. En avril 1926, la revue du Deutsche Werkbund *Die Form* publie un article de Johannes Molzahn, créateur proche du Bauhaus, qui dégage l'essentiel des réflexions de l'avant-garde du logo : « L'esprit de la marque est un absolu, la forme est exclusivement déterminée par des lois optico-mécaniques qui guident la création. Ici, la fonction crée la forme tout comme dans le domaine de l'ingénierie mécanique. En réalité, la question de la marque n'est pas un problème d'abord artistique, mais bien plutôt un problème technico-scientifique et concrètement psychique. Comme dans le cas de la machine, la forme esthétique n'est ici rien d'autre que le résultat d'une construction parfaite, l'objectif étant l'excellence des performances. » Cette philosophie est concrétisée le plus clairement dans les réalisations pionnières de Wilhelm Deffke et Karl Schulpig [→ 12]. De nombreux designers internationaux de la génération suivante, comme Paul Rand ou Yusaku Kamekura, ont eux aussi cité le Bauhaus et ses acquis comme des influences importantes pour leur travail.

Mais c'est seulement au cours des années 1940 que le logo moderne commence à s'imposer largement dans le cadre de nouveaux projets ou lors du remaniement de signes déjà existants. Pour finir, à partir des années 1950, le mouvement de la typographie suisse – parfois appelé « International Typographic Style », fondé lui aussi par des avant-gardistes des années 1920, apportera une contribution décisive à la percée définitive de la création graphique moderne, notamment sur le plan international [→ 13]. Dans une Suisse moins directement touchée par la Seconde Guerre mondiale, les idées et les orientations du graphisme international ont pu continuer de se développer et, à la fin de la guerre, elles vont être saluées par une nouvelle génération de graphistes – d'abord dans les pays voisins. Une contribution non négligeable à la diffusion du style suisse a été apportée par la revue *Graphis*, fondée en 1944 à Zurich, et par sa publication annuelle *Graphis Annual*. C'est surtout cette dernière, avec sa sélection de projets réalisés dans le monde entier, qui fut le média le plus influent de l'époque. Elle atteignit et influença des créateurs des cinq continents. Dans le domaine de la couverture de livre ou de l'affiche, le style suisse, considéré rétrospectivement, marque une phase révolue de l'histoire du design. S'il a donné le ton de la création à son époque, ce style sera ensuite modifié au moins en partie par de nouvelles influences – notamment celle du Pop Art. L'empreinte qu'il a laissée dans le domaine du logo a toutefois été telle qu'il faut considérer les créations de cette époque comme une véritable césure dans l'évolution du média. Certains paramètres fondamentaux qui ont révolutionné la technique de conception aussi bien que la perception des marques commerciales ont alors été appliqués et explorés pour la première fois dans toutes leurs implications.

unitymedia

DC COMICS™

Rio2016

Sony Ericsson

Thomas Cook Group

at&t

16

Three-dimensional logos,
used chiefly or almost exclusively
in color applications

Dreidimensionale Logos,
die hauptsächlich oder sogar
ausschließlich in farbiger
Anwendung funktionieren

Logos tridimensionnels
fonctionnant principalement,
voire exclusivement en couleurs

35

Au cours des années 1960, le logo élargit encore son champ d'application avec l'apparition de systèmes de corporate design conçus jusqu'aux moindres détails. Des images d'entreprise homogènes, entièrement normalisées en termes de couleurs, de typographie, de langage visuel ou d'autres aspects, s'imposent alors progressivement. Le systématisme et l'ordre réglés viennent désormais remplacer le traitement individuel du signe [→ 14+15]. Jusqu'à l'apparition du manuel de conception, les entreprises utilisaient leur logo de façon très différente selon les médias de communication (affiche, rapport de gestion etc.), souvent dans des versions ludiques. Sauf exception, ces changements n'altéraient guère l'aspect fondamental des logos. Avec la révolution numérique des années 1990 dans la production médiatique, on relève toutefois de vrais changements dans la conception de logos. Dans un premier temps, les nouvelles possibilités offertes par la conception graphique assistée par ordinateur conduisent à des actualisations plutôt cosmétiques de nombreux signes. L'ajout d'une ombre portée et l'insertion d'autres effets tridimensionnels sont alors les interventions les plus courantes. Au cours de ces dernières années se sont aussi imposés de plus en plus souvent des logos purement tridimensionnels [→ 16]. Leur complexité en termes de couleurs et de design fait que les logos en 3D ne peuvent être produits en version monochrome sans perte d'aspects importants du design. Les anciennes règles de base qui excluaient la couleur ou l'excès de détails pour des raisons liées à des problèmes de reproductibilité n'ont plus cours aujourd'hui grâce aux progrès des techniques d'impression.

Le logo offre donc aujourd'hui apparemment plus d'espace de liberté créatrice que jamais. Cela rend d'autant plus nécessaire d'avoir une vue d'ensemble des paramètres fondamentaux du design, somme toute limités en nombre. Pour le présent ouvrage, plusieurs milliers de logos modernes – surtout des années 1950 aux années 1980 – ont été réunis et analysés du point de vue de formel. Les trois chapitres principaux « Géométrique », « Effet » et « Typographique », eux-mêmes subdivisés en nombreuses sous-catégories, présentent les principales formes fondamentales et possibilités créatives que l'on peut recenser dans cette somme représentative de logos. En feuilletant cette compilation, la première impression sera peut-être que tout a déjà existé. Mais à y regarder de plus près, on réalisera clairement que la combinaison des paramètres de création présentés recèle encore des possibilités illimitées qu'il s'agit de découvrir lors du travail de conception.

VIVA MODERNISM!
R. Roger Remington

Modernism, in its broadest definition, is contemporary thought, character or practice. More specifically, Modernism describes for the arts a set of cultural tendencies and associated cultural movements, affirming the power of human beings to make, improve and reshape their environment. Modernism is the projection of an ideology encompassing awareness of the production process and the final destination of its products.

The quintessential Modernist designer Massimo Vignelli sets the birth of Modernism as coinciding with the publication of the Diderot and d'Alembert *Encyclopédie* in the middle of the 18th century. This work was the great contribution of the Enlightenment, a unique moment of transition in the history of mankind from an agrarian society to an industrial one, from a religion-dominated culture to a liberal and progressive vision of the world. In the encyclopedia was to be found the last expression of crafts and an early view of the new Machine Era. Also evident was the recognition of the need for a different way of designing artifacts. No longer was the artisan the master of the end product, but a new figure was emerging, someone devising products manufactured by machines, from glass to china, from steel to fabrics, from paper to type and more. The Enlightenment generated a new way of thinking as people looked forward to a new social order. The French Revolution accelerated man's evolution and gave new strength to ideas. The modern man was born, liberated from the bind of oppressing and confining boundaries from the past. New horizons stimulated minds in every area from the sciences to the arts, from politics to commerce. The advent of the steam engine at the beginning of the 19th century brought power to industry. Products of all kinds had to be designed for the new production processes. Mechanization took command, from railways to textiles. Even agriculture was mechanized. Steel bridges spanned the new era. Everything was now designed, at the beginning in a rather naive way and later in a more conscious way, thus expressing the new technologies and the new sensibilities. Industrial and technological change always gives rise to social change which, in turn, affects artistic expression. Creative expressions become a mirror, always reflecting society.

Marx and Engels provided a voice for the needs of a different social justice. A new way of seeing the human condition gave rise to new ideologies covering every aspect of the nascent society emerging from the Industrial Revolution. In the middle of the 19th century, William Morris reacted against the stylistic commonality caused by the improper use of the new industrial processes, advocating a new attention to the design of products, from furniture to textiles.

The design and building of London's Crystal Palace heralded the emergence of Modernism through architecture. This unique building of cast-iron and glass was constructed in 1851 for the Great Exhibition at Hyde Park which showcased the newest products of many nations. Its design forecast by years the glass curtain walls of Gropius's architecture of the 1920s.

The profile of the modern designer was therefore starting to take shape. At the beginning of the 20th century in Germany, Peter Behrens was already the model for the modern industrial designer, covering with his work the whole field of design, applying new mental processes and new expressions. He was the first designer to face the industrial needs of communication and the real inventor of corporate identity, the expression of a company vision and commitment to integrity and quality. Behrens was also a founding member of the Deutsche Werkbund, which played a major role in integrating design and industry. A noteworthy publication of the Werkbund from 1921 entitled *XX Eigen-Marken* (Twenty Personal Brands) presented for the first time a collection of identity marks and logotypes from its members, many of which break with traditional forms of identity of the period.

Other European avant-garde movements each did their best to radically sever connections with the traditional past and contribute to shaping modern design thought and practice. This new wave of creative thought and activity cut across many boundaries beyond design to painting, sculpture, architecture, dance, music, poetry and more. Contributors came from many parts of Europe. The Constructivists in Russia were the major players of the European avant-garde and El Lissitzky was the seminal father of this movement. For this break-away Modernist, "Not even the new was new enough for him."[1] The Cubist painters in Paris suggested new ways of seeing the world and shaping visual form. The De Stijl group in the Netherlands brought their utterly unique inventions to this initiative to break away dramatically from traditional forms. One of their members, painter Piet Mondrian, wrote: "At every moment of the past all variations of the past were 'new.' But it was not THE new. We should not forget that we stand at the end of a culture, at the end of everything old."[2] The Futurists in Italy and the Dada group in Switzerland and Berlin were instrumental in liberating typography.

The geographic center of much of this dynamic change was Germany. In 1927, led by Kurt Schwitters, designers from many parts of Germany came together to form a group known as the "Ring Neue Werbegestalter" (Circle of Modern Advertising Designers). Among its members were Jan Tschichold, Max Burchartz, Willi Baumeister, along with many others. This group of graphic designers held exhibitions and meetings throughout Germany showing off their progressive graphics and advocating avant-garde approaches in their work. Much of the Modernist European expression in design became unified at the Bauhaus in Germany. This experimental school, especially in its Dessau phase, was the first to determine the ideological and formal boundaries of the design profession, its enriched sensitivities and sense of purpose.

ALLGEMEINE ELEKTRICITÆTS-GESELLSCHAFT BERLIN

A.E.G.-SCHEINWERFER MIT ZEISS-SPIEGEL

17

AEG booklet from 1909 using
the company's visual identity
created by Peter Behrens

AEG-Werbebroschüre von
1909 im von Peter Behrens
entwickelten Erscheinungsbild

Brochure AEG de 1909 utilisant
l'identité visuelle de la firme
créée par Peter Behrens

Poster proposal by Wilhelm Deffke
for the Werkbund exhibition of 1914

Plakatentwurf zur Werkbund-
Ausstellung 1914 von
Wilhelm Deffke

Proposition d'affiche pour
l'exposition du Werkbund
de 1914 par Wilhelm Deffke

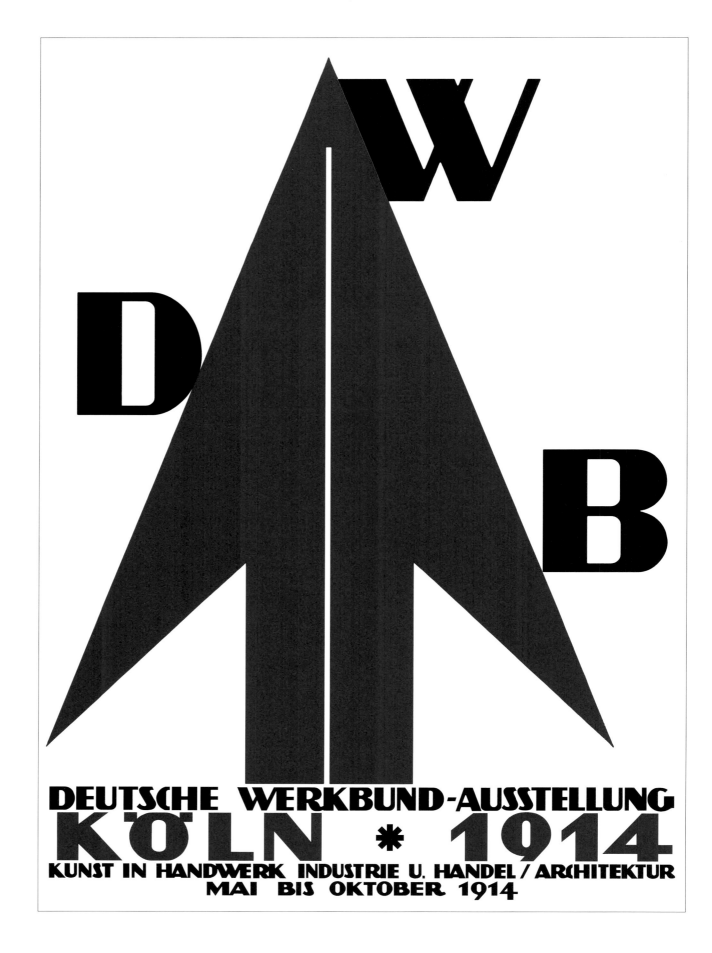

The thrust of European Modernism was brought to America prior to World War II and, following the conflict on the crest of America's post-war economic boom, corporate identity became the goal of most businesses and industries. Every firm needed a new corporate logo or symbol, and a modern look became the norm for every business. Progressive American designers such as Lester Beall, Paul Rand and William Golden met the challenge and thus began the golden age of corporate identity in the United States. This worldwide impetus was to last well into the 1970s.

In the late 1980s, the ideals of Modernism were being critically reviewed and tested. Deconstructivism was a trend born from the postmodernist wish to replace Modernism. Skeptics were asking, is Modernism just a style? Designers were also asking if a new design approach had temporary or permanent values. In response to their critics, objective minds felt that it was necessary to understand the difference between developing and replacing. As Vignelli has strongly stated, "Replacing Modernism implied a misunderstanding of the basic notion of Modernism. It is not a style but a dynamic attitude in continuous flux, with solid foundations based on rational processes. Styles are just the opposite, ephemeral manifestations of the speculative desires of producers."[3] While there remain doubters, for many of its supporters today Modernism is alive and well, because its *raison d'être* is permanent and its imperatives are historically valid. Its critics and its advocates continue to argue the case. In spite of this philosophical dichotomy of view, the Modernists still hold to their utopian goal of making the world better by design.

References Cited

[1] El Lissitzky: unpublished work
[2] Hollis, Richard: *Swiss Graphic Design*; Yale University Press, New Haven 2006; p.15
[3] Vignelli, Massimo: About Modernism; personal letter, 2012

Es lebe die Moderne!
R. Roger Remington

Ganz allgemein gesprochen versteht man unter „Moderne" zeitgenössisches Denken, Sein und Handeln. In engeren Kontext der Kunst ist die Moderne eine Reihe kultureller und verwandter Strömungen, die uns die Fähigkeit des Menschen bestätigen, seine Umgebung zu formen, zu verbessern und umzugestalten. Sie ist die Vorausschau einer Ideologie, zu der ein Verständnis für den Herstellungsprozess und die endgültige Bestimmung ihrer Produkte gehören.

Massimo Vignelli, der archetypische Designer der Moderne, nennt als Geburtsstunde seiner Epoche die Veröffentlichung von Diderots und d'Alemberts *Encyclopédie* in der Mitte des 18. Jahrhunderts. Dieses Werk gilt als großartigste Leistung der Aufklärung, einer in der Geschichte der Menschheit einzigartigen Übergangzeit von der Agrar- zur Industriegesellschaft, von einer durch die Religion bestimmten Kultur zu einer toleranten, fortschrittlichen Weltsicht. In der Enzyklopädie traten ein letztes Mal die Handwerke in den Vordergrund, gleichzeitig bot sie einen ersten Blick auf das neue Maschinenzeitalter. Zudem wurde dort bereits von der Notwendigkeit gesprochen, neue Methoden zur Gestaltung von Gegenständen zu entwickeln. Nicht mehr der Handwerker war Meister des Endprodukts, ein neuer Berufsstand bildete sich heraus: einer, der die von Maschinen hergestellten Produkte ersann, ob nun aus Glas oder Porzellan, Eisen oder Stoff, Papier oder Schrifttypen. Im Zuge der Aufklärung entwickelte sich eine neue Art des Denkens, die Menschen lebten in Aussicht auf eine neue soziale Ordnung. Die Französische Revolution trieb die Evolution des Menschen noch weiter voran, neue Gedanken verschafften sich Raum. Der moderne Mensch wurde geboren, ein Mensch, den keine erdrückenden, beengenden Schranken mehr behinderten. Neue Horizonte regten in allen Bereichen das Denken an, ob in der Wissenschaft oder der Kunst, in der Politik oder im Handel. Das Aufkommen der Dampfkraft Anfang des 19. Jahrhunderts versorgte die Industrie mit Energie. Hilfsmittel aller Art für die neuen Produktionsabläufe mussten entworfen werden, die Mechanisierung hielt überall Einzug, ob bei der Eisenbahn oder in der Textilindustrie. Selbst die Landwirtschaft wurde mechanisiert. Stahlbrücken überspannten die neue Ära. Alles war nun gestaltet – anfangs noch eher naiv, später sehr bewusst. In der Gestaltung fanden die neuen Technologien und das neue Empfinden ihren Ausdruck. Industrielle und technische Neuerungen haben immer auch soziale Veränderungen zur Folge, die wiederum die künstlerische Ausdruckskraft beeinflussen. Der kreative Ausdruck ist ein Spiegel, der unweigerlich die Gesellschaft reflektiert.

Marx und Engels verliehen der Notwendigkeit einer sozialen Gerechtigkeit ihre Stimme. Eine neue Sicht auf die *conditio humana* ließ neue Ideologien erstehen, in denen jeder Aspekt der Gesellschaft, die sich gerade aus der industriellen Revolution löste, abgedeckt wurde. Mitte des 19. Jahrhunderts plädierte William Morris als Reaktion auf die einfallslose Gestaltung von Objekten, zurückzuführen auf

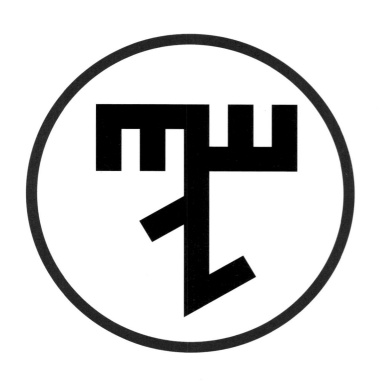

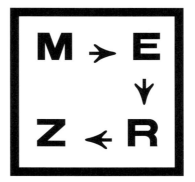

19

Logotypes by Karl Bültmann,
Kurt Schwitters, Hans Karl Michel
and Otto Firle (from left to right)
from the early 1920s

Logoentwürfe von Karl Bültmann,
Kurt Schwitters, Hans Karl
Michel und Otto Firle (von links
nach rechts) aus den frühen
1920er-Jahren

Logos conçus au début des
années 1920 par (de g. à dr.)
Karl Bültmann, Kurt Schwitters,
Hans Karl Michel et Otto Firle

MAX KÖRNER

CARL SCHULPIG
Zur Ausführung gewählt

MAX HERTWIG
Engste Wahl

KARL MICHEL
Engste Wahl

CARL SCHULPIG

MAX HERTWIG

GEORG BREITWIESER

MAX HERTWIG

PAUL SÜSSMANN D. J.

GEORG BREITWIESER

HEINZ KEUNE

SIGNET-WETTBEWERB

Der Bund der deutschen Gebrauchsgraphiker erließ im August 1919 unter seinen Mitgliedern einen Wettbewerb für ein Bundessignet. Die Preisrichter, Lucian Bernhard und Professor Bruno Paul, Mitglieder des Ehrenausschusses, haben aus den 93 Einsendungen, deren hohen Durchschnittswert sie anerkennend feststellten, die hier abgebildeten 16 Entwürfe in engere Wahl gezogen und die letzte Entscheidung zwischen den drei Arbeiten von Schulpig, Hertwig und Michel getroffen. Wie der Bund in seinen „Mitteilungen" bekannt gibt, entschied gegen Michels Entwurf, der künstlerisch als der beste erschien, der Einwand, daß er einen gewissen kirchlichen oder freimauerischen Einschlag aufweise, gegen Hertwigs reife Schriftlösung das Bedenken, daß sie auch mit andern Buchstaben denkbar sei und wahrscheinlich bald zahlreiche unerwünschte Nachahmung fände. So wurde endgiltig Schulpigs Zeichen zur Ausführung gewählt, dessen Schrift zwar nicht restlos befriedigte, für den aber der packende, einprägsame Zug sprach, der sowohl die Graphik gut versinnbildlicht, wie dem Kampfcharakter des Bundes angepaßt scheint. — Der Verein der Plakatfreunde wünscht dem ihm befreundeten Bund der deutschen Gebrauchsgraphiker: In hoc signo vinces!

HANS HEIMBECK

O. H. W. HADANK

KARL MICHEL

WALTER HARTUNG

H. TH. HOYER

20

Results of a logo competition for the "Bund der deutschen Gebrauchsgraphiker" (German Designers Association) in 1920. The design by Karl Schulpig was used until the 1960s.

Ergebnisse des Logowettbewerbs für den „Bund der deutschen Gebrauchsgraphiker" aus dem Jahr 1920. Der Entwurf von Karl Schulpig wurde bis in die 1960er-Jahre verwendet.

Résultats du concours de logos ouvert en 1920 pour l' « Union ces graphistes allemands » (Bund der deutschen Gebrauchsgraphiker). Le projet de Karl Schulpig sera utilisé jusque dans les années 1960.

46

den falschen Einsatz der neuen industriellen Herstellungsweisen, für eine größere Aufmerksamkeit gegenüber der Gestaltung von Gegenständen, vom Möbelstück bis zur Textilie.

Mit Entwurf und Errichtung des Londoner Crystal Palace war die Moderne schließlich auch in der Architektur angekommen. Dieses unvergleichliche Bauwerk aus Gusseisen und Glas wurde 1851 für die Great Exhibition im Londoner Hyde Park errichtet, bei der die neuesten Produkte aus aller Herren Länder vorgestellt wurden. Seine Gestaltung nahm die gläsernen Vorhangfassaden von Walter Gropius aus den 1920er-Jahren um Jahrzehnte vorweg.

Allmählich bildete sich ein Profil des modernen Designers heraus. In Deutschland galt Peter Behrens zu Anfang des 20. Jahrhunderts als Vorbild des modernen Industriedesigners. Seine Arbeit deckte alle Bereiche der Gestaltung ab und ließ neue Denkprozesse und neue Ausdrucksformen einfließen. Als erster Designer beschäftigte er sich auch mit den Ansprüchen der Industrie hinsichtlich ihrer Kommunikation. Er ist der eigentliche Erfinder der Corporate Identity, dem Ausdruck einer Firmenvision und der Verpflichtung zu Integrität und Qualität. Behrens war außerdem Gründungsmitglied des Deutschen Werkbunds, der eine wesentliche Rolle beim Zusammenspiel von Gestaltung und Industrie einnahm. Eine einflussreiche Veröffentlichung des Werkbunds aus dem Jahr 1921 mit dem Titel *XX Eigen-Marken* stellte erstmalig eine Reihe von Markenzeichen und Logotypen seiner Mitglieder vor, die vielfach mit den traditionellen Signets der damaligen Zeit brachen.

Auch andere europäische Bewegungen der Avantgarde lösten nach Kräften alle Verbindungen zur Vergangenheit und warteten mit eigenen Vorstellungen auf, um das moderne Design in Theorie und Praxis weiterzuentwickeln. Diese neue Welle kreativen Denkens und Handelns erstreckte sich über die bloße Gestaltung hinaus bis hin zu Malerei, Bildhauerei, Architektur, Tanz, Musik, Lyrik und weiter. Die Beiträge stammten aus vielen Teilen Europas. Die russischen Konstruktivisten führten die Liga der europäischen Avantgarde an, mit El Lissitzky als bahnbrechender Gründungsvater der Bewegung. Für den revolutionären Vertreter der Moderne war „nicht einmal das Neue neu genug".[1] Die Pariser Maler des Kubismus legten neue Möglichkeiten nahe, die Welt zu sehen und visuelle Formen zu gestalten. Die niederländische Gruppe De Stijl sagte sich mit ihren eigenwilligen Erfindungen radikal von den traditionellen Formen los. Wie eines ihrer Mitglieder, der Maler Piet Mondrian, schrieb: „In jedem Moment der Vergangenheit waren alle Variationen der Vergangenheit ‚neu'. Aber es war nicht DAS Neue. Wir dürfen nicht vergessen, dass wir am Ende einer Kultur stehen, am Ende alles Alten."[2] Die Futuristen in Italien und die Dadaisten in der Schweiz und Berlin waren maßgeblich daran beteiligt, die Typografie zu befreien.

Geografischer Mittelpunkt vieler dieser dynamischen Veränderungen war Deutschland. Unter dem Vorsitz von Kurt Schwitters trafen sich 1927 Designer aus allen Teilen des Landes zur Gründung der als

Ring Neuer Werbegestalter bekannten Gruppe. Dieser Kreis von Grafikern, dem neben Jan Tschichold, Max Burchartz und Willi Baumeister viele andere angehörten, organisierte in ganz Deutschland Ausstellungen und Versammlungen, in denen sie ihre fortschrittliche Grafik präsentierten und avantgardistische Ansätze ihres Gewerbes propagierten. Ein Großteil der europäischen Strömungen der Moderne fand sich im deutschen Bauhaus wieder. Diese experimentelle Schule legte, vor allem in ihrer Zeit in Dessau, als Erste die ideologischen und formalen Grenzen des gestaltenden Berufs fest und sprach von dem dafür erforderlichen Einfühlungsvermögen und dem Vorrang der Zweckdienlichkeit.

Der Grundgedanke der europäischen Moderne war schon vor dem Zweiten Weltkrieg nach Amerika gelangt. Im gewaltigen wirtschaftlichen Aufschwung der Nachkriegszeit verlangten die meisten Unternehmen und Industrien der USA nach einer Corporate Identity. Jede Firma benötigte ein neues Logo oder Symbol, ein moderner Look wurde Norm für jedes Unternehmen. Fortschrittliche amerikanische Designer wie Lester Beall, Paul Rand und William Golden nahmen die Herausforderung an, und damit begann in den Vereinigten Staaten das goldene Zeitalter der Corporate Identity – ein weltweiter Siegeszug, der sich bis in die 1970er-Jahre hinein fortsetzen sollte.

Ende der 1980er-Jahre wurden die Ideale der Moderne einer kritischen Neubewertung unterzogen. Der Dekonstruktivismus als Trend entstand aus dem postmodernen Wunsch heraus, die Moderne abzulösen. Skeptiker erhoben die Frage, ob die Moderne nicht ein bloßer Stil sei. Auch Designer dachten darüber nach, ob ein neuer Gestaltungsansatz kurzzeitige oder dauerhafte Werte darstelle. Als Reaktion auf diese Kritik vertraten objektive Beteiligte die Ansicht, dass es notwendig sei, den Unterschied zwischen Entwickeln und Ersetzen zu verstehen. Wie Vignelli so nachdrücklich feststellte: „Die Moderne zu ersetzen – dem Gedanken liegt ein Missverständnis vom Grundkonzept der Moderne zugrunde. Sie ist kein Stil, sondern eine dynamische Einstellung, die ständig im Fluss ist, aber ein solides, auf rationalen Abläufen beruhendes Fundament hat. Ein Stil ist genau das Gegenteil davon, eine flüchtige Manifestation der spekulativen Wünsche der Hersteller."[3] Zweifler gibt es nach wie vor, aber für viele Fürsprecher der Moderne ist sie heute so jung wie eh und je, weil ihr Daseinsgrund nie veraltet und ihre Ansprüche historisch gerechtfertigt sind. Kritiker und Verteidiger stehen sich nach wie vor gegenüber. Und trotz dieser philosophischen Gegensätze halten die Vertreter der Moderne an ihrem utopischen Ziel fest, die Welt durch Design besser zu machen.

Literaturzitate

[1] Lissitzky, El: Unveröffentlichte Arbeit
[2] Hollis, Richard: *Swiss Graphic Design*; Yale University Press, New Haven 2006; S. 15
[3] Vignelli, Massimo: Über Modernismus; Persönlicher Brief, 2012

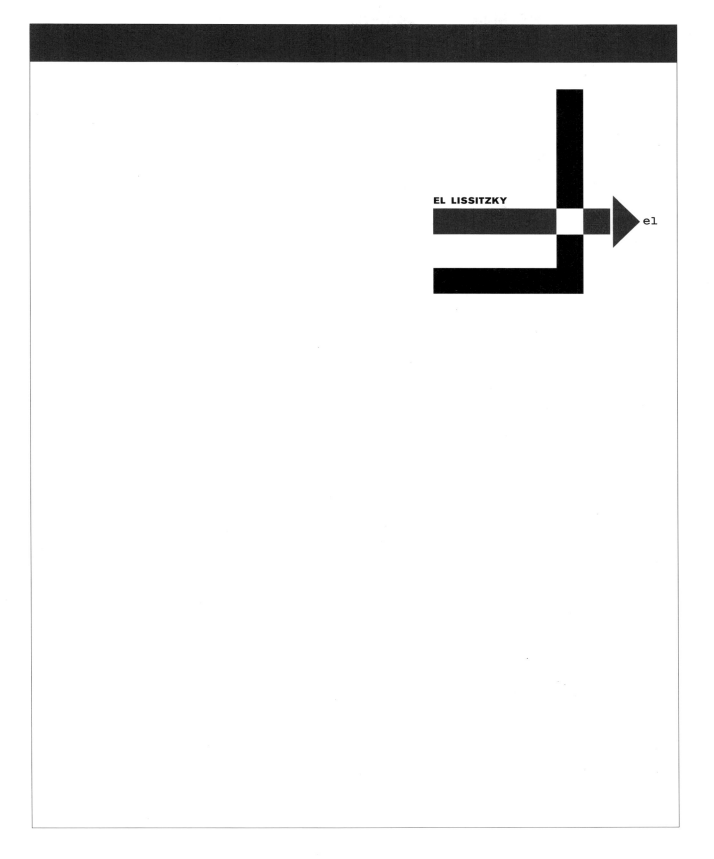

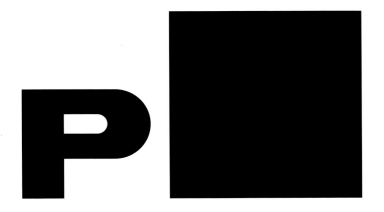

21

Letterhead with the personal
mark of El Lissitzky, 1924

Briefbogen mit der Eigenmarke
von El Lissitzky, 1924

Feuille de papier à lettres
avec la marque personnelle
d'El Lissitzky, 1924

22

Personal mark of Piet Zwart,
1927

Eigenmarke von Piet Zwart,
1927

Marque personnelle de
Piet Zwart, 1927

The sign of good television

When this symbol shines out from a television screen, it identifies, for viewers and advertisers alike, the network where they're most likely to find what they're looking for:

...where 6 of television's 10 most popular shows' are broadcast

...where average ratings are higher than on any other network'

...where television's solid-success package programs come from... shows like Mama, Toast of the Town, Studio One, Suspense, Burns & Allen, Talent Scouts

...where the new hits will *keep* coming from: I Love Lucy, Frank Sinatra, Corliss Archer, See It Now, An Affair of State, Out There, My Friend Irma

...where 59 national advertisers... including 15 of America's 20 biggest... are profitably doing business today."

"This is the CBS Television Network"

Nielsen TV Program Popularity Index (October)
**(October 1)*

Newsfilm tells the world...

Newsfilm is global not only in its coverage of news, but also in its distribution. There are subscriber stations around the world. In England, Denmark, Holland and Luxembourg. In Australia and Japan. In Hawaii and Alaska. In Canada, Cuba, Mexico and Argentina.

There are three basic reasons for *Newsfilm*'s worldwide growth. Its news coverage is fast, professional, complete. It is a product of CBS News, known the world over as broadcasting's finest newsgathering organization. And third, *Newsfilm* is the *only* news service produced especially and exclusively for the use of television stations.

One major subscriber to this service is Independent Television News Limited, the network news service for Great Britain's commercial television system. According to Editor Geoffrey Cox of ITN: "*Newsfilm* has been of immense value to us. We have been able to rely on it with complete confidence as the foundation of our foreign coverage... not only in the United States but throughout the rest of the world. Particularly, *Newsfilm*'s reporting of major happenings has been outstanding."

A word to the worldly-wise: *Newsfilm* is available to *all stations*, at home and abroad. Get complete information from...

CBS TELEVISION FILM SALES, INC.
the most film programs for all stations

TARGET In 1965 CBS Television achieved a nine-year objective: delivering the most popular programs to the largest audience at the lowest cost in all television.

23

Examples of print advertising for CBS Television, designed by William Golden in 1951 and using his "eye" symbol as main characteristic

Beispiele für Werbung des Fernsehsenders CBS, 1951 von William Golden entworfen, bei der sein markantes „Eye"-Symbol im Mittelpunkt steht

Publicités de la chaîne de télévision CBS, conçues en 1951 par William Golden autour du célèbre «eye symbol»

Vive la modernité !
R. Roger Remington

Dans son acception la plus large, la modernité est une pensée, un caractère ou une pratique attachés à la contemporanéité. Dans l'art, la modernité décrit un ensemble de tendances culturelles et de mouvements qui affirment le pouvoir de l'être humain de créer, améliorer et remanier son environnement. La modernité est la projection d'une idéologie consciente du processus de production et de la destination finale de ses produits.

Massimo Vignelli, designer moderne par excellence, fait remonter la naissance de la modernité à la publication de l'*Encyclopédie* de Diderot et d'Alembert au milieu du XVIIIe siècle. Ce travail a été la grande manifestation des Lumières, ce moment unique dans l'histoire de l'humanité qui marque le passage d'une société agraire à une société industrielle, d'une culture dominée par la religion à une vision du monde progressive et libérale. Dans l'*Encyclopédie* se trouvent à la fois la dernière expression de l'artisanat et une première approche de la nouvelle ère des machines. S'y manifeste aussi comme une évidence la nécessité de concevoir les objets manufacturés selon d'autres critères. L'artisan n'est plus le maître du produit final : un nouvel acteur apparaît, qui dessine les produits fabriqués par des machines − du verre à la porcelaine, de l'acier aux étoffes, du papier aux caractères d'imprimerie. Les Lumières ont donné naissance à une nouvelle manière de penser au moment où les gens vivaient dans l'attente d'un nouvel ordre social. Plus tard, la Révolution française donne un coup d'accélérateur à l'évolution humaine et insuffle une nouvelle vigueur à ces idées. L'homme moderne est né, l'homme libéré des chaînes de l'oppression et des limitations contraignantes du passé. De nouveaux horizons stimulent les esprits dans tous les domaines, des sciences aux arts, de la politique au commerce. Au début du XIXe siècle, l'avènement de la machine à vapeur stimule puissamment l'industrie. Les produits de tout type doivent être dessinés en fonction des nouveaux processus de fabrication. La mécanisation prend les rênes − du chemin de fer au textile. L'agriculture elle-même se mécanise. Les ponts en acier se tendent au-dessus de l'ère nouvelle. Tous les objets sont désormais « designés », d'abord un peu naïvement, plus tard d'une manière consciente qui permet aux nouvelles technologies et sensibilités de s'exprimer. Les évolutions industrielles et technologiques entraînent toujours dans leur sillage des changements sociaux qui affectent à leur tour l'expression artistique. Les expressions créatives deviennent toujours un miroir qui reflète la société.

Marx et Engels se sont fait les porte-parole du besoin d'une justice sociale différente. Une nouvelle manière d'aborder la condition humaine donne naissance à de nouvelles idéologies qui couvrent tous les aspects de la société née de la révolution industrielle. Au milieu du XIXe siècle, William Morris réagit contre la morosité stylistique due à l'utilisation impropre des nouveaux processus industriels et prône une attention nouvelle au design des produits − des meubles aux tissus.

La conception et la construction du Crystal Palace à Londres annoncent l'émergence de la modernité en architecture. Ce bâtiment tout à fait unique en fonte et en verre fut construit à Hyde Park à l'occasion de l'Exposition universelle de 1851, qui présentait les produits les plus récents de nombreuses nations. Son design anticipait de bien des années les murs-rideaux en verre que l'architecte Gropius allait concevoir dans les années 1920.

Le profil du designer moderne commence à prendre forme. Dès le début du XXe siècle, en Allemagne, Peter Behrens est le modèle du designer industriel moderne. Son travail couvre tout le champ d'application du design en s'appuyant sur des processus mentaux et des modes d'expression inédits. Behrens fut le premier designer à répondre au besoin de communication de l'industrie et le véritable inventeur de l'identité graphique, qui donne une expression visuelle à l'engagement d'intégrité et de qualité de l'entreprise. Behrens fut aussi membre fondateur du Deutscher Werkbund, qui jouera un rôle de premier plan en conciliant design et industrie. En 1921, une mémorable publication du Werkbund intitulée *XX Eigen-Marken* (Vingt marques maison) présente pour la première fois un recueil de marques et de logotypes créés par ses membres, dont beaucoup rompent avec les formes d'identité graphique traditionnelles qui prévalent à l'époque.

D'autres mouvements d'avant-garde européens ont contribué de leur mieux à rompre les ponts avec le passé traditionnel et à élaborer la pensée et les pratiques du design moderne. Cette nouvelle vague d'activité intellectuelle et créative déborde vers bien des domaines situés au-delà du design : peinture, sculpture, architecture, danse, musique, poésie etc. Ses contributeurs sont originaires de nombreuses régions d'Europe. Les constructivistes russes sont les principaux acteurs de l'avant-garde européenne. El Lissitzky est le père absolu du mouvement. Pour ce champion de la modernité, « même la nouveauté n'était pas assez nouvelle. »[1] À Paris, les peintres cubistes inaugurent de nouvelles manières de voir le monde et de concevoir la forme visuelle. En Hollande, les membres du groupe De Stijl enrichissent de leurs inventions tout à fait uniques cet effort pour se libérer radicalement des formes traditionnelles. L'un d'entre eux, le peintre Piet Mondrian, écrit alors : « De tout temps, toutes les variations passées ont été "nouvelles". Mais ce n'était pas LA nouveauté. N'oublions pas que nous nous trouvons à la fin d'une culture, à la fin de tout ce qui est ancien. »[2] Les futuristes en Italie et les dadaïstes en Suisse et à Berlin ont joué un rôle majeur dans la libération de la typographie.

Le centre de toute cette dynamique du changement est l'Allemagne. En 1927, des designers de nombreuses régions d'Allemagne forment autour de Kurt Schwitters un groupe connu sous le nom de « Ring Neuer Werbegestalter » (Cercle des nouveaux graphistes publicitaires), dont les membres comptent notamment Jan Tschichold, Max Burchartz, Willi Baumeister, pour n'en citer que quelques-uns.

Spread from identity style guide for
Connecticut General Life Insurance,
designed by Lester Beall in 1958

Doppelseite aus dem Design-
manual der Connecticut
General Life Insurance, 1958
von Lester Beall entwickelt

Double page du manuel de design
graphique de la Connecticut General
Life Insurance, développé en 1958
par Lester Beall

25

Massimo Vignelli's visual identity
for American Airlines, 1967

Massimo Vignellis Erscheinungsbild
für die Fluggesellschaft American
Airlines, 1967

L'identité visuelle de la compagnie
aérienne American Airlines conçue
par Massimo Vignelli, 1967

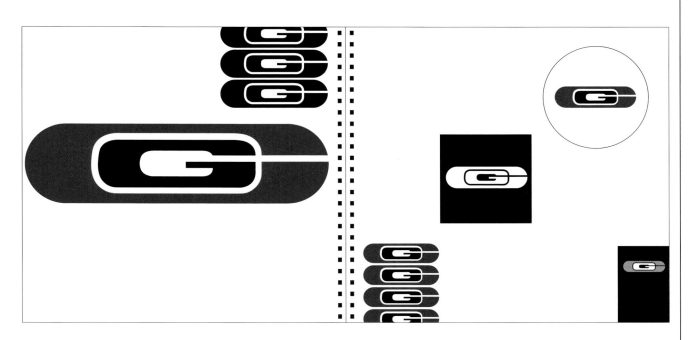

Ce groupe de graphistes organise des expositions et des rencontres dans toute l'Allemagne, présentant leur graphismes progressifs et défendant l'approche avant-gardiste de leur travail. Une bonne part de l'expression moderne européenne a été unifiée au Bauhaus en Allemagne. Cette école expérimentale, particulièrement pendant la phase de Dessau, fut la première à définir les lignes idéologiques et formelles du métier de designer, de ses sensibilités enrichies et de son sens utilitaire.

La vague de la modernité arrive aux États-Unis avant la Seconde Guerre mondiale. À l'apogée du boom économique d'après-guerre, la définition de l'identité visuelle devient l'objectif de la plupart des entreprises et industries américaines. Toutes ont alors besoin d'un nouveau logo ou symbole. Une image moderne est la norme pour toute entreprise. Les designers américains progressistes comme Lester Beall, Paul Rand et William Golden relèvent le défi, marquant le début de l'âge d'or de la *corporate identity* aux États-Unis. Les effets de cette dynamique mondiale seront encore perceptibles pendant une bonne partie des années 1970.

À la fin des années 1980, une révision critique soumet les idéaux de la modernité à rude épreuve. Le déconstructivisme est une mode née du désir de remplacer la modernité. Les sceptiques se demandent si la modernité n'est qu'un style et les designers s'interrogent à leur tour pour savoir si une nouvelle approche du design est porteuse de valeurs temporaires ou permanentes. En réponse à leurs critiques, les esprits objectifs ressentent la nécessité de faire comprendre la différence entre remplacement et évolution. Comme Vignelli l'a déclaré avec une grande pertinence : «Remplacer la modernité relevait d'un malentendu touchant la notion fondamentale de modernité. La modernité n'est pas seulement un style, mais une attitude dynamique en perpétuel mouvement, avec des bases solides reposant sur des processus rationnels. Les styles en sont l'exact contraire : des manifestations éphémères des désirs spéculatifs des fabricants. »[3] Si les incrédules persistent, pour beaucoup de ses défenseurs la modernité est aujourd'hui vivante et se porte bien parce que sa *raison d'être* est d'ordre permanent et que ses impératifs ont une validité historique. Entre et défenseurs de la modernité, le débat se poursuit. Malgré la divergence des points de vue, les modernes restent fidèles à leur objectif utopique d'améliorer le monde par le design.

Références des citations

[1] Lissitzky, El : Travail non publié
[2] Hollis, Richard : *Swiss Graphic Design*, Yale University Press, New Haven 2006, p. 15
[3] Massimo Vignelli à propos de la modernité : lettre personnelle, 2012

R. Roger Remington is Vignelli Distinguished Professor of Design at the Vignelli Center for Design Studies at Rochester Institute of Technology, Rochester, New York, USA.

R. Roger Remington ist Vignelli Distinguished Professor of Design des Vignelli Center for Design Studies am Rochester Institute of Technology, Rochester, New York, USA.

R. Roger Remington est un éminent professeur de design du Vignelli Center for Design Studies au Rochester Institute of Technology, Rochester, New York, USA.

Geometric Geometrisch Géométrique

Geometric

Different periods in the relatively short history of design are marked either by a trend towards greater simplicity or a counter-trend away from it. Such changes of approach were probably at the root of the conflict many graphic artists experienced between free artistic expression and commercial design. Modernist designers gladly seized on the rules and visual vocabulary of geometry. Circles, triangles, rectangles and squares were able to transmit clear and emphatic signs. Many successful logos also incorporated visual references to the advertiser's name and/or line of business. This sometimes means that a second or even a third look at the logo is required to interpret the full meaning.

Die unterschiedlichen Epochen der noch relativ jungen Design-geschichte sind bestimmt durch den Trend hin zu bzw. den Gegen-trend weg von einer verstärkten Sachlichkeit in der Gestaltung. Hier spiegelt sich vermutlich der in vielen Gestalterpersönlichkeiten steckende Zwiespalt zwischen freiem künstlerischem Ausdruck und einem – weniger anfechtbaren – verwissenschaftlichten Ent-wurf wider. Modernistische Gestalter griffen die Geometrie mit ihrer Formensprache und ihrem Regelwerk jedenfalls dankbar auf. Aus Kreisen, Dreiecken, Rechtecken oder Quadraten konstruierten sie eindeutige und kraftvolle Zeichen. Das Einfügen von visuellen Hinwei-sen auf den Namen oder die Tätigkeit des jeweiligen Unternehmens gelang dennoch in vielen Fällen. Hierzu ist beim Betrachter jedoch mitunter ein zweiter oder dritter Blick auf das Zeichen notwendig.

Les différentes époques de l'histoire encore relativement jeune du graphisme sont marquées par la tendance à une sobriété créative accrue, ou bien par le courant opposé qui s'en éloigne. Ceci traduit sans doute le dilemme de bien des graphiste entre création artistique libre et travail le plus scientifique possible, c'est-à-dire inattaquable. Le fait est que les graphistes modernes ont été heureux d'accueillir dans leur travail la géométrie, avec son langage formel et son cortège de règles. A partir de cercles, de triangles, de rectangles ou de carrés, ils ont conçu des signes aussi clairs que puissants. L'intégration de références visuelles aux noms ou à l'activité des entreprises concer-nées n'en a pas moins été réussie dans bien des cas. Il est vrai que ces réalisations nécessitent parfois un second ou un troisième regard.

Anguleux

Eckig

Angular

Artwood Büromöbel
Office furniture
1960s · Ernst Roch · CA

Light Publicity
Design
1962 · Makoto Wada · JP

The Mite Corporation
Electronics
1960s · Lester Beall · US

Brouers Møbelfabrik
Furniture
1970s · Anonymous · DK

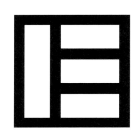

Enciclopedia Fatos e Fotos
Publishing
1966 · Pinto Ziraldo · BR

Werbeagentur Atelier Robert Pütz
Advertising
1965 · Robert Pütz · DE

Günter Bläse Werbeagentur
Advertising
1950s · Günter Bläse · DE

Fischer Baugesellschaft
Construction company
1972 · Gerold Schmidt · DE

Salev
Electronics
1969 · Bucher-Crémières · FR

Brasibel SA
Textiles
1967 · Alexandre Wollner · BR

Film/Funk/Fernsehwissenschaftliche Bibliothek Berlin
Library
1965 · Herbert Prüget · DE-GDR

Securit SA
Office furniture
1961 · Alexandre Wollner · BR

Catesbys
Delivery service
1964 · Peter Ray · UK

Klingenthal
Textiles
1960s · Anonymous · DE

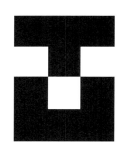

Betonwerk Teltow
Cement
1965 · Andreas Nießen · DE-GDR

Dewag-Dia-Dresden
Photographic services
1965 · Johannes Brase · DE-GDR

M. Medicke
Industrial trade
1965 · Peter Mantwill · DE-GDR

Takahashi Shoji
Industrial recycling
1960s · Nakajo Masayoshi · JP

Stuhlfabrik Körner
Furniture
1965 · Reiner Wiegang · DE-GDR

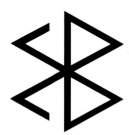

Ernst Beutler
Interior design
1940s · Hans Hartmann · CH

Empire Hotel, Rio de Janeiro
1960s · Aloísio Magalhães/PVDI · BR

Hamburger Illustrierte
Magazine
1970s · Ekkehart Rustmeier · DE

**Projektierung für die Bindemittel-
und Betonindustrie Dessau**
Construction company
1965 · Karl Thewalt · DE-GDR

Möbelkombinat Erfurt
Furniture
1965 · Reiner & Sigrid Wiegang · DE-GDR

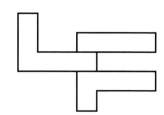

**2nd Congresso Panamericano
de Arquitetos, São Paulo**
Architectural congress
1962 · João Carlos Cauduro · BR

Lamm-Frates Company
Real estate
1971 · Crawford Dunn · US

Fernsehgerätewerke Stassfurt
Televisions
1965 · Heinz Unzner · DE-GDR

**Hannelore Lüling
Verlagsbuchhandlung Erlangen**
Bookstore
1973 · Anonymous · DE

Companhia General de Minas
Mining
1962 · Alexandre Wollner · BR

Sanyo Electric
1970 · Tomoichi Nishiwaki,
Inada Akira · JP

Eduard Franke Apparatebau
Electrical
1965 · Reiner Wiegang · DE-GDR

Kind Stahlmöbelfabrik
Furniture
1960s · Wolfgang Schmittel · DE

GT Tisch-Hydraulik
Hydraulic systems
1970 · Heiko Groschke · DE

Sola y Tortas
Lighting systems
1972 · Lydia Casellas · ES

Transformatorenwerk Falkensee
Machinery
1965 · Herbert Prüget · DE-GDR

Riverside Housing
1957 · Ernst Roch/
Design Collaborative · CA

Taller Cubano
Automobile repairs
1966 · Reynaldo Da Costa · VE

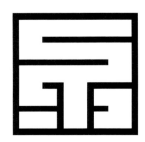

**Europäisch-Arabische Bank,
Frankfurt am Main**
1973 · Heinz Schwabe · DE

Betonwerke Berlin
Cement
1965 · Manfred Kloppert · DE-GDR

Tecnizoo
Stockbreeding
1963 · Walter Del Frate · IT

Galeria Folha
Art gallery
1961 · Willys de Castro,
Hércules Barsotti · BR

Seibert-Stinnes
Warehousing
1973 · Heinz Schwabe · DE

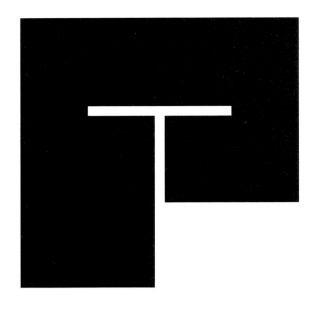

Indústrias Paramount
Clothing
1963 · Alexandre Wollner · BR

Marketing Italia S.p.A.
Research institute
1960s · Cecco Re · IT

id Druck
Printing
1960 · Herbert W. Kapitzki · DE

Little, Brown
Publishing
1960s · Push Pin Studios · US

Georges Streiff
1960s · Roger-Virgile Geiser · CH

RAI Radiotelevisione Italiana
Broadcasting
1954 · Erberto Carboni · IT

World Design Conference Tokyo
1960 · Takashi Kono · JP

Gassmann & Menge
1965 · Fritz Deutschendorf · DE-GDR

Giovanni Brunazzi
Design
1960s · Giovanni Brunazzi · IT

Ediciones Mundonuevo
Publishing
1950s · Rómulo Macció · AR

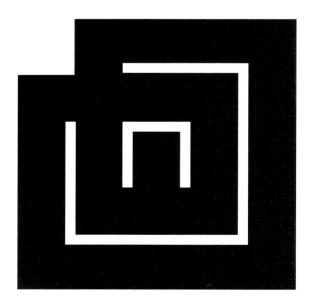

Witthöft Werk für Spulenkörper & Isoliererzeugnisse
Heating technology
1965 · Johannes Brase · DE-GDR

Philosophische Bibliothek, Hamburg
Publishing
1989 · Jens Peter Mardersteig · DE

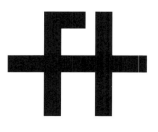

Preben Schou
Furniture
1970s · Anonymous · DK

Allende & Brea
Lawyers
1960s · Gustavo Balcells · AR

Form und Technik
Industrial design
1960s · Wolfgang Schmittel · DE

Data Pathing
Data processing
1971 · Harry Murphy, Victor Langer/
Harry Murphy & Friends · US

**Lehr-und Leistungsschau
Neubrandenburg**
Trade fair
1965 · Ludwig Bonitz · DE-GDR

George F. Eber
Architecture
1960s · Ernst Roch · CA

Estro Armonico:Club
Record label
1960s · Jacques Richez · BE

Harry A. Jarvis
Fuel oil
1960s · Nedo Mion Ferrario · VE

Weimar-Werk
Machinery
1965 · Fritz Deutschendorf · DE-GDR

Harcourt Brace Jovanovich
Publishing
1972 · Anonymous · US

Turnpike Engineering
1964 · Kramer, Miller, Lomden,
Glassman Inc. · US

Jana
1970s · Hannes Schober,
Wolfram Reinhardt · DE

**Ingenieurbüro für Planung und
Steuerungssysteme**
Planning and control systems
1973 · Heinz Schwabe · DE

RAI Edizioni ERI
Publishing
1966 · Paolo Bargis · IT

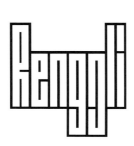

Renggli
Interior design
1960s · Carlo L. Vivarelli · CH

Muster-Schmidt Verlagsgesellschaft
Publishing
1905 · Christian Hansen-Schmidt · DE

P.I.E. Facilities
Life insurance
1971 · Arthur Eckstein · US

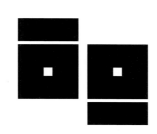

Action Graphique Paris
Design
1959 · Gérard Ifert · FR

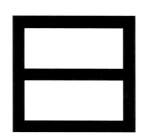

Nikken Setsukei
Architecture
1970 · Hiromu Hara · JP

**Teatro de Arena da Guanabara,
Rio de Janeiro**
Theater
1967 · Pinto Ziraldo · BR

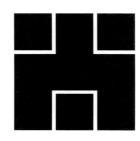

Brafor
Furniture
1965 · Aloísio Magalhães/PVDI · BR

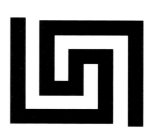

Stuttgarter Gardinenfabrik
Curtains
1960s · Otl Aicher · DE

Tall Oaks
Construction company
1969 · Patricia Turnbull · CA

Bonifica
Landscape planning
1968 · Enzo Mari · IT

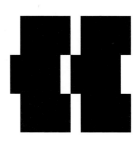

Associazione Italiana Prefabbricazione
Prefabricated buildings
1964 · Bob Noorda/
Unimark International · IT

Holzform
Carpentry
1970 · Hannes Schober,
Wolfram Reinhardt · DE

I.J.J. Koroknay & Associates
Urban planning
1967 · Imre Koroknay · CA

Flèche

Pfeil

Arrow

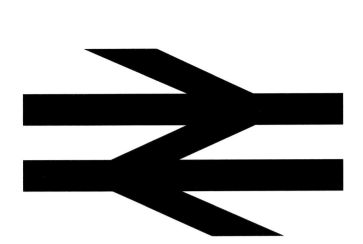

British Railways Board
Public transport
1964 · Gerald Barney, Milner Gray, Rupert Armstrong,
Collis Clements/Design Research Unit · UK

Nederlandse Spoorwegen
Public transport
1967 · Tel Design Associated · NL

Treffpunkt
Television show
1979 · Odermatt+Tissi · CH

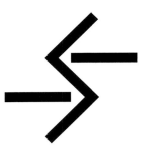

Steiner
Import-export
1958 · Marcel Wyss · CH

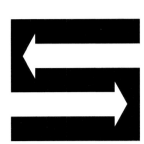

Shannon Car Ferry
1968 · Eric Patton · UK

Electricity Council
1968 · Nicholas Jenkins · UK

Ministerium für Verkehr
Department of transport
(proposed design)
1970s · Helmut Schmid · DE

International University Exchange
Student exchange program
1955 · Ralph Prins · NL

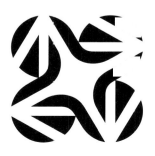

Steetfinder
Maps
1971 · Arie J. Geurts · US

Metro
Public transport
1972 · Jesús Emilio Franco/
Diseño Industrial-Publicidad · VE

International Marketing Corporation
1975 · James Lienhart · US

Educational Tour
Student travel organization
1969 · Walter J. Diethelm,
Jürg Grüninger · CH

New Brunswick Telephone Co.
Telecommunications
1966 · Ernst Roch/
Design Collaborative · CA

Alcu Team Nixdorf
Computer systems
1971 · Ludvík Feller · DE

Assist A.S.B.L.
Student travel organization
1966 · Michel Olyff · BE

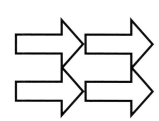

**Review of Educational Cybernetics
& Applied Linguistics**
Academic journal
1968 · Ian McLaren · UK

Flugaggregate
Aircraft technology
1972 · Max Graf von Pückler,
Norbert Schramp · DE

Lambert Lepage Labbé, Montreal
Audio-visual communication
1968 · Claude Gauthier · CA

Welthandelsfirma
Import-export
1980 · Odermatt+Tissi · CH

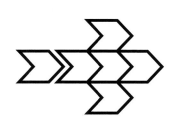

Ullian
Publishing
1962 · Etienne Bucher · FR

Hochvakuum
Vacuum products
1965 · Herbert Prüget · DE-GDR

Büro für Handelsförderung
Trade promotion
1960s · Roger-Virgile Geiser · CH

SIMAT Italestero
Postal services
1971 · Ornella Noorda · IT

Committee of Aluminum Producers
1960s · Saul Bass · US

Chemdorff
Chemicals
1970 · Francisco Marco Vilar/
Grupo de Diseño · ES

Museum of Fine Arts, Montreal
1970 · Fritz Gottschalk/
Gottschalk+Ash · CA

Hammaslaboratorio Hamtek
Dental laboratory
1966 · Juhani Parikka/
Markkinointi Viherjuuri · FI

Companhia Brasileira de Projetos
Construction company
1967 · João Carlos Cauduro,
Ludovico Antonio Martino · BR

Polskie Koleje Państwowe
Public transport
1960s · Josef Słobosz · PL

J. C. Stackhouse Studios
Design
1968 · J. C. Stackhouse Studios · CA

VEB Hochspannungswerk
Electricity
1965 · Berthold Resch · DE-GDR

Reinhardt Klinkhardt
Air filtration
1965 · Horst Hilbert · DE-GDR

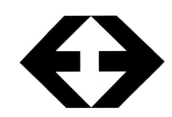

Austral Líneas Aéreas
Airline
1966 · Guillermo Gonzáles Ruiz · AR

Import-Export
1960s · Andrzej Zbrozek · PL

Touchstone Books
Publishing
1970 · John Condon · US

Heben Fördern Lagern Seibert-Stinnes
Storage technology
1973 · Heinz Schwabe · DE

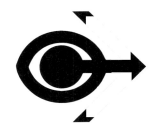

Centre d'Etudes et de Développement des Relations Internationales
Student exchange program
1968 · Jacques Douin · FR

Ferrovie Nord Milano
Public transport
1981 · R. Nava, D. Soffientini, A. Ubertazzi · IT

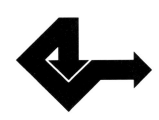

Boyer
Craft supplier
1969 · Alain Pontecorvo · FR

Stelko
Electronics
1969 · Morten Peetz-Schou · DK

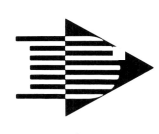

Dusal Instruments
Industrial manufacture
1960s · Eckstein-Stone · US

Hispanic Center, Salt Lake City
Cultural center
1979 · Scott Engen · US

Transitalia
Travel agency
1977 · Giovanni Brunazzi · IT

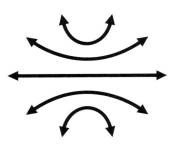

Corning Class
Works foundation
1974 · Robert Hagenhofer · US

Arthur & Spencer
Haulier
1969 · Peter G. Ulmer · CA

Robert Cantieni
Printing
1968 · Christian Lang · CH

Rastal Glasveredlung
Glass
1973 · Lothar Böhm · DE

Mark Five
Investment
1971 · Allan W. Miller · US

Applied Power Industries
Machinery
1960s · J. Budd Steinhilber/ Vie Design Studios · US

Westinghouse Electric Corporation
Management convention
1969 · Peter Megert · US

Schweizerische Reisekasse
Travel fund
1960s · Rudolf Bircher · CH

Jefferson Buslines
· Public transport
1973 · Peter Seitz · US

Meca
Highway advertising
1970 · Studio González Ruiz & Shakespear · AR

Western Center on Law and Poverty
Social services support center
1969 · Rod Dyer · US

SGS
Microcircuit sales conference
1965 · Bob Noorda/ Unimark International · IT

Brasil Travel Agency
1960s · Magalhães, Noronha & Pontual · BR

Galeria Seta
Art gallery
1963 · Willys de Castro, Hércules Barsotti · BR

Asbestos
1970s · Woudhuysen Inc. · UK

Flugsýningin 1969
Aviation history exhibition
1969 · Thröstur Magnusson, Hilmar
Sigurdsson/Argus Advertising · IS

WCVB-TV Channel 5
Broadcasting
1970s · Lance Wyman · US

Dynam Publicité
Advertising
1965 · Anonymous · BE

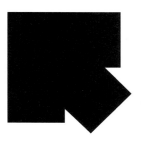

Montello Tour
Tourism
1977 · Peter Vetter · IT

Ediciones de Occidente
Publishing
1964 · Amand Domènech · ES

**New Brunswick
Hydro-Electric Company**
Energy supplier
1971 · Chris Yaneff · CA

Centro de Información CNC
Information center
1968 · Félix Beltrán · CU

Kutsuna Shoji
Manufacturing
1974 · Koichi Watanabe · JP

Karl Künzle
1970 · Michael Baviera · CH

Controle Qualtiss
Textiles
1961 · Gérard Ifert · FR

Treffpunkt Industrie
Trade organization
1960s · Walter Brudi · DE

Coco Ernesto Transportes
Transport
1976 · Jorge Sposari · AR

Carlo Reggiani
Plastics
1968 · Vittorio Antinori · IT

Carrefour de la Belle Epine
Shopping center
1969 · Théodore Stamatakis/
Créations Stama · FR

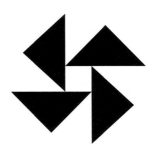

Sarag
Advertising
1965 · Anonymous · DE

**Centre National de la
Formation Permanente**
Education
1970 · Rémy Peignot · FR

Exposición Ferroviaria Internacional
Rail transport exhibition
1968 · Ricardo Blanco · AR

Fotograbado Vene
Prepress services
1967 · Gerd Leufert · VE

Statens Informasjonstjeneste
Information center
1968 · Paul Brand · NO

Asbestos Eastern Transport
Transport
1960 · Jean Morin · CA

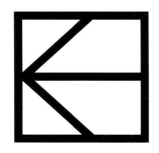

Kurt Huber
Advertising
1950s · Kurt Huber · CH

Edward Hughes
Design
1973 · Edward Hughes · US

Park City Hospital
1978 · Joe Dieter · US

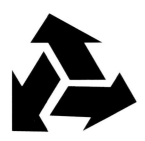

Comercializadora de Banano Comunbana-Panama
Foods
1978 · Dicken Castro · CO

City of Emeryville
City identity
1973 · William Carson,
Douglas Williams · US

Internationale Verpackungsausstellung
Packaging exhibition
1960s · Adolf Flückiger · CH

Schwabengarage
Parking lot
1940s · Hans Gaensslen · DE

Interpol
International police organization
(proposed design)
1944 · Max Huber · IT

Kiewit Computation Center
Integrated computing
1966 · Frank Lieberman · US

Elitera Verlag
Publishing
1971 · Wolfram Geister · DE

Consorcio Intermex
1973 · Ernesto Lehfeld · MX

Glasgow Airport
1965 · Kinneir, Calvert & Associates · UK

Ximenes Hnos
Import-export
1960s · Gerd Leufert · VE

**Salon de l'Audiovisuel et
de la Communication**
1970 · Daniel Maurel/
Chourgnoz Publicité · FR

Ingeniörforlaget
Publishing
1967 · Bruno Oldani · NO

Cedec
Swimming club
1972 · Jean Delaunay/Look · FR

Museum Voor Schone Kunsten, Ghent
Art museum
1967 · Antoon de Vijlder · BE

National Design Council
Industrial design body
1962 · Allan Robb Fleming · CA

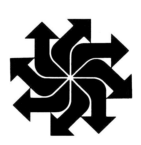

Cominag
1981 · Florent Garnier · FR

Instituto Mexicano de Opinión Pública
Market research
1975 · Ernesto Lehfeld · MX

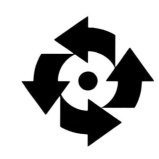

Jean Oertli
Tools
1946 · Hans Neuburg · CH

Hillier Parker May & Rowden
Real estate
1970 · Michael Tucker · UK

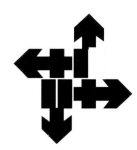

Feria de Muestras de Barcelona
Exhibition
1969 · Ribas & Creus · ES

Medalist Manufacturing Company
Heating technology
1968 · Randall R. Roth · US

The Celdic Report
Health survey
1970 · Leslie Smart · CA

New York State Urban Development
State-subsidized housing
1980 · Arnold Saks · US

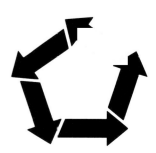

Pentair
Air-conditioning
1980 · Bror B. Zetterborg · FI

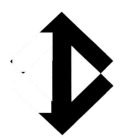

Companhia do Metropolitano São Paulo
Public transport
1967 · João Carlos Cauduro,
Ludovico Antonio Martino · BR

Polo Consultoria e Planejamento
City planning
1969 · João Carlos Cauduro,
Ludovico Antonio Martino · BR

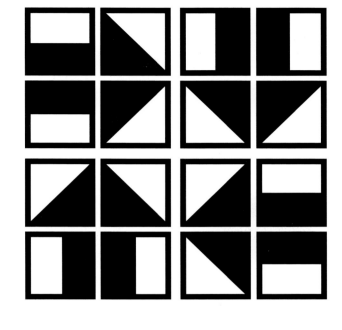

St. Paul Skyways
Transportation
1970 · Peter Seitz · US

National & Commercial Banking Group
1968 · Mark Woodhams/
Allied International Designers · UK

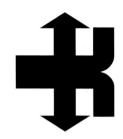

Suomen Ulkomaankauppaliitto
Import-export
1959 · Kosti A. Antikainen · FI

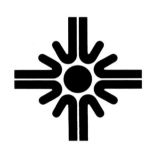

Union Carbide Corporation
Chemicals
1975 · Richard Yeager · US

West Coast Landscape Construction
Landscape design
1960s · Conrad E. Angone · US

Camera di Commercio I.A.A. di Milano
Chamber of commerce
(part of integrated logo system)
1972 · Mimmo Castellano · IT

Carolina Trade Zone
Free trade zone
1975 · Robert A. Gale · US

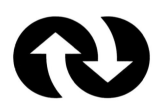

New Life Movement Association
Civic education
1975 · Kiyoshi Kyoi · JP

Metro São Paolo
Public transport
1978 · PVDI · BR

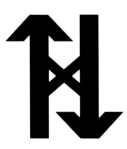

Preludin
Appetite suppressant
1960s · George Giusti · US

Werbeagentur Gerber, Geiß, Kunert & Co.
Advertising
1972 · Rainer E. Kunert · DE

Abakonverlag
Publishing
1975 · Helmut Lortz · DE

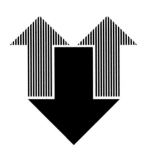

Pest Control of Cambridge
1953 · Henrion Design Associates · UK

Haulier
1950s · Heinz Schwabe · DE

Corporación Casa de la Juventud
Youth hostel
1981 · Gustavo Gómez-Casallas · CO

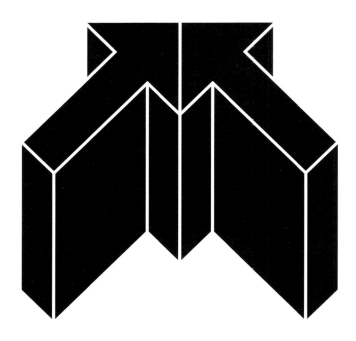

Ministerio del Comercio Exterior
Foreign trade
1973 · Félix Beltrán · CU

**Home & Dominion
Investments of Canada**
1969 · Arthur Irizawa/
Stewart & Morrison · CA

Brødr. Søyland
Construction machinery
1965 · Erik Fjellberg · NO

Asphalt Roofing
Building materials
1983 · Terry Lesniewicz/Al Navarre · US

Nippon Illustrators Conference
1969 · Shigeo Fukuda · JP

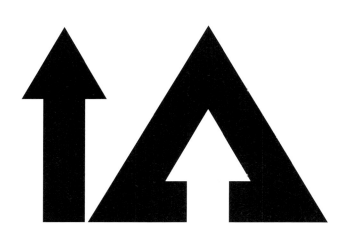

International Instant Archery Association
1971 · David L. Burke · US

US Air Force Systems Command
Military research and development
1961 · Ben Dennis · US

Scal GP
Aluminum
1967 · Roman Duszek/
Lonsdale Design · FR

Road Construction Enterprise
Highway construction
1980 · Ivan Dvoršak,
Matjaz Bertonceli · YU

Constructions Métalique
Machinery
1950s · Jacques Nathan-Garamond · FR

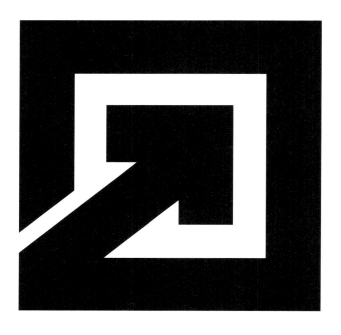

Design-Zentrum Baden-Württemberg
Design association
1956 · Herbert W. Kapitzki · DE

Gozdno Gospodarstvo Novo Mesto
Forestry
1976 · Ivan Dvoršak · YU

Bunka
Publishing
1970 · Shigeo Fukuda · JP

J. R. Geigy
Pharmaceuticals
1960s · Toshihiro Katayama · JP

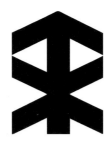

Quebec Pavilion, Expo '67, Montreal
World's fair stand
1967 · Frank Lipari/
Gazette Printing Company · CA

Vereinigte Schweizer Rheinsalinen
Salt
1960s · Ferdi Afflerbach · CH

La Nouvelle Encyclopédie
Publishing
1960s · Christin Delorme · FR

Nihon Jutaku Prefab
Prefabricated houses
1960s · Yusaku Kamekura · JP

Crédit Lyonnais Bank
1971 · Daniel Morel/
Chourgnoz Publicité · FR

Ciba
Pharmaceuticals
1958 · Ernst Roch/
Design Collaborative · CA

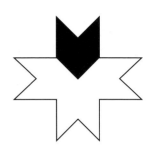

John Sandwick Studios
Design
1969 · Bill Hyde · US

Sanshin Electric
Telecommunications
1968 · Hiroshi Ohchi · JP

Helwig
Agricultural machinery
1960s · Wolfgang Schmittel · DE

I.F.P.
Oil drilling
1968 · Etienne Bucher · FR

Auto-Test
Automobile electrics
1970 · Michel Martina · FR

Caudano Casa e Giardino
Home and garden center
1972 · Emanuele Centazzo/Sitcap · IT

Holzindustrie Altmark, Tangerhütte
Timber reclamation
1965 · Karl Müller · DE-GDR

S.V.T. Société du Verre
Textiles
1964 · Philippe Caza · FR

Norris Industries
Fire and safety equipment
1960s · Eskil Ohlsson/
Solow-Wexton · US

Impuls Werbung Horst Kraus
Advertising
1961 · Anonymous · DE

George W. Barton & Associates
Road planning
1960s · R. Nelson/
W. Bartsch Associates · US

Indústrias Villares
Construction company
1967 · João Carlos Cauduro,
Ludovico Antonio Martino · BR

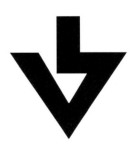

Virax
Precision tools
1960s · Rémy Peignot · FR

Rohm and Haas
Chemicals
1960s · Lester Beall · US

Polttoaine GHH
Fuel oil
1967 · Seppo Polameri · FI

Moldoplast
Plastics
1965 · Amand Domènech · ES

Kibag
Construction materials
1979 · Odermatt+Tissi · CH

Swissair
Airline
1952 · Rudolf Bircher · CH

King Racing
Drag and bike racing
1980 · Thomas Ohmer,
Courtney Reeser · US

Nankai Tuun
Express shipping
1960s · Yoshio Amaya · JP

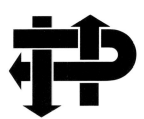

Pockman Manufacturing
Poultry farming equipment
1960s · R.W. Mutch & Co. · US

Trade Union of Building Workers
1960 · Franciszek Winiarski · PL

Japan Socialist Party
1961 · Makoto Wada · JP

Ville de Montréal
City administration
1964 · Jacques Roy/
Jacques Guillon Designers · CA

Placement Services
Employment agency
1972 · Ed Bohon · US

Caribbean Communications
Investment
1968 · Heiner Hegemann/
Chermayeff & Geismar · US

Budapesti Metró
Public transport
1968 · Crescencia Zelenák · HU

Presspali
Deep drilling
1970 · Giovanni Brunazzi · IT

Romfield Building Corporation
Construction company
1965 · Chris Yaneff · CA

Chaums Apparel
Clothing
1970 · Vance Jonson · US

Nishimura Shiko
Paper
1969 · Tomoichi Nishiwaki · JP

Polator
Import-export
1964 · Martti A. Mykkänen · FI

Sidbec Steel
1965 · Frank Lipari/
Gazette Printing Company · CA

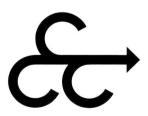

Corporate Communications Company
Advertising
1965 · Lou Frimkess/
Advertising Designers · US

Nihon Industrial Newspaper
1969 · Shigeo Fukuda · JP

G. Priestner
Haulier
1964 · Kenneth Hollick · UK

Seatrain Lines
Container transport
1964 · Tom Geismar/
Chermayeff & Geismar · US

Dynastructures
Space engineering
1963 · Kramer, Miller,
Lomden, Glassman Inc. · US

Neuenschwander, Bern
Thermal engineering
1950s · Robert Sessler · CH

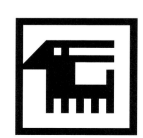

MÉM Kiállítási Iroda
Agriculture
1967 · István Szekeres · HU

G. Stasen
Investment
1968 · Randall R. Roth · US

R. E. Suter Lichtpausanstalt
Reprographics
1940s · Robert Sessler · CH

Acciones y Valores
Broker
1979 · Fernando Rión · MX

Gifts on the Green
Gift store
1967 · Herman & Lees Associates · US

Kenneth Harris
Hearing aid consulting
1960s · Ron Ford · UK

Soundguide
Metal workshop
1960s · David Caplan · UK

AP Bauunternehmung
Construction company
1950s · Emanuel Bosshardt · CH

Green Arrow
Publishing
1983 · Makoto Yoshida · JP

**Centre National de la Recherche
Scientifique**
Government research organization
1971 · J. Picart le Doux · FR

Comsip Automation
Electronics
1969 · Jacques Nathan-Garamond · FR

Crédit Mutuel Hypothécaire
Bank
1968 · Gilles Fiszman · BE

Gottlieb Pfenninger
Electronics
1950s · Rose-Marie
Joray-Muchenberger · CH

R. Pape
Antennas
1971 · Peter Riefenstahl · DE

United Investment Services
1967 · Chris Yaneff · CA

**Städtebau Entwicklungs-
und Sanierungsgesellschaft**
Urban development
1970s · Hanns Lohrer · DE

Cagneuve
Engineering
1967 · Etienne Bucher · FR

Up Magazine
1970 · Ave Pildas · US

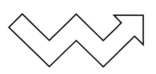

De Wolf
Advertising
1960s · De Wolf · BE

East Dayton Tool & Die Company
Tool manufacturer
1960 · J. Budd Steinhilber/
Vie Design Studios · US

Hecker Elektronik
Electronics
1976 · Manfred Wutke · DE

La Voce Repubblicana
Newspaper
1973 · Michele Spera · IT

Vereinigte Zellstoff, Pirna
Paper
1965 · Johannes Brase · DE-GDR

The Education Directory
Communications
1978 · Ner Beck · US

Harold Hare
Real estate
1968 · Leslie Smart · CA

Walther + Moser Elektroapparate
Electronics
1950s · Hans Rudolf Lauterburg · CH

Mac
Advertising film production
1970 · Tomás Vellvé · ES

Bede Aircraft
Kit-plane manufacturer
1961 · Read Viemeister/
Vie Design Studios · US

Europäischer Allergiekongress, Basel
Health symposium
1962 · Roland Aeschlimann · CH

Svit
Pulp processing
1960s · Milan Vesely · CZ

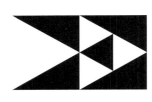

Edgewood Furniture
1961 · Tom Geismar/
Chermayeff & Geismar · US

Solnhofener Plattenwerke
Tiles
1974 · Rolf Müller · DE

Aero-Cargo
Air freight
1965 · Félix Beltrán · CU

Gould
Electronics
1970 · Peter Teubner/
RVI Corp. · US

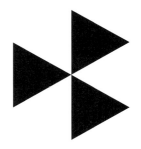

Diethelm Werbeagentur
Advertising
1964 · Walter J. Diethelm · CH

Widom Wein & Partners
Construction company
1979 · Ray Engle · US

M. H. D. Odziez Włókno
Textiles
1964 · Andrzej Zbrozek · PL

Publi-Syrthese & R. L. Dupuy
Advertising
1965 · Anonymous · BE

Moffitt & McDaniel
Architecture
1971 · Ray Engle · US

Studio Books
Publishing
1969 · Jiří Rathouský · CZ

Pittsburgh Wholesale Distributors
Toys
1968 · Philip Seefeld/
Unimark International · US

Ansar Mosaic
Mosaic design
1967 · Ivor Kamlish · UK

Inženjerski Projektni Zavod
Engineering
1973 · Sanja Iveković · YU

Jewish Foundation
Cultural organization
1960s · Ivan Chermayeff, Heiner
Hegemann/Chermayeff & Geismar · US

Japan General Arts Corporation
1970 · Gan Hosoya · JP

Industry Training Board, Harrow
1967 · Kenneth Hollick · UK

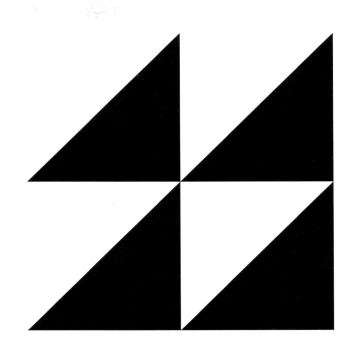

SJV Warmtecentrum
Thermal engineering
1966 · Benno Wissing/Total Design · NL

Steenkolen Handelvereeniging
Trade association
1966 · Total Design · NL

Roger Mayer
Advertising
1960 · Roger Mayer · CH

50 Jahre Technikmagazin
Magazine commemoration
1950s · Paul Sollberger · CH

A-P García, Barcelona
Advertising
1968 · Tomás Vellvé · ES

P. A. Fitzgerald & Co.
Engineering
1960s · Raymond Kyne · IE

Sofia Fashion Center
1960s · Lüdmil Mehandjiev · BG

**Hongkong and Shanghai
Banking Corporation**
1983 · Henry Steiner · HK

German Pavilion, Expo '61, Turin
World's fair stand
1961 · Karl-Oskar Blase · DE

W. S. Inwalidów
1972 · Kazimierz Mann,
Jarosław Jasiński · PL

Nizzoli Associati
Urban planning
1965 · A. G. Fronzoni · IT

Triedro
Furniture
1971 · Michele Spera · IT

Norconsult
Management consultancy
1968 · Bruno Oldani · NO

Novum
Design group
1958 · Helmut Lortz · DE

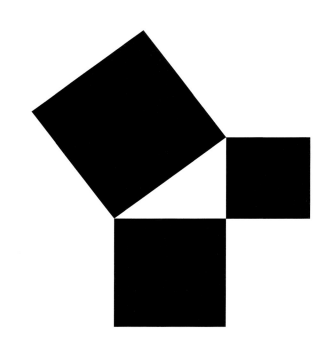

Financial Parameters, Willowdale
Investment
1970 · Manfred Gotthans, Chris Yaneff/Chris Yaneff · CA

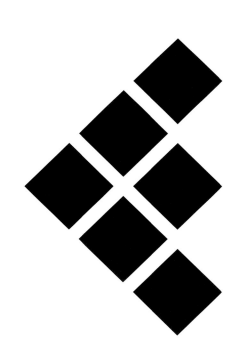

FRESPO Fresas de Exportación
Import-export
1977 · Jaime Gutierrez Lega · CO

Center for Advanced Engineering Study
Institute of technology
1969 · Dietmar R. Winkler · US

**Alumni Association of the
Massachusetts Institute of Technology**
1967 · Dietmar R. Winkler · US

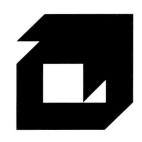

Aeberhard & Co.
Packaging
1969 · Ruedi Peter · CH

Karl H. Stittgen
Jeweler
1966 · Friedrich Peter · CA

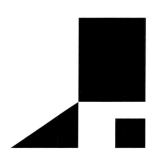

Schuhhersteller
Footwear
1972 · Jerzy Leontiew · PL

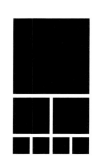

**Brazilian Institute of
Geography and Statistics**
1960s · Magalhães,
Noronha & Pontual · BR

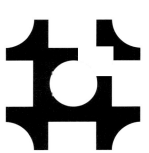

Holland, Hannen & Cubitts
Construction company
1958 · Romek Marber · UK

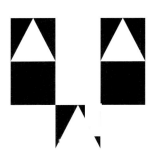

S. C. Fromagerie
Foods
1965 · Luc Van Malderen · BE

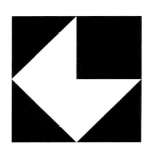

J. L. Møllers Møbelfabrik
Furniture
1960s · Anonymous · DK

Otaka Design Production
Advertising
1975 · Tckeshi Otaka · JP

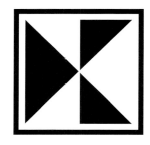

Karl Krämer Verlag
Publishing
1957 · Gottfried Prölß · DE

Fiação e Tecelagem Sant'Ana
Weaving
1972 · João Carlos Cauduro,
Ludovico Antonio Martino · BR

Associated Industrial Consultants
Engineering research
1960 · Henrion Design Associates · UK

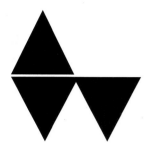

Ault & Wiborg
Inks
1967 · David Caplan · UK

CTV Television Network, Toronto
1966 · E. J. Morrison/
Stewart & Morrison · CA

Primary Mathematics Teaching
Education
1960s · Ivan Dodd · UK

Studio Sansoni
Design
1969 · Piero Sansoni · IT

University of Alberta, Faculty of Arts
Art department
1960s · Walter Jungkind · CA

Ogier Boudoul
Tools
1967 · Gérard Guerre/Technés · FR

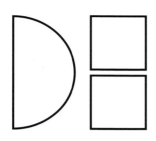

**Facta Werbeagentur Hans-Dieter
Richartz und Alfons Bürger**
Advertising
1975 · Facta Werbeagentur · DE

Ikedamura Aseduction
Planning office
1980 · Norio Ikeda · JP

KD-Kommunikation
Public relations
1969 · Morten Peetz-Schou · DK

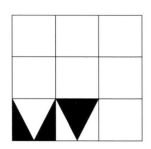

Münchner Volkshochschule
Education
1973 · Rolf Müller · DE

Typographische Gesellschaft München
Design association
1979 · Rolf Müller · DE

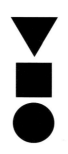

Victor N. Cohen
Advertising
1960 · Victor N. Cohen · CH

Stabilimenti Chimici Italiani
Chemicals
1968 · A. G. Fronzoni · IT

Villa Cerro Industries
Agricultural machinery
1969 · Ferruccio Ferri/Ferri Pubblicità · IT

Mlad
Wooden toys
1974 · František Bobáň · CZ

Gense
Stainless steel
1960s · Rolf Lagerson, Stig Bark · SE

Religioni Oggi Dialogo
Magazine
1970 · Michele Spera · IT

Domo
Grocers
1956 · Hanns Lohrer · DE

American Motors Corporation
Automobile company
1969 · Walter P. Margulies/
Lippincott & Margulies · US

Bardtenschlager Verlag
Publishing
1970 · Anonymous · DE

Divadlo za Branou
Theater
1960s · Ludvík Feller · CZ

Koch Möbel
Furniture
1964 · Klaus Grözinger · DE

Milani & Kobi Werbeagentur
Advertising
1969 · Hans Knöpfli · CH

Praxis und Röntgeneinrichtungen AG
Medical equipment
1965 · Peter Kräuchi · CH

Ribbon
Pharmacy
1979 · Giancarlo Iliprandi · IT

Deciep
1972 · Félix Beltrán · CU

Standard International Corporation
Industrial manufacture and design
1960s · Malcolm Grear · US

Kramer Werbeagentur
Advertising
1950s · Kramer Werbeagentur · DE

Sten Jacobsson Konsult
Management consultancy
1950s · Lars Bramberg · SE

E. Weber & Cie
Vending machines
1961 · Rudolf Bircher · CH

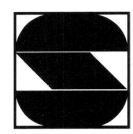

Scfety Products
1970 · Luis Ortega de Uhler · ES

**Research Laboratory of
Architectural Space**
1975 · Akisato Ueda · JP

Rothenhäusler & Wälchli
Advertising
1965 · Anonymous · CH

American Home
Magazine
1968 · Tony Russell/
Russell & Hinrichs · US

G. Simmen Schreibmaschinen
Typewriters
1966 · Walter J. Diethelm · CH

Kruger Pulp and Paper
1965 · Ernst Roch/
Design Collaborative · CA

Donegal Quartzite
1978 · Richard Eckersley · IE

Panalogic
Digital imaging systems
1972 · R. Roger Remington · US

Techno-Einkaufs Gesellschaft
Electronics
1968 · Paul Klahn · DE

Deutsche Bank
(proposed design)
1972 · Heinz Schwabe · DE

Club You May
Nightclub
1969 · Tomoichi Nishiwaki,
Akisato Ueda · JP

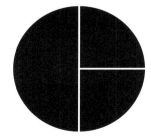

Chicago Graphics
Printing
1970s · James Lienhart · US

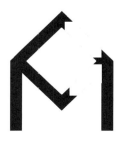

Mächler Metallbau, Cham
Metalworks
1957 · Robert Geisser · CH

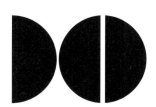

Delfim
Fishing
1969 · João Carlos Cauduro,
Ludovico Antonio Martino · BR

L'Electro Porcelaine
Electronics
1971 · Gérard Guerre/Technés · FR

Kippis
Restaurant furniture
1969 · Osmo Omenamäki · FI

Industrial Trainers
1965 · John Gibbs, T. J. Attwood/
Unit Five Design · UK

Schweizerische Bundesbahn, Bern
Federal railway
1970 · Kurt Wirth · CH

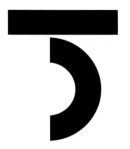

Institut d'Esthétique Industrielle, Brussels
Industrial design institute
1960 · Michel Olyff · BE

J. B. Rasmussen & Co.
Furniture
1969 · Michele Spera · IT

Rassegna Repubblicana
Magazine
1970 · Michele Spera · IT

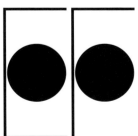

L'Electricfil
Electronics
1969 · Gérard Guerre,
Sylvaine Collignon/Technés · FR

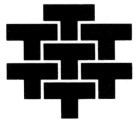

Tarmac
Engineering
1969 · Ronald Armstrong/
Design Research Unit · UK

Intomart Qualitatief
Publishing
1980 · Daphne Duijvelshoff · NL

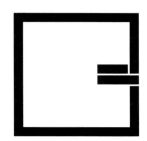

**Eindhoven School for
Graphic Techniques**
1966 · Bear Cornet · NL

Selection Consultants
Management consultancy
1965 · John Gibbs,
T. J. Attwood/Unit Five Design · UK

Wolfgang Mirbach
Photographer
1982 · Herbert Wenn · DE

Summa Corporation
Business investment management
1971 · Mario Zamparelli,
Jean-Claude Müller · US

Lemke Graphische Kunstanstalt, Berlin
Printing
1960 · Hans Adolf Albitz · DE

Order-Mation
Electronic automation
1963 · David J. Goodman/
Porter & Goodman Design · US

The Nissei Theater
1966 · Gan Hosoya · JP

Oral Editora
Publishing
1968 · Pinto Ziraldo · BR

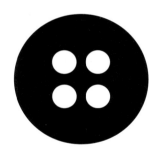

Muestra
Market research
1961 · Rómulo Macció · AR

Target
Supermarket chain
1970 · Unimark International · US

Meritalia
Furniture
1967 · Paolo Bon · IT

Crystalex Nový Bor
Glass
1983 · Vincenc Kutáč,
Stanislav Kovár · CZ

Dois Pontos
1970 · PVDI · BR

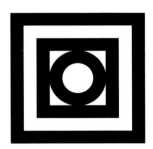

Polygraph-Export
International trade
1965 · Dieter Lehmann · DE-GDR

Graphis Press
Printing
1968 · John Tomkins · UK

Meibundo
Bookstore
1973 · Yasaburo Kuwayama · JP

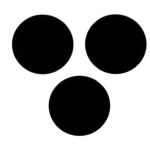

Silberkugel
Restaurant
1960s · Ruedi Külling/
Delpire-Advico · CH

P. Bork
Design
1960s · Anonymous · DK

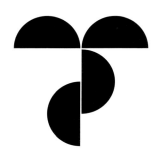

Mario Dias Costa
1950s · Marcel Wyss · CH

Design Workshops, London
Construction company
1966 · Philip Sharland/
Negus & Negus · UK

Pagliano Arredamenti
Furniture
1970 · Giovanni Brunazzi · IT

Hutmacher Breiter
Millinery
1970 · Oanh Pham Phu · DE

Coronado Pálace Hotel, São Paulo
1968 · João Carlos Cauduro,
Ludovico Antonio Martino · BR

Pam
Fuel oil
1966 · Benno Wissing,
George Koizumi/Total Design · NL

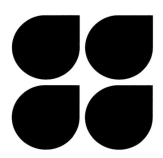

Pam
Fuel oil
1966 · Benno Wissing,
George Koizumi/Total Design · NL

Eiran Lämpö
Plumbing
1969 · Jukka Veistola/Sok · FI

Gruppo Bodino
Architecture
1979 · Giovanni Brunazzi · IT

Creative Capital Corporation
Real estate
1970 · Robert Hagenhofer · US

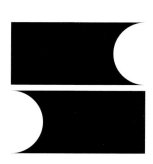

Shin Nihon Jitsugyo
Chemicals
1970 · Kazuo Tanaka · JP

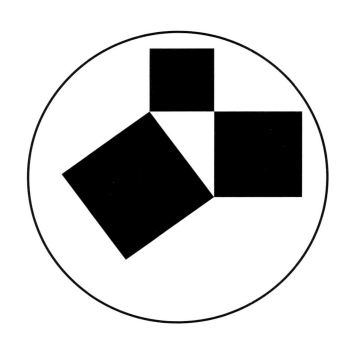

Deutsche Feinmechanik und Optik
Trade organization for optical products
1982 · Rolf Müller · DE

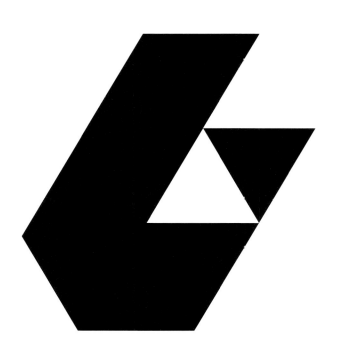

Trefil
Heavy industry
1972 · João Carlos Cauduro, Ludovico Antonio Martino · BR

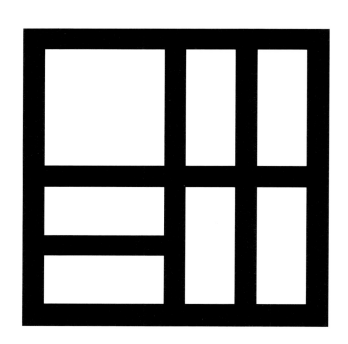

Light Metal Founders Association
1968 · Roger O. Denning · UK

Natursteinwerke, Zöblitz
Natural stone supplier
1965 · Sigrid Hopf · DE-GDR

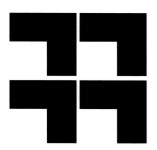

E. M. Középületé Vállalat
State building authority
1969 · Ilona H. Müller · HU

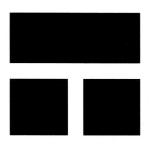

Telle
Furniture
1964 · Hans R. Woodtli · CH

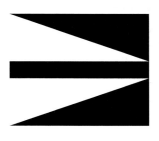

The British National Export Council
1962 · Negus & Negus · UK

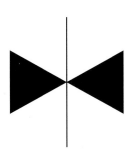

Hugo Boss Kosmetik
Cosmetics
1973 · Heinz Schwabe · DE

Colección Teatro
Publishing
1962 · Rómulo Macció · AR

Westransco Freight
International shipping
1967 · James Cross · US

Linnepe
Publishing
1972 · Anonymous · DE

Kenroc
Building materials
1970 · Pete Dodd/
Creative Resources · CA

McIntosh's Sports Cottage
Sporting goods
1970s · Kate Keating Associates · US

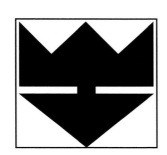

Terra-Bio-Chemie
Chemicals
1967 · Paul Klahn · DE

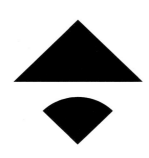

Viscosuisse
Textiles
1965 · Hans Hurter · CH

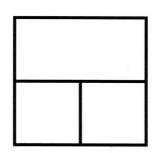

Taniguchi, Takamiya & Associates
Architecture
1980 · Takenobu Igarashi,
Akinori Nagao · JP

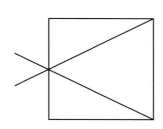

Ekkehard Kuschner
Photographer
1967 · Ulrich Maass · DE

Tecnika
Real estate
1979 · Carlo Malerba · IT

Swisspack
Trade fair for packaging solutions
1970 · Donald Brun · CH

Ytong
Building materials
1963 · Josef P. Grabner · CH

British Ministry of Transport Test Station
Vehicle certification
1959 · Kinneir, Calvert & Associates · UK

Associated Colleges of the Midwest
1968 · Charles MacMurray/
Latham Tyler Jensen · US

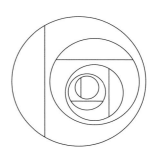

Universitets Etnografiske
Ethnographic museum
1968 · Paul Brand · NO

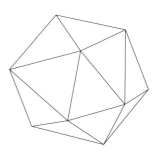

Robert Zeidman Associates
Industrial design
1960s · George Tscherny · US

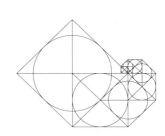

Hans Winterhager
Engineering
1960s · Klaus Winterhager · DE

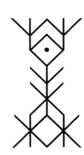

Shinichi Kusamori
Publishing
1969 · Makoto Wada · JP

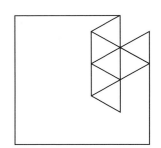

The Design Partnership
Design group
1968 · Henry Robertz · US

Gesellschaft Gronauer Wald
Real estate
1969 · Wolfgang Heuwinkel · DE

Alfred Schwendtner
Architecture
1968 · Franz Kuchenbauer · DE

Kanbe
Textiles
1973 · Akisato Ueda · JP

Finaldi
Electronics and telecommunications
1975 · A. G. Fronzoni · IT

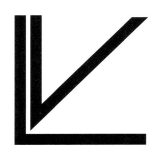

Leske Verlag
Publishing
1960s · Hanswerner Klein · DE

Ingenieursbureau Croot
Engineering
1962 · Ralph Prins · NL

Urs Walther
Electronics
1961 · Hans Knöpfli · CH

Pacific Data Images
Computer animation
1983 · Kip Reynolds · US

Arteper
Art center
1972 · A. G. Fronzoni · IT

Československý Spisovatel
Publishing
1960s · Ludvík Feller · CZ

Annual of Architects
1971 · Dicken Castro · CO

Tequila Mexicano
Alcoholic drinks
1982 · Félix Beltrán,
Teresa Echartea · CU/MX

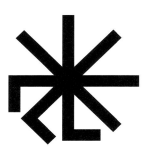

Photolithographic School
1960s · Gerd Leufert · VE

East Kilbride Development Corporation
Urban planning
1965 · James Smith · UK

Idle Lease
Leasing services
1979 · Masami Taki · JP

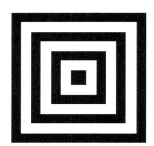

Macmillan of Canada
Publishing
1967 · Leslie Smart · CA

Schweizer Theater-Verband
Theater union
1988 · Niklaus Troxler · CH

Informatica
Business consulting
1975 · R. Nava, D. Soffientini,
G. Romani, A. Ubertazzi · IT

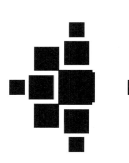

Soft Energy Systems
1978 · Carlo Malerba · IT

Diatech
1989 · Gil L. Strunck · BR

Filmalpha
Film production
1987 · A. G. Fronzoni · IT

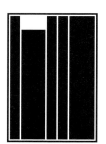

Fehr'scher Taschenbuchladen, St. Gallen
Bookstore
1960s · Jost Hochuli · CH

Siofor
Pharmaceuticals
1977 · Maurizio Milani · IT

Kobe Shinbun Shuppan
Publishing
1975 · Yoshitake Komoriya · JP

Tscharnergut Immobilien
Real estate
1960 · Peter Kräuchi · CH

Fisons Overseas
Fertilizer
1964 · John Harrison · UK

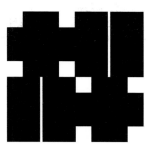

Ajuntament de Barcelona
City council
1963 · Ribas & Creus · ES

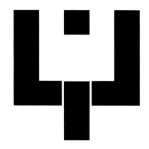

Landwirtschaftlicher Informationsdienst
Agriculture
1963 · Hans Knöpfli · CH

Congreso Interamericano de Vivienda
Housing congress
1968 · Gerd Leufert · VE

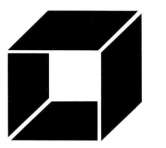

Akustik-Ground Tongeräte
Sound equipment
1980 · Klaus Richter · DE

T & M
Plastics
1981 · Yonefusa Yamada, Yuko Ishida · JP

Kulturhistorisches Museum
1965 · Hans Schlapmann · DE-GDR

Kirchentreffen
Church assembly
1983 · Herbert Wenn · DE

Chemical Industry
1983 · László Lendvai, Sára Ernő · HU

Companhia de Cigarros Souza Cruz
Cigars
1970 · Aloísio Magalhães/PVDI · BR

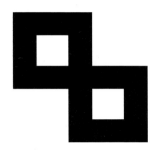

Alco Bauzubehörgesellschaft
Construction materials
1962 · Klaus Grözinger · DE

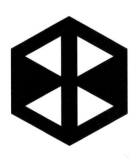

Schmolz & Bickenbach
Steel
1957 · Wolf D. Zimmermann · DE

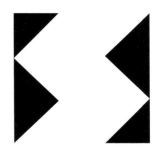

S. J. Surnamer
Printing
1970 · Robert Hagenhofer · US

Chrysler
Automobiles
1962 · Lippincott & Margulies · US

Peter Raacke
Industrial design
1961 · Robert Sessler · CH/DE

Cincinnati Science Center
Museum
1970 · Stan Brod · US

Arsonsisi
Paints
1948 · Walter Ballmer · IT

Itaipú Hidrelétrica Binacional
Energy supplier
1974 · PVDI · BR

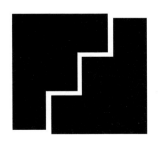

Financiera Faciema
Bank
1975 · Guillermo Gonzáles Ruiz · AR

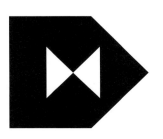

London Rubber Industries
Rubber products
1963 · David Harris · UK

Kies- & Betonwerk Gerwisch
Cement
1965 · Horst Jacob · DE-GDR

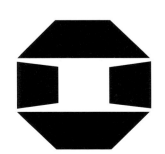

Icomi Minérios
Mining
1962 · PVDI · BR

Stafford-Corley Realtors
Real estate
1970 · Bob Swisher · US

Svenska Stalpressnings
Pressed steel
1960s · Bertil Andersson-Bertilson · SE

R. S. Stokvis & Zonen
Radio equipment
1960 · A. G. Schillemans · NL

Nissan Koku Service
Travel agency
1981 · Tadasu Fukano · JP

Water Systems Council
Well water
1967 · David L. Burke · US

Buchreihe über Sozialarbeit
Publishing
1980 · Anonymous · DE

Tachibanayaki Seitosho
Ceramics
1981 · Kazuharu Fuji · JP

Graphicart
Printing machinery
1960s · Walter Bonani · IT

Lawron Industries
Plastics
1969 · Carl Brett/
Hiller Rinaldo Associates · CA

The Nihon Keizai Shimbun
Economics journal
1966 · Hiromu Hara/
Nippon Design Center · JP

Officine Metallurgiche Cornaglia
Metallurgical products
1968 · Egidio Bonfante, Mavi Ferrando · IT

Cincinnati Health Careers
Medical employment
1974 · Stan Brod, Monica Brown · US

The Windrifter
Motel and restaurant
1973 · Richard J. Morgado · US

Arbeitsgemeinschaft der Regionalpresse
Press association
1967 · Erich Hänzi · CH

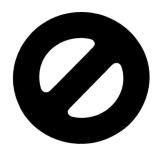

Urban Research Conference, Tokyo
Urban development
1970 · David L. Burke · US

Pharmacia AS
Pharmaceuticals
1966 · Armin Hofmann · CH

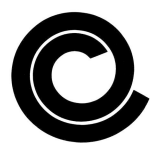

Willi Pfanner
Printing
1968 · Christian Lippauer · CH

Rupel Boom
Glass
1964 · Rob Buytaert · BE

id Druck
Printing (proposed design)
1960 · Herbert W. Kapitzki · DE

Marushoku
Supermarket chain
1980 · Akira Hirata, Junko Naito · JP

Disco-Partes
Automobile parts
1968 · John Lange · VE

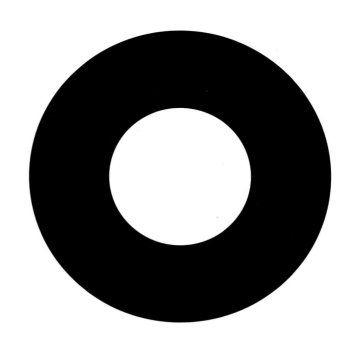

Blue Circle Group
Cement and paints
1966 · Henrion Design Associates · UK

Sunpark Onoda
Shopping center
1983 · Akira Hirata, Koji Mori · JP

Meneba
Grain mill
1970 · John Lloyd/
Allied International Designers · UK

Nihon Kachiku Jinko Juseishi Kyokai
Cattle insemination
1983 · Yasuhisa Iguchi · JP

United Shoe Machinery Corporation
Footwear machinery
1960s · Lippincott & Margulies · US

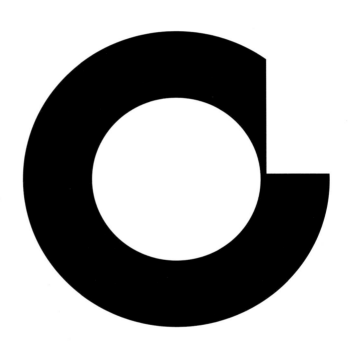

Girsberger
Furniture
1955 · Carl B. Graf · CH

Dayton Hudson Corporation
Retail
1970s · Vance Jonson · US

Futuro Fibreglass Homes
Housing design
1971 · Michel Lincourt · CA

S. F. Mokes & Co.
Engineering
1967 · Chandrashekhar Kamat/
Design Research Unit · UK

Credit Bank
1960s · Gérard Miedinger · CH

CBS Television
Broadcasting
1951 · William Golden · US

Jiyukokumin-sha
Publishing
1974 · Yasaburo Kuwcyama · JP

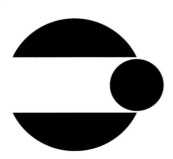

TransCanada Pipelines
Energy supplier
1969 · E. J. Morrison/
Stewart & Morrison · CA

**Kulturelles Zentrum der Sonja
Henie-Niels Onstad Foundation**
Cultural center
1968 · Odermatt+Tissi · CH

Government of Toronto
1970 · Peter G. Ulmer/
Stewart & Morrison · CA

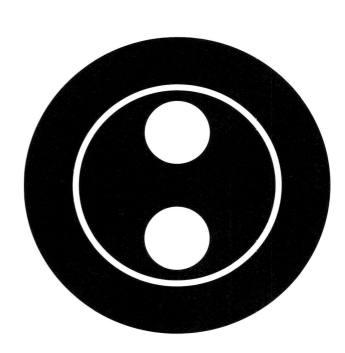

Milgrom
Textiles
1970 · Rolf Strub/Mafia · FR

Kantonspolizei Zürich
Police
1960s · Walter Sonderer · CH

Enertec
Solar energy
1979 · Jorge Sposari · AR

Pecivo
Foods
1982 · Judita Skalar · YU

Ishimaru
1971 · Ikko Tanaka · JP

Meer-Terrasse
Real estate
1976 · Bruno K. Wiese · DE

G. J. Møbler
Furniture
1965 · Claus Rostrup · DK

Schule für Kinder Stiftung
Charity
1985 · Niklaus Troxler · CH

California Industrial Vision Service
Image processing
1980 · Koji Takei/
Thomas Ohmer · JP/US

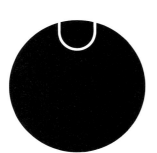

Polar Universiade '70
Sports contest
1968 · Jukka Veistola, Tapio
Korpisaari, Antti Laiho/Sok · FI

Chamebel
Aluminum windows
1967 · Luc Van Malderen,
Servaas Goddijn · BE

**International Union of
Geodesy and Geophysics**
1968 · Hansruedi Widmer/Devico AG · CH

Jung-Kang Spice
Spices
1960s · T. S. Jisang · CN

Fujisankei Kokukusha
Advertising
1978 · Ippo Miyamoto,
Tadashi Ishikawa · JP

Asahikawa Shinyo
Bank
1975 · Kazumasa Nagai · JP

Stress Free Plastics
1969 · Ralph Whitworth/
William's Advertisement Offices · UK

Jardine Fleming & Co.
Investment bank
1972 · Henry Steiner · US

Minami-nihon
Broadcasting
1983 · Kazumasa Nagai · JP

Roland Heiler Versicherung
Insurance
1967 · Kurt Weidemann · DE

Kurobe Shopping Center Merci
1982 · Akitoshi Tsunczaki · JP

Japan Amateur Sports Association
1974 · Kazumasa Nagai · JP

Le Point
Publishing
1966 · Michel Waxman · BE

Gebrüder Villinger
Printing
1960s · René Villinger · CH

Yamane Works
Plumbing
1973 · Kazumasa Nagai · JP

Seiko Shoji
1983 · Yasuhisa Iguchi · JP

Deutsche Aerospace
German aerospace (proposed design)
1970s · Bruno K. Wiese · DE

Kawakichi
Wallpapers
1973 · Kazumasa Nagai · JP

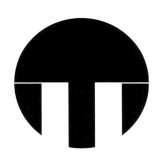

The Table Takahashi
Manufacturing
1960s · Nakajo Masayoshi · JP

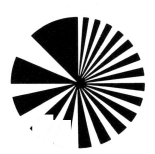

Suzuharu
Precision machinery
1967 · Kenichi Yoshioka · JP

Sanyo Shokai
Photography
1980 · Tetsuya Ota · JP

Corso-Sport Áruház
Sporting goods
1983 · István Szekeres · HU

Idéalement, une marque commerciale pousse l'abstraction et la polysémie à l'extrême sans rien perdre de sa lisibilité. Habituellement, les marques commerciales sont une sorte de métaphore et, d'un certain point de vue, elles doivent être comprises comme une représentation visuelle de la pensée.
Saul Bass

Idealerweise reizt ein Markenzeichen die Grenzen der Abstraktion und Mehrdeutigkeit aus, ohne seine Lesbarkeit einzubüßen. Gemeinhin sind Markenzeichen eine Art Metapher und in gewisser Hinsicht als Sichtbarmachung des Denkens zu verstehen.
Saul Bass

The ideal trademark is one that is pushed to its utmost limits in terms of abstraction and ambiguity, yet is still readable. Trademarks are usually metaphors of one kind or another. And are, in a certain sense, thinking made visible.
Saul Bass

Kurt Hochreutener
Advertising
1960s · Kurt Hochreutener · CH

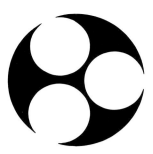

Corporación Financiera del Tolima
Finance
1971 · Dicken Castro · CO

Saffa
Working women's congress
1960s · Soland-Schatzmann · CH

Corn Nuts
Foods
1963 · G. Dean Smith · US

The Citizens Bank of Kuwait
1980 · Young Jae Cho · KR

Spare Tire
Tire inflator
1962 · Jerry Berman · US

W. Oertli
Fuel oil
1950 · Hans Neuburg · CH

Computer Terminal Corporation
Computing
1960s · Raymond Loewy,
William Snaith · US

Indústrias Romi
Machinery
1972 · João Carlos Cauduro,
Ludovico Antonio Martino · BR

OriolAvia Soviet Avstriskoe
Aviation
1967 · Vladimir Chaika · RU

Termocalor Radiator
Heating
1975 · Paolo Gotti, Maurizio Osti · IT

General Sirtering Corporation
Metal products
1963 · James Lienhart/RVI Corp. · US

Royal Micrographics
Microphotography systems
1969 · Primo Angeli · US

Centrais Elétricas de São Paulo
Energy supplier
1966 · João Carlos Cauduro,
Ludovico Antonio Martino · BR

Takane Keikaku
Sports facility
1982 · Shigeo Fukuda · JP

Opticon
Optics
1969 · Matthew Leibowitz · US

Märwiler Most
Fruit juices
1956 · Gottfried Honegger · CH

Albert Ryf
Haircare products
1963 · Edgar Küng · CH

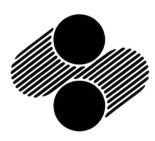

Istituto Geografico de Agostini
Printing
1979 · Giovanni Brunazzi · IT

Chicago Circle Center
Education
1964 · J.R. Weiss/
The Design Partnership · US

Nippon Cultural Broadcasting Systems
1958 · Kenji Ito · JP

Cordier
Cosmetics
1957 · Michel Olyff · BE

France Vision
Film production
1971 · Jean Delaunay/Look · FR

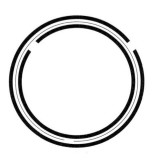

Envair Corporation
Environmental control systems
1969 · Hayward R. Blake/
The Design Partnership · US

ABC7 Los Angeles
Broadcasting
1970s · G. Dean Smith · US

Ove Engström
Design
1983 · Ove Engström,
Ingvar Johansson · SE

**Public Organization for Safety Tests
on Motor Vehicles**
1960s · Lars Bramberg · SE

Youth Employment Agency
1982 · Damien Harrington · IE

Ajinomoto
Food, pharmaceuticals
1969 · Mitsuo Katsui · JP

Eurocitel
Film production
1968 · André Chante/
Hollenstein Création · FR

Echter Verlag
Publishing
1979 · Ludwig Maria Beck · DE

Turnover Cradle
Door hinges
1960s · Lee Mason/
Allen, Dorsey & Hatfield · AU

Confezioni Coo
Clothing
1960s · Iris & Bruno Pippa · IT

Hagiwara
Textiles
1980 · Masahiro Abe · JP

Luminator
Engineering
1967 · H. B. Smith · US

Stoy, Hayward & Co.
Management consultancy
1970 · Peter Wildbur/
BDMW Associates · UK

Lykes Pasco
Juice packaging
1960s · Charles MacMurray/
Latham Tyler Jensen · US

Der Kinderbuchverlag
Publishing
1971 · Sonja Wunderlich · DE-GDR

VEB Plastpackungswerk
Packaging
1965 · Dieter Herzschuh · DE-GDR

**Technical Association of the
Pulp and Paper Industry**
1969 · Bradbury Thompson · US

Bos en Lommerschool
School
1971 · Jan Jaring · NL

Oehler & Co.
Machinery
1959 · Paul Bühlmann · CH

Ropan Film
Film production
1972 · Sudarshan Dheer · IN

Umebachi Kogyo
Appliances
1976 · Michio Ogura · JP

Cinéma Arenberg
Arthouse cinema
1968 · Gilles Fiszman · BE

Sterilite Plastic
Plastics
1970 · Joe Selame · US

Howard Miller Clock Co.
Watches
1960s · Irving Harper/
George Nelson & Co. · US

Towa Shoko
Building materials
1982 · Takeo Sugaya · JP

Saffa Divisione Chimica
Chemicals
1967 · Walter Del Frate · IT

Poonam International Hotels
1973 · Sudarshan Dheer · IN

Obrist & Co.
Pipes
1955 · Paul Bühlmann · CH

Siebdruck Dürst
Printing
1950s · Otto Dürst · CH

Schweizerischer Werkbund, Bern
Craft association
1962 · Marcel Wyss · CH

The George Wicken Group
Real estate
1968 · Collis Clements · UK

Central National Bank
1980 · Silvio Gayton · US

Audiomat
Language studies
1968 · Philippe Caza · FR

Hakone Open-Air Museum
1968 · Hiromu Hara/
Nippon Design Center · JP

Welti-Furrer
Haulier
1970 · Hansruedi Scheller · CH

Vozila Gorica
Automobiles
1963 · Oskar Kogoj · YU

Atami New Fujiya Hotel
1963 · Yoshio Hayashi · JP

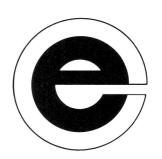

Concord Enterprises
1973 · Ronald Cutro · US

**Dental Laboratorium
J. Geuzebroek**
1970 · Jan Jaring · NL

Istha Industriele Ontwerpers
Design
1967 · A. G. Schillemans · NL

Wädenswil Bank
1966 · Eugen & Max Lenz · CH

Versandhaus Mauritius
Mail-order
1969 · Herbert Post · DE

Hikari
Plastics
1950s · Hiroshi Ohchi · JP

Ceag Grubenlampen
Mining lamps
1963 · Walter Breker · DE

Visual Books Editions Alpha
Publishing
1960s · Henri Steiner · CH

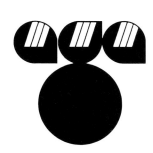

Asociación de Empresarios de Artes Gráficas de Asturias
Graphic designers association
1973 · José Santamarina · ES

Gesellschaft der Ludwig von Roll'schen Eisenwerke
Ironworks
1940s · Hans Neuburg · CH

Chr. Jensen Møbelsnedkeri
Furniture
1960s · Anonymous · DK

Wanner
Insulction
1970 · Michel Waxman · BE

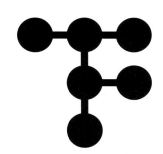

Telefusion
Broadcasting
1962 · Atelier Stadelmann Bisig · CH

Adolf Fehler
Electronics
1940s · Hans Neuburg · CH

Einspritzgerätewerk, Aken
Machinery
1965 · Henry Siebert · DE-GDR

Boehringer Kinderpräparate
Pharmaceuticcls
1965 · Wolf D. Zimmermann · DE

Rüesch Bohrer, Zurich
Drill manufacturer
1945 · Carlo L. Vivarelli · CH

Courtiers d'Assurance Associés
Insurance
1968 · Remo Muratore · IT

Fuji Speedway Co.
Motor sports
1965 · Yoshio Hayashi · JP

Polychimie
Chemicals
1968 · Etienne Bucher · FR

Max Weishaupt Pyria
Oil and gas burners
1968 · Ruedi Rüegg · DE

J. R. Geigy
Pharmaceuticals
1956 · Jörg Hamburger · CH

Verlag für Wirtschafts und Steuersachverständige
Publishing
1950 · Hanns Lohrer · DE

Worbla
Paper
1960 · Marcel Wyss · CH

Herman Ohme Associates
Tourism
1960s · Hy Farber · US

Altdorfer
Furniture
1940s · Pierre Gauchat · CH

Boso Shigyo
Paper
1977 · Takeshi Nakajima, Takeo Sugaya · JP

Mod'elle Boutique
1969 · A. G. Schillemans · NL

The League of Women Voters of Massachusetts
Democratic organization
1971 · Joe Selame · US

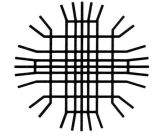

Carlos Celis Arquitectos, Caracas
Architect
1969 · Gerd Leufert · VE

Varuhuset Gyllen
Grocers
1969 · Ove Engström, Siv Lundkvist · SE

Shigeto Insatsu
Printing
1981 · Masahiro Shimizu · JP

Verband Internationaler Vertrieb
Import-export
1970 · Ekkehart Rustmeier · DE

Conseil du Centenaire de la Confédération
Commemorative foundation
1966 · George Huel · CA

Percy & Halden
Automobile-care products
1966 · Eurographics · UK

Leamington Hotel, Oakland
1969 · Jerry Berman · US

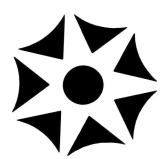

San Francisco Seven
Design
1960s · San Francisco Seven · US

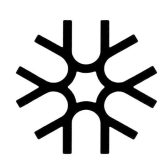

Union
1970s · Robert Hagenhofer · US

Slieve Bawn Co-operative
Crafts
1974 · Peter Dabinett · IE

Canadian Industrial Editors Association
1970 · Leslie Smart · CA

Hobelwerk Zürich
Carpentry
1970s · Frédéric Riz à Porta · CH

Copp Clark
Financial markets advisor
1973 · Gottschalk+Ash · CA

Etnografski Muzej
Ethnographic museum
1979 · Miloš Ćirić · YU

Visiting Arts Unit
Exhibition council
1981 · Peter Wildbur · UK

Postisäästöpankki
Bank
1960 · Pauli Numminen · FI

Congress of City Planning
1978 · Guillermo Gonzáles Ruiz · AR

American Institute for Cities of the New World
1960s · Chermayeff & Geismar · US

Nationales Hilfswerk
Charity
1950s · Paul Sollberger · CH

Ilmarinen - Eläkevakuutus
Insurance
1966 · Teuvo Gunnar Luostarinen/
Mainos Taucher Reklam · FI

Miles Laboratories
Pharmaceutical research
1967 · Morton Goldsholl · US

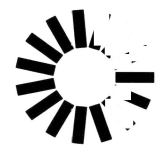

Solite
Aggregates
1965 · Ian Bradbery · UK

Pharmaceutical Services
1960s · Tom Geismar/
Chermayeff & Geismar · US

Bill Armstrong Studio
Recording studio
1973 · Cato Hibberd Design · AU

Gruen Lighting
Residential lighting
1950s · Louis Danziger · US

Creative Resources
Public relations
1969 · Pete Dodd/
Creative Resources · CA

Schwaderlapp Keramik
Ceramics
1962 · Jupp Ernst · DE

Werkzeugmaschinenwerke, Chemnitz
Machine tools
1965 · Wolfgang Hoepfner · DE-GDR

Nederlandse Filmacademie
Film academy
1966 · Jan Jaring · NL

Ontario Automobile
Automobiles
1968 · Raymond Lee · CA

Oakbrook Terrace Shopping Center
1962 · Saul Bass · US

**Faculdade de Arquitetura e Urbanismo
da Universidade de São Paulo**
Architecture and urban planning dept., USP
1960 · Ludovico Antonio Martino · BR

Rek-O-Kut
Audio services
1960 · George Nelson,
Richard Shiffer · US

Abitibi Provincial Papers
Paper
1969 · James D. Taylor/
Rous & Mann Press · CA

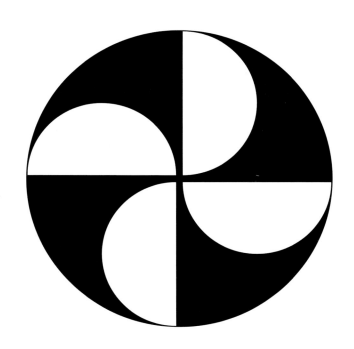

People Plus
Employment agency
1970 · Leslie Smart · CA

Companhia Sol de Seguros
Insurance
1960s · Aloísio Magalhães/PVDI · BR

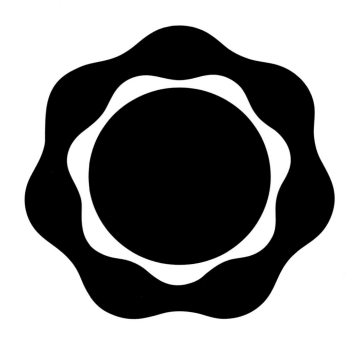

National Museum of Ethnology
1977 · Mitsuo Katsui · JP

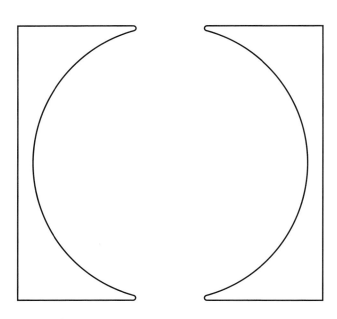

Gertrude Lempp Kerbis
Architecture
1961 · Hayward R. Blake · US

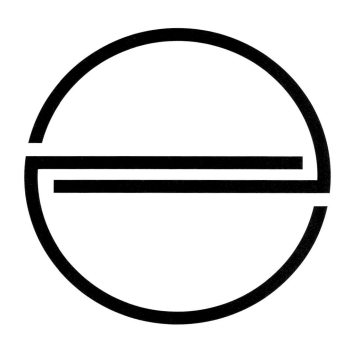

Krankenpflegeschule Zürich
Medical school
1960s · Students of Kunstgewerbeschule Zürich · CH

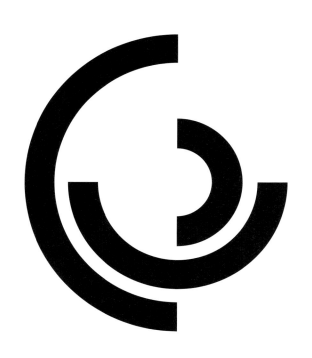

12th Triennale di Milano
Architecture and industrial art exhibition
1959 · Roberto Sambonet · IT

HB Ice Cream
1967 · Talmadge,
Drummond & Partners · UK

North Manchester School of Nursing
Medical school
1968 · Robert Davies · UK

WBAP
Broadcasting
1963 · Crawford Dunn · US

Fathers of Confederation
1960s · Fritz Gottschalk · CA

Certina
Watches
1956 · Carl B. Graf · CH

Gerd Hatje Verlag
Publishing
1968 · Wim Crouwel · NL

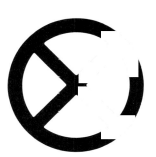

Ateljé Lyktan
Lighting
1960s · Anonymous · SE

Co-Graphics
Printing
1958 · A. E. Eddenden · CA

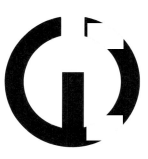

Ritz Italora
Watches
1972 · Da Centro Disegno · IT

F.lli Oggioni
Furniture
1958 · Giulio Confalonieri, Ilio Negri · IT

Someron Kutomo
Textiles
1967 · Rolf Christianson · FI

San Lorenzo
Silverware
1970 · G. & R. Associati · IT

Columbia Schallplatten
Record label
1957 · Marcel Wyss · CH

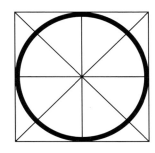

Teleac
Educational television
1963 · Wim Crouwel/Total Design · NL

Feldmühle
Paper
1963 · Wolfgang Heuwinkel · DE

Exportbank
Bank
1960s · Gérard Miedinger · CH

Antriebe-Gesellschaft
Engineering
1960 · Peter Kräuchi · CH

S. B. R. Radio- und Fernsehgesellschaft
Broadcasting
1969 · Dechy-Publicité · BE

Omniscreen
Printing
1961 · Wim Crouwel/Total Design · NL

Hotellerie Rigi
Hotel
1960s · Gérard Miedinger · CH

Cora Very Americano
Alcoholic drinks
1972 · Emanuele Centazzo/Sitcap · IT

Oxford Development Company
Real estate
1980 · Francis R. Esteban · US

Izrom
Light-bulbs
1972 · Asher Kalderon · IL

R. S. Stokvis & Zonen
Electronics
1960 · A. G. Schillemans · NL

Electron Optics
Research laboratory
1974 · Maria Mazzara · US

Cipag
Boilers
1968 · Michel Gallay · CH

P. Wellhauser Super-Jet
Lawn sprinkler
1959 · Michel Martina · CH/FR

Pelgrim
Gas supplier
1968 · A. G. Schillemans · NL

Eastman Machine Co.
Machinery for the textile industry
1961 · Crosby, Fletcher, Forbes · UK

Inhilco
Restaurant
1974 · Milton Glaser · US

Ashby Marine
Boat motors
1960 · Romek Marber · UK

Hydroscience
Water pollution control
1970s · Robert Hagenhofer · US

Global Tours & Travel
Travel agency
1964 · Crosby, Fletcher, Forbes · UK

Staten Island Mental Health Society
1970s · Robert Hagenhofer · US

Japan Scientific Societies Press
Publishing
1982 · Hiroshi Manzen · JP

Büro Memminger
Embroidery machinery
1960 · Hanns Lohrer · DE

Ryman
Office supplies
1962 · Kinneir, Calvert & Associates · UK

Südalumin
Aluminum products
1962 · Hans Kuh · DE

Tam O'Shanter Glen
Construction company
1970 · Raymond Lee · CA

Crosignani Arti
Typography and lithography
1963 · Piero Ottinetti · IT

George Glenn
Poultry farm
1960s · Rolf Harder · CA

Augenoptik in der DDR
Trade association
1965 · Werner Liebscher · DE-GDR

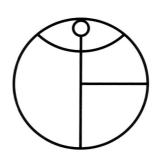

Gymnaestrada Basel
Gymnastics world cup
1968 · Herbert Leupin · CH

Toyo Printing Company
1963 · Porter & Goodman Design · US

Internationale Schützenunion
Sports association
1960s · Eugen & Max Lenz · CH

Cooper & Beatty
Typesetting and printing
1960s · Anthony Mann · CA

Management Organization
1970 · James Lienhart/RVI Corp. · US

Luottokontrolli Oy
Bank
1965 · Seppo Polameri · FI

Ediciones Infinito
Publishing
1954 · Carlos Alberto
Méndez Mosquera · AR

Kulturkreis Hard
Cultural association
1978 · Othmar Motter · AT

Maschinen- und Apparatebau, Chemnitz
Machinery
1965 · Max Mehlig · DE-GDR

Enastur
Energy supplier
1975 · José Santamarina · ES

Konsum
Wines
1965 · Erhard Müller · DE-GDR

Martin Rosette
Design
1965 · Martin Rosette · DE-GDR

Togal-Werk Schmidt
Pharmaceuticals
1940s · G. F. Schmidt · CH

VEG Saatzucht Zierpflanzen
Flowers
1965 · Herbert Vogel · DE-GDR

Verzinkerei Worb
Galvanization
1950s · Werner Vogelsanger · CH

Fabryka Samochodów Warszawie
Automobiles
1980 · Tytus Walczak · PL

W. H. Smith & Son
Office supplies
1965 · Woudhuysen Inc. · UK

Holzverarbeitung, Querfurt
Woodworking
1965 · Bernhard Wille · DE-GDR

Publireiac
Advertising film production
1968 · Pino Tovaglia · IT

Kyodo-Sekiyu
Oil
1966 · Ikko Tanaka · JP

Chatelaine Home Courses
1965 · Leslie Smart · CA

Hyspa
Sports exhibition
1961 · Hans Neuburg · CH

Building Centre
Architecture and design
1960s · Milner Gray/
Design Research Unit · UK

Meßgeräte Holle
Measuring instruments
1965 · Rudolf Purke · DE-GDR

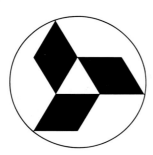

**Arbeitsgemeinschaft
des Kunsthandwerks NRW**
Arts and crafts association
1960 · Walter Breker · DE

Messegelände Düsseldorf
Trade fair (proposed design)
1967 · Coordt von Mannstein · DE

Schule für Sprachtherapie
Speech therapy
1950s · Josef Müller-Brockmann · CH

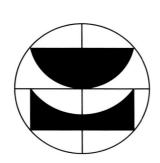

Societies of Industrial Design
Design group
1950s · Djordje Milanovic · YU

China Handelskontor
Trade association
1969 · Wolfgang Heuwinkel · DE

Amersfoortse Gemeenschap
Exhibition hall
1960s · Leendert Stofbergen · NL

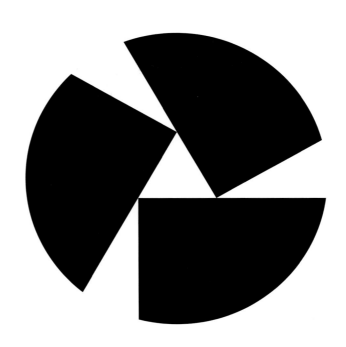

Banco Nacional
Bank
1974 · PVDI · BR

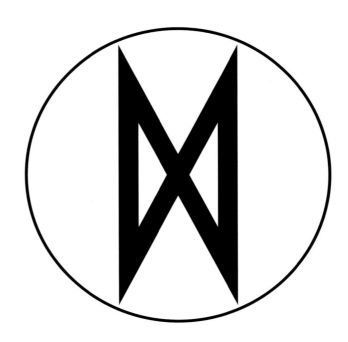

Melitta-Werke
Coffee
1950 · Jupp Ernst · DE

Odakyu
Department store
1961 · Yoshio Hayashi · JP

Sender Freies Berlin
Broadcasting
1970s · Atelier 13 · DE

Brockmann
Timber merchant
1974 · Walter Breker · DE

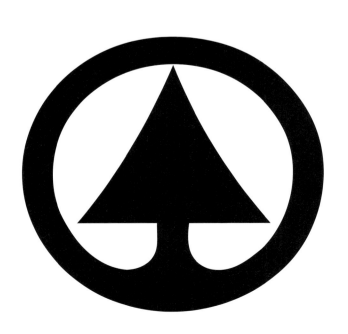

Spar
Supermarket chain
1968 · Raymond Loewy/CEI · UK

Bernische Kraftwerke
Energy supplier
1970 · Erich Hänzi · CH

Manifestica Graficke
Design association
1979 · Miloš Ćirić · YU

Great Western United Corporation
Sugar refiner
1969 · Pieter van Delft/
Unimark International · US

Niagara University Art Festival
1966 · Richard De Natale · US

Philippine Airlines
1968 · Primo Angeli, Jerry Leonhard · US

California Dairy Association
1966 · Thomas Laufer · US

Boise Cascade Corporation
Land development
1963 · G. Dean Smith · US

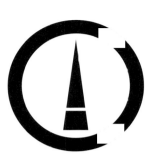

Audax
Audio equipment
1959 · George Nelson · US

Chicago Center for Research Studies
1968 · Bruce Beck/
The Design Partnership · US

Zmaj
Batteries
1968 · Grega Košak · YU

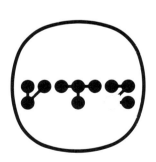

Radio-televizija Zagreb
Broadcasting
1971 · Jože Brumen · YU

Fabrika Ambalaze
Packaging
1959 · Albert Kastelec · YU

Fleischerei Timm, Bad Doberan
Butcher
1965 · Klaus Grosche · DE-GDR

Journal of the History of Biology
Academic journal
1968 · David Ford · US

VEB Feinwerktechnik, Dresden
Engineering
1965 · Johannes Brase · DE-GDR

Jelen Forest
1963 · Miloš Ćirić · YU

Filmo
Film production
1960s · Josef P. Grabner · CH

Heating systems
1960s · Havas Conseil · FR

R. S. Stokvis & Zonen
Electronics (proposed design)
1960 · A. G. Schillemans · NL

RSSA Komi
Civil airline
1960s · Igor Borisovič,
Leonid Nikolaevič Rabičev · RU

Perlmuttknopffabrik, Kelbra
Buttons
1965 · Christa Gabriel · DE-GDR

Kobe Shinkotsu
Haulier
1979 · Ikuya Kimura · JP

Schweizerischer Orientierungslauf
Sports event
1964 · Hansruedi Scheller · CH

Państwowe Zakłady Mechaniczne
Pumps
1969 · Jan Hollender · PL

Mac Fisheries
Supermarket chain
1952 · Hans Schleger · UK

Karten-Druckerei Karl Werner
Printing
1957 · Hermann Eidenbenz · CH

Women's College Hospital
Teaching hospital
1968 · Patricia Turnbull · CA

Građevno Arhitektonsko Projektno
Civil engineering
1970s · Ivan Picelij · YU

Suomen Tennisliitto
Tennis club
1968 · Heikki Ahtiala/
Mainos Taucher Reklam · FI

Département de la Creuse
City council
1970 · Jean Delaunay/Look · FR

Signa Design Consultants
1953 · Louis le Brocquy · IE

Centralni Komitet SKJ
Political organization
1968 · Dragoslav Stojanovic · YU

Schwermaschinenbau S. M. Kirow
Machinery
1965 · Günther & Käthe
Mickwausch · DE-GDR

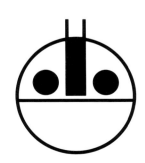

Refratechnik Albert
Refractory materials
1959 · Walter Breker · DE

Publicity
State department store
1975 · Asher Kalderon · IL

Promien Liqúids
1966 · Jarosław Jasiński · PL

Verband der Volkstheater
Theater association
1970s · Peter Steiner · DE

VEB SPEMAFA Spezialmaschinen
Machinery
1965 · Günter Hiller · DE-GDR

Libreria A-Zeta
Bookstore
1971 · Giovanni Brunazzi · IT

Omecsa Construction
Plumbing
1977 · Ernesto Lehfeld · MX

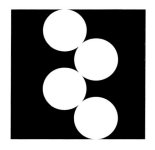

Ross-Ellis
Printing
1961 · Ernst Roch/
Design Collaborative · CA

Telimena
Fashion house
1960s · Władysław Stańczykowski · PL

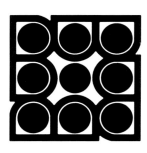

Brüllmann
Prepress services
1966 · Kurt Weidemann · DE

Swiss Cheque
Banking
1960s · Gérard Miedinger · CH

Congreso Nacional des Artes Gráficas
Design congress
1966 · Josep Pla-Narbona · ES

De Doelen
Concert organizers
1966 · Benno Wissing/Total Design · NL

W. Euler
Paper
1961 · Willy Faltin · DE

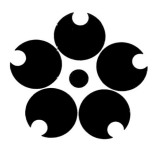

Expo '70, Osaka
World's fair
1966 · Takeshi Otaka · JP

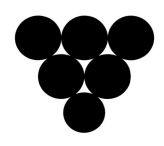

**Associazione Amazori
del Vino Fratres Bibones**
Wine
1969 · Giovanni Brunazzi · IT

**Stichting Actie
Zending & Werelddiaconaat 1968**
Charity
1967 · Sjoerd Bylsma · NL

Corelli Financial Group
Investment
1977 · Gustavo Gómez-Casallas · CO

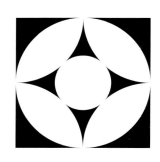

Nuffic
Education
1969 · Ralph Prins · NL

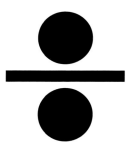

Willy Bosshard
Advertising
1960 · Willy Bosshard · CH

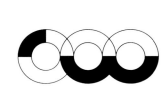

Rudolf Werder
Prepress services
1969 · Gisela Buomberger/
Atelier Rudolf Bircher · CH

The Bifurcated & Tubular Rivet Company
Rivets
1966 · Ulrich Haupt/
Allied International Designers · UK

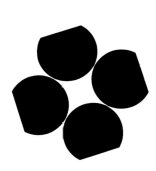

Osaka Art Festival
1965 · Takeshi Otaka · JP

German Pavilion, Expo '70, Osaka
World's fair stand
1970 · Karl-Oskar Blase · DE

**Spital für Klinische
Psychiatrie, Littenheid**
Hospital
1970 · Emanuel Bosshardt · CH

Vereinigung Zentrum, Witikon
Shopping center
1969 · Ernst & Ursula Hiestand · CH

Chribska
Glass
1965 · Stanislav Kovár · CZ

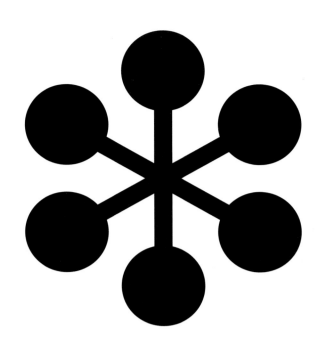

Hyvon-Kudeneule
Clothing
1950 · Matti Viherjuuri · FI

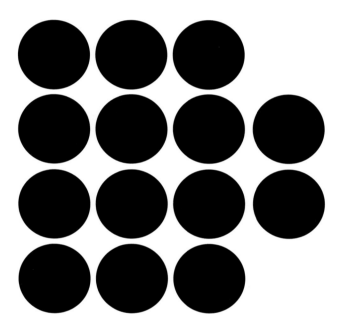

Cristallerie Daum
Glass
1970 · Leen Averink · FR

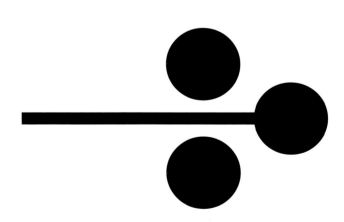

Claude Jones
Pawnbroker
1960s · Geoffrey Woollard · UK

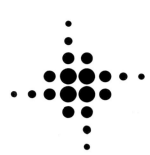

Kalbro Corporation
Computing
1979 · Richard Yeager · US

Závody Tažkého Strojárstva
Engineering
1973 · František Bobáň · CZ

Grafische Maschinengesellschaft
Printing machinery
1960s · Paul Moser · CH

T. Hürlimann
Heating technology
1968 · Edi Doswald · CH

Fiorucci
Cold meats
1975 · Rinaldo Cutini · IT

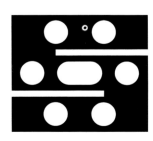

Systemprofile, Stuttgart
Furniture
1973 · Heinz Schwabe · DE

Vollstädt
Cannery
1965 · Klaus Neumeister · DE-GDR

Automobil Club der Schweiz
Automobile drivers association
1950s · Josef Müller-Brockmann · CH

Leipziger Gummiwarenfabrik
Rubber products
1965 · Horst Hilbert · DE-GDR

Kemian Työntekijäin Liitto
1970 · Olof Eriksson · FI

Gebrüder Sulzer
Pumps and looms
1960s · A. Frei · CH

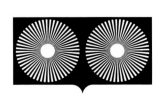

Òliba
Record label
1970 · Francesc Guitart · ES

Deutsche Unfallverhütung
Accident prevention
1960s · Sigrid & Hans Lämmle · DE

Laboratoires d'Etudes Cosmétologiques
Cosmetics
1969 · Jacques Nathan-Garamond,
L. Barmache · FR

Fédération des Travailleurs du Québec
Workers union
1968 · Pierre-Yves Pelletier · CA

Vestebene
Clothing
1969 · Giorgio Maltisotto, Sitcap · IT

Société Industrielle de Lunetterie
Eyewear
1969 · Pierre Lissac/Pezet Publicité · FR

Needham, Louis and Brorby
Advertising
1960s · Morton Goldsholl · US

Pharmaceutical Centre
1975 · Ernst Roch · CA

Die Brücke
Cultural association
1960s · Peter Riefenstahl · DE

Hemus
Pencils
1960s · Anton Metchknev · BG

Spühler
Color photo reproductions
1960s · Heini Schmid · CH

Deutsche Waffenbörse, Stuttgart
Weapons
1971 · Michael Herold · DE

Kunstanstalt Krugmann
Printing
1960s · Karlheinz Schillinger · DE

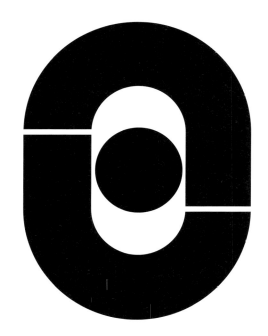

Asbest Technik
Asbestos
1972 · Hansruedi Scheller · CH

Raymond Lee & Associates
Advertising
1969 · Raymond Lee · CA

Classic Jewelers
1973 · Henry Steiner · US

Syndicat National des Assurances Vie
Insurance
1970 · Pham Ngoc Tuan · FR

Brewers Warehousing
Beer sales
1964 · Hans Kleefeld/
Stewart & Morrison · CA

Patterson Plaza
Shopping center
1979 · Henry Steiner, Paul Cheung ·
US/HK

**Verband der Reform und
Diätfachgeschäfte der Schweiz**
Health and diet foods
1971 · Walter J. Diethelm · CH

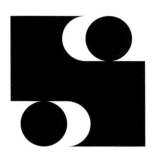

Karol Syta
Design
1960s · Karol Syta · PL

**Faculdade de Ciências Médicas da
Santa Casa de Misericórdia de SP**
Medical university
1963 · Ludovico Antonio Martino · BR

Industrial Management
1965 · Zdeněk Ziegler · CZ

Screen Gems
Film production
1965 · Tom Geismar/
Chermayeff & Geismar · US

Karl Feldmann
Tools
1967 · Klaus Winterhager · DE

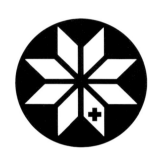

Norges Røde Kors
Winter mountain safety
1968 · Bruno Oldani · NO

Union
Workers union
1976 · František Bobáň · CZ

Maac
Design
1972 · Shin Matsunaga · JP

Maruishi
Millinery
1980 · Yonefusa Yamada,
Shin Szaki · JP

Brno Exhibition of Inventions
1972 · Jan Rajlich, Miroslav Holek · CZ

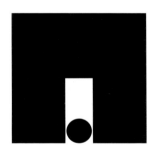

Meracie Prístoje
Measuring instruments
1968 · František Bobáň · PL

Handelsschule
Business school
1960s · Jupp Ernst · DE

Chinaware Factory
1960s · Ryuichi Yamashiro · JP

Onimus-Outils
Transportation
1950s · Robert Sessler · CH

Bundespreis Gute Form
Industrial design award
1969 · Walter Breker · DE

Gernay Delbecque
Tents and awnings
1965 · Julian Key · BE

ICSID Annual Congress
Design congress
1967 · Laurent Marquart/
Jacques Guillon Designers · CA

Gesellschaft für Gerichtliche Medien
Legal publishing
1965 · Gerhard Voigt · DE-GDR

Lincocin Upjohn Company
Pharmaceuticals
1960s · Will Burtin · US

Nederlandse Reassurantie Groep
Insurance
1968 · Hartmut Kowalke,
Christine Witt/Total Design · NL

With more than 3,000 shops, the Kobe-based Daiei Inc. is one of Japan's biggest supermarket chains. The company was launched in 1957 with the opening of a single drugstore. By the beginning of the 1970s the small retailer had grown to become market leader in the Japanese supermarket sector and the company needed an expertly designed corporate logo. An in-house team took on the task in 1973 with the help of the branding agency PAOS, and the new logo took the form of a circle with a piece chopped off. The image became the focal point of the company's entire corporate design. It appears in several versions on labeling, packaging, and even on staff uniforms. Over the decades, simply by playing with different blends of colors and outlines, designers have come up with vibrant variations of the logo that have helped to make Daiei one of Japan's flagship brands. The logo was replaced in 2005 by a new design from a different agency.

The Daiei Inc. mit Hauptsitz in Kobe gehört heute mit über 3.000 Geschäften zu den größten japanischen Supermarktketten. Gegründet wurde das Unternehmen 1957 mit der Eröffnung eines einzelnen Drogeriegeschäftes. Bereits Anfang der 1970er-Jahre war aus dem kleinen Einzelhändler der japanische Branchenmarktführer geworden, und eine Professionalisierung des visuellen Auftritts war notwendig. In Zusammenarbeit mit der Brandingagentur PAOS nahm 1973 ein hausinternes CI-Team die Arbeit auf. Ein angeschnittener Kreis wurde als neues Logo entwickelt und in den Mittelpunkt des gesamten Corporate Designs gestellt. Er findet sich in unterschiedlichster Gestaltung bei Beschriftungen, Verpackungen und sogar der Mitarbeiterbekleidung wieder. Allein durch das geregelte Spiel mit wenigen Variationsarten etwa durch Farben und Linien ergaben sich unzählige Möglichkeiten und ein lebendiger Auftritt, der Daiei über viele Jahrzehnte zu einer der japanischen Vorzeigemarken machte. 2005 wurde das Logo durch den Entwurf einer anderen Agentur ersetzt.

Avec plus de 3000 magasins, The Daiei Inc., sise à Kobe, est aujourd'hui une des plus grandes chaînes de supermarchés japonais. L'entreprise fut fondée en 1957 avec l'ouverture d'un seul magasin, une droguerie. Dès le début des années 1970, le petit détaillant était déjà le leader japonais du secteur, et une professionnalisation de l'identité visuelle s'avéra nécessaire. En collaboration avec l'agence de branding PAOS, une équipe interne d'identité de marque se mit au travail en 1973. Comme nouveau logo, on développa le concept d'un cercle coupé, qui devint le centre de l'identité visuelle de la marque. Ce cercle se retrouve sous les formes les plus diverses dans les écritures, les emballages, et même sur les vêtements de travail des employés. Le jeu réglé et la déclinaison de quelques variantes, notamment en termes de couleurs et de lignes, suffisaient à produire d'innombrables possibilités et une image vivante qui a fait de Daiei une des marques phares du Japon pendant de nombreuses décennies. En 2005, le logo fut remplacé par le projet d'une autre agence.

PAOS Inc. was founded in Tokyo in 1968 by the Japanese art director Motoo Nakanishi (*1938). Over the years the company has been commissioned to create more than 100 corporate design projects. Among these have been prizewinning designs for internationally known and respected clients such as Kenwood, Mazda and TDK. Since the 1980s, PAOS has opened a number of branches in cities including New York, Beijing and Shanghai. It continues to work successfully as a consultancy for identity and marketing strategies.

PAOS Inc. wurde 1968 vom japanischen Art Director Motoo Nakanishi (*1938) in Tokio gegründet. Das Unternehmen wurde über die Jahre mit der Realisierung von über 100 Corporate-Design-Projekten beauftragt. Es entstanden international bekannte, geschätzte und prämierte Identitäten für Auftraggeber wie Kenwood, Mazda oder TDK. Ab den 1980er-Jahren eröffnete PAOS mehrere Büros unter anderem in New York, Peking und Shanghai. Bis heute ist das Unternehmen als Beratungsagentur für Identity- und Markenstrategien erfolgreich.

PAOS Inc. a été fondé en 1968 à Tokyo par le directeur artistique japonais Motoo Nakanishi (*1938). Au fil du temps, l'entreprise a été chargée de la réalisation de plus de cent projets de corporate design. Ont ainsi vu le jour des identités visuelles internationalement connues, respectées et primées pour des entreprises comme Kenwood, Mazda ou TDK. À partir des années 1980, PAOS ouvre plusieurs bureaux à l'étranger, notamment à New York, Pékin, Shanghai. L'entreprise connaît aujourd'hui encore le succès comme agence de conseil en stratégie d'identité et de marque.

The Daiei Inc.

1975 · Rei Yoshimura/PAOS Inc. · JP

Neutral Helvetica was a conscious choice for the corporate typeface, in order not to distract the viewer's attention from the Daiei logo. The designers made a point of experimenting with duplication, resolution and color, and also published a manual showing in detail how they applied the results when creating the logo.

Ganz bewusst hat man die neutrale Helvetica als Unternehmensschrift gewählt, die dem Daiei-Logo keine visuelle Konkurrenz macht. Neben dem gewollten Spiel mit Verdopplung, Farbigkeit und Rasterung des Logos wurden sämtliche Details zur Verwendung klar definiert und in einem umfangreichen Manual festgehalten.

L'Helvetica fut délibérément choisie comme fonte pour l'entreprise parce que sa neutralité n'entrait pas en conflit avec le logo Daiei. À côté du jeu voulu sur le redoublement, le coloris et le tramage du logo, l'utilisation de chaque détail fut clairement définie et explicitée dans un vaste manuel.

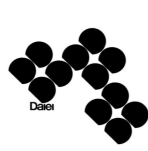
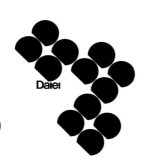

アイウエオカキクケコサシ
スセソタチツテトナニヌネ
ガギグゲパピプペアィゥェ
アイウエオカキクケコサシ
スセソタチツテドナニヌネ
ガギグゲパピプペアィゥェ
店社明食式商品売加告株広
あいうえおかきアイウエオカキ
店社明食式商品売加告株広
あいうえおかきアイウエオカキ
ABCDEFGHIJKLMNO
abcdefghi12345678
ABCDEFGHIJKLMNO
abcdefghi12345678

ダイエーグループ。
ショッパーズプラザ。
キャプテンクック
ブルーマウンテン
クリスティ クリスティ
リトルチャイルド
プレイカンパニー
ビーエムワイ
ダイエーニュース

ダイエー教育センター
ダイエー専門店街
ダイエー駐車場
神戸流通センター
お客様入口
Blue Mountain
Young Mate
Sonnet
Daiei News

株式会社 ダイエー

株式会社 ダイエー

株式会社 ダイエー

The Daiei, Inc.

株式会社 ダイエー
大阪府吹田市豊津町9番1号 〒564

株式会社 ダイエー
大阪府吹田市豊津町9番1号 〒564
電話（ダイヤルイン）

株式会社 ダイエー
東京都品川区西五反田7-22-17 〒141
電話 東京(03)493-4711

The Daiei, Inc.
9-1 Toyotsu-cho, Suita, Osaka

The Daiei, Inc.
9-1 Toyotsu-cho, Suita
Osaka, Japan
Telephone 06-386-1147
Telex 523-8422 DAIEI-J
Cable DAIEI INC. SUITA

株式会社 ダイエー
大阪府吹田市豊津町9番1号 〒564

株式会社 ダイエー
東京都品川区西五反田7-22-17 〒141
電話 東京(03)493-4711

株式会社 ダイエー
東部地区本部
東京都品川区西五反田7-22-17 〒141
電話 東京(03)493-4711

The Daiei, Inc.

株式会社 ダイエー
西宮分室 兵庫県西宮市
〒662 電話 西宮(0798)67-3161

株式会社 ダイエー
西部店

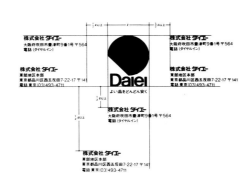

株式会社 ダイエー
大阪府吹田市豊津町9番1号 〒564
電話（ダイヤルイン）

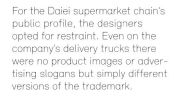

For the Daiei supermarket chain's public profile, the designers opted for restraint. Even on the company's delivery trucks there were no product images or advertising slogans but simply different versions of the trademark.

Bei der Außendarstellung der Daiei-Supermärkte wurde der moderne und zurückhaltende Gesamtauftritt der Marke konsequent gepflegt. Selbst die Lieferwagen des Unternehmens enthalten keine Produktabbildungen oder Werbeaussagen, sondern zeigen lediglich verschiedene Varianten des Markenzeichens.

Pour la représentation extérieure des supermarchés Daiei, l'identité visuelle globale, moderne et sobre, de la marque fut cultivée de manière conséquente. Même les camions de l'entreprise ne présentent ni image de produit, ni message publicitaire, mais simplement différentes variantes de la marque commerciale.

The Daiei group made extensive use of the multi-faceted logo in packaging designs for its own-label products. Such an array of variations on the logo made for high-quality packaging with each version inextricably linked to the master brand.

Die vielfältigen Spielarten, die das Erscheinungsbild mit sich brachte, wurden bei Entwürfen für Verpackungen von Eigenprodukten der Daiei-Gruppe ausgiebig genutzt. Die Produkte erhielten einen eigenen hochwertigen Charakter, standen jedoch trotz allen Variantenreichtums immer in untrennbarer Verbindung zur Hauptmarke.

Les nombreuses déclinaisons découlant de l'identité visuelle furent abondamment utilisées sur les emballages des produits du groupe Daiei, qui reçurent leur propre caractère haut de gamme tout en restant toujours indissolublement liés à la marque principale malgré la richesse des variantes.

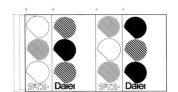

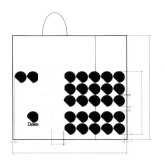

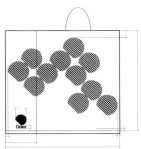

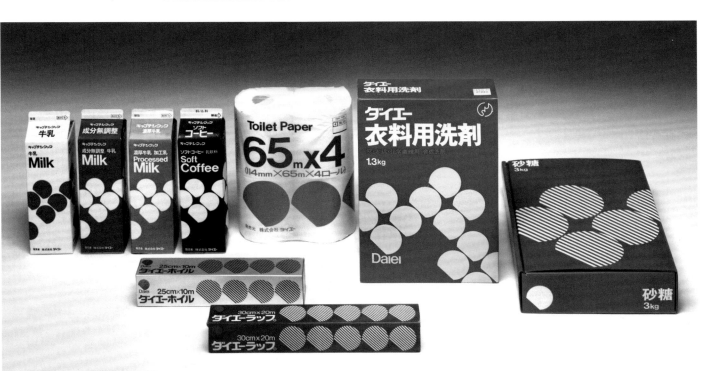

Croix

Kreuz

Cross

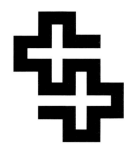

Patentamt St. Gallen
Patents office
1968 · Robert Geisser · CH

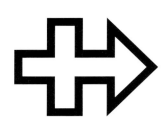

**Konservative
Christlichsoziale Volkspartei**
Political party
1960 · Robert Geisser · CH

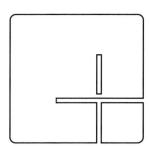

Omnium Technique Hôtelier
Engineering
1967 · Gérard Ifert/Publicis · FR

Helvetas Fonds für Entwicklungshilfe
Development aid
1965 · Christian Lang · CH

Methodistenkirche der Schweiz
Church
1968 · Emanuel Bosshardt · CH

Schweizerische Textilindustrie
Textiles
1960s · Ernst Jaggi · CH

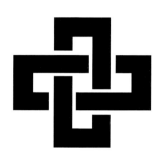

Sulzberger & Co.
Bank
1966 · Hans Hartmann · CH

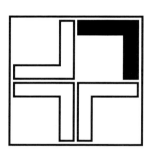

System Three
Market research
1966 · Ian Bradbery · UK

National Dental Hospital
1976 · Guillermo Gonzáles Ruiz · AR

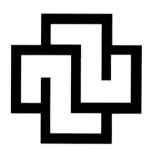

Schweizerische Kreditanstalt
Bank
1967 · Willy Wermelinger · CH

Sharp Grossmont Hospital
1973 · Calvin Woo · US

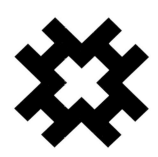

Hollister
Mecical supplies
1979 · Jack Weiss, Randi Robin · US

Schweizer Radio
Broadcasting
1978 · Roland Hirter · CH

Schweizer Europahilfe
Aid agency
1940s · Eugen & Max Lenz · CH

Schweizer Reederei
Shipping
1950s · Marcel Wyss · CH

Stiftung Schweizer Spitzensport
Sports foundation
1972 · Hansruedi Scheller · CH

Religious Television Programs
Broadcasting
1968 · Yvon Laroche · CA

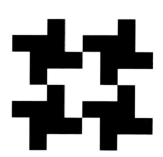

Maestrelli
Textiles
1960s · Franco Grignani · IT

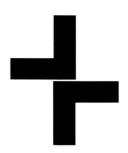

Marler Haley
Exhibition materials
1961 · June Fraser/
Design Research Unit · UK

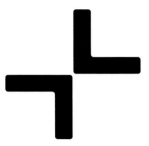

Low's
Printing
1962 · Hayward R. Blake · US

Stephan Zucker & Associates
Real estate
1981 · Azar Khosrovi-Ivorsohk · US

Rohrleitungsbau Finow
Pipes
1965 · Werner Rudolph · DE-GDR

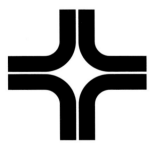

Toronto Council of Catholic Men
1968 · William Newton,
Jurgen Hoffmann · CA

Canadian Guild of Crafts
National crafts trust
1964 · Heiner Hegemann/
Chermayeff & Geismar · CA

Tokamachi
Textiles
1963 · Takashi Kono · JP

Da Costa & Asociados CA
Market research
1969 · Reynaldo Da Costa · VE

Blutzentrale, Stuttgart
Blood donation
1970s · Hannes Schober,
Wolfram Reinhardt · DE

Asia
Ski manufacturing
1960s · Gan Hosoya · JP

Ekco Containers
1960s · Don Marvine/
Latham Tyler Jensen · US

Pitney Bowes
Business equipment
1971 · Robert A. Gale · US

Brookvent
Ventilation systems
1964 · Henrion Design Associates · UK

**Verband Schweizerischer
Stickerei-Exporteure**
Clothing
1960s · Otto Krämer · CH

Gaudenzia Drug Rehabilitation Center
1971 · Richard Yeager,
Mike Chapman · US

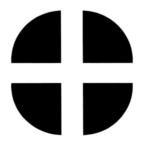

Pavia Municipality Town Hall
1981 · R. Nava, D. Soffientini,
A. Ubertazzi · IT

Beekman Downtown Hospital
1969 · Philip Gips · US

St. Luke's Hospital
1972 · Terry Lesniewicz, Al Navarre · US

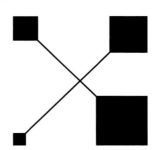

Museo de Arte, Caracas
Museum
1983 · Gerd Leufert · VE

Shintoku Electronic
1968 · Hiromu Hara/
Nippon Design Center · JP

I Propilei
Publishing
1965 · Daniele Baroni · IT

**Associazione Campeggiatori
Turistici d'Italia**
Camping association
1971 · Giovanni Brunazzi · IT

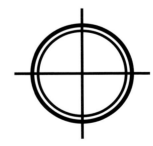

Junger Instruments AB
Precision technology
1968 · Geoffrey Woollard/
Allied International Designers · UK

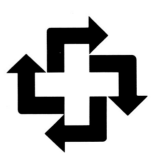

Hospital Management Systems Society
Healthcare organization
1967 · Beau Gardner · US

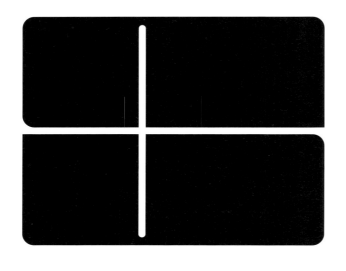

Scandinavian Windows
1969 · David J. Plumb · UK

Aannemerscombinatie Bouw Binnenziekenhuis
Hospital
1969 · Ben Bos/Total Design · NL

Salisbury Theological College
1967 · Keith Murgatroyd · UK

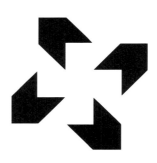

Hospital Consortium
Medical center alliance
1974 · Michael Vanderbyl · US

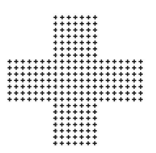

Red Cross International, Havana
Aid agency
1958 · Félix Beltrán · CU

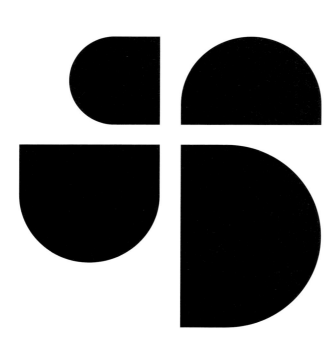

F. Hoekendijk Kerk
Church
1971 · Jan Jaring · NL

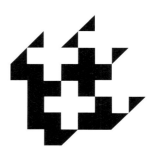

Medical Leasing Company
Healthcare
1975 · Charlotte Potts · US

Capital Planning Resources
Real estate
1974 · Mike Quon · US

Japan Textile Association
1967 · Takashi Kono · JP

Eurocross
Transportation
1972 · John Nash/
Richard, Nash & Friends · UK

K+K Medical
Medical supplies
1982 · Scott Engen · US

Merrill Lynch, Pierce, Fenner & Smith
Stockbrokers
1962 · Lester Beall · US

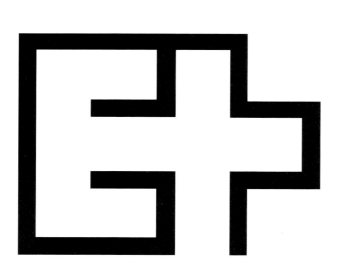

Schweizerische Landesausstellung, Lausanne
Exhibition
1964 · Armin Hofmann · CH

Bouwmij Janssen
Construction company
1964 · Marcel Pijpers · NL

Schweizerische Kreditanstalt
Bank (proposed design)
1967 · Jörg Hamburger · CH

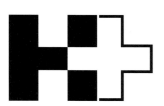

Hospicare
Hospital services
1969 · Detlef Hallerbach · US

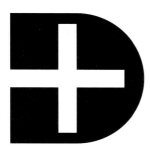

Dillman+Danaher
Investment
1970 · Allan W. Miller · US

Kirchengemeinde Buchthalten
Church
1960s · Peter G. Ulmer · CH

Haig & Haig
Whiskey (proposed design)
1964 · Paul Frick · US

Sacill
1941 · Max Huber · IT

Kashiwaba Neurosurgery
Hospital
1982 · Shin Ikeda · JP

Senior Jesuits Program
Religious organization
1978 · Edward Hughes · US

Dreesen + Poersch
Advertising
1965 · Anonymous · DE

W. B. Cross
Dairy products
1970 · Ron Richards · CA

The Glenbrook Hospital
1974 · Edward Hughes · US

Expo '64, Lausanne
World's fair (proposed design)
1964 · Kurt Wirth · CH

B+S Sägewerk
Sawmill
1960s · Hans-Joachim Brauer · DE

Hôpital Notre-Dame, Montreal
Hospital
1970 · George Huel · CA

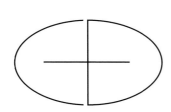

Communication+Design
1972 · Gerold Schmidt · DE

Fahrni & Palermo
Brakes
1960s · Roger-Virgile Geiser · CH

4th Congress of Red Cross International, Havana
Aid conference
1962 · Félix Beltrán · CU

Pharmacies Modernes
Pharmacy chain
1961 · Rolf Harder/
Design Collaborative · CA

University of Utah Medical Center
Health center
1980 · Michael Richards,
Bill Swensen · US

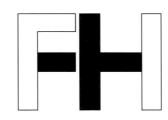

Fédération Horlogère, Biel
Watches
1961 · GGK · CH

M+N+P
Design
1960 · Aloísio Magalhães, Luiz Fernando
Noronha, Artur Lício Pontual · BR

Hospitales Unidos de Barcelona
Hospital association
1959 · Ribas & Creus · ES

Kent County Memorial Hospital
1981 · George Delany · US

Mental Health
Medical equipment
1979 · Ken'ichi Hirose · JP

Cryer & Marchant
Photography
1965 · Tony Forster · UK

Points

Punkte

Dots

Attco
Theatrical staging and lighting
1967 · Clarence Lee · US

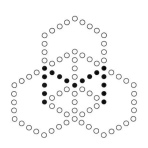

Metra International
Management consultancy
1958 · Henrion Design Associates · UK

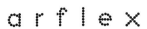

Macom
Computer equipment
1960s · Alfons Boehm · CH

Con-centra-bau
Construction company
1971 · Wolf D. Zimmermann · DE

Roggero & Tortia Poligrafico
Printing
1969 · Giovanni Brunazzi · IT

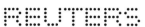

Arflex
Furniture
1960s · Albe Steiner · IT

Gucker and Goldstein
Lace importers
1962 · Robert P. Gersin · US

Sigen
Nuclear research
1975 · Giovanni Brunazzi · IT

Reuters
News agency
1966 · Crosby, Fletcher, Forbes · UK

Grand Dinner Theater
1982 · Joseph Boggs · US

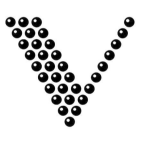

Vide
1978 · Silvio Coppola · IT

Studio Doveri
Design
1983 · Claudio Doveri · IT

Grays of Cambridge
Sporting goods
1963 · David Harris · UK

Pritchard Wood and Partners
Advertising
1964 · Henrion Design Associates · UK

**Sociéte Générale des
Coopératives de Consommation**
Supermarket chain
1966 · Raymond Loewy/CEI · FR

Holmen Paper
1965 · Crosby, Fletcher, Forbes · UK

Business Computers
1968 · Talmadge, Drummond &
Partners · UK

**The American Library
Association, Chicago**
1965 · Vance Jonson · US

Jeune France
Political youth organization
1972 · Jean Delaunay/Look · FR

Rautatiekirjakauppa
Public transport
1964 · Bror B. Zetterborg · FI

Matvörur Hf.
Foods
1969 · Thröstur Magnusson, Hilmar
Sigurdsson/Argus Advertising · IS

Liikkeenjohdon Valmennus-Rastor
Education
1968 · Juhani Parikka/
Markkinointi Viherjuuri · FI

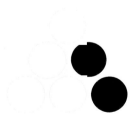

Escuela de Administración Pública
School
1971 · Dicken Castro · CO

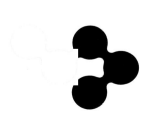

Nishikawa Sangyo
Bedding materials
1976 · Mitsuo Ishida, Shoji Sato · JP

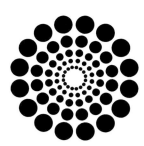

Exhibition Services
1960s · Erberto Carboni · IT

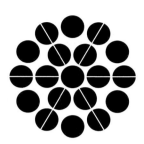

Kosmos
Flowers
1967 · Jan Jaring · NL

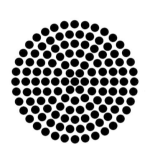

Cumberland Furniture Corporation
Office furniture
1960s · Rudolph de Harak · US

Roosevelt University
1971 · Edward Hughes · US

Everbrite Electric
1970s · Tomoko Miho/
George Nelson & Co. · US

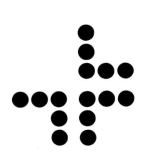

Jen Elettronica
Electronics
1979 · Beppe Benenti · IT

Aid Association for Lutherans
Insurance
1968 · Morton Goldsholl · US

Centro Médico Docente La Trinidad
Hospital
1972 · Gerd Leufert · VE

Halftone House
Printing colors
1965 · Tom Woodward · US

Conicit
Research institute
1970 · Gerd Leufert · VE

Taichi Shoji
Public relations
1981 · Ishine Nituma,
Taijiro Nakayama · JP

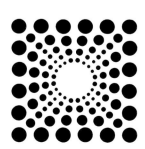

Kim Lighting
1970 · Ray Engle · US

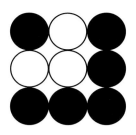

Video 9
Broadcasting
1973 · Anne-Marie Latrémolière/
Hollenstein Création · FR

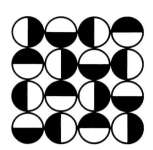

Color, Línea, Luz
Art exhibition
1969 · Gerd Leufert · VE

Banco del Estado
Bank
1977 · Dicken Castro · CO

Labora Mannheim
Laboratory equipment
1974 · Erwin Poell · DE

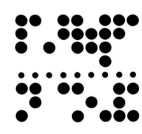

Engels & van Ooststroom
Design
1968 · Frits W. van Ooststroom · NL

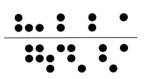

**Van Dien, van Uden, Besançon,
Koppenberg & Co.**
Accounting
1968 · Louis Swart · NL

Figuratif

Figürlich

Figurative

Das Aktuelle Bild der DEWAG
Advertising services
1965 · Herbert Prüget · DE-GDR

AGM
Miniature models
1967 · Bob Gill · US/UK

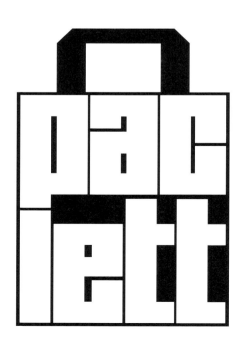

Paclett
Paper
1960s · Ingo & Christine Friel · DE

International Paper Company
Paper and packaging
1959 · Lester Beall · US

Lake Forest Open Lands Association
Environmental body
1968 · Bruce Beck · US

F lli Franchi
Seeds
1968 · Piero Ottinetti · IT

Tabakblatt Kristinus
Cigarettes
1960s · Bruno K. Wiese · DE

Sungarden
Real estate
1973 · John Spatchurst · AU

Research Park
Real estate
1963 · Read Viemeister/
Vie Des gn Studios · US

Editorial Fabril
Publishing
1962 · Rómulo Macció · AR

O.E.C.D.
Trade organization
1964 · Jacques Nathan-Garamond · FR

Middlechurch Home of Winnipeg
Nursing home
1965 · William Mayrs · CA

System Truck Painting
Vehicle painting
1964 · James Cross · US

Baumschule
Tree nursery
1960s · Helmuth Kurtz · CH

Cousances
Kitchen appliances
1972 · Jean Delaunay/Look · FR

Janss Canejo Community
Neighborhood organization
1964 · Ken Parkhurst · US

Jöns
Transportation
1970s · Heinz Schwabe · DE

Baumschule Ketzin Havel
Tree nursery
1965 · Herbert Prüget · DE-GDR

Florex Pentti Kauhanen
Flowers
1968 · Eka Lainio/
Markkinointi Viherjuuri · FI

The Marin Jewish Community Center
Cultural organization
1960s · Robert Pease · US

Curling Club Basel
Sports organization
1967 · Jürg Spahr · CH

**Canadian Society of Landscape
Architects**
1966 · Jacques E. Charette · CA

Jay Ski Village
Ski resort
1967 · Ken Parkhurst · US

Robert's Dairy Company
Foods
1960 · Thomas Laufer & Associates · US

Müller & Kalkow
Soap
1965 · Heinz Israel · DE-GDR

Canadian Pulp & Paper Association
1967 · William Kissiloff/
Kissiloff & Wimmershoff · CA

Air Canada
Airline
1963 · Hans Kleefeld/
Stewart & Morrison · CA

Autark
Measuring instruments
1940s · Walter Herdeg · CH

Film Projects
Film production
1960s · Joe Caroff/
Design Associates · US

Sheridan Nurseries
Landscape architecture
1968 · Manfred Gotthans/
Chris Yaneff · CA

Uniplan
Bank
1969 · Raymond Gid · FR

Assofrutta Etnea
Fruits
1970 · Sergio Salaroli · IT

Alessio Bassi
Metal goods
1960s · Giancarlo Guerrini · IT

VEB Fernmeldewerk
Telecommunications
1965 · Alfons Hopf · DE-GDR

Studio Friel
Design
1960s · Ingo & Christine Friel · DE

Vitam
Fruits
1948 · Max Huber/Studio Boggeri · IT

Liberazione e Sviluppo
Development aid
1971 · Ilio Negri · IT

Märkisches Museum
Museum of local history
1965 · Günter Henkel · DE-GDR

Mondial Toys
Children's toys
1972 · Walter Del Frate · IT

Cercle du Livre Economique
Publishing
1968 · Lonsdale Design · FR

Musik-Biennale
Music festival
1965 · Herbert Prüget · DE-GDR

Emanuel Turowski
Telecommunications
1953 · Gerd Leufert · VE

Cordon Bleu de Venezuela
Canned foods
1963 · Nedo Mion Ferrario · VE

Shiroya
Laundry
1965 · Mitsuhiko Sasao/
McCann Erickson-Hakuhodo · JP

Landwirtschaftsausstellung der GDR
Exhibition
1965 · Kar. Thewalt · DE-GDR

Steelcase
Furniture
1970 · Vance Jonson · US

Il Mulino
Publishing
1968 · Walter Hergenröther · IT

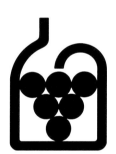

Ermolao
Wines
1968 · Enzo Scarton/Alfa Studio · IT

Oy Airam
Light-bulbs
1961 · Kyösti Varis · FI

Rand McNally & Company
Publishing
1964 · Bruce Beck/
The Design Partnership · US

Danish Agricultural Marketing Board
Food products
1963 · Adam Moltke · DK

Garnfabrik
Yarns
1950s · Heinz Schwabe · DE

RAI Radiotelefortuna
Television lottery
1967 · Pino Tovaglia · IT

VVB Werkzeugmaschinenwerke
Machine tools
1965 · Wolfgang Hoepfner · DE-GDR

Liviana
Clothing
1965 · Enzo Scarton/Alfa Studio · IT

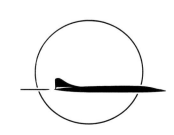

Flughafen Hamburg
Airport
1974 · Studio Freudenthal · DE

Hallesches Laternenfest
City festival
1965 · Gerhard Voigt · DE-GDR

Mál & Menning
Publishing
1968 · Thröstur Magnusson, Hilmar
Sigurdsson/Argus Advertising · IS

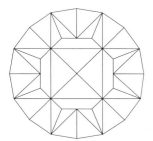

Poikien Kaupunki
Education
1968 · Bror B. Zetterborg · FI

Rous & Mann Press
Printing
1968 · James D. Taylor/
Rous & Mann Press · CA

Nancy Martin
Writer
1965 · Jerry Braude · US

Sebastiani Gioielli
Jeweler
1964 · Bob Noorda/
Unimark International · IT

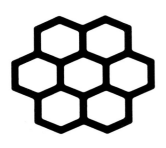

Industriezweigakademie
Electrical projects
1965 · Gerhard Voigt · DE-GDR

Venezuelan Supply
Industrial gloves
1952 · Gerd Leufert · VE

Oppi
School furniture
1968 · Osmo Omenamäki · FI

Hjertegarn
Yarns
1964 · Morten Peetz-Schou · DK

Nihon-Reiyon
Textiles
1965 · Shigeo Fukuda · JP

Consejo de Artesanías
World crafts council
1965 · Gerd Leufert · VE

Société Générale de Relations Publiques
Public relations
1955 · Jacques Nathan-Garamond · FR

Martin-Senour
Paints
1956 · Morton Goldsholl · US

Post Magazine
1969 · Shigeo Fukuda · JP

Osaka Seisyonen Bunka No Kai
Cultural association
1960s · Yoshio Amaya · JP

Lois Moinat
Furniture
1940s · Walter Herdeg · CH

Ariston Elettrodomestici
Home appliances
1963 · Vittorio Antinori · IT

Moreschi
Footwear
1963 · A. G. Fronzoni · IT

Yokota
Thread manufacturing
1969 · Takeshi Otaka · JP

**Comédiens Associés
du Québec**
Federation of actors
1971 · Raymond Bellemare · CA

Sveriges Biodlares Riksförbund
Federation of beekeepers
1969 · Ove Engström · SE

**Stichting Collectieve Propaganda
van het Nederlandse Boek**
Dutch commission for book promotion
1960s · Benno Wissing · NL

Teatro Estable de Maracay
Theater
1967 · Gerd Leufert · VE

Berg- & Hüttenindustrie
Metallurgy
1965 · Werner Duda · DE-GDR

Fonema Idiomas
Language school
1971 · Pérez Sánchez · ES

Japan Agricultural Co-op Associations
Bank
1968 · Yoshio Hayashi · JP

Bonving Skofabrik
Footwear
1960s · Fritjof Pedersén · SE

Spielzeugmechanik Pfaffschwende
Toys
1965 · Walter Seifert · DE-GDR

Carol Cutner
Photographer
1969 · Bob Gill · US/UK

Bild und Heimat Reichenbach
Publishing
1965 · Peter Mantwill · DE-GDR

Association d'Hospitalisation du Québec
Healthcare organization
1966 · Pierre-Yves Pelletier · CA

Walther Raebel & Sohn
Clothing
1965 · Karl-Jürgen Härtel · DE-GDR

15th Festival Internazionale del Teatro Universitario
Theater festival
1967 · Franco M. Ricci · IT

Western Savings Bank
1969 · Walter P. Margulies/
Lippincott & Margulies · US

Täuber & Sohn Verlag
Publishing
1960s · Toni Burghart · DE

Nordisk Lettmetall
Metalworks
1950 · Walter Sauer · DE

Wm. S. Merrell
Pharmacy
1965 · Ernst Roch/
Design Collaborative · CA

Shimoda Prince
Hotel chain
1973 · Shigeo Katsuoka · JP

Barber-Ellis of Canada
Office supplies
1964 · Manfred Gotthans/
Chris Yaneff · CA

Kulturgruppe Schiffsmontage
Cultural association
1965 · Hans Schlapmann · DE-GDR

La Caffetteria
Coffee shop
1964 · Vittorio Antinori · IT

Festival Internacional do Film
Film festival
1965 · Pinto Ziraldo · BR

Falken Verlag, Heinz von Känel
Publishing
1940s · Eugen & Max Lenz · CH

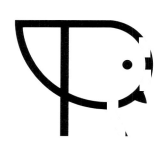

Incubatoio Ronchi
Poultry farming
1964 · Veniero Bertolotti/Studio 4 · IT

Parvulario Tagore
Girls' primary school
1967 · José Baqués · ES

Canadian Arthritis & Rheumatism Society
Healthcare
1965 · Eiko Pech/Stewart & Morrison · CA

Spring Pond Apartments
Real estate
1968 · Robert Ivers · US

Boles-Aero
Travel agency
1962 · Jerry Braude · US

Park Bellows Apartments
Real estate
1968 · Robert Pease,
Bryce Browning · US

Slendaire
Cosmetics
1965 · Jan Hollender · PL

Canada Decalcomania
Decal manufacturer
1968 · Chris Yaneff · CA

Lanificio Rivetti
Textiles
1968 · Silvio Coppola · IT

André B. Thomas
Communication and marketing
1971 · Raymond Bellemare · CA

Cresta Rossa
Poultry
1968 · Gianni Venturino/
Studio Pentagono · IT

Schützenverband
Sports association
1960s · Eugen & Max Lenz · CH

Heberlein & Co.
Textiles
1940s · Walter Käch · CH

Association of the Swedish Book Trade
1969 · Erik Ellegaard Frederiksen · DK

Heibon Shuppan
Publishing
1965 · Tadashi Ohashi · JP

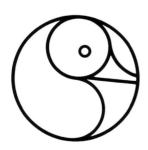

Soc. Convectio
Cookers
1970s · Stefano Simoni · IT

Fulford Dodds
Baby products
1961 · Hans Kleefeld/
Stewart & Morrison · CA

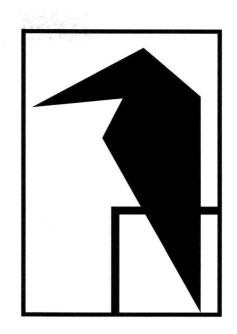

Ravenstein Verlag
Publishing
1955 · Hans Kramer · DE

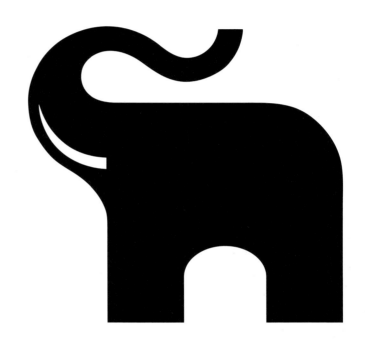

L'Elefante
Furniture
1967 · Bob Noorda/Unimark International · IT

Uusikivalehti
Magazine
1950s · Martti A. Mykkänen · FI

Fritz Feinhals Werbeberater
Advertising
1953 · Heinz Schwabe · DE

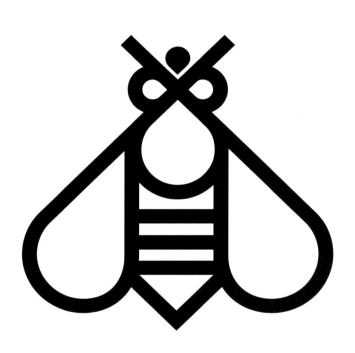

Krefina Bank
1960s · Robert Geisser · CH

Kyodo Nyugyo
Dairy products
1965 · Ikko Tanaka · JP

Kammgarnspinnerei, Brandenburg
Yarns
1965 · Heinz Weber · DE-GDR

F.lli Turccolo
Foods
1968 · Enzo Scarton/Alfa Studio · IT

Ainsa - Artículos Industriales
Leather
1969 · Ribas & Creus · ES

Marzotto
Textiles
1966 · Bob Noorda/
Unimark International · IT

Ricardo Fayos
Leather and wool
1968 · Ernesto Moradell Català · ES

Vollhumon Düngemittel
Fertilizers
1960s · Erich Buchegger · AT

Haraldssøn
Office supplies
1967 · Paul Brand · NO

Serrature Meroni
Locksmiths
1967 · Fiero Sansoni · IT

Gutter
Cranes
1961 · Piero Ottinetti · IT

Redding Zoo
1971 · Adrian Loos · US

Club du Safari International
1971 · Leen Averink · FR

Monarch Machinery
Knitting machines
1965 · Manfred Gotthans/
Chris Yaneff · CA

H. Zwart & Co.
Wood
1962 · J. Weston Advertising Design · US

VEB Saalemühlen
Mills
1965 · Gerhard Brose · DE-GDR

Lamperti Cotonificio
Cotton
1964 · Silvio Coppola · IT

New York Aquarium
1970 · Edward Marson · US

Marzotto
Textiles
1964 · Bob Noorda/
Unimark International · IT

Playboy Magazine
1953 · Arthur Paul · US

Storkline
Infants' furniture
1960 · Morton Goldsholl · US

Yonen Geizyutu
Children's books
1960s · Yoshio Amaya · JP

Pirelli Sapsa
Textiles
1967 · Salvatore Gregorietti/
Unimark International · IT

Penguin Children's Books
Publishing
1960s · Henrion Design Associates · UK

Pelican Films
Film production
1961 · S. Neil Fujita · US

Amore & Pollastrini
Fish
1963 · Vittorio Antinori · IT

Gin-Marke - Illva
Distillery
1958 · Walter Del Frate · IT

Ente Provinciale per il Turismo
Tourist office
1969 · Bob Noorda/
Unimark International · IT

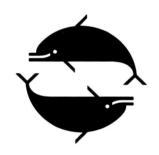

Montreal Aquarium
1967 · Ernst Roch/
Design Collaborative · CA

Religious Television Programs
Broadcasting
1966 · Pierre-Yves Pelletier · CA

Ditta Impermeabili San Giorgio
Raincoats
1960s · Giulio Confalonieri · IT

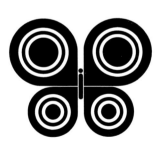

Joyce Shoes
Footwear
1970 · Joseph Bottoni · US

Exlibris
1950s · René Althaus · CH

O'Keefe's Fisheries
1956 · Ernst Roch/
Design Collaborative · CA

Clay-Adams
Medical instruments
1967 · Bruce Blackburn/
Chermayeff & Geismar · US

Glen Cove
Real estate
1968 · F. Everett Forbes · US

Maui Surf Hotel
1969 · Clarence Lee · US

Izumimoto Syoten
Pet shop for tropical fish
1960s · Yoshio Amaya · JP

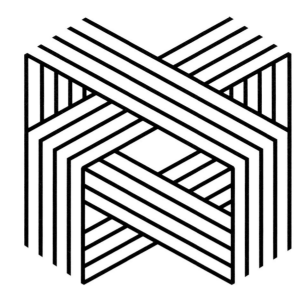

Grand Prix du Ruban d'Or de l'Emballage
Packaging award
1969 · Daniel Maurel/Chourgnoz Publicité · FR

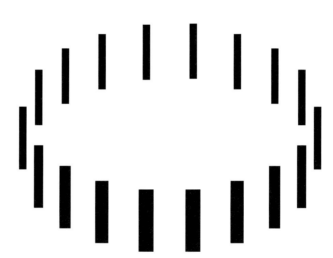

Deutsches Filmmuseum
Film museum
1984 · Philipp Teufel, Günter Illner · DE

Nylon de México
Clothing
1970s · Lance Wyman · US

Studio Troisi
Design
1968 · Alfredo Troisi · IT

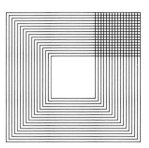

Rochester Institute of Technology,
Television Center
Broadcasting research
1968 · R. Roger Remington · US

Erik Ellegaard Frederiksen
Industrial design
1960 · Erik Ellegaard Frederiksen · DK

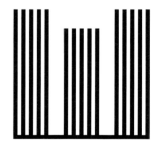

Ensemble Productions
Record label
1970 · J. & A. Breukelman
Design Associates · CA

16th Congresso da ISSCT
Sugar cane manufacturers congress
1976 · PVDI · BR

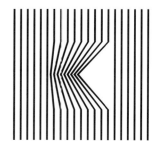

Walter O. Koinzer
1967 · B. Keller/Studio CKR · DE

Arflex
Furniture
1971 · Giancarlo Iliprandi · IT

IASA Indústrias de Azulejos
Tiles
1971 · Roberto Amaro Lanari · BR

Asociación Argentina de Psicoterapia
Psychotherapy
1971 · Norberto H. Coppola · AR

Aboa Development
1974 · Akisato Ueda · JP

Eina
Design school
1967 · Pérez Sánchez · ES

Hotel & Public Building Equipment Group
Interior design
1967 · Negus & Negus · UK

Ingrid
Cosmetics
1970 · Franco Grignani · IT

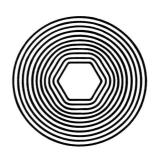

Balbuena
Jeweler
1974 · José Santamarina · ES

Department of Health & Social Security
Government office
1970 · Woudhuysen Inc. · UK

Sterling Life
Insurance
1981 · Kenneth Hollick · UK

Phototype Satzherstellung
Typesetting
1967 · Walter Landmann,
Heinz Friedrich · DE

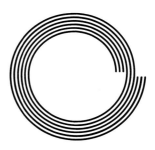

Constant Haute Coiffure
Hairdresser
1967 · Yvon Laroche · CA

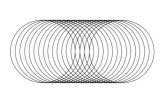

Meacham Companies
1969 · Robert P. Gersin · US

Palacio de Pioneros, Havana
Youth center
1975 · Félix Beltrán · CU

Life Engineering
1973 · Go Okazawa,
Makoto Yoshida · JP

Optical Peripherals Laboratory
Optical memory storage
1982 · Tim Larsen · US

Istituto Luce
Lighting
1972 · Ettore Vitale · IT

Elektro Gruber
Electronics
1970 · Heinz Kröhl, Peter Offenberg · DE

Kurt Steinwendtner
Film production
1960s · Kurt Schwarz · AT

Variolan
Construction company
1975 · Keith Murgatroyd,
Tony Forster · UK

Centre Georges Pompidou
Cultural center
1975 · Jean Widmer · FR

Toyama Museum of Modern Art
1981 · Tatsuo Okonu · JP

Cofremca
Market analysis
1973 · Daniel Sinay/
Hollenstein Création · FR

Van Gelder
Paper
1968 · Karen Munck/
Allied International Designers · UK

Bagnasco
Restaurant chain
1968 · Piero Ottinetti · IT

Urban Renewal Development
1966 · Richard De Natale · US

SGMI
Construction company
1971 · Jean Delaunay/Look · FR

Olympic Games, Moscow 1980
1980 · Vlad mir Arsentyev · RU

Republic Corporation
Holding company
1968 · Robert Miles Runyan · US

University of Notre Dame
1969 · Hayward R. Blake · US

Promicron
Electronics
1960s · Walter Ballmer · CH

Electrorama
Lighting
1970 · Jean Delaunay/Look · FR

Vibrodyne
Polishing and vibratory finishing
1962 · Read Viemeister · US

Transamerica Pyramid
Skyscraper
1969 · Jerry Berman · US

Continental Airlines
1968 · Saul Bass & Associates · US

Union Générale Cinématographique
Cinema operator
1970 · Jean Delaunay/Look · FR

Projuventud
1979 · Dicken Castro · CO

Nordidakt 1969
School bookfair
1969 · Thröstur Magnusson, Hilmar
Sigurdsson/Argus Advertising · IS

Rockwell International
Manufacturing conglomerate
1968 · Saul Bass & Associates · US

Orthopaedic Hospital
1981 · James Cross · US

Médiavision
Film distribution
1971 · Jean Delaunay/Look · FR

Barkow
Fuel oil
1960s · Primo Angeli · US

Cimeo Milan
Import-export
1980 · Félix Beltrán · CU/MX

Ondulato Umbro
Paper
1974 · Rinaldo Cutini · IT

Le Canne
Hotel
1972 · A. G. Fronzoni · IT

Edition Tusch
Publishing
1972 · Anonymous · AT

**American Association
of Department Stores**
Retail federation
1970s · Vincent Ceci · US

Banco Noroeste
Bank
1973 · Joãc Carlos Cauduro,
Ludovico Antonio Martino · BR

Nijverdal ten Cate
Textiles
1960 · Gerard Wernars · NL

Stalling Filmsatz
Typesetting
1975 · Bruno K. Wiese · DE

Cefina JMW
Jewish social-work foundation
1969 · Otto Treumann · NL

Teamtex
Textiles
1976 · Odermatt+Tissi · CH

Marco
Bookstore
1971 · Pierluigi Cerri, Vittorio Gregotti,
Pierluigi Nicolin · IT

Santiago Textil
Clothing
1975 · Jorge Canales · MX

Centro de Documentación Política
Political research and publishing
1978 · Ernesto Lehfeld · MX

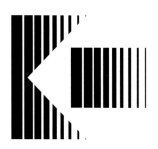

Kennecorp
Rubber products
1973 · Terry Lesniewicz, Al Navarre · US

Instituto Postal Telegráfico
Telecommunications
1979 · Nedo Mion Ferrario · IT/VE

Mettler & Co.
Textiles
1969 · Odermatt+Tissi · CH

Raffold
Conveyor systems
1970 · David J. Plumb · UK

Grebsa Cibernética
Cybernetics
1981 · Morfos Diseño · MX

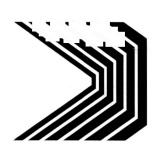

Architectural Symposium
1967 · Gerd Leufert · VE

União São Paulo
Import-export
1973 · PVDI · BR

ON Associates
Music publishing
1970 · Shin Nagamatsu,
Kyoji Nakatani · JP

Sistemas Drupal
Printing
1975 · Gerd Leufert,
Ladislaus Popper · VE

The I Club
Private club
1982 · Henry Steiner,
Jennings Ku · HK

Ministerstwo Przemysłu Lekkiego
Ministry of light industry
1960s · Witold Surowiecki · PL

Hochschule für Verkehrswesen
Transport science
1970 · Gert Wunderlich · DE-GDR

Companhia Brasileira de Sintéticos
Synthetic fibers
1969 · Alexandre Wollner · BR

The Tudor Press
Publishing
1970 · Gavin Healey · UK

Yamada Co.
Textile fibers
1974 · Akisato Ueda · JP

Rangau Quelle
Mineral water
1979 · Manfred Wutke · DE

Intergast Internationale
Exhibition
1960s · Peter Wehr · DE

Grupo Cinco
Architecture
1978 · Allan W. Miller/Animex · MX

Nero Giroldi
Reinforced concrete
1960s · Franco Grignani · IT

Johnson & Nephew
Wires
1972 · John Harrison, John Brewer, Barry
O'Dwyer/Stewart Morrison Harrison · UK

Equipamento de Hoy
Furniture
1971 · Ricardo Blanco · AR

Herreria Rodriguez
Metalworks
1982 · Jose Luis Aguirre · IT

Key Services
Management consultancy
1970 · Gavin Healey · UK

Nawinta Mineralbrunnen
Mineral water
1979 · Manfred Wutke · DE

Stiftung Volkswagenwerk
Humanities and science research funding
1965 · Klaus Grözinger,
Peter Riefenstahl · DE

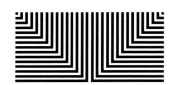

Ministerio de la Industria Ligera
Government office for
light industries
1980 · Félix Beltrán · CU

Klimaanlagen-Hersteller
Air-conditioning
1961 · Helmut Keppler · DE

Laboratoires Sarbach
Pharmaceutical laboratory
1966 · Erich Brenzinger/
Chourgnoz Publicité · FR

Healey Mills Associates
Design
1968 · Gavin Healey, Denis Mills · UK

David Rossi
Jeweler
1970 · Giovanni Brunazzi · IT

Mediart Communications
Public relations
1983 · Shigeo Katsuoka, Tako Ikeda · JP

Queenswear
Textiles
1973 · Rolf Harder · CA

Agence Katimavik
Public relations
1968 · George Huel · CA

Vereinigte Mineralquellen der Schweiz
Mineral water producers organization
1960s · Christian Lang · CH

**Ministry of Transport
Computer Center**
1979 · Velizar Petrov · BG

Keikyu Inawashiro
Resort
1985 · Shigeo Katsuoka,
Hiroko Tsukada · JP

Stamps Sales
1973 · Ernesto Lehfeld · MX

Skandinaviska Banken
Bank
1972 · Tor A. Pettersen/
Lock Pettersen · UK/SE

Tokyo Advertising
1966 · Kazumasa Nagai/
Nippon Design Center · JP

Suruga Bank
1965 · Kazumasa Nagai · JP

Industrial Design USA
Exhibition
1966 · George Nelson · US

Saumweber & Stecher
Construction company
1974 · Oanh Pham Phu · DE

Tack Leisure Building
1977 · Shintaro Ajioka · JP

Transair
Airline
1969 · Silvio Coppola · IT

TUC
Theater
1977 · Claude Dietrich · PE

Contravision
Printing
1972 · Bank & Miles · UK

Woolmark
International wool secretariat
1964 · Franco Grignani · IT

FRANKONA

Frankona Rückversicherung
Insurance
1979 · Rolf Müller · DE

Drogerie Kohler
Pharmacy
1969 · Atelier Stadelmann Bisig · CH

Gilbey Vintners
Wines
1968 · Unimark International · UK

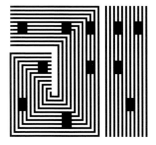

Puls
Fashion
1968 · Michel Coudeyre/Snip · FR

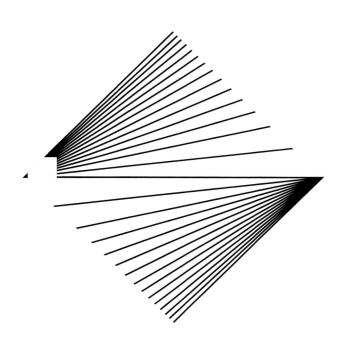

Chemiefaserkongress
Congress on synthetic fibers
1975 · Rolf Müller · DE

Asturiana de Informática
Computer systems
1967 · José Santamarina/
Elias & Santamarina · ES

Colt Heating & Ventilation
1965 · Henrion Design Associates · UK

Gevacolor Gevaert
Film processing
1960s · Gerard Wernars · NL

Vantage Planning Systems
Architectural systems
1975 · Jack Evans · US

Fränkische Gobelin Manufaktur
Textiles
1980 · Christof Gassner · DE

Cefilac
Metalworks
1971 · Florent Garnier · FR

Teppichfabrik Niedek-Velour
Carpets
1983 · Paul Effert · DE

Waterman Paterson Candy International
Water treatment
1966 · Holmes Kitley Associates · UK

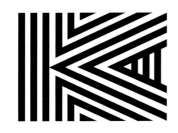

Kremer Automation
Electronics
1970 · Abram Games · UK

Tréfileries de Châtillon-Gorcy
Metalworks
1968 · Philippe Gentil · FR

Taubman Shopping Center
1971 · Robert P. Gersin · US

J. Ulbach & Cia.
Pharmaceuticals
1978 · Enric Huguet · ES

Sandgren & Murtha
Wood
1960s · Ad Tolhuis · US

Cantoni
Cotton mill
1960s · M. Schneider/Studio Boggeri · IT

Fukusuke
Commemorative event
1981 · Helmut Schmid · DE/JP

Toyo Jitsugyo
Marble surface care
1982 · Masahiro Shimizu · JP

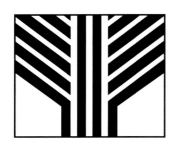

Totem
Paints
1968 · Franco M. Ricci · IT

**Companhia Serviços
de Engenharia Servienge**
Road construction
1967 · Joaquim Redig · BR

Yoshino
Interior design
1976 · Koichi Watanabe · JP

Kyowa Kodoku Seihan
Wooden boards
1978 · Yukishia Takakita · JP

**Government of Ontario
Department of Trade & Development**
1969 · Stewart & Morrison · CA

Estudio Uno
Design
1979 · Gerd Leufert · VE

Rayflex
Textiles
1960s · Norman Gorbaty/
Ken Kirkwood Agency · US

Engen-Graphic
Design
1977 · Scott Engen · US

Moatti
Antiques
1972 · Jean Delaunay/Look · FR

Ilford
Photographic materials
1966 · Ronald Armstrong/
Design Research Unit · UK

The Fiber Union
1982 · Joe Dieter · US

Museo de Arte Moderno Jesús Soto
Museum of modern art
1970 · Gerd Leufert · VE

Fonacot
Furniture design competition
1978 · Jorge Sposari · AR

Imasco
Consumer goods
1970 · Rolf Harder, Ernst Roch/
Design Collaborative · CA

VEB Feintuch
Clothing
1965 · Heidtraud Stenker · DE-GDR

Industrias de Alta Tecnología
Technological development
1978 · Alfonso Capetillo Ponce,
Jack Vermonden · MX

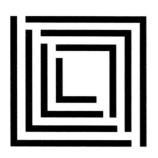

Karl Langen Klischeefabrik
Prepress services
1955 · Hans Karl Rodenkirchen · DE

Station Hotel, Kyoto
1960s · Yorikazu Hirata · JP

Oleon Laboratoire
Cosmetics
1972 · Jean Delaunay/Look · FR

Community Krsko Region
Flag
1982 · Judita Skalar · YU

Omniafili
1963 · Max Huber · IT

**Japanese Association for
Expo '70, Osaka**
World's fair organization
1969 · Nakajo Masayoshi · JP

Uitgeverij Spaarnestad
Publishing
1968 · Tel Design Associated · NL

Trust Funds
Financial fund
1981 · George Tscherny · US

Pacific Fuel Trading
1983 · Tatsuhito Yamamoto · JP

Construtora Queiroz Galvão
Road construction
1968 · Joaquim Redig · BR

Soifer
Glass
1977 · Jorge Sposari · AR

Kahma
Supermarket chain
1981 · Kinya Zen, Takaaki Yoshinobu · JP

Karaca Holding
1978 · Selahattin Sönmez · TR

Rogers Broadcasting
1965 · Manfred Gotthans,
Chris Yaneff · CA

Écrire avec des images présente l'avantage d'être direct, concis et concentré. Une image peut représenter toute une série d'associations qui ne pourraient souvent être expliquées qu'en utilisant beaucoup de mots. Une image peut être la représentation de quelque chose que nous pouvons dire. En tant que symbole, elle peut représenter une idée abstraite et en tout cas non visuelle.

Herbert Bayer

Mit Bildern zu schreiben hat den Vorteil, direkt, kurz und bündig zu sein. Ein Bild kann für eine komplexe Abfolge von Assoziationen stehen, die häufig nur mit vielen Worten zu erklären wäre, und kann etwas repräsentieren, das sich verbal ausdrücken lässt. Als Symbol kann es für eine abstrakte und eigentlich nicht visuelle Idee stehen.

Herbert Bayer

Picture writing has the advantage of directness, short-ness and concentration. A picture can stand for a whole complex of associations which often only many words can communicate. A picture can be the representation of something we can say. As a symbol, it may stand for an abstract and otherwise unvisual idea.

Herbert Bayer

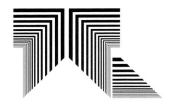

Técnicas de Comunicación
Advertising
1969 · Francesc Guitart · ES

Science Research Associates
Educational publisher
1976 · Edward Hughes · US

Prime Jewelry
1983 · Ryuji Hirotani · JP

Universidad Simón Bolívar
University
1969 · Gerd Leufert · VE

Printing Convention 1975
1975 · Joe Sonderman,
Mike Hogelin · US

Overseas Computer Consultants
Computing
1970 · Peter Wildbur · UK

**Canadian Conference on
Church and Society**
1968 · Julien Hébert · CA

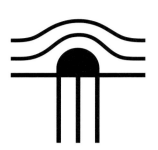

Tabasa
Road construction
1969 · Enric Huguet · ES

Kreißelmeier Verlag
Publishing
1962 · Werner Maier · DE

Performance Maximus
Sports center
1968 · J. R. Weiss/
The Design Partnership · US

Lodex
Textiles
1967 · Andrzej Bertrandt · PL

Seminar Services
Education
1970 · Appelbaum & Curtis · US

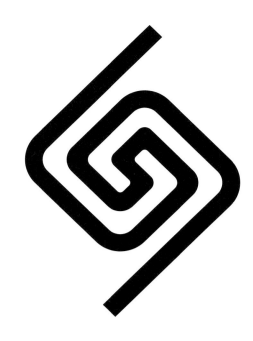

Gütesiegel Echt Silber
Silver quality-mark
1975 · Hans Karl Rodenkirchen · DE

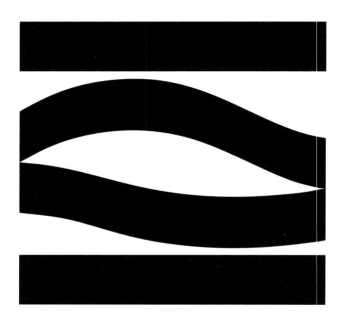

AZ Grupo Gráfico
Design
1970 · Pedro Ariño · ES

C.O.N.I.
Commemorative event
1972 · Mimmo Castellano, Michele Spera · IT

Tennis Unlimited
Sports club
1968 · Appelbaum & Curtis · US

17 Printmakers from England
Art exhibition
1970 · Álvaro Sotillo · VE

Ligue Electrique du Québec
Electronics
1966 · Laurent Marquart/
Jacques Guillon Designers · CA

Reeva Perkins
Silversmith
1968 · Allan D. Rae · CA

Industrie und Handelskammer
Trade organization
1979 · Rolf Müller · DE

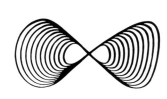

Admiral Corporation
Electronics
1960s · Morton Goldsholl
Design Associates · US

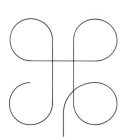

Hanataba
Nightclub
1960s · Takeshi Otaka · JP

The Whiskey House
Import-export
1960s · Giulio Confalonieri · IT

**Companhia Nacional
de Tecidos Nova América**
Textiles
1968 · Joaquim Redig · BR

Publistrade
Advertising
1964 · Piero Ottinetti · IT

Dechy Publicité
Advertising
1962 · Dechy Publicité · BE

Partito Repubblicano Italiano
Political party
1970 · Michele Spera · IT

Ediciones Poligrafa
Publishing
1963 · Joan Pedragosa · ES

Cattle Ranch
1965 · Frank Lipari/
Gazette Printing Company · CA

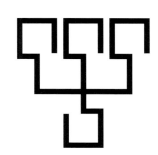

Gifu Medico Support
Healthcare
1980 · Norihiko Watanabe,
Mariko Ozawa · JP

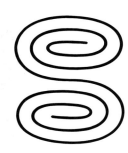

Steiger & Deschler Webereien
Weaving
1950s · Otl Aicher · DE

**Design Competition for
Mainichi Newspapers**
1963 · Makoto Wada · JP

Keio
Department store
1962 · Yoshio Hayashi · JP

Smith Fruit Farms
Foods
1968 · Allan D. Rae · CA

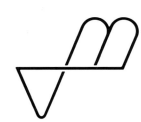

Hans Marseille Verlag
Publishing
1986 · Anonymous · DE

Ravizzini
Ropes
1955 · Pino Tovaglia · IT

Sarriö
Paper
1970 · Amand Domènech · ES

A. Alan Perkins
Architecture
1968 · Allan D. Rae · CA

IVAP
Prefabrication technology
1960 · Mimmo Castellano · IT

In the run-up to the 1968 Olympic Games in Mexico City, the chairman of the organizing committee, the architect Pedro Ramírez Vázquez, launched an international competition to design the graphics for the games. The winners were a team that included the British industrial designer Peter Murdoch and the young American graphic designer Lance Wyman, whose typographic logo was based on the five Olympic rings. In 1966, Wyman was commissioned to produce the graphic design for "Mexico 68." Working from the basic concept of the logo, he developed and supervised a visual program embracing color, typography, pictograms and graphics, using the five-ring image in a wide variety of ways. The result was seen as a quantum leap in the development of conceptual design solutions, which set an internationally esteemed example for later projects of its kind.

Für die Entwicklung von Architektur und Grafik der Olympischen Spiele von Mexico City 1968 initiierte der als Vorsitzender des Organisationskomitees eingesetzte Architekt Pedro Ramírez Vázquez einen internationalen Wettbewerb. Im Team mit dem britischen Industriedesigner Peter Murdoch beteiligte sich der junge Amerikaner Lance Wyman an der Ausschreibung und gewann mit seinem typografischen Logoentwurf, der auf den Kreisen der olympischen Ringe basiert. Wyman wurde 1966 zum Gestaltungsbeauftragten der Spiele von „Mexico 68" berufen. Aus dem Grundkonzept des Logos entwickelte er ein visuelles Programm mit Farben, Typografie, Piktogrammen und Mustern. Unter seiner Leitung wurde das Erscheinungsbild umfassend umgesetzt. Das Ergebnis stellte sich als Quantensprung in der Entwicklung von konzeptionellen Designentwürfen heraus und wurde zu einem international beachteten Vorbild für viele spätere Arbeiten in diesem Bereich.

Pour le développement des architectures et des graphismes des jeux Olympiques de Mexico en 1968, l'architecte Pedro Ramírez Vázquez, président du Comité d'Organisation, lança un concours international. Faisant équipe avec le designer industriel britannique Peter Murdoch, le jeune Américain Lance Wyman remporta l'appel d'offres grâce à son projet de logotype reposant sur les cercles des anneaux olympiques. En 1966, Wyman fut nommé responsable du design des jeux Olympiques de « Mexico 68 ». À partir du concept de base du logo, il développa tout un programme visuel avec couleurs, typographie, pictogrammes et motifs. Sous sa direction, l'identité visuelle des jeux Olympiques s'étendit à tous les aspects. Le résultat s'avéra être un saut quantique dans le développement de projets graphiques conceptuels et devint un modèle internationalement remarqué pour bien des travaux réalisés plus tard dans ce domaine.

Olympic Games, Mexico 1968

1968 · Lance Wyman · US/MX

Lance Wyman (*1937) took a degree in industrial design but it was not until after graduation that he discovered his passion for graphic design. He started out on his career in 1960, working in the design department of General Motors. He later joined the office of the designer George Nelson. Between 1966 and 1971 he practiced in Mexico, before opening his own studio in New York, which today continues to specialize in the creation of corporate identities. Since 1973, Wyman has lectured on a regular basis at the Parsons School of Design.

Lance Wyman (*1937) studierte zunächst Industriedesign. Erst nach dem Studium entdeckte er seine Begeisterung für Grafik und begann 1960 seine Laufbahn u. a. in der Designabteilung von General Motors und als Angestellter im Büro von George Nelson. Zwischen 1966 und 1971 war er als Gestalter in Mexiko tätig. Anschließend eröffnete er ein eigenes Büro in New York, das sich bis heute auf die Entwicklung von Firmenidentitäten spezialisiert. Seit 1973 ist Wyman regelmäßig als Dozent an der Parsons School of Design tätig.

Lance Wyman (*1937) a d'abord suivi des études de design industriel. Ce n'est qu'après celles-ci qu'il se découvre une passion pour le graphisme. En 1960, il commence notamment sa carrière au département de design de General Motors et comme collaborateur du bureau de George Nelson. De 1966 à 1971, il travaille comme graphiste à Mexico, puis il ouvre son propre bureau à New York et se spécialise jusqu'à ce jour dans le développement d'identités d'entreprises. Wyman enseigne régulièrement à la Parsons School of Design depuis 1973.

ABCDEFGHIJKLMNOPQ
RSTUVWXYZ $<?>!&:;,. ""
1234567890

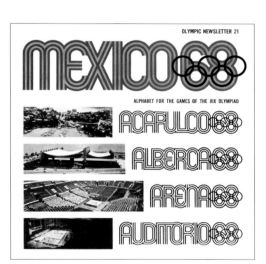

The starting point for the Mexico Olympics design was the idea of connecting the Olympic rings with the slogan "Mexico 68." Based on this, the design team developed an instantly recognizable typeface, which would then be used as lettering at the various venues where Olympic events were staged.

Ausgangspunkt der Designlösung war die Idee, die olympischen Ringe mit dem Schriftzug „Mexico 68" zu verbinden. Aus diesem Ergebnis wurde eine eigene Schriftart entwickelt, die unter anderem die Logo-Schriftzüge aller Spielstätten bestimmte.

L'argument de départ de la solution graphique était d'associer entre eux les anneaux olympiques et l'inscription « Mexico 68 ». À partir du résultat fut ensuite développée une écriture spécifique qui finit notamment par définir les logotypes de l'ensemble des sites olympiques.

Wyman designed pictograms
for each of the 20 Olympic sports,
all made to fit with the style of the
logo. As part of the overall graphics system the boxes with rounded
corners were used for other signage and as photo frames.

Passend zum Logo entwarf
Wyman 20 Piktogramme für
die olympischen Sportarten.
Die Boxen mit den abgerundeten
Ecken dienten im Gesamtdesign
auch als Träger für Fotos und
weitere Informationszeichen.

Dans le même esprit que le logo,
Wyman développa 20 picto-
grammes désignant les disci-
plines olympiques. Dans le design
global, les carrés aux angles
arrondis servirent aussi de fonds
pour des photos et d'autres
signes informatifs.

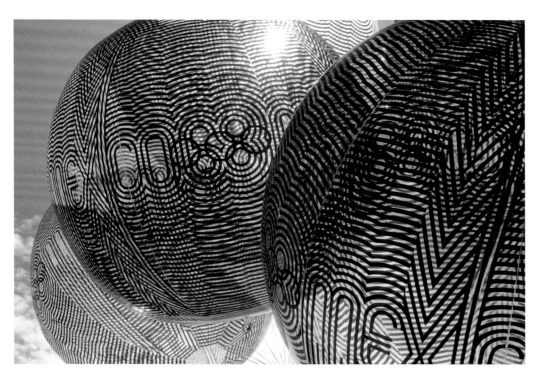

A latticework image developed from the logo was a prominent design feature at the 1968 Mexico Olympics. This instantly recognizable pattern was used repeatedly, for everything from postage stamps to the paved areas around the stadia.

Ein aus dem Logoentwurf entwickeltes Linienraster war bestimmendes Gestaltungselement der Olympischen Spiele 1968. Von Briefmarken bis hin zum Bodenbelag um die Stadien herum wurde das Muster mit hohem Wiedererkennungseffekt vielfältig eingesetzt.

La trame linéaire développée à partir du projet de logo fut l'élément graphique déterminant des jeux Olympiques de 1968. Des timbres postaux aux revêtements de sol aux abords des stades, ce motif fut introduit sous les formes les plus diverses avec un formidable effet de reconnaissance.

Oblique

Schräg

Skewed

Belair
Airline
1979 · Armin Vogt · CH

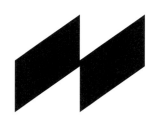

Nagase Rubber
Sporting goods
1979 · Kazuo Tajima · JP

ERCOA
Machinery
1975 · Elías García Benavides · ES

Base Finanza
Investment
1987 · A. G. Fronzoni · IT

Seiyu Stores
Supermarket chain
1974 · Jitsuo Hoashi · JP

Indian Airlines
1973 · Benoy Sarkar · IN

Frigerio
Haulier
1983 · R. Nava, D. Soffientini,
A. Ubertazzi · IT

Sogiplast
Plastics
1982 · R. Nava, D. Soffientini,
A. Ubertazzi · IT

Estudio Actual
Art gallery
1968 · Nedo Mion Ferrario · IT/VE

Fukuoka City
Public Transport
1979 · Fumio Koyoda · JP

Tower Industries
Stone surfaces
1981 · Thomas Ohmer, Koji Takei · US/JP

Melbourne Whiting
Construction company
1968 · Hans R. Woodtli · CH

Homare Bowling Center
Sports facility
1972 · Shuji Torigoe · JP

Zürich Versicherungsgesellschaft
Insurance
1971 · Jörg Hamburger · CH

Exposervice
Exhibition promotion
1979 · Ernst Roch · CA

Merinoteks
Yarns
1970s · Andrzej Stypułkowski · PL

Volker Zahm
Advertising
1967 · Oanh Pham Phu · DE

Mizuno Print
Printing
1976 · Kazuharu Fuji · JP

Elektrowatt Zürich
Energy and industry holding company
1973 · Odermatt+Tissi · CH

vh Verlag
Publishing
1970s · Helmut Schmid · DE

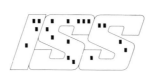

International Scientific Systems
Data processing
1963 · Fletcher, Forbes, Gill · UK

Morse Shoe
Footwear
1968 · Herman & Lees Associates · US

Leykam
Paper
1981 · Madeleine Bujatti · AT

S+E
Industrial goods
1970s · Ekkehart Rustmeier · DE

Valextra
Leather and plastic goods
1971 · Giulio Confalonieri · IT

Fiat Costruzioni & Impianti
Automobile engineering
1972 · Giovanni Brunazzi · IT

Legler Industria Tessile
Textiles
1968 · Jörg Hamburger · CH

Kingsway Public Relations
Communications company
1973 · Kate Osbar · UK

Yoshioka Photography Studio
1980 · Yonefusa Yamada · JP

**International Audio-Visual
Technical Centre, Antwerp**
1968 · Rob Buytaert · BE

Messaggeria Emiliana
Parcel service
1963 · Valeriano Piozzi/Piozzi & Cima · IT

Via Rail Canada
Public transport
1978 · Anonymous · CA

Academic Aye Computer
Computing
1980 · Minoru Takahashi · JP

Overseas Marketing Corporation
Technological development
1967 · Chandrashekhar Kamat/
Design Research Unit · UK

Sterling Projects
Property developer
1970s · Jack Evans · US

VAW
1970s · Heinz Schwabe · DE

Matthews Real Estate
1979 · Duane Wiens, Arvid Wallen · US

Thomas Laufer & Associates
Design
1968 · Thomas Laufer · US

Panart
Artist management
1969 · Rod Dyer · US

Flughafen Immobilien Gesellschaft
Real estate
1970s · Peter G. Ulmer · CH

Istituto di Studi di Servizio Sociale
Research institute
1970 · Michele Spera · IT

Yeye
Cosmetics
1967 · Armando Milani · IT

Fiat

1967 · Armin Vogt · CH/IT

Ever since the mid-1950s, Jean Reiwald, owner of a small advertising agency in Basel, had dreamed of combining his profession with his passion for Italian automobiles. After applying to a series of companies to be allowed to present his work, he was finally appointed Fiat's advertising consultant for Switzerland in 1960. He quickly rose to the position of advertising advisor at Fiat headquarters in Turin, where one of his tasks was coming up with ideas on how to combine the company logo with the different types of automobile Fiat produced. It was then the turn of Reiwald's art director, Armin Vogt, to meet the challenge and develop a Fiat logo, a single unifying image to be used for all the corporation's products. In 1968, the new corporate design was introduced internationally. Vogt's design continued to be used, albeit with several modifications, until 1999.

Der Besitzer einer kleinen Werbeagentur in Basel Jean Reiwald träumte bereits Mitte der 1950er-Jahre davon, seine Vorliebe für italienische Autos mit dem Beruf zu verbinden. Nach zahlreichen Gesuchen um eine Präsentation berief man ihn 1960 schließlich zum Werbeberater für Fiat in der Schweiz. Schnell stieg er zum Ansprechpartner bei der Konzernzentrale in Turin auf, auch als man bei Fiat nach einer Lösung suchte, um das Firmenlogo mit der Typenbezeichnung der unterschiedlichen Automodelle zu verbinden. Reiwalds damaliger Art Director Armin Vogt entwickelte daraufhin ein neues Fiat-Logo, das in ein integriertes Markensystem eingebettet die Herausforderung überzeugend einfach umsetzte. Im Jahr 1968 wurde der neue Markenauftritt international eingeführt. Auch wenn das Design mehrfach angepasst wurde, war das von Vogt entworfene Logo bis 1999 in Verwendung.

Dès le milieu des années 1950, Jean Reiwald, propriétaire d'une petite agence publicitaire bâloise, rêvait de pouvoir concilier son métier et sa passion pour les voitures italiennes. En 1960, après toute une série de tentatives pour présenter ses idées, il fut finalement nommé conseiller publicitaire de Fiat Suisse. Reiwald devint rapidement un interlocuteur privilégié auprès de la centrale turinoise, notamment lorsqu'on chercha une solution pour combiner le logo Fiat et le nom des modèles de la marque. Armin Vogt, directeur artistique de Reiwald, développa alors un nouveau logo Fiat qui, intégré dans un système global d'identité visuelle, apportait une solution convaincante à ce défi. En 1968, la nouvelle image de la marque fut introduite au plan international. Même si le design général fut plusieurs fois remanié, le logo conçu par Vogt continua d'être utilisé jusqu'en 1999.

Armin Vogt (*1938) trained in several different design studios between 1954 and 1960, as well as attending the Zurich School of Arts and Crafts. After time spent working in Paris and Milan, between 1963 and 1969, he was art director at Jean Reiwald's advertising agency in Basel. Since 1970 he has had his own studio in Basel, working in every field of graphic design. He is also a gallery owner, publisher and lecturer, and a member of several Swiss design organizations.

Armin Vogt (*1938) erhielt seine Ausbildung zwischen 1954 und 1960 in verschiedenen Ateliers sowie an der Kunstgewerbeschule Zürich. Nach Stationen in Paris und Mailand war er von 1963 bis 1969 Art Director bei der Jean-Reiwald-Werbeagentur in Basel. Seit 1970 ist er mit eigenem Studio in Basel in allen Bereichen des Grafikdesigns tätig. Neben seiner gestalterischen Tätigkeit ist er als Galerist, Verleger und Dozent aktiv und engagiert sich in verschiedenen schweizerischen Designverbänden.

Armin Vogt (*1938) s'est formé entre 1954 et 1960 dans différents ateliers et à l'École des arts et métiers de Zurich. De 1963 à 1969, après un passage par Paris et Milan, il travaille comme directeur artistique de l'agence publicitaire bâloise Jean Reiwald. À partir de 1970, il est actif dans tous les domaines du graphisme au travers de son propre studio bâlois. À côté de son activité professionnelle, Vogt travaille aussi comme galeriste, éditeur, enseignant, et s'engage dans différentes associations de graphistes en Suisse.

The design consisted of Univers Italic type set at an angle of 16 degrees, each letter encased in a box. The use of different colors and configurations gave each brand and model its unique identity.

Ausgerichtet am 16-Grad-Winkel der Schrift Univers Italic wurde das System aus Boxen konstruiert, in der jeweils ein Buchstabe eingesetzt war. Mittels unterschiedlicher Farbigkeiten und Anordnung der Boxen erhielten Modelle sowie Submarken ihre eigenständige Identität.

Le système de cases contenant chacune une lettre fut développé à partir de l'angle de 16° de la fonte Univers Italic. Les modèles et les sous-marques reçurent leur identité particulière grâce à l'utilisation de différents arrangements et coloris.

Based on the concept developed
by Armin Vogt and his colleagues
at Jean Reiwald's advertising
agency, various designers exper-
imented imaginatively with shapes,
fonts and colors to create posters,
adverts and brochures for international use.

Auf Basis der von Armin Vogt
und seinen Kollegen bei der
Jean-Reiwald-Werbeagentur
entwickelten Grundlagen spielen
international verwendete Plakate,
Anzeigen und Broschüren verschiedener Gestalter kreativ mit
den Elementen des Erscheinungsbildes: Form, Schrift und Farbe.

Sur la base des principes développés par Armin Vogt et ses collègues au sein de l'agence publicitaire Jean Reiwald, les affiches,
annonces et brochures créées par
différents graphistes pour une
utilisation internationale, jouent de
manière créative avec les éléments
de l'identité visuelle : forme, police
de caractères et couleur.

The Fiat trademark was so
readily recognizable, even when
it appeared in a truncated version,
that it could be used for a variety
of communications, such as
adverts and invitation cards.

Der hohe Wiedererkennungseffekt des Fiat-Markenzeichens,
selbst in unvollständiger Dar-
stellung, machte es für unterschiedliche Medienanwendungen
wie Ankündigungsanzeigen oder
Einladungskarten einsetzbar.

Le haut degré de reconnaissance
de la marque Fiat, produit par
le logo même incomplet, permit
de l'utiliser dans différents médias
comme des cartons des annonces
ou d'invitation presse.

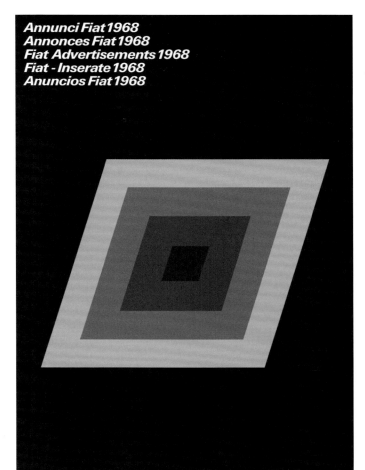

Annunci Fiat 1968
Annonces Fiat 1968
Fiat Advertisements 1968
Fiat - Inserate 1968
Anuncios Fiat 1968

Fiat (Suisse) SA
1211 Genève 13 FIAT

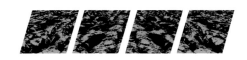

Fiat a le plaisir de présenter au public
ses nouvelles voitures
au 40ème Salon International
de l'Automobile de Genève.

Fiat (Suisse) SA
1211 Genève 13 FIAT
Stands 8 et 8 bis

Arrondi

Rund

Round

Labor Abbigliamento
Clothing
1972 · Giovanni Brunazzi · IT

Aldo Maspero
Furniture
1971 · Studio GSZ · IT

**Institut für Latein-Amerikanische
Studien der Universität St. Gallen**
Education
1981 · Jost Hochuli · CH

Ole Lynggaard
Goldsmith
1969 · Morten Peetz-Schou · DK

Resch-Verlag
Publishing
1977 · Karl Pfeifle · AT

Groupe Kastuan
Urban planning
1970 · Pham Ngoc Tuan · FR

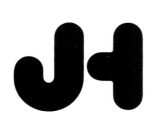

Jeff Hirsh
Furniture
1976 · Mike Quon · US

Handi Polstermöbel
Furniture
1970s · Werner Hartz · DE

Argos Industrial
Textiles
1958 · Alexandre Wollner · BR

Kunimatsuya
Retail
1979 · Koichi Watanabe · JP

Cerámica Zanon
Ceramic tiles
1978 · Eduardo A. Cánovas · AR

Hamburger Sparkasse
Bank
1970s · Ekkehart Rustmeier · DE

Docenave Navegação
Shipping operator
1967 · PVDI · BR

SIF Società Fonografica
Record label
1967 · Italo Lupi · IT

Volumobili CA
Interior design
1969 · Gerd Leufert · VE

Franck Olivier
Clothing
1970 · Jean Delaunay/Look · FR

SG6
Technology sales conference
1967 · Salvatore Gregorietti/
Unimark International · IT

Etcetera
1966 · Nakajo Masayoshi · JP

Gebrüder Reichert & Söhne
Neon lighting
1950s · Pierre Gauchat · CH

Nortextil
Clothing
1966 · Paul Brand · NO

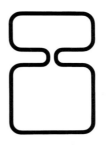

I Neofigurativi
Publishing
1967 · Franco M. Ricci · IT

Plica

Plica Rohrfabrik Rüschlikon
Pipes
1960s · Rudolf Bircher · CH

Centro Tecnico Confederale
Investment
1972 · Mimmo Castellano · IT

Amsterdam Creative Team
Design
1972 · Ben Bos · NL

Schappe International
1965 · Hanns Lohrer · DE

Leela
Clothing
1960s · Henry Steiner · HK

Napako
Metalworks
1981 · Jiří Rathouský · CZ

Tsukamoto Gakuin
Education
1969 · Tomoichi Nishiwaki · JP

Imai Seisakusho
Cleaners and ovens
1981 · Kanju Morohoshi · JP

Rebi
Foods
1971 · Alain Pontecorvo/
Chourgnoz Publicité · FR

Bernazzoli
Furniture
1970 · Franco M. Ricci · IT

Verband der Deutschen Textilindustrie
Textiles organization
1971 · Hanns Lohrer · DE

Sapio
Olive oil
1971 · Mimmo Castellano · IT

Patient Care Products
Healthcare
1978 · Appelbaum & Curtis · US

Isuzu
Vehicle and engine manufacturer
1980 · Isuzu Design Department · JP

Skema Srl
Magazine
1969 · Marco Caroli · IT

Antonio Ratti
Silk
1970 · Giulio Confalonieri · IT

Ideal Science Industry
Printing
1979 · Shigeo Fukuda · JP

Fazenda Buracão
Agriculture
1970 · João Carlos Cauduro/
Ludovico Antonio Martino · BR

Vides Cinematografica
Film production
1972 · Michele Spera · IT

VIETA

Vieta
Audio equipment
1968 · Pérez Sánchez · ES

Carré

Quadrat

Square

Design-Garamond
Industrial design
1968 · Jacques Nathan-Garamond · FR

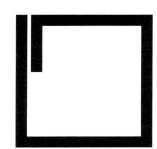

E. H. Schelling Rümlang
Container trade
1960 · Odermatt+Tissi · CH

William C. Shopsin
Architecture
1960s · Anonymous · US

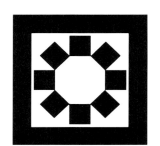

Institut de Formation
par le Groupe, Montréal
1964 · Rolf Harder/
Design Collaborative · CA

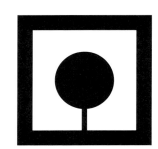

Robert Feller
Horticulture
1963 · Hans Knöpfli · CH

Riam
Furniture
1972 · Almerico de Angelis · IT

Asgard-Verlag Dr. Werner Hippe
Publishing
1969 · Schulz-Haller · DE

7-Air
Airline
1969 · Atelier Stadelmann Bisig · CH

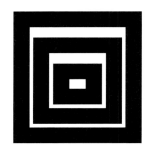

Galerie Godard Lefort
Art gallery
1964 · Fritz Gottschalk/
Gottschalk+Ash · CA

Sidro
Steel tubing
1959 · Wim Crouwel · NL

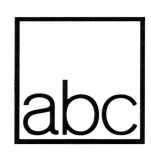

Thomas Porzellan
China
1963 · Ruedi Rüegg · CH

Iveco
Vehicle manufacturer
1978 · Carlo Malerba · IT

Kunsteisbahn und
Schwimmbadgenossenschaft
Skating rink and swimming pool
1965 · Peter G. Ulmer · CH

El Al
Airline
1963 · Otto Treumann · NL

Indústrias Zillo
Industrial trading
1972 · Aloísio Magalhães/PVDI · BR

Palazzi Editori
Publishing
1963 · Max Huber · IT

Schweizerische Volksbank
Bank
1960s · Helmuth Kurtz · CH

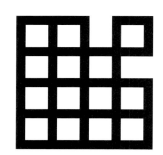

Taka Design Production
Design
1981 · Shinichi Takahara · JP

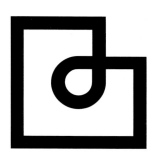

Complejo Plástico, Isla Margarita
Art center
1970 · Nedo Mion Ferrario · VE

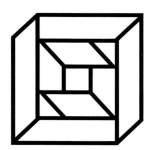

Essedi Editrice
Publishing
1972 · Giancarlo Iliprandi · IT

Hans-Kjell Larsen
Architecture
1970 · Paul Brand · NO

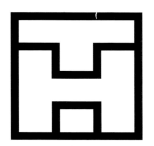

Thomas I. Hull
Insurance
1967 · Chris Yaneff · CA

Walter Nievergelt Klischeeanstalt
Prepress services
1960s · Walter Bangerter · CH

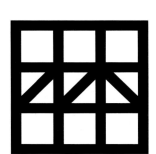

Smith Construction
1958 · Ernst Roch, Rolf Harder/
Design Collaborative · CA

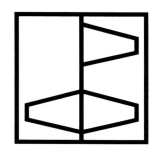

Plieger
Sanitation
1958 · Wim Crouwel/Total Design · NL

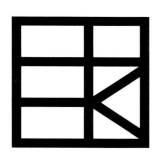

Universität der Künste, Berlin
Arts university
1960s · Helmut Lortz · DE

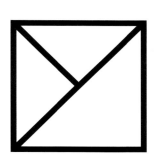

Yamada Design Room
1968 · Yonefusa Yamada · JP

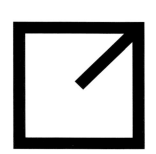

Astoris
1973 · R. Nava, D. Soffientini,
A. Ubertazzi · IT

Maria Mazzara
Design
1970 · Maria Mazzara · US

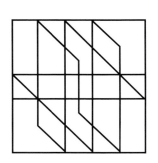

Schauspielgemeinschaft Zürich
Actors association
1954 · Leo Gantenbein · CH

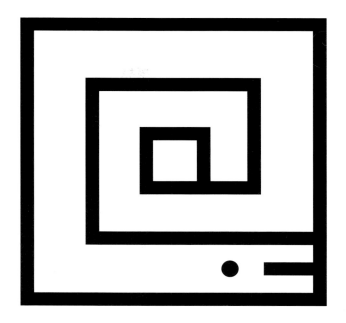

Marktgass-Passage Apotheke
Pharmacy
1964 · Paul Sollberger · CH

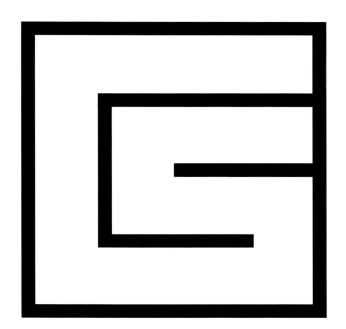

Carl Steinherr
Design
1964 · Carl Steinherr · NL

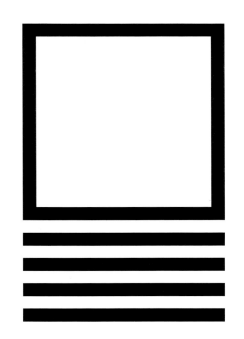

La Cie J. B. Rolland & Fils
Paper
1960 · George Huel · CA

Larson Enterprises
Photographic reflectors
1963 · James Cross · US

Angelo Valaguzza
Luggage
1970 · Pino Tovaglia · IT

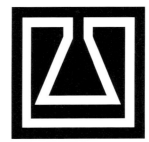

Laboratori Cosmochimici
Chemicals
1950 · Walter Ballmer · CH

Constructora Los Alamos
Construction company
1969 · José Santamarina/
Elias & Santamarina · ES

Keenan Pipe & Supply Company
Pipes and fittings
1968 · Thomas Laufer
& Associates · US

Luciana Valcarenghi
Antiques
1957 · Albe Steiner · IT

Phoenix Rheinrohr
Steelworks
1950s · Anonymous · DE

Klik
Photographic accessories
1969 · Ribas & Creus · ES

Joseph P. Kennedy Foundation
Charity
1960s · Raymond Loewy,
William Snaith · US

Tenax
Refractory materials
1947 · Carlo L. Vivarelli/
Studio Boggeri · IT

Adresser Service
1968 · Paul Brand · NO

Bramin
Furniture
1960s · Anonymous · DK

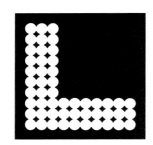

LaSalle Steel
Steelworks
1962 · Morton Goldsholl · US

BS
Tires
1959 · Ilio Negri · IT

Direkt Mailing Service
Delivery service
1968 · Paul Brand · NO

Apotheke Ehrensberger
Pharmacy
1950s · Helmuth Kurtz · CH

Nomos Verlagsgesellschaft
Publishing
1963 · Willy Fleckhaus · DE

Studio Fotografico F. B.
Photo studio
1964 · Veniero Bertolotti/Studio 4 · IT

Nordisk Film
Film production
1968 · Paul Brand · NO

System-Offner
Varnishing and paint finishing
1963 · Hanns Lohrer · DE

Telemeccanica Elettrica
Electronics
1958 · Bob Noorda/
Unimark International · IT

Jermi
Silks
1965 · Walter Del Frate · IT

De Forenede Papirfabrikker
Paper
1967 · Morten Peetz-Schou,
Krister Appelfeldt · DK

Elektro
Electronics
1960s · Josef Týfa · CZ

Comitato per la Seta Italiana
Committee for Italian silk
1960s · Franco Grignani · IT

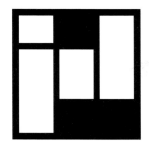

International Research & Development
Research and development
1964 · David Caplan · UK

Kohlenversorgungs AG
Coal
1963 · Igildo Biesele · CH

Veeder-Root
Counting control devices
1960s · Chermayeff & Geismar · US

Schweizer Tabak
Tobacco
1950s · Adolf Flückiger · CH

Are Bildarchiv
Image archive
1973 · Helmut Schmid · DE

Structural Products
Aluminum
1958 · Fred Witzig · US

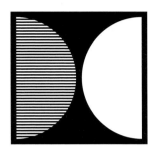

Papierfabrik Cham
Paper
1968 · Paul Leber/Leber & Schmid · CH

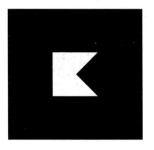

Textilhaus Kemmerling
Clothing
1950s · Robert Sessler · CH

K. Täumer & Söhne Ziegeldächer
Roofer
1961 · Otto Kuchenbauer · DE

Hamac-Hansella
Packaging machines
1960 · Wolf D. Zimmermann · DE

Torii & Co.
Pharmaceuticals
1977 · Kazuo Tanaka · JP

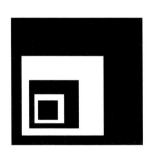

Ospinas y Cia.
Construction company
1974 · Dicken Castro · CO

PR-Consult
Public relations
1967 · Paul Brand · NO

Eugen Schmidt
Furniture
1955 · Helmut Lortz · DE

Hyspan
Expansion joints
1982 · Calvin Woo, Mike Whalen · US

Edil Glass
1978 · Walter Hergenröther · IT

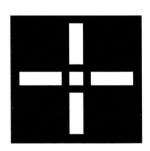

Aero Exploration
Aerial photography
1967 · Eckhard Neumann · DE

Harcourt, Brace and World
Publishing
1962 · Tom Geismar/
Chermayeff & Geismar · US

Ingstroi
Highway construction
1982 · Nicolay Pecareff · BG

Luc Dugardyn
Architecture
1960 · Michel Olyff · BE

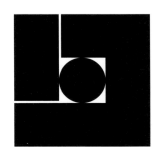

Klaus Becker
Insurance
1965 · Klaus Winterhager · DE

Aprior
Swiss watch industry syndicate
1969 · Julien van der Wal · CH

Scott Paper
Toilet paper
1960s · Hiram Ash/
George Nelson & Co. · US

Home Store
1973 · João Carlos Cauduro,
Ludovico Antonio Martino · BR

Litton Industries
Electrical systems
1958 · Robert Miles Runyan · US

Hogarotel 7
Hotel industry congress
1967 · Ernesto Moradell Català · ES

Novotar
Concrete construction
1973 · František Bobáň · CZ

Tuna Çelik
Metalworks
1982 · Burhan Tastan · TR

Nava Officine Grafiche
Printing
1968 · Max Huber · IT

Polifarma
Pharmaceuticals
1967 · Carmelo Cremonesi/
Stile-Advertising · IT

Rising Sun
1978 · Tadashi Ishikawa,
Hideko Sakado · JP

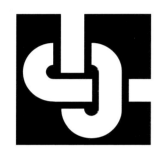

Van Besouw
Looms
1968 · Gerard Wernars · NL

Zins
Clothing
1967 · Daniel Maurel/
Chourgnoz Publicité · FR

William Paton Sales
Braided cords
1963 · Eurographics · UK

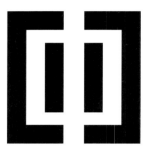

Toiminimi Mome
Door handles
1969 · Eka Lainio/
Markkinointi Viherjuuri · FI

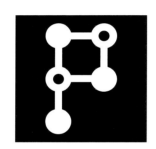

Toyo Rayon
Synthetic fibers
1962 · Makoto Wada · JP

Československé Státní Aerolinie
Airline (proposed design)
1960s · Jiří Rathouský · CZ

Oliver Tyrone Corporation
Real estate
1970 · Francis R. Esteban · US

Marsol
Polyvinyls
1970 · Ilio Negri · IT

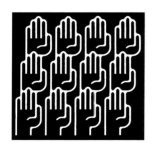

Mani Tese
Sustainability
1970 · Pino Tovaglia · IT

Schillemans Ontwerper
Design
1969 · A. G. Schillemans · NL

Shepherd Building Group
Construction company
1964 · Eurographics · UK

Anliker & Co.
Elevators
1955 · Hans Neuburg · CH

Albert Uldry Siebdruckerei
Printing
1960s · Kurt Wirth · CH

Viktoria Verlag
Publishing
1950s · Kurt Toggweiler · CH

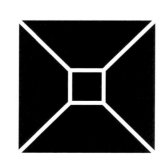

The Lab Memorial Library
Social science training
1969 · Hayward R. Blake/
The Design Partnership · US

Alag
Construction company
1960 · Hans Knöpfli · CH

Polaha & Somers
1970 · Ronald Cutro · US

**Raymond Chabot
Martin Paré & Associates**
Accounting
1982 · Vasco Ceccon · CA

Aerhotel
Hotel
1968 · Pino Tovaglia · IT

Nippon Unit Load
Container companies
1977 · Koichi Watanabe · JP

Marchiorello
Clothing
1969 · Pino Tovaglia · IT

Sarriõ
Paper
1970 · Tomás Vellvé · ES

Hüttemann-Holzbau
Carpentry
1970 · Ulrich Schürmann · DE

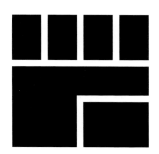

Editorial Estela
Publishing
1971 · Enric Satué · ES

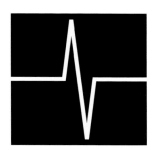

Electro Physical Instruments
1966 · Ernst Roch/
Design Collaborative · CA

**Rochester Institute of Technology
Information Center**
1966 · R. Roger Remington · US

Rakennustaiteen Seura
Architects association
1956 · Jukka Pellinen · FI

Embratur
Tourism
1977 · PVDI · BR

Amt für Sozialversicherung
Social security
1960s · Walter Bangerter · CH

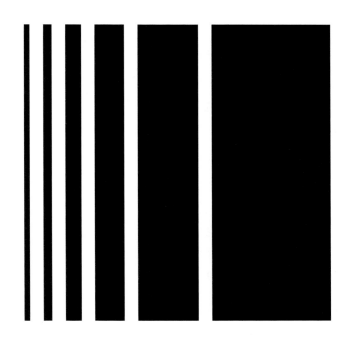

Registro Tumori del Piemonte e la Valle D'Aosta
Cancer research institute
1971 · Giovanni Brunazzi · IT

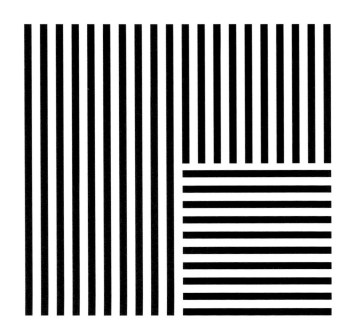

Centro di Cultura G. Puecher
Cultural center
1969 · Franco Grignani · IT

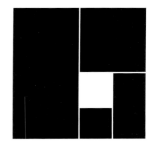

Galerie Schindler
Art gallery
1962 · Paul Sollberger · CH

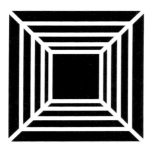

Glendale Center Theater
1979 · Scott Engen · US

Ministerio de Desarrollo Económico
Ministry of economic development
1968 · Dicken Castro · CO

Goldmann Cegos
Education
1969 · Carlo Eruni · IT

San Francisco Executive Park
Office campus
1981 · Harry Murphy · US

Domus Ricera
Publishing
1956 · Giulio Confalonieri · IT

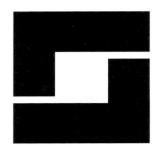

Schäfer Architekten
Architecture
1950s · Georges Calame · CH

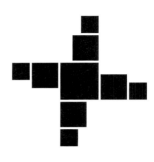

Instituto de Desarrollo Urbano
Urban planning
1973 · Dicken Castro · CO

Instituto de Diseño
Design institute
1964 · Gerd Leufert · VE

Werb'-Günther
Advertising and publishing
1965 · Hace Frey · DE

**Municipality of the City of
Buenos Aires**
1979 · Eduardo A. Cánovas · AR

Eurodomus
Interior design book series
1956 · Giulio Confalonieri · IT

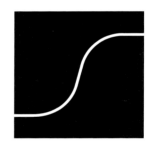

Symphonic Electronic Corporation
Consumer electronics
1969 · Jean Morin, John Murray · CA

**Bundesvereinigung
Deutscher Heimstätten**
Housing association
1971 · G. W. Hörnig · DE

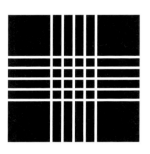

Kinnasand
Curtains and carpets
1960s · Anonymous · SE

ASM
1972 · Max Huber · IT

Alfred Scherz Verlag
Publishing
1953 · Paul Sollberger · CH

Woningbouwvereniging de Goede Woning
Construction company
1970 · Ralph Prins · NL

Versandhaus Neckermann
Mail-order (proposed design)
1960s · Wolfgang Freitag · DE

Terimobel
Real estate
1967 · Julian Key · BE

Papier und Druck
Printing
1960s · Gregor Kintzel · DE

Mursten og Fliser Producenter
Bricks
1969 · Ove von Späth · DK

Ansbacher Siegel
Printing
1970s · Robert Hagenhofer · US

La Banque Caraïbe
Bank
1983 · Harry Murphy · US

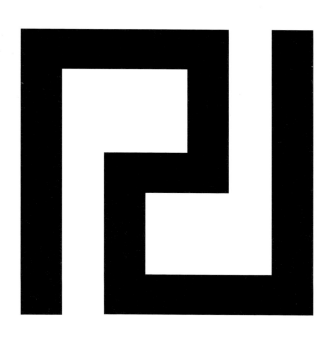

Peter Doehler
Management consultancy
1968 · Oanh Pham Phu · DE

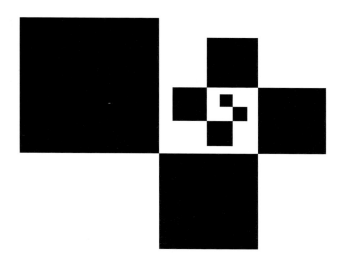

Larsen Design Office
1976 · Tim Larsen · US

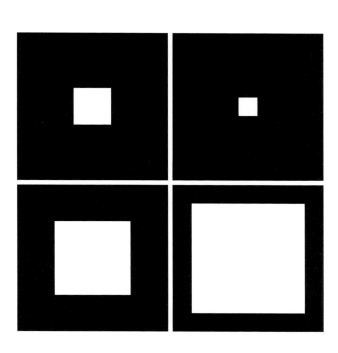

Olivetti Systed
Educational institution
1971 · Walter Ballmer · IT

Gottlieb Kistler-Söhne
Sawmill
1959 · Odermatt+Tissi · CH

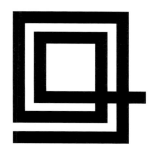

Olivetti
Business machines
1956 · Marcello Nizzoli · IT

Verlag Dr. M. Schulze
Publishing
1978 · Hansherbert Buschhüter ·
DE-GDR

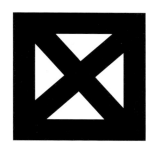

**Stichting Culturele
Integratie van Noord en Zuid**
Cultural association
1968 · Rob Buytaert · BE

Salon International de Galeries Pilotes
Exhibition
1960s · Roger-Virgile Geiser · CH

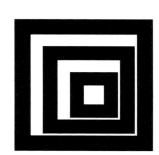

Mostra Mercato d'Arte Contemporanea
Art fair
1963 · Piero Sansoni · IT

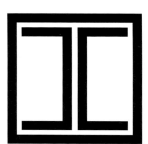

Jacob Bek
Metalworks
1961 · Winfried J. Jokisch · DE

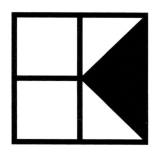

Knudsen Creamery Company
Dairy products
1968 · Vance Jonson · US

Packaging Direction
Packaging
1968 · Susumu Kimura · JP

Norsk Hytteformidling
Apartments
1969 · Paul Brand · NO

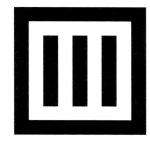

Orma
Metalworks
1957 · A. G. Fronzoni · IT

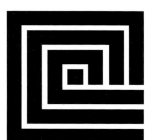

Galleria D'Arte San Fedele
Art gallery
1969 · Franco Grignani · IT

Dreieck

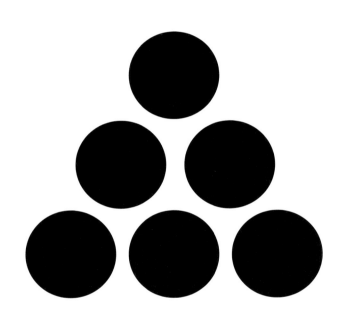

Tequila Mexicano
Liquor
1982 · Félix Beltrán · CU/MX

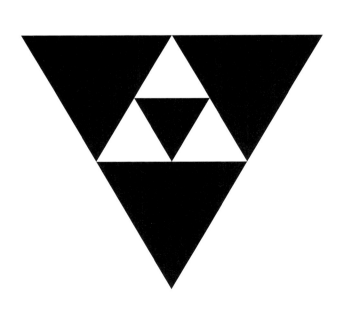

Delfim Araújo SA
Investment
1966 · João Carlos Cauduro, Ludovico Antonio Martino · BR

Gralglas
Glass
1950 · Otl Aicher · DE

Gomes de Almeida Fernandes
Construction company
1964 · Paulo de Tarso Mello,
Cleuton Sampaio · BR

Delta Costruzioni Meccaniche
Pharmaceutical equipment
1969 · Ilio Negri · IT

Augusto Avanzini
Adhesive products
1964 · Dante Bighi · IT

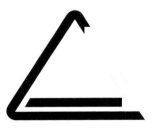

Companhia Brasileira de Embalagens
Packaging
1961 · Alexandre Wollner · BR

Ateneo de Caracas
Cultural institute
1963 · Nedo Mion Ferrario · VE

Delta Werbegesellschaft
Advertising
1972 · Gerold Schmidt · DE

Asakura Architects & Associates
1971 · Hiroshi Manzen · JP

Alpeadria Dos Ljubljana
Tourism
1931 · Ivan Dvoršak · YU

Art Grafische Werkstätten
Design
1960s · Ryszard Dudzicki · PL

Helvetia Feuer
Insurance
1961 · Karl Gerstner/GGK · CH

Christian Broadcasting Network
1982 · George McGinnis · US

Alpine
Sporting goods
1980 · John M. Alexander · US

Reggio Leasing
1989 · Silvio Coppola · IT

Editora Delta
Publishing
1960s · Aloísio Magalhães/PVDI · BR

Roussel Uclaf
Pharmaceuticals
1963 · Raymond Loewy/CEI · FR

Adjeleian & Associates
Engineering
1967 · Jacques E. Charette · CA

Association of Canadian Distillers
Trade association
1971 · Manfred Gotthans, Chris
Yaneff/Chris Yaneff · CA

Industrial Trade Union
1950s · Walter Sauer · DE

Kashiyama
Clothing
1977 · Kazumasa Nagai · JP

Intercontinentale Assicurazioni
Insurance
1970 · Vittorio Antinori · IT

Alpha Techno
Chemicals
1982 · Kazufumi Hamada,
Akira Hirata, Hiroshi Mori · JP

Kreis Deckt Dächer, Dübendorf
Roofers
1961 · Hansruedi Scheller · CH

A. Diethelm
Painting tools and supplies
1957 · Carlo L. Vivarelli · CH

Crivelli Arte
Art gallery
1972 · G. & R. Associati · IT

Select
1982 · Yoshihiro Kishimoto · JP

Anton Lihl
Advertising
1970 · Oanh Pham Phu · DE

Packer Enterprises
Investment
1983 · Yarom Vardimon · IR

Salón Internacional del Automóvil
Automobile show
1968 · Tomás Vellvé · ES

Seterie Argenti
Textiles
1986 · Max Huber · IT

Asbestzementwerk Magdeburg
Asbestos
1965 · Horst Jacob · DE-GDR

Verlag für Technik und Wirtschaft
Publishing
1969 · Heinz Kröhl, Peter Offenberg · DE

Amann Möbel
Furniture
1972 · Werner Hartz · DE

Max R. Diethelm
Architecture
1964 · Walter J. Diethelm · CH

Staatliche Schule für Kunst und Handwerk
Art school
1946 · Robert Sessler · CH/DE

Insinööriliitto
Engineering association
1962 · Olof Eriksson · FI

Carl A. Donald Excavation
1957 · Ernst Roch/
Design Collaborative · CA

Associated Spring
Industrial trade
1958 · Armin Müller · US

Delta Acceptance Corporation
Financial services
1964 · Chris Yaneff · CA

Gérard Miedinger
Design
1960s · Gérard Miedinger · CH

Hotel Kirishima
1960s · Kenji Ito · JP

Mountain and Molehill
Public relations
1960s · Mountain and Molehill · UK

Aerhotel
Hotel
1968 · Franco Grignani · IT

Amerada Bridge & Steel Erectors
Construction engineering
1965 · Terry Logan/
J. Walter Thompson · CA

National Parks & Monuments, Dublin
1969 · Damien Harrington/
Kilkenny Design Workshops · IE

Fibreboard Paper Products
1960s · Anonymous · US

Alpa
Sailing boats
1966 · Sergio Privitera/P&T · IT

Forest History Society
Educational institution
1960s · Russell A. Sandgren · US

Tidningen Arbetet
Paper
1968 · Bertil Andersson-Bertilson · SE

Blue Mountain Pottery
1965 · Manfred Gotthans,
Chris Yaneff/Chris Yaneff · CA

Monte Ávila Editores
Publishers
1968 · Gerd Leufert · VE

Interwerba
Advertising
1965 · Interwerba · CH

Spółdzielnia Rybołówstwa
Fishing cooperative
1960s · Ryszard Dudzicki · PL

Pow Wow in the Pines
Cultural gathering
1970s · George E. Hands/
Center for Industrial Design · US

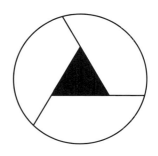

Triad Institute for Urban Research
1969 · Charles Fuhrman · US

Berlin Hilton
Hotel
1960s · Anonymous · DE

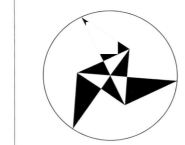

Tri
Advertising
1960s · Tri · US

Vision Photography
1969 · Rod Dyer · US

P. Barberini
Optical products
1964 · Till Neuburg · CH

Western Motor Company
Automobiles
1952 · Anonymous · US

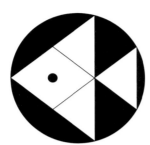

Textil Fischer
Textiles
1950s · Kurt Toggweiler · CH

Vance Industries
Plumbing supplier
1963 · Randall R. Roth · US

**Escuela Superior de
Administración Pública**
Higher education
1970 · Claude Dietrich · PE

Maansiirto Tampere
Exhibition
1965 · Rolf Christianson · FI

Vow
Textiles
1969 · Akira Hirata, Junko Naito · JP

WDR Westdeutscher Rundfunk
Broadcasting
1968 · Graphicteam Köln · DE

McLean
1981 · Keith Murgatroyd · UK

André Piccoli Architekt
Architecture
1950s · Marcel Wyss · CH

Møbelfabriken Trekanten
Furniture
1960s · Anonymous · DK

Den Danske Landmandsbank
Bank
1967 · Acton Bjørn · DK

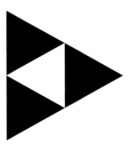

Peter Kwasny
Spray paints
1964 · Werner Keidel · DE

União
Petroleum derivatives
1969 · Alexandre Wollner · BR

Salesco
Furniture
1960s · Anonymous · DK

Andreas F. Achenbach Verlag
Publishing
1977 · Anonymous · DE

Exhibit House International
1967 · Heiner Hegemann/
Chermayeff & Geismar · CA

Gruppo Operativo di Ricerca
Research institute
1966 · Till Neuburg · CH

**Centennial of Confederation
of Canada**
Commemorative event
1966 · Stuart Ash/Gottschalk+Ash · CA

Rakennuspuusepanteollisuus
Product certificate
1963 · Bror B. Zetterborg · FI

Løvig Hedensted Møbelfabrik
Furniture
1960s · Anonymous · DK

Effect

Effekt

Effet

Simply playing with basic geometric shapes can provide a variety of graphic solutions. Even so, it is only by adding extra effects that designers can exploit the full range of possibilities. Among typical techniques currently used in logo design are mirror imaging, duplication and cropping. In the main, a finished logo design will not be the result of a single set of specifications. The most exciting and idiosyncratic logos rely simultaneously on several effects. A look at more recent work reveals that, whatever the new and constantly changing trends may be, designers are still happy to fall back on the methods described on the following pages.

Das Spiel mit den einfachen geometrischen Grundformen erlaubt bereits eine Vielzahl unterschiedlicher grafischer Lösungen. Erst durch die Anwendung weiterer Effekte lässt sich jedoch die ganze Bandbreite an Möglichkeiten ausschöpfen. Ein Fokus auf Methoden wie Spiegelung, Verdopplung oder Zerschneiden verdeutlicht gängige Schemata in der Gestaltung von Logos. Oft fand in den realisierten Zeichen nicht nur ein einzelner Gestaltungsparameter Anwendung, vielmehr führte die Kombination mehrerer Effekte zu spannungsreichen und individuellen Logoentwürfen. Untersucht man Arbeiten neueren Datums, erweisen sich die im folgenden beschriebenen Methoden – unabhängig von sich verändernden Gestaltungstrends – als noch immer in Anwendung.

Le jeu sur les formes géométriques fondamentales offre déjà un grand nombre de possibilités graphiques. C'est seulement par l'application d'effets supplémentaires que toute la palette des possibilités peut être épuisée. Une concentration sur des méthodes comme la réflexion, le redoublement ou le découpage fait apparaître des schémas courants dans la création de logos. Souvent, le signe final ne procède pas seulement d'un seul paramètre de création. Au contraire, c'est la combinaison de plusieurs effets qui produit des résultats captivants et individuels. Lorsqu'on analyse des réalisations récentes, on s'aperçoit que les méthodes décrites ci-après ont conservé toute leur validité – indépendamment des tendances changeantes de la création.

Coupé

Abgeschnitten

Cut-off

G.E.A.P.
Typesetting
1978 · Alfredo de Santis · IT

Sumi Imoto Bowling Office
Office building
1960s · Sumio Hasegawa · JP

Meridional Companhia de Seguros
Insurance
1960s · Joaquim Redig · BR

Gerber
Advertising
1960s · Gerber Werbeagentur · CH

Maurice Barthalon
Electricity
1968 · Gérard Guerre/Technés · FR

Prestressed Concrete of Colorado
Construction materials
1975 · Unit 1 · US

Bernhard Handgrätinger
Electronics
1962 · Winfried J. Jokisch · DE

Fairchild
Publishing
1966 · Philip Franznick/
Franznick & Charney · US

National Homes Construction
Construction company
1976 · Barrett & Gaby · US

Arti Present Messebau
Exhibition systems
1970s · Hannes Schober,
Wolfram Reinhardt · DE

Infobau
Construction company
1972 · Werner Hartz · DE

Eddie Barclay
Record label
1983 · Julien van der Wal · CH

Rotbuch Verlag
Publishing
1975 · W. Tatlin · DE

Demonte Bouw
Construction company
1971 · Jan Jaring · NL

Fiat Centro Culturale
Cultural association
1965 · Giovanni Brunazzi · IT

Celebrity House
Restaurant chain
1969 · Hess & Antupit · US

Universidad de Ingenieria
Engineering university
1965 · Claude Dietrich · PE

Montgomery Communications
Broadcasting
1982 · George Tscherny · US

Galleria Milano
Art gallery
1963 · Giulio Confalonieri · IT

Grandi Motori Trieste
Engineering
1970 · Giovanni Brunazzi · IT

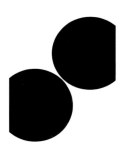

Club Selector
Nightclub
1964 · Takeshi Otaka · JP

Coquina Oil Corporation
1970 · RVI Corp. · US

Buenos Aires City Hall
1971 · Studio González Ruiz &
Shakespear · AR

Cordex
TV sets
1962 · Lala Méndez Mosquera · AR

Gazette Printing
1969 · William J. Campbell · CA

Jacques Bellemare
Design
1969 · Jacques Bellemare · CA

Gubler
Printing
1969 · Hans Knöpfli · CH

Hotel Takase
1967 · Takeshi Otaka · JP

Delaware Management Fund
Investment
1969 · Kramer, Miller, Lomden,
Glassman Inc. · US

Nicholas J. Green
Photography
1968 · Tony Forster · UK

Miyata
Beauty salon
1978 · Toshinori Nozaki · JP

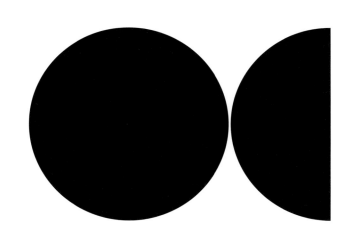

Optima Corporation
1978 · Lewis van der Beken, Norm Holtzman · US

Comforto
Furniture
1974 · Ettore Vitale · IT

Claude Neon Limited

1973 · Gottschalk+Ash · CA

Gottschalk+Ash was founded in Montreal in 1966 as a graphic design partnership between the Canadian Stuart Ash (*1942) and the Swiss Fritz Gottschalk (*1937). The practice grew fast and the two partners and their team were soon much in demand for corporate design projects for international companies like Air Canada, HypoVereinsbank and EniChem. Gottschalk+Ash offices were opened internationally and, then as now, brand communications and orientation systems remain at the heart of the company, which has branches in Toronto, Calgary and Zurich.

Gottschalk+Ash wurde 1966 als Ateliergemeinschaft des Kanadiers Stuart Ash (*1942) und des Schweizers Fritz Gottschalk (*1937) in Montreal gegründet. Das Büro wuchs schnell, und die beiden wurden mit ihrem Team zu gefragten Ansprechpartnern für Corporate-Design-Projekte internationaler Unternehmen wie Air Canada, HypoVereinsbank oder EniChem. Internationale Ableger des Büros entstanden. Bis heute sind Markenkommunikation und Orientierungssysteme die Schwerpunkte des Unternehmens mit Büros in Toronto, Calgary und Zürich.

Gottschalk+Ash a été fondé en 1966 à Montréal comme communauté d'atelier du Canadien Stuart Ash (*1942) et du Suisse Fritz Gottschalk (*1937). L'agence connaît ensuite un essor rapide, et les deux graphistes et leur équipe deviennent des interlocuteurs très demandés pour les corporate designs d'entreprises internationales comme Air Canada, HypoVereinsbank ou EniChem. Des bureaux seront ensuite créés à l'international. Jusqu'à aujourd'hui, la communication d'entreprise et les systèmes signalétiques constituent le cœur de métier de l'entreprise implantée à Toronto, Calgary et Zurich.

In 1973, several Canadian companies in the outdoor advertising sector joined forces with the aim of offering clients a comprehensive, nationwide service. Because the name of one of the firms involved, Claude Neon, was already so well known, it was decided to adopt the same name for the new organization. However, when it came to design, the watchword was innovation rather than tradition. The Gottschalk+Ash design studio, with its two founders and their colleague Freddy Jaggi, was contracted to create a new kind of design system. Instead of a single logo, they came up with five versions of an incomplete letter "C". Instead of having one company color, there were four, arranged together in different combinations. The result was a scheme with plenty of possibilities for change, with each version looking slightly different but always consistent. With hindsight, the Claude Neon logo can be seen as an early example of a flexible but recognizable corporate identity.

Mehrere kanadische Unternehmen aus dem Bereich der Außenwerbung schlossen sich 1973 mit dem Ziel zusammen, einen landesweiten umfassenden Werbeservice bieten zu können. Claude Neon, eine der fusionierenden Firmen, lieferte den Namen für das neue Unternehmen, da er aufgrund seiner Historie den größten Bekanntheitsgrad versprach. Beim Design setzte man jedoch auf Innovation statt auf Tradition. Das Designbüro Gottschalk+Ash wurde beauftragt, und die beiden Firmengründer konzipierten gemeinsam mit ihrem Mitarbeiter Freddy Jaggi ein neuartiges Designsystem. Statt eines einzigen Logos gab es fünf Varianten des unvollständigen Buchstabens „C", und statt einer Hausfarbe gab es vier, die jeweils miteinander arrangiert wurden. Aus der Kombination ergab sich ein System mit zahlreichen Variationsmöglichkeiten, das immer leicht unterschiedlich aussah, aber stets einheitlich wirkte. Rückblickend ist das Design von Claude Neon ein früher Vertreter flexibler, systematischer Erscheinungsbilder.

En 1973, plusieurs entreprises canadiennes du secteur de la publicité extérieure fusionnèrent pour pouvoir fournir des services publicitaires dans le cadre d'une couverture globale du pays. Claude Neon, une de ces firmes, livra le nom de la nouvelle entreprise parce que son histoire était celle qui promettait la meilleure notoriété. Pour le design, on préféra miser sur l'innovation plutôt que sur la tradition. L'agence de graphisme Gottschalk+Ash fut retenue, et ses deux fondateurs et leur collaborateur Freddy Jaggi développèrent un système graphique d'un genre inédit. Au lieu d'un logo unique, ils créèrent cinq variantes de la lettre « C » incomplète ; et au lieu d'une seule couleur définissant l'identité visuelle, il y en avait quatre qui pouvaient être arrangées entre elles. De cette combinatoire résultait un système permettant de nombreuses variations présentant un aspect légèrement différent tout en restant toujours homogène. Rétrospectivement, le design de Claude Neon apparaît comme un premier cas d'image de marque à la fois systématique et flexible.

Five versions of the initial letter "C" of the company name were used for the Claude Neon logo, complemented by a palette of four colors in various combinations. The result was a versatile, but still simple design system.

Das „C" aus dem Firmennamen wurde in fünf Varianten zum Logo von Claude Neon. Ergänzt durch eine Palette aus vier Farben, die jeweils miteinander kombiniert werden konnten, ergab sich ein variantenreiches und dennoch einfaches Designsystem.

L'initiale « C » de la marque commerciale devint le logo de Claude Neon au travers de cinq variantes. Complétée par une palette de quatre couleurs combinables entre elles, il en résulta un système graphique à la fois simple et riche en variantes.

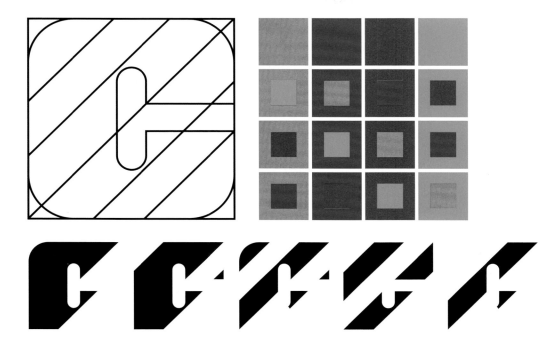

The neutral Helvetica typeface was chosen for the Claude Neon design. These large-scale billboards the company used for its advertising throughout Canada show how clearly legible the white lettering was when set against a brightly colored background.

Die neutrale Schriftart Helvetica ergänzte das Design von Claude Neon. Zu den kräftigen Grundfarben konnte sie in Weiß mit idealer Lesbarkeit platziert werden, wie diese Großflächenplakate zeigen, die als Eigenwerbung des Unternehmens in ganz Kanada zu sehen waren.

La fonte neutre Helvetica venait compléter le design de Claude Neon. En blanc, elle se superposait de manière parfaitement lisible aux couleurs vives du fond, comme le montrent ces affiches publicitaires autopromotionnelles que l'on a pu voir dans tout le Canada.

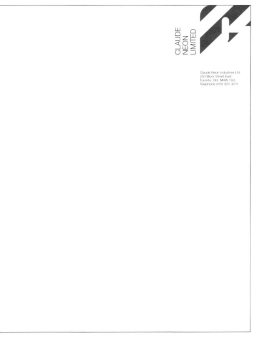

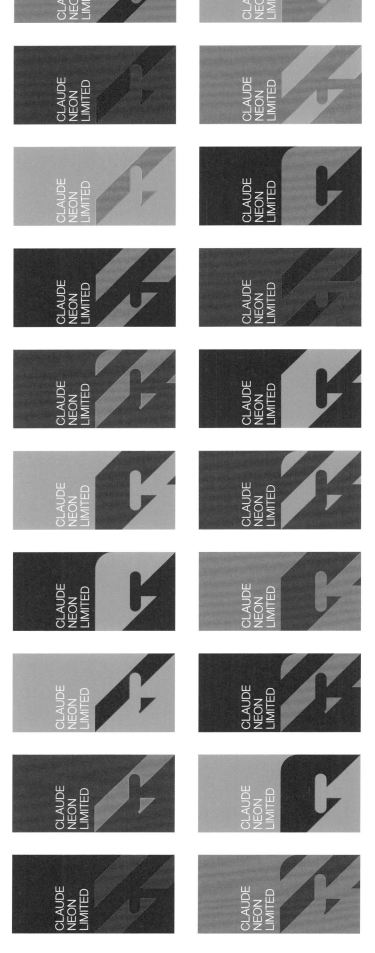

It was on business cards, however, that the design concept came into its own. There were 60 possible combinations of color and logo and each employee was given a full set with all the variations. Even more visual variety was created with the development of the same concept for use in prospectuses and on posters.

Vor allem bei den Visitenkarten wurde das Designkonzept betont. Es waren 60 verschiedene Farb- und Logokombinationen möglich, und jeder Mitarbeiter erhielt einen kompletten Satz mit allen Varianten. Für Prospekttitel und Plakate wurden auf Basis dieses Systems ergänzend verschiedene Muster generiert, die für zusätzliche visuelle Abwechslung sorgten.

Le concept graphique était particulièrement mis en valeur sur les cartes de visite. Soixante combinaisons couleurs/logo étaient possibles, et chaque collaborateur en recevait un jeu complet avec toutes les variantes. Pour les titres de prospectus et les affiches, différents motifs complémentaires produits sur la base de cette systématique accroissaient encore la diversité.

Claude Neon
Electrical Sign
Products

Canadian
Outdoor Rates

1974

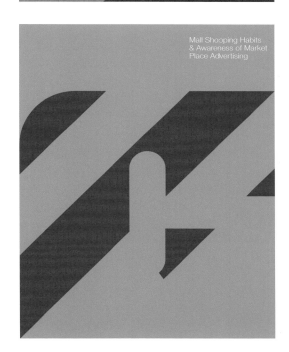

Mall Shooping Habits
& Awareness of Market
Place Advertising

This is
Claude Neon

Claude Nèon   Claude Neon
Limitée   Limited

Rapport Annuel   Annual Report
au 31 décembre   December 31,
1972   1972

Fractionné

Zerteilt

Split

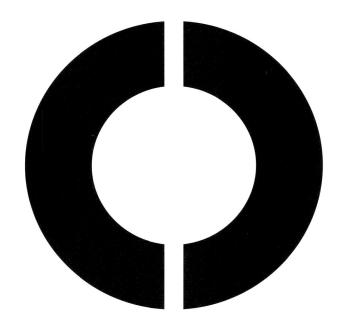

Clenet Coachworks
Automobiles
1977 · Marty Neumeier · US

Sanyo
Electronics
1963 · Shigeo Fukuda · JP

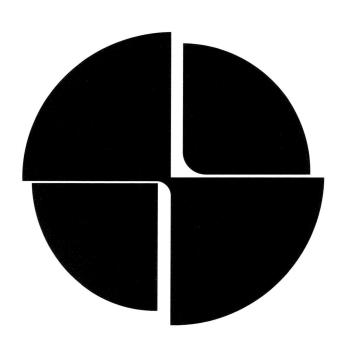

CO.FE.MO. di P. Moreschi & Figli
Metal processing
1967 · Pietro Amadei · IT

Yee-Bradley
Airport engineers
1969 · Clarence Lee · US

Tokyo Financing Bank
1969 · Yoshio Hayashi · JP

Pepsi-Cola
Beverage
1960s · Ivan Chermayeff,
Gene Secander · US

Fantini Elettronica
Electronics
1965 · Giovanni Brunazzi · IT

Multicenter
Art gallery
1972 · Giulio Confalonieri · IT

Österreichischer Bundesverlag
Publishing
1980 · Anonymous · AT

International Ocean Exposition
1973 · Kazumasa Nagai · JP

Atelier Chourgnoz
Design studio
1960s · Jean-Marie Chourgnoz · FR

Válvulas Hydra
Hydraulic valves
1966 · Alexandre Wollner · BR

Teleflex
Cable systems
1968 · David L. Burke · US

Toyo Jozo
Wines
1968 · Kazumasa Nagai · JP

Ontario Recreation Society
Recreational therapy
1971 · John S. Brown · CA

Ontario Institute for Studies in Education
Teachers' college
1969 · Leslie Smart · CA

River Steel
Steel plant
1971 · Kenichi Yoshioka · JP

Schlösser
Plastics
1960s · Hanns Lohrer · DE

Kemdex
Dental hygiene
1966 · Anonymous · DE

Frank Neubauer
Design
1965 · Jürgen Hammer · DE-GDR

Turun Kala
Foods
1962 · Bror B. Zetterborg · FI

Italsider
Steel industry
1962 · Mimmo Castellano · IT

Holiday Universal
Network of health centers
1970 · S. Neil Fujita · US

Hammer Neubauer Grafikerkollektiv
Design
1965 · Jürgen Hammer · DE-GDR

Delco
Packaging
1963 · Lance Wyman · US

Companhia Coronado de Hoteis
Hotel chain
1968 · João Carlos Cauduro,
Ludovico Antonio Martino · BR

Riehm, Bretz & Co.
1965 · Graphicteam Köln · DE

Shinden Kiki Laboratory
Electronics
1970 · Fumiko Ichikawa/
Yoshioka Design Room · JP

Kailani Building
Apartments
1968 · Clarence Lee, Claire Treat · US

Lindholms Bil
Automobile sales
1970 · Ove Engström · SE

Usines du Pied-Selle
Kitchens
1964 · Raymond Loewy/CEI · FR

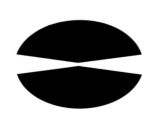

Kold Kist
Foods
1962 · Thomas Laufer · US

Cramer Druck
Printing
1972 · Gerold Schmidt · DE

**5th International Labour
Film Festival, Montreal**
1967 · Georges Beaupré · CA

Longo
Inks
1970 · Walter Hergenröther · IT

**Bundesverband der Deutschen
Luft- und Raumfahrtindustrie**
Aircraft and space industry association
1976 · Rolf Müller · DE

Statens Informasjonstjeneste
National parks
1966 · Paul Brand · NO

**Weather Engineering
Corporation of Canada**
Weather studies group
1957 · Allan Harrison · CA

Sogien
Packaging materials
1976 · Yoshikatsu Tami · JP

Stanrey
Metal goods
1960s · Roy W. Madison · US

Komeito
Political party
1970 · Hiroshi Ohchi · JP

Gouda Garden
Yarns
1969 · Ralph Prins · NL

Sanko Kogyo
Engineering parts
1976 · Yoshihiro Kishimoto · JP

Scic
Kitchens
1965 · Franco M. Ricci · IT

Communications USA
Exhibition
1965 · Arnold Saks, James S Ward · US

Reel Image Productions
Film studio
1971 · Paul M. Levy · US

Ediciones Unidas
Publishing
1971 · Francesc Guitart · ES

ICOMI - Indústria Comércio de Minérios
Mining
1960s · Aloísio Magalhães/PVDI · BR

Society of Typographic Designers
1966 · James D. Taylor/
Rous & Mann Press · CA

Thomson C.S.F.
Electronics
1969 · Alain Carrier · FR

Passagen Verlag
Publishing
1985 · Anonymous · AT

Bopp und Reuther Messtechnik
Measuring instruments
1976 · Rolf Müller · DE

WC4 TV
Broadcasting
1971 · G. Dean Smith · US

D. W. Graham and Associates
Landscape architecture
1963 · Georges Beaupré · CA

Instituto de Ciencia Animal
Livestock management and research
1969 · Félix Beltrán · CU

Laverne International
Furniture
1965 · James S. Ward, Arnold Saks · US

Centro de Turismo Nova Lindóia
Tourism
1962 · Alexandre Wollner · BR

Södahl
Furniture
1960s · Anonymous · DK

Centro Arredamento Moderno
Interior design
1973 · Amedeo Bergamasco · IT

Ceramica Gresparma
Floor tiles
1965 · Franco M. Ricci · IT

Brown, Jensen and Garloff
Media production
1981 · Tim Larsen · US

Urban Research Corporation
Development
1968 · David L. Burke · US

Art Metal
Office furniture
1960s · Lester Beall · US

Torii & Co.
Pharmaceuticals
1978 · Kazuo Tanaka · JP

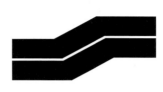

Les Entreprises Transport
Transportation
1969 · Jean Morin, Tony Hobbs · CA

Valextra
Leather goods
1962 · A. G. Fronzoni · IT

Lutherisches Verlagshaus
Publishing
1981 · Anonymous · DE

Lime Waterproofing
1961 · Appelbaum & Curtis · US

Insinööritoimisto Y. Pitkänen
Engineering
1967 · Seppo Polameri · FI

Shield Furniture
1967 · Rod Dyer, George Osaki,
Roland Young · US

Tie-Ja Vesirakennushallitus
Highways and waterways
1968 · Pentti Rahikainen · FI

Werbeagentur Zühlke
Advertising
1965 · Anonymous · DE

Arkia
Airline
1971 · Asher Kalderon · IL

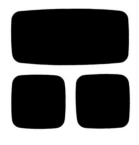

Trapinex
Printing
1968 · Raymond Gid · FR

Tokyo Zokei College
Art school
1967 · Mitsuo Katsui · JP

The Bunker-Ramo Corporation
Computer systems
1960s · Lester Beall · US

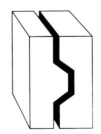

Harvey Cowan
Architecture
1969 · James Donahue/
Cooper & Beatty · CA

Universidade De Brasília
University
1963 · PVDI · BR

Terra Furniture
1969 · Frank R. Cheatham,
David J. Goodman · US

Sirti
Electronics
1968 · Pino Tovaglia · IT

Energy Storing System
1981 · Ove Engström · SE

Marathon Realty
Real estate
1977 · Stuart Ash/
Gottschalk+Ash · CA

Urological Surgery Center
Hospital
1979 · Eduardo A. Cánovas · AR

Moody Moore and Partners
Architecture
1966 · James Cross · US

Typographic Québec
Typesetting
1969 · James Donahue/
Cooper & Beatty · CA

Mobilia
Furniture
1966 · Claude Dietrich · PE

Universal
Travel agency
1971 · Jean Delaunay · FR

Milano Cinema
1977 · Alfredo de Santis · IT

Centro Profesional de Dibujantes
Graphic designers association
1959 · Nedo Mion Ferrario · VE

Ytong-Bolagen
Building materials
1965 · Robert Geisser · CH

British Shoe Corporation
1971 · R. M. Godin, Miles Walker/
Newton & Godin · UK

Nakamura Architecture Office
1959 · Hiroshi Ohchi · JP

Kobashi Photo Studio
1974 · Ken'ichi Hirose · JP

Women's Fashion Factory
1965 · Jan Hollender · PL

Editorial Tiempo Nuevo
Publishing
1970 · John Lange · VE

Katimavik
Billboard marketing
1970 · Yvon Laroche,
Pierre-Yves Pelletier · CA

Photoronic Typographers
Typesetting
1970 · James Liennart · US

Klöpfer
Mining
1960s · Hanns Lohrer · DE

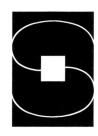

Sorge
Weaving
1960s · Hanns Lohrer · DE

S.E.I.
Encyclopedia
1968 · Giorgio Maltisotto/Sitcap · IT

Industries Valcartier
Plastics
1968 · Laurent Marquart/
Jacques Guillon Designers · CA

**Recordati Industria Chimica
e Farmaceutica**
Pharmaceuticals and chemicals
1971 · Ilio Negri · IT

Tynes Møbler
Furniture
1970 · Bruno Oldani · NO

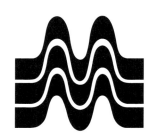

Marcona Mining Corporation
1969 · Robert Pease · US

Washington Mutual
Savings bank
1968 · Ken Parkhurst · US

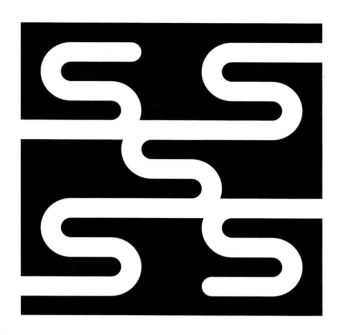

Sturm Söhne Solingen
Climate technology
1970 · Hans Karl Rodenkirchen · DE

Celstar
Polystyrene products
1970 · Bruno Oldani · NO

Norbrasite Comércio e Importação
Paper
1969 · Alexandre Wollner · BR

Peter Revson
Motor racing
1972 · Robert Miles Runyan, Ron Jefferies/
Robert Miles Runyan & Associates · US

TelCom
Broadcasting consultant
1970 · Tom Woodward · US

Eastman Kodak
Photographic equipment
1983 · Joe Selame · US

Maestro
Foods
1970 · Morten Peetz-Schou · DK

Kinsho Co.
Textiles
1971 · Tomoichi Nishiwaki · JP

Kailua Chamber of Commerce
1973 · Thomas Starr,
Randall Swatek · US

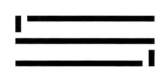

Schneidereit Immobilien
Real estate
1972 · Hans Karl Rodenkirchen · DE

Torii & Co.
Pharmaceuticals
1975 · Kazuo Tanaka · JP

Quorum Corporation
Acquisitions and development
1983 · Denise Spaulding · US

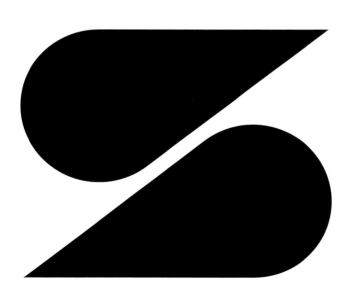

Sakata International
Trading
1983 · Ikuya Kimura · JP

Typographie Métro
Typesetting
1966 · Pierre-Yves Pelletier · CA

Standard Desk
Office furniture
1964 · Ernst Roch/
Design Collaborative · CA

Kellock Factors
Investment bank
1976 · Kenneth Hollick · UK

Wood Lighting Industries
1982 · Ray Engle · US

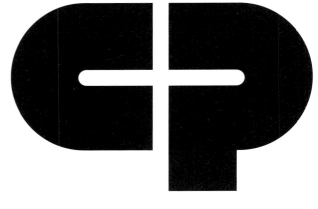

Continental Petroleum
1979 · J. Barton · US

Libra Rotoget
Research institute
1972 · Alfredo Troisi · IT

Olin Mathieson
Chemicals
1970s · Lippincott & Margulies · US

Lartel
Textiles
1979 · Alfonso Capetillo Ponce · MX

Tibbetts
Paint
1964 · Manfred Gotthans/
Chris Yaneff · CA

Kaneda Enterprises
1983 · Hiroshi Toida · JP

NV Versicherung
Insurance
1960s · Otto Rieger · DE

Watchtower Society
Religious group
1970 · Yasaburo Kuwayama · JP

Rothschild Group
Financial consultancy
1979 · Diana Graham · US

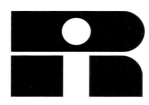

Inter-Rückversicherungs AG
Insurance
1964 · Paul Bühlmann · CH

Landesverband Bayerischer Bauinnungen
Trade association
1970 · Wolf D. Zimmermann · DE

Ets Bouvet
Steel industry
1965 · Jean Delaunay/Look · FR

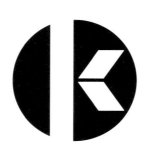

Osakeyhtiö Konttoritarpeita
Engineering
1959 · Jukka Pellinen · FI

Alphabet Shop
Typesetting and signage
1971 · Richard Wittosch · US

Gruppo Uno
Cultural association
1968 · Michele Spera · IT

Wiener + Deville
Advertising
1965 · Anonymous · CH

Ferrante Petroli
Fuel oil
1969 · Mimmo Castellano · IT

Michel Olyff
Design
1960s · Michel Olyff · BE

Hanabusa
Planning office
1979 · Toshio Sunohara · JP

**American Computer and
Communications Company**
Computer services
1971 · Conrad E. Angone · US

Times Watch
Watches
1966 · Mimmo Castellano · IT

Pussy - Agencia de Modelos
Modeling agency
1969 · Pedro Ariño · ES

Christian Kortmann
Meat-processing machinery
1965 · Reiner Wiegang · DE-GDR

Aksel Kjersgaard
Furniture
1960s · Anonymous · DK

Tipofilm Cortometraggi Pubblicitari
Advertising
1965 · Enzo Careccia/Opit Pubblicità · IT

Isy Bernard
Cosmetics
1964 · Hans Karl Rodenkirchen · DE

**Verband Baugewerblicher
Unternehmer Bayerns**
Trade association
1970 · Wolf D. Zimmermann · DE

De Donato Editore
Publishing
1968 · Daniele Baroni · IT

Imprimerie Jouve
Printing
1950s · Aldo Calabresi · IT/FR

Univerzitetna Knjižnica Maribor
University
1983 · Ivan Dvoršak · YU

Holland & Josenhans
Publishing
1975 · Bernhard Wanzel · DE

Console Foods
1983 · Gary Ball · US

Industria Petrolifera Sacca
Fuel oil
1972 · Silvio Coppola · IT

Ifanger
Turning tools
1960s · Milo Schraner · CH

Cross Company
Machine builders
1981 · Mark Topczewski, Frances
Ullenberg, Ken Eichenbaum · US

Van Abbemuseum, Eindhoven
Modern and contemporary art museum
1960s · Wim Crouwel · NL

Monogram Industries
Portable toilets
1968 · James Cross · US

Tessitura di Giussano
Textiles
1970 · Silvio Coppola · IT

National Theatre, London
1971 · Henrion Design Associates · UK

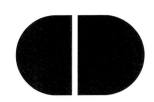

Centro Di
Publishing
1968 · A. G. Fronzoni · IT

Imprimerie Daynac
Printing
1967 · Philippe Gentil · FR

System- und Flugelektronik
Flight systems development
1972 · Rainer E. Kunert · DE

Kommunalentwicklung Baden-Württemberg
Local development
1970s · Hanns Lohrer · DE

Tanaka Soshoku
Interior design
1983 · Shigenobu Nagaishi · JP

Università Internazionale dell'Arte
University
1968 · Bob Noorda/
Unimark International · IT

International Motorsport Association of Canada
1969 · William Newton, Bill Hedges · CA

Spence Hurtt
Real estate
1960 · Ken Parkhurst · US

F.lli de Dominicis
Patent office
1968 · Patrizia Pataccini/
Studio Cortesi · IT

Ramón Sopena
Publishing
1964 · Ribas & Creus · ES

Torrefazione Veneta
Coffee roasting
1972 · Edoardo Salvestrini · IT

TV2
Broadcasting
1966 · Guillermo Gonzáles Ruiz · AR

Lloyd Chester Associated
Public relations
1972 · Mike Quon · US

Engineering Products of Canada
1966 · Jacques Roy/
Jacques Guillon Designers · CA

Deutsche Grundbesitz-Investmentgesellschaft
Real estate investment
1973 · Heinz Schwabe · DE

Research III
Chemical research institute
1963 · Gerry Rosentswieg/
The Graphics Studio · US

Servizi Finanziari Internazionali
Financial services
1968 · Ilio Negri · IT

Menswear Association of Britain
1965 · Michael Tucker · UK

IBM Western Region
Computer systems
1968 · Gerry Rosentswieg · US

Deutsche Bank
(proposed design)
1972 · Heinz Schwabe · DE

Röntgen Technische Dienst
X-rays
1964 · Charles Jongejans · NL

Unione Italiana di Riassicurazione
Insurance
1978 · Ettore Vitale · IT

Teach Yourself Books
Publishing
1969 · Peter Cope · UK

Teatro Popolare di Roma
Theater
1975 · Rinaldo Cutini · IT

Léon Ullmann
Publishing
1963 · Jacques Douin · FR

Marketing Improvements
Market analysis
1964 · Fletcher, Forbes, Gill · UK

Head/Ellerman
Management consultancy
1970 · James Lienhart · US

Kokusai
Road construction
1960s · Kazumasa Nagai · JP

Groep De Bondt
Construction company
1968 · Rob Buytaert · BE

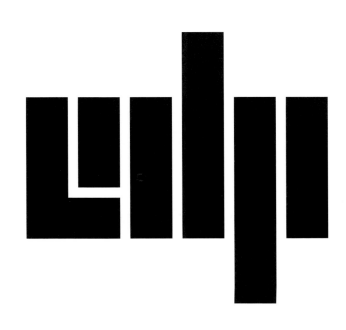

EDP Technology
Computer software
1968 · Arnold Saks · US

Nomina
Research institute
1982 · Rolf Müller · DE

Pillar
Construction company
1968 · John Gibbs/Unit Five Design · UK

Tate & Lyle
Sugar
1967 · Henrion Design Associates · UK

Jilly's
Fast-food chain
1972 · John Harrison, Barry
O'Dwyer/Stewart Morrison Harrison · UK

Aebi & Co.
Engineering works
1950s · Eugen Jordi · CH

Moggi
Toys
1968 · Sergio Salaroli · IT

Dane Brog
Liquor
1970 · Heinz Schwabe · DE

Comité de Solidaridad con Vietnam
Political committee
1967 · Félix Beltrán · CU

TTX
Glass
1966 · Claude Dietrich · PE

**San Francisco
Rehabilitation Workshop**
1964 · Michel Dattel · US

**Schifflukenabdeckung
und Pollerfertigung**
Ship components
1965 · Ludwig Bonitz · DE-GDR

Av-Producenterna
Television and radio technology
1969 · Olle Eksell · SE

Ministerio de Trabajo y Comunidades
Government office
1966 · Claude Dietrich · PE

Kouler Gallery
Art gallery
1966 · David L. Burke · US

Instituto Cubano del Petróleo
Fuel oil
1968 · Félix Beltrán · CU

Cesa
Radio components
1970 · Luciano Francesconi · IT

Human Relations Bureau of Los Angeles
Urban integration
1968 · Michel Dattel · US

House of Packaging
1967 · Rod Dyer · US

Production Systems International
Oil and gas
1968 · George K. Buckow Jr./
Communications Group · US

FAMIA
Consumer fair
1970 · Michael Herold · DE

D.K.P. Naviera
Shipping
1969 · Yvon Laroche · CA

Lennart Larsson Rörled
1981 · Hans Kündig · SE

Yamada Shomei Lighting
1968 · Mitsuo Katsui · JP

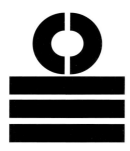

Captain's Card
Travel agency
1970 · Lund & Lommer · DK

Westinghouse Design Center
Research and development
1969 · Peter Megert · US

Chestnut Mountain Park, Toronto
1970 · William Newton, Ludwig Scharfe/
Paul Arthur Associates · CA

Light House
Lamps
1963 · Bruno Oldani · NO

**Bygningsartikkelgrossistenes
Landsforbund**
Exhibition
1970 · Bruno Oldani · NO

**Young Homebuilders
of Northern California**
1969 · Robert Pease · US

L'Artiere
Gift shop
1972 · Franco M. Ricci · IT

TV 7 Mar del Plata
Broadcasting
1966 · Guillermo Gonzáles Ruiz · AR

Keramische Werke
Ceramics
1965 · Martin Rosette · DE-GDR

Torniotecnica
Precision machinery
1970 · Ilio Negri · IT

Noritsu
Boilers
1967 · Takeshi Otaka · JP

Promociones Artísticas y Diseño
Design promotion
1966 · Gerd Leufert · VE

York Regional School of Nursing
1968 · William Newton · CA

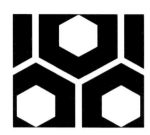

Ceramiche della Robbia
Ceramics
1966 · Andrea Rossi · IT

Joyo Bank
1965 · Yoshio Hayashi · JP

**Howard, Needles, Tammen
and Bergendorff Architects**
1970 · Eugene Belline/
Unimark International · US

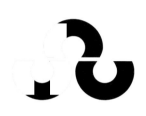

The Science Council of Canada
Scientific advisory group
1970 · Peter Steiner/
Gottschalk+Ash · CA

Cantoni
Textiles
1960s · Studio Boggeri · IT

New Ocean Engineering
Technology institute
1968 · Dietmar R. Winkler · US

Cronmatch
Matches
1965 · W. M. de Majo · UK

Messerform
Cutlery
1958 · Hans Karl Rodenkirchen · DE

TV 3 Film Festival
Broadcaster's film festival
1969 · Studio González Ruiz &
Shakespear · AR

Ontario Pavilion, Expo '70, Osaka
World's fair stand
1969 · Ken Young/
Stewart & Morrison · CA

Aluchrome Corrosion Treatment
1981 · Ove Engström,
Torgny Gustavsson · SE

Rabitz Druck
Printing
1961 · Hans Karl Rodenkirchen · DE

Plus
1972 · Kazumasa Nagai · JP

Oice
Mediation committee
1965 · Italo Lupi · IT

Optik Meier
Optician
1967 · Anonymous · DE

VEB Uhrenkombinat
Watches
1965 · Lothar Barutzki · DE-GDR

Drumlin Farms
Agriculture
1968 · Manfred Gotthans/
Chris Yaneff · CA

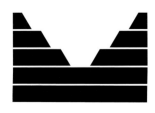

Summa Corporation
Mining
1973 · Mario Zamparelli,
Jean-Claude Müller · US

Atlantic Richfield Company
Petrochemicals
1970s · Carol Lipperl, Tomoko Miho · US

Duplication

Verdopplung

Duplication

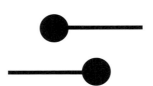

Schlagzeuginstrumentenfabrik
Johannes Link
Musical instruments
1950s · Otl Aicher · DE

Karl Kessel
1965 · Félix Beltrán · CU

Bellasich & Bossi
Publishing
1967 · Silvio Coppola · IT

Grossman
Publishing
1960s · Everett Aison · US

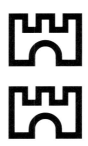

Livraria 2 Cidades
Bookstore
1962 · Ludovico Antonio Martino · BR

Gremio de Maestros Impresores
de Barcelona
Printing association
1969 · Ribas & Creus · ES

Housing Development Corporation
1970 · Manfred Gotthans,
Chris Yaneff · CA

Illy Caffé
Coffee
1959 · Dante Bighi · IT

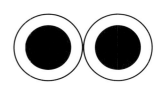

Bofinger+Reinhardt
Design
1970s · Bofinger+Reinhardt · DE

Ferrer Internacional
Pharmaceuticals
1970 · Francisco Marco Vilar/
Grupo de Diseño · ES

Studio d'Ingegneria
Industrial engineers
1973 · Alfredo Troisi · IT

Gugelmann & Cie
Textiles
1960s · Hansruedi Widmer/
Devico AG · CH

Indústrias Cosmo
Record turntables
1962 · Josep Pla-Narbona · ES

Architetti Associati
Architecture
1973 · Michele Spera · IT

Weston Woods
Film production
1960 · Jon Aron · US

Wunderwald-Krawatten
Ties
1950 · Walther Bergmann · DE

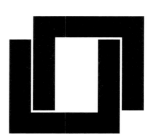

Champlain Container Corporation
Transportation
1960s · Stuart Ash/Gottschalk+Ash · CA

Grupo Cobalto
Cinemas
1969 · Álvaro Sotillo · VE

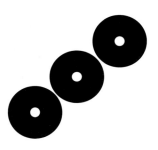

All-Terrain Vehicle
Off-road vehicles
1969 · Leslie & Philip Smart · CA

Takarabune
Clothing
1982 · Shuzo Murase,
Jun Yoshida, Toshinori Nozaki · JP

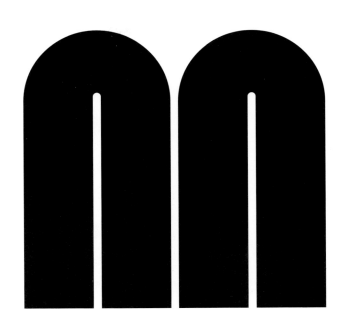

Paul Maurel
Bookstore and art gallery
1968 · Daniel Maurel/Chourgnoz Publicité · FR

Olle Eksell Design
Design
1969 · Olle Eksell · SE

Eishucha
Teas
1969 · Iwasaki Shinji/
Yoshioka Design Room · JP

Tra Ital
Pipe technology
1972 · Corinna Ferrari · IT

Vereinigte Böhmische Glasindustrie
Glass
1950 · Walter Sauer · DE

Smith Stevens Architects
1971 · Paul M. Levy · US

Contal Construction Continental
Construction company
1960s · Roberto Amaro Lanari · BR

Towers Merchants
Grocery
1966 · Chris Yaneff · CA

Marine Sciences Corporation
Underwater research
1961 · Frank R. Cheatham/
Porter & Goodman Design · US

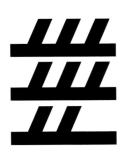

Württembergischer Kunstverein
Art association
1979 · Kurt Weidemann · DE

H. H. Ehrlich, Erfurt
Metal constructions
1965 · Karl-Jürgen Härtel · DE-GDR

Augusto Bedoya
Customs office
1967 · Claude Dietrich · PE

Helsingin Kaupungin Sähkölaitos
Electronics
1960 · Martti A. Mykkänen · FI

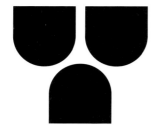

Banque Transatlantique
Bank
1970 · Daniel Maurel/
Chourgnoz Publicité · FR

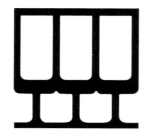

Glaswerke Ilmenau
Glass
1965 · Karlheinz Herke · DE-GDR

St. Cloud Library
Public library
1975 · Peter Seitz · US

Bombones Keops-Blanxart
Chocolates
1965 · Ribas & Creus · ES

Totalgas
Fuel oil
1965 · Ilio Negri, Michele Provinciali,
Pino Tovaglia · IT

Nährmittelwerk
Foods
1940s · Gust Hahn · DE

Piazza y Valdez Ingenieros
Construction company
1967 · Claude Dietrich · PE

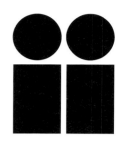

Studio Idea II
Advertising
1970 · Renato Romiti/Studio Idea II · IT

Preussag
Steelworks
1969 · Hans J. Mundt · DE

House of Ronnie
Fashion
1971 · Tony Russell/
Russell & Hinrichs · US

Centro Studi Piemontesi
Library
1973 · Giovanni Brunazzi · IT

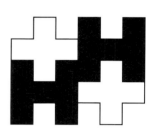

Asociación para el Desarrollo Hospitalario
Hospital association
1969 · Ribas & Creus · ES

Miracle Ear
Hearing aids
1981 · Peter Seitz · US

Howarth & Smith Monotype
Typesetting
1963 · Carl Brett/
Hiller Rinaldo Associates · CA

Minnesota Zoo
1978 · Peter Seitz · US

Metropolitan Life Insurance
1967 · Sandgren & Murtha · US

**Junior Women's
Association of Wheaton**
1968 · James Lienhart/RVI Corp. · US

Johnny Shapiro Menswear
Clothing
1967 · Raymond Lee · CA

Banco de Desenvolvimento do Paraná
Industrial banking
1968 · JMM Publicidade · BR

The Canadian Welfare Council
Social welfare
1968 · Jacques E. Charette · CA

Slippstodin
Shipbuilding
1966 · Kristjan Kristjansson · IS

Neckermann
Mail-order (proposed design)
1960s · Luis Pals · DE

Bense Bau
Construction company
1970 · Werner Hartz · DE

Centro Stampa Minerva
Printing
1968 · Remo Muratore · IT

Heller
Radio advertising
1967 · Robert Pease · US

The Twentieth Century Fund
Research institute
1968 · Edward Deniega Jr. · US

Sodeho
Hotel association
1967 · Gérard Guerre/Technés · FR

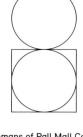

Rothmans of Pall Mall Canada
Cigarettes
1965 · James D. Taylor/
Rous & Mann Press · CA

Sbrissa
Foods
1964 · Enzo Scarton/Alfa Studio · IT

Good Design Corner
1960 · Takashi Kono · JP

Mab & Mya
Textiles
1962 · Bertil Andersson-Bertilson · SE

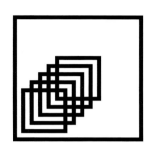

Akitt & Swanson
Architecture
1971 · Ernst Barenscher · CA

Comitato per la Seta Italiana
Silk marketing
1962 · Franco Grignani · IT

Hotel Residencia Montemar
1969 · José Santamarina/
Elias & Santamarina · ES

Everoy
Refrigerators
1961 · Marcello Minale,
Brian Tattersfield · UK

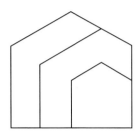

Whitehall Development
Construction company
1968 · Michael Van Elsen/
Hiller Rinaldo Associates · CA

Junket Dessert
Foods
1960 · Appelbaum & Curtis · US

Niigata-nippo
Newspaper
1950s · Yusaku Kamekura · JP

Bolsa de Valores do Rio de Janeiro
Stock exchange
1966 · Nelson Motta, Renato Landim · BR

Grace
Jeweler
1982 · Koichi Nakai, Ichiro Nakai, Tetsuo
Hiro, Tetsuo Togasawa · JP

Peter Murdoch
Furniture
1960s · Lance Wyman · US

WW
Pharmacy
1960s · Herbert Auchli · CH

Imprimerie Monnier
Printing
1965 · Théodore Stamatakis/
Créations Stama · FR

Momicor
Chemical research laboratories
1977 · Armando Milani,
Maurizio Milani · IT

Hennessy Industries
Automobile accessories
1967 · Jerry Braude · US

Collana Discografica
Recording series
1950s · Cecco Re · IT

Carlo Ciarli
Advertising
1968 · Carlo Ciarli · IT

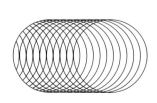

Helipot
Potentiometers
1947 · Lou Frimkess · US

Trame

Raster

Grid

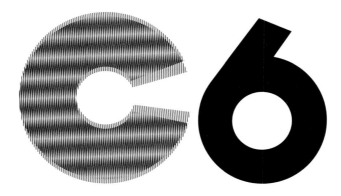

Cinema Six
Movie rentals
1968 · Bob Gill · US/UK

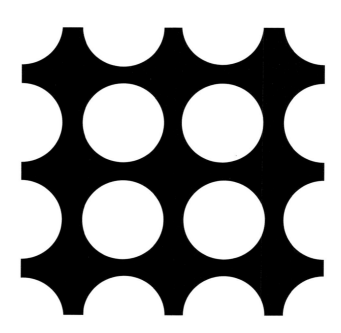

Ratiobau
Property development
1965 · Hanns Lohrer · DE

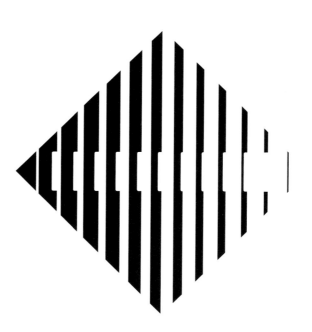

Dai-ichi-shoji
Chemical products
1968 · Hiroshi Ohchi · JP

Photolabor Klischeeanstalt
Photographic laboratory
1960s · F. G. Boes · DE

Schwitter Klischees
Prepress services
1962 · Karl Gerstner · CH

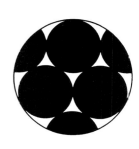

Cantarelli
Animal feed
1969 · Franco M. Ricci · DE

Lemon Tree Productions
Music productions
1968 · Clarence Lee · US

Cromoherma
Chemicals
1969 · Tomás Vellvé · ES

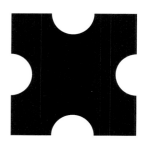

Xellos Havana
Stamps
1970 · Félix Beltrán · CU

Kodak Paris
Photographic equipment
1970s · Bucher-Crémières · FR

**Gütezeichen für Erzeugnisse
der Deutschen Emailindustrie**
Enamel quality-mark
1986 · Bruno K. Wiese · DE

Alpina Shoes
Footwear
1969 · Tomaž Kržišnik · SI

Ciba Photochemie
Photochemicals
1970s · Annemarie Staehlin,
Erwin Giger · CH

Agroquímica Rafard
Chemicals
1977 · PVDI · BR

Sato Design Room
1978 · Shigeru Sato · JP

Coloplast
Healthcare products
1988 · Hans Due · DK

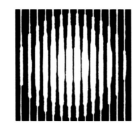

Skan Camera G-M Laboratories
1968 · Henry Robertz/
The Design Partnership · US

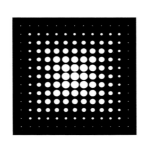

Reclamo-Standard
Printing
1967 · Bruno Oldani · NO

Ljós & Orka
Light installations
1968 · Thröstur Magnusson, Hilmar
Sigurdsson/Argus Advertising · IS

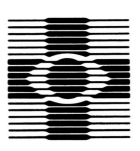

Highland Baptist Hospital
1981 · Tony Bead · US

**Research Center for
Personality Development**
Research institute
1970s · Dick Krueger · US

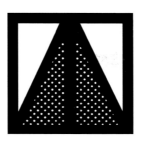

Asunaro Academy
Publishing
1983 · Yoshihiko Kurobe · JP

Pflugshaupt
Gardening
1963 · Atelier Stadelmann Bisig · CH

Komisija za Zastitu Okoline pri RK SOH
Environmental commission
1973 · Dalibor Martinis · YU

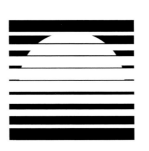

Tundra Books
Publishing
1968 · Rolf Harder/
Design Collaborative · CA

Terituono
Raincoats
1965 · Theodoor Manson · IT

Jerusalem Economic Conference
1983 · Asher Kalderon · IL

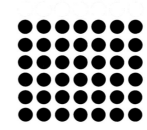

**Secretaria de Educação e Cultura
do Estado da Guanabara**
Ministry of education and culture
1969 · Aristo Rabin · BR

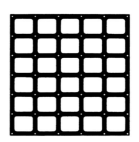

El Farol
Oil company magazine
1969 · Gerd Leufert · VE

Imbalplast
Wrapping paper
1967 · Ilio Negri · IT

Leidschenhage Shopping Center
1968 · Benno Wissing/
Total Design · NL

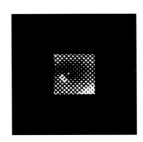

Speakeasy Club
Nightclub
1967 · Crosby, Fletcher, Forbes · UK

Continental Bank Money Card
Bank card
1970s · James Lienhart · US

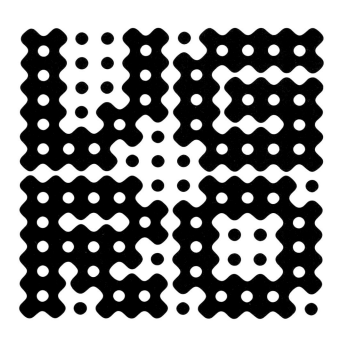

Vereniging van Grafische Reproductie Ondernemingen
Association for graphic reproduction
1958 · Gerard Wernars · NL

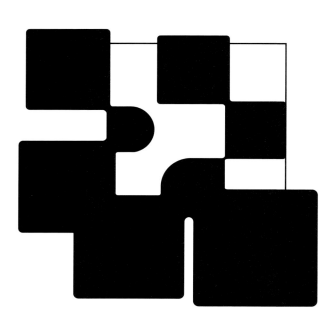

Schwitter Klischees
Prepress services
1959 · Karl Gerstner · CH

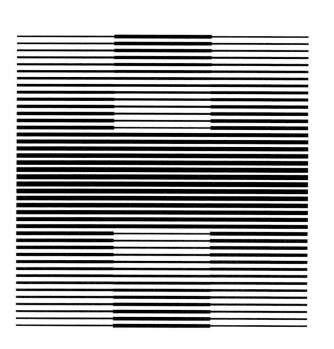

Hauserman
Movable walls
1970 · Paul M. Levy · US

Banque Nationale de Paris
Bank
1974 · Rudi Meyer · FR

Bather Belrose Boje
Civil engineering
1981 · Tim Larsen · US

Bennetts
Printing
1970 · Jack Evans · US

Bodensee
Nightclub
1974 · Othmar Motter · AT

Pitino Gim Mario
Flooring
1968 · Armando Milani · IT

Galería de Arte Nacional
Art gallery
1977 · Álvaro Sotillo · VE

Nikkei Printing
1973 · Koichi Takahashi · JP

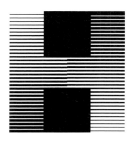

Ebesa
Perfumery
1977 · G. Edwards · MX

The Krystal Company
Fast-food chain
1975 · Chermayeff & Geismar · US

Lucentum Baloncesto
Sports association
1979 · Fernando Medina · ES

Media Services, University of Utah
1983 · Scott Engen · US

The Court, San Francisco
1978 · Michael Vanderbyl · US

Optica Piñile
1981 · José Santamarina/
Elias & Santamarina · ES

Tecnolyte
Lighting
1971 · Ettore Vitale · IT

Bund Freischaffender Foto-Designer
Association of freelance photo designers
1986 · Rolf Müller · DE

Camera di Commercio I.A.A. di Milano
Chamber of commerce
1972 · Mimmo Castellano · IT

Protech Security Systems
Home and office security
1983 · Silvio Gayton · US

Enrico Tronconi
Lighting
1971 · Ilio Negri · IT

ENEL
Energy supplier
1967 · Ilio Negri · IT

Medium
Furniture
1972 · Pérez Sánchez · ES

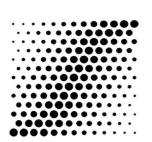

Peter Seitz & Associates
Design
1988 · Peter Seitz · US

Oakland Treecrop Company
Orchards
1969 · Carl Seltzer · US

Vallecchi Editore
Children's books
1973 · Mimmo Castellano · IT

Eyssa
Electronics
1971 · Pérez Sánchez · ES

Siggraph
Computer graphics conference
1984 · Peter Seitz · US

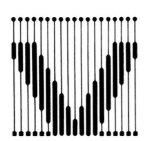

La Vivienda
Accounting
1977 · Gerd Leufert · VE

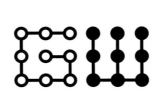

Great Western Research Corporation
Engineering
1965 · Vance Jonson · US

European Home Study Council
Distance learning
1969 · Carl Steinherr · NL/SE

Struthers Electronics Corporation
1976 · Arthur Eckstein · US

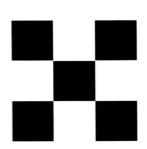

Passpoint Auto Wash
Car-wash
1969 · Heinz Waibl/
Unimark International · IT

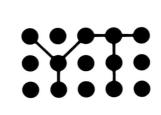

Yoshihiro Tatsuki
Photography
1965 · Makoto Wada · JP

Stoomvaart Maatschappij
Transportation
1969 · Will van Sambeek
Design Associates · NL

Sigma Diffusion
1969 · Florent Garnier · FR

First Fidelity Bank
1983 · Harry Murphy,
Kimberly Lentz · US

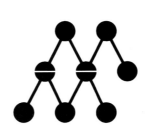

Suzuki
Clothing
1969 · Shigeo Fukuda · JP

Television Opinion Panel
Television voting
1969 · John Gibbs/Unit Five Design · UK

Banco Andrade Arnaud
Bank
1960 · DPZ · BR

Bank of Dallas
1982 · Jack Evans · US

McHenry Medical Group
1965 · Bruce Beck · US

Staff Selection & Services
Management consultancy
1968 · Gilles Fiszman · BE

Ondulex-Doublex
Piston rings
1965 · Philippe Caza · FR

General Graphis
Printing
1964 · Sjoerd Bylsma · NL

Ets Ch. Pautry-Tetras
Aluminum
1970 · Michel Gallay · FR

Camargo Campos
Construction company
1977 · João Carlos Cauduro,
Ludovico Antonio Martino · BR

Fog & Mørup
Furniture
1960s · Anonymous · DK

Secura
Insurance
1960s · Diggelmann & Mennel · CH

GB
Publishing
1950 · Raoul A. Brink · DE

Fredericia Stolefabrik
Furniture
1960s · Anonymous · DK

Thymos Corporation
1975 · Don Davis · US

Nils Nessim
Carpets
1958 · Olle Eksell · SE

VEB Funkwerk
Audio technology
1965 · Fritz Deutschendorf · DE-GDR

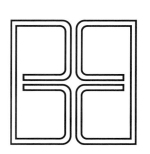

Deutsche Bibelgesellschaft
Publishing
1980 · Atelier Ade · DE

Lima
Foods
1963 · Antoon de Vijlder · BE

Dominici Frères
Cheese
1971 · Jacqueline Gachet/
Chourgnoz Publicité · FR

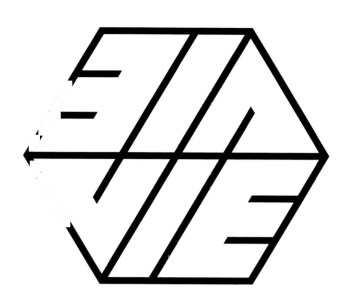

Vermont Import & Export
Sporting goods
1962 · Stephen Dunne/Unimark International · US

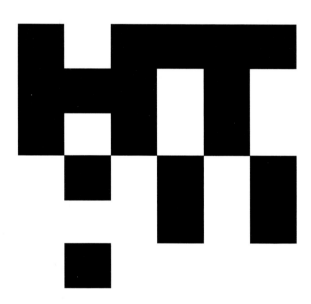

Heinz Terhardt
Photography
1965 · Anonymous · DE

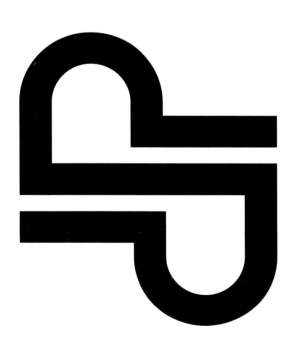

Pavarini
Furniture
1946 · Walter Ballmer · IT

Granula
Plastics
1962 · Paul Bühlmann · CH

Terme di Salsomaggiore
Spa
1970 · Carlo Bruni · IT

Major Holdings & Development
Property management
1969 · John S. Brown · CA

Dascucci Pelletteria
Leather products
1978 · Carlo Marchionni · IT

Continental Plaza
Office building
1972 · Ronald Cutro · US

Jeugdkerk
Youth church
1960 · Wim Crouwel · NL

Rose-Marie Joray
Design
1960s · Rose-Marie
Joray-Muchenberger · CH

Peter Bos
Television production
1968 · Jan Jaring · NL

Publi-pistas
Advertising
1969 · Enric Huguet · ES

Drukkerij Steven
Printing
1966 · Antoon de Vijlder · BE

Benoît de Pierpont
Design
1969 · Benoît de Pierpont · BE

Ryno Scientific
Contact lenses
1968 · Beau Gardner · US

New Man
Clothing
1968 · Raymond Loewy/CEI · FR

Mobil Wall
Furniture
1964 · Heinz Waibl · IT

British Celanese
Acetates and chemicals
1969 · Raymond E. Meylan/Artes Graphicae · UK

Union of Municipal and Government Employees
1968 · Thröstur Magnusson, Hilmar Sigurdsson/Argus Advertising · IS

Economic and Investment Bank
1950s · Fridolin Müller · CH

Metropolitana Milanese
Public transport
1963 · Bob Noorda/
Unimark International · IT

Kasparian
Furniture
1955 · Allen Porter/
Porter & Goodman Design · US

Petri-Presse/Buchdruckerei Benno Schwabe & Co.
Printing
1940s · Imre Reiner · CH

G. Spinelli & Co.
Printing
1964 · Leone Sbrana · IT

Cultural Presentations
1968 · Arnold Saks · US

Lease Plan Nederland
Automobile hire
1967 · Ralph Prins · NL

Browning, Day, Pollk Associates
Architecture
1975 · Robert L. Willis, Vicky Ko · US

Librairie des Sciences
Bookstore
1968 · Michel Waxman · BE

Road Safety
Department of transport
1969 · Clarence Lee · US

Fon Graphics
Design
1977 · Burhan Tastan · TR

TT Group
Textiles
1960s · Anonymous · DK

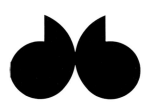

Decoradora Marina Blanco
Interior design
1969 · José Santamarina/
Elias & Santamarina · ES

Manuel Albo
City tours
1979 · Yutaka Sato · JP

Total Oil
Fuel oil
1963 · Ilio Negri, Giulio Confalonieri · IT

Seilerei Haas
Ropes
1960s · Ernst Roch · CA

De Baak
Management institute
1970 · Helmut Salden · NL

Drogerie Büchi
Pharmacy
1970s · Hansruedi Scheller · CH

Robin Nordwell
Metal industry
1965 · E. J. Morrison, Arthur Irizawa/
Stewart & Morrison · CA

Cambridge Computer Services
1960s · Herbert Spencer · UK

European Community, Brussels
1973 · Dieter Urban · DE

Adria Bank
1980 · Peter Skalar · YU

Lauber AG
Transportation
1958 · Müller+Eichenberger · CH

**Art Directors & Designers
Association of New Orleans**
1960s · Donald C. Smith · US

Transnitro
Transportation
1972 · Arnold Saks, Karl Hartig · US

Centro de Cultura Mediterránea
Cultural center
1973 · Tomás Vellvé · ES

Narai Hotel
1960s · Kim Pai · TH

Van Manen & Co.
Printing
1969 · A. G. Schillemans · NL

Programming db
Broadcasting
1968 · Tom Woodward · US

Möbelkombinat Wi-We-Na
Furniture
1965 · Bernhard Wille · DE-GDR

Nago
Nutritional products
1940s · Albert Rüegg · CH

db Drogerie Bazaar
Pharmacy
1970s · Anonymous · NL

R. Jenni
Music production
1950s · Marcel Wyss · CH

Kompressionswerk Benneckstein
Automobile parts
1965 · Bernhard Wille · DE-GDR

Bühler Buchdruck
Printing
1940s · Albert Rüegg · CH

Movomatic
Electronics
1940s · Hans Kasser · CH

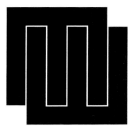

Michael Marin
Architecture
1971 · Jean-Marie Chourgnoz/
Chourgnoz Publicité · FR

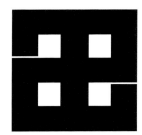

Alfons Eder
Design
1958 · Alfons Eder · FI

Centro Cultural Tercer Mundo
Cultural center
1969 · Emiro Lobo · VE

Klünder-Keramik
Ceramics
1965 · Georg Hülsse · DE-GDR

Metal 2 Indústria Metalurgica
Metal foundry
1963 · João Carlos Cauduro · BR

Editions Edigraf
Publishing
1966 · Maurice Leclercq · BE

Cafetin
Cafeteria
1967 · Gerd Leufert · VE

Studelec
Electrical engineers
1967 · Gérard Guerre/Technés · FR

Popea
Cosmetics
1945 · Rudolf Bircher · CH

Otto Rohrbach Autospenglerei
Automobile bodyshop
1960s · Marcel Wyss · CH

Nepentha
Nightclub
1969 · Giulio Confalonieri · IT

City Engraving
Printing
1968 · Eurographics · UK

**Wächter Industrie- und
Wirtschaftswerbung**
Advertising
1965 · Anonymous · DE

Kilkenny Design Workshops
Design center
1963 · Louis le Brocquy · UK

Syn-Bouw
Construction company
1962 · Bear Cornet · NL

**6th International Congress of the
Society of Industrial Designers**
1968 · Roger O. Denning · UK

C. Danel
Furniture
1960s · Anonymous · SE

Laroche Pelletier Graphistes, Montreal
Design
1968 · Yvon Laroche,
Pierre-Yves Pelletier · CA

Editorial Primera Plana
Publishing
1967 · Ricardo Blanco · AR

Diversified Products
Wholesale
1964 · Frank R. Cheatham · US

Schraubenfabrik
Screws
1950s · Paul Jacopin · CH

H. Würgler & Sohn
Sporting goods
1940s · Walter Herdeg · CH

Löw & Manz Loma Bausysteme
Architecture
1966 · Igildo Biesele · CH

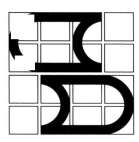

Enciclopedia della Stampa
Encyclopedia of printing
1968 · Giovanni Brunazzi · IT

Acuerdo de Cartagena
Trade agreement
1970 · Claude Dietrich · PE

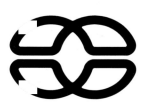

Lamper
Furniture
1970 · Francesc Guitart · ES

Nakamura
Patent office
1973 · Koichi Watanabe · JP

Matsubara Shirts
Clothing
1975 · Akisato Ueda · JP

Papierfabrik Seetal
Paper
1960s · Hans Weber · CH

Partner Werbeagentur
Advertising
1965 · Anonymous · DE

Dansilar
Stockings
1955 · Hanns Lohrer · DE

Normdrehteile
Metallic goods
1965 · Walter Höhne · DE-GDR

Mamekawa Jidosha
Automobile dealer
1979 · Osamu Ogawa, Hajime Fuji · JP

Bemberg
Silk quality-mark
1952 · M. Schneider/Studio Boggeri · IT

Camer
Plastics
1971 · Francisco Marco Vilar/
Grupo de Diseño · ES

Norpapp Industri
Packaging
1970 · Paul Brand · NO

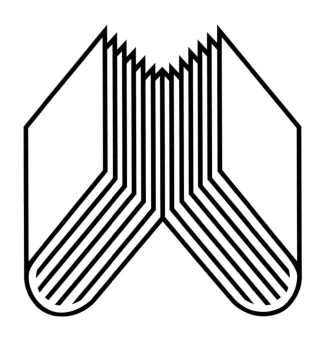

Biblioteca Nacional
National library
1971 · Gerd Leufert · VE

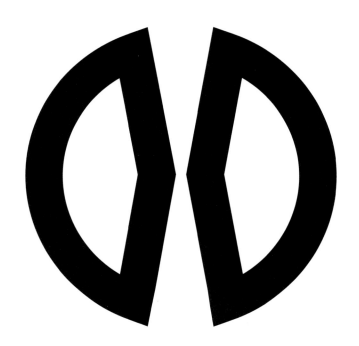

Savage Sloan
Design
1961 · Savage Sloan · CA

Hotel Zürich
1960s · Eugen & Max Lenz · CH

Niepce
Exhibition
1950s · Jacques Nathan-Garamond · FR

Ladrillera Santafe
Building materials
1978 · Gustavo Gómez-Casallas,
Rodrigo Fernández · CO

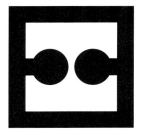

**Harvard Studies in
Technology and Society**
Publishing
1968 · David Ford · US

Vector
Aerospace systems
1962 · Matthew Leibowitz · US

Hypko & Klausch
Clothing
1965 · Jürgen Förster · DE-GDR

Skandia Shop
Sporting goods
1970 · Knut Yran · NO

Turmhotel, Bad Zurzach
Hotel
1960s · Ernst Keller · CH

Globex Design
Exhibition
1970 · Yvon Laroche,
Pierre-Yves Pelletier · CA

D. C. Heath
Publishing
1970 · Herman & Lees Associates · US

Pharos-Verlag Hansrudolf Schwabe
Publishing
1961 · Peter Megert · CH

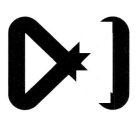

Draper Dobie & Co.
Stock trading
1969 · Manfred Gotthans/
Chris Yaneff · CA

Parkhotel am See
Hotel
1960s · Erich Hänzi · CH

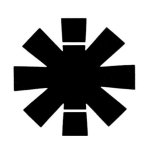

Banco do Estado de Minas Gerais
Bank
1968 · Pinto Ziraldo · BR

National Grain
Agriculture
1966 · William Mayrs · CA

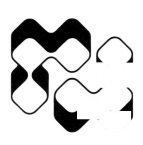

Berenschot, Bosboom
Management consultancy
1969 · Jaap Frank · NL

Short Line
Transportation
1960s · Malcolm Grear · US

Serem
Care for the disabled
1970s · Julián Santamaría · ES

Olida Caby
Foods
1969 · Lonsdale Design · FR

Schwind Radiohandel
Radios
1940s · Walter Herdeg · CH

Sutro and Co.
Stockbrokers
1970 · G. Dean Smith · US

Stierli & Kobelt
Metal goods
1960s · Peter Schaufelberger · CH

Euroviet
Cultural center
1960s · Oanh Pham Phu · DE

Institutet för Färgfoto
Photography
1969 · Bertil Andersson-Bertilson · SE

Werbegesellschaft
Advertising
1961 · Helmut Keppler · DE

Freies Gymnasium Zürich
School
1972 · Hansruedi Scheller · CH

Corporate Concept
Architecture
1968 · Louis Stuart · NL

Nadaman
Restaurant
1960 · Takeshi Otaka · JP

R. J. Associates
Architectural services
1970 · Frederick A. Usher/
Usher & Follis Design · US

Corporación Consultors
Engineering
1983 · Allan W. Miller · US

Light
Electricity services
1966 · PVDI · BR

Agol-Chemie
Chemicals
1960 · Werner Mühlemann · CH

Magis Farmaceutici
Pharmaceuticals
1974 · Armando Milani,
Maurizio Milani · IT

Il Parnaso
Publishing
1964 · Hazy Osterwalder/
Studio Boggeri · IT

Ando Sekimen Kogyo
Beer
1969 · Takeshi Otaka · JP

Nonaka Shokudo
Restaurant
1974 · Shuji Torigoe · JP

Irish Flock
Cables
1968 · George Daulby/
BDMW Associates · UK

Professional Photographers of America
Photographers association
1965 · James Lienhart/RVI Corp. · US

Nihon Shurui Hanbai
Foods and beverages
1979 · Shigeo Katsuoka · JP

Itran
Medical visual training systems
1970 · Jay Hanson · US

Hi-Tide
Fish products
1967 · Nicholas Jenkins · UK

Lapponia
Jeweler
1968 · Eka Lainio/
Markkinointi Viherjuuri · FI

El Nuevo Grupo
Theater
1967 · John Lange · VE

Norte Sur
Travel agency
1960s · Gerd Leufert · VE

Measuring Instruments
1970s · Toru Otsuka · JP

Deutscher Heilverband
Medical association
1960s · Otto Rieger · DE

Kalos
Watchmaker
1969 · Franco M. Ricci · IT

Rest-Glow
Lighting
1965 · Ernst Roch/
Design Collaborative · CA

Turner Color Works
Paint
1960s · Tetsuo Katayama · JP

Churchman's
Tobacco
1960s · John Harris/
Allied Industrial Designers · UK

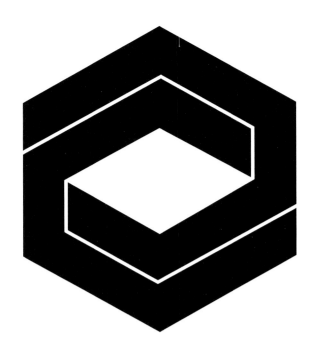

Association of Food Retailers
1960s · Hans Hartmann · CH

International Janitor
Heating systems
1968 · Ulrich Haupt/
Allied International Designers · UK

Vantage Home Builders
Construction company
1978 · John R. Rieben · US

Coronado Shopping Center
1970s · Gollin, Bright & Zolotow · US

Torii & Co.
Pharmaceuticals
1963 · Yoshio Hayashi · JP

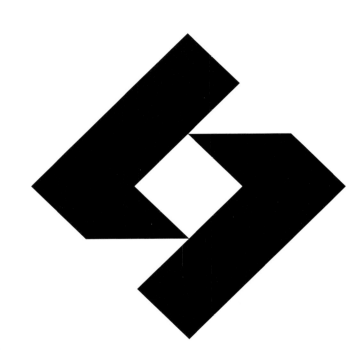

Saupe-Präzisions Drehmaschinen
Precision lathes
1965 · Joachim Gessner · DE-GDR

Anthroposan Heilmittel
Pharmaceuticals
1965 · Jürgen Förster · DE-GDR

J. Mosterd
Air cleaning machines
1971 · Jan Jaring · NL

Instituto de Diseño de Caracas
Design school
1970 · Manuel Espinoza · VE

Laidlaw Lumber
Timber
1963 · Rudy Eswarin/
Stewart & Morrison · CA

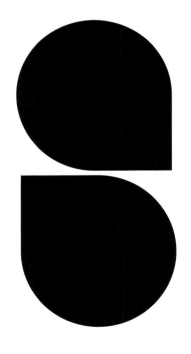

Giselle Subero
Art gallery
1964 · Nedo Mion Ferrario · VE

TV 2 Cultura
Broadcasting
1968 · João Carlos Cauduro,
Ludovico Antonio Martino · BR

Sanibel Monoprix
Sanitary products
1966 · Jean Delaunay/Havas Conseil · FR

Noble Lowndes International
Insurance
1968 · David Caplan · UK

Calcestruzzi Centro Italia
Construction materials
1970 · Francesco Burcini/Studio A · IT

Randstad
Employment agency
1967 · Ben Bos/Total Design · NL

Getreidekombinat Rostock
Agriculture
1965 · Ludwig Bonitz · DE-GDR

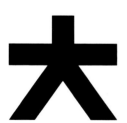

Ecos
Security services
1969 · Ricardo Blanco · AR

Universidad Tecnológica Nacional
University
1966 · Ricardo Blanco · AR

Baumwollspinnerei Leinefelde
Weaving
1965 · Dietrich Bauer · DE-GDR

Löser-Bauunternehmung
Construction company
1965 · Anne Askenasy · DE-GDR

Ber Gold Inc.
1976 · Stuart Ash/Gottschalk+Ash · CA

Royal Garden Hotel
1960s · Ronald Armstrong · UK

Skilift Netschbühl
Ski lift
1971 · Hans Hartmann · CH

Petite Maison Shimazaki
Clothing
1977 · Akira Hirata, Hiroshi Tada · JP

British Transport Docks Board
1964 · Ben John, Ed Stone/
Unit Five Design · UK

Herman Miller
Furniture
1947 · George Nelson, Irving Harper · US

Heidolph-Elektro
Electronics
1967 · Oanh Pham Phu · DE

W. Plüss Offset- und Buchdruck
Printing
1960s · Hansruedi Scheller · CH

Rank Xerox
Photocopiers
1950s · Marcello Minale · UK

Druckerei Nöthen
Printing
1938 · Walter Breker · DE

Aoki Printing
1979 · Yoshikatsu Tami · JP

Offset-Haus
Printing
1960s · Walter Bangerter · CH

The Conservation Trust of Puerto Rico
Ecological and heritage conservation
1968 · Chermayeff & Geismar · US

Browne & Nolan
Printing, publishing and packaging
1964 · Collis Clements · UK

Roto Smeets
Printing
1968 · Marcel Pijpers · NL

Zeefdrukkerij B. Wijtmans
Printing
1966 · Bear Cornet · NL

Tanner
Model aircraft
1950s · Marcel Wyss · CH

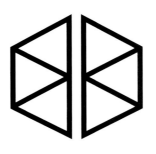

Kristall Verlag
Publishing
1979 · Anonymous · DE

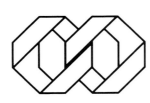

**Instituto Brasileiro de
Mercado de Capitais**
Business school
1970 · Luiz Sérgio Coelho de Sampaio · BR

Diamond Crystal Salt
Salt
1960s · Dickens Design Group · US

Algenova
Aeronautical company
1964 · A. G. Fronzoni · IT

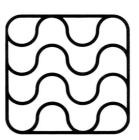

Dutch Pavilion, Expo '70, Osaka
World's fair stand
1969 · Total Design · NL

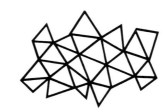

Fiat Service
Automobile repairs
1958 · Giovanni Brunazzi · IT

Longo
Office supplies
1966 · Walter Hergenröther · IT

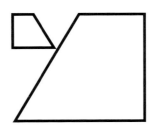

Metall
Machinery
1966 · Jan Jaring · NL

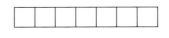

Jean Reiwald
Advertising
1960s · Jean Reiwald · CH

**Farmaceutische Industrie
de Watermolen**
Pharmaceuticals
1968 · Jaap Frank · NL

Visual Design Program
Design education
1970 · Manuel Espinoza · VE

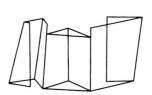

Camera di Commercio I.A.A. di Carrara
Chamber of commerce
1968 · Michele Spera · IT

F.M.E.
Canning
1961 · Ralph Prins · NL

Furnas
Energy supplier
1971 · PVDI · BR

Freelance Forum
International holding
1978 · Joe Vera, Monserrat Rota · MX

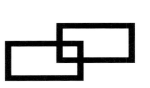

Fred Heer
Design and advertising
1960s · Fred Heer · CH

C. Casacuberta
Printing
1966 · Tomás Vellvé · ES

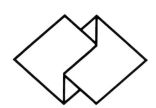

Asociación de Industriales de Artes Gráficas
Graphics industry
1968 · Nedo Mion Ferrario · VE

Camera di Commercio I.A.A. di Milano
Chamber of commerce
(part of integrated logo system)
1972 · Mimmo Castellano · IT

Honbo Office
Real estate
1979 · Takenobu Igarashi · JP

Cadil
Construction company
1975 · Armando Ferraro Senior · VE

Probursa
Stockbroker
1978 · Joe Vera · MX

Watkinson Library
College library
1960s · William Wondriska · US

Multiprocessors
Furniture
1981 · Gustavo Gómez-Casallas,
Rodrigo Fernández · CO

Lausen & Lange
1960s · Herbert W. Kapitzki · DE

Olympic Games, Montreal 1976
1976 · George Huel · CA

Banco Mercantil do Brasil
Bank
1969 · Aloísio Magalhães/PVDI · BR

Maruko Birumen
Property management
1977 · Yasaburo Kuwayama · JP

Impossibilia
Book series
1973 · Gerd Leufert · VE

Kowa Kogei Group
Typesetting
1977 · Yasaburo Kuwayama · JP

Gobbetto
Interior design
1975 · R. Nava, D. Soffientini,
G. Romani, A. Ubertazzi · IT

Continter
Transportation
1978 · R. Nava, D. Soffientini,
G. Romani, A. Ubertazzi · IT

Broome County
Transportation
1960s · Fritz Gottschalk/
Gottschalk+Ash · CA

Ets Roland
Paper bags
1962 · Raymond Loewy/CEI · FR

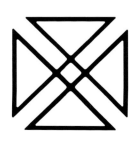

Quarto Centenário do Rio de Janeiro
Commemorative event (proposed design)
1963 · Aloísio Magalhães/PVDI · BR

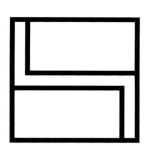

Wilkhahn Sitzmöbel
Furniture
1964 · Rolf Müller · DE

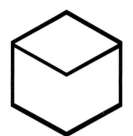

**Canadian Department
of Public Works**
1969 · Ken Patton · CA

Quarto Centenário do Rio de Janeiro
Commemorative event
1963 · Aloísio Magalhães/PVDI · BR

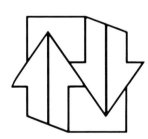

Del Libro sin Arco, Caracas
Publishing
1971 · Gerd Leufert · VE

Interdéveloppement
Management consultancy
1968 · Lonsdale Design · FR

Immobiliare Pizzetti
Real estate
1978 · Armando Milani,
Maurizio Milani · IT

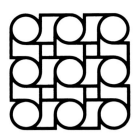

Revista del Colegio de Arquitectos
Architectural magazine
1970 · Álvaro Sotillo · VE

Office National Industriel de l'Azote
Fertilizers
1963 · Jacques Douin · FR

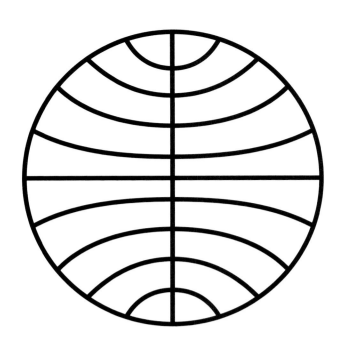

Pan American Airlines
1950 · Edward Larrabee Barnes,
Charles Forberg, Ivan Chermayeff · US

Beckers
Inks
1968 · Stig Arbman · SE

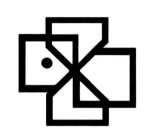

Saldos de Papel
Paper
1983 · Olga Dorantes/
Saxdid Diseño · MX

Herbacin
Cosmetics
1965 · Walter Seifert · DE-GDR

Advertisers Inserts
Advertising
1982 · Ronald Cutro · US

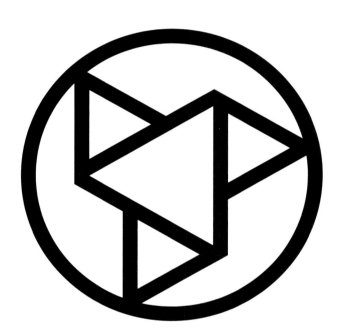

Pieter Schoen
Paint
1963 · Karel Suyling · NL

Werbeagentur Kurt Huber
Design
1960 · Kurt Huber · CH

Centro Commerciale Americano
Import-export
1967 · Carlo Bruni · IT

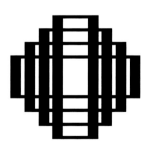

Chelsear Industries
1973 · Robert A. Gale · US

Hunziker
Exhibition space
1960s · Paul Bühlmann · CH

Spectrum Möbel
Furniture
1960 · Teun Teunissen van Manen · NL

Sosiaalihuollon Keskusliitto
Social services
1958 · Olof Eriksson · FI

Deutscher Packungs-Wettbewerb
Packaging competition
1963 · Anonymous · DE

Vallecchi Editore
Publishing
1964 · Bob Noorca/
Unimark International · IT

Stephen Biondi DeCicco
Art studio services
1958 · Charles MacMurray/
Latham Tyler Jensen · US

The Vanier Institute of the Family
Families organization
1969 · John Kobold/
Hiller Rinaldo Associates · CA

L'Opéra de Québec
Opera
1971 · Yvon Laroche,
Pierre-Yves Pelletier · CA

Laboratoire de Cosmétologie Biologique
Cosmetics
1968 · Gilles Fiszman · FR

Manifattura Valle dell'Orco
Plastics
1952 · Egidio Bonfante · IT

Matsuura Kensetu
Construction company
1980 · Kazutoshi Uemoto · JP

Gillette
Safety razors
1969 · Wolfgang Schmittel · DE

Internationale Verkehrsausstellung München
Transport exhibition
1963 · Ernst Ruchay · DE

Renda Priori & Cia.
Foods
1965 · Rafael Rodrigues · BR

Residence Villaferrata
1972 · Renato Romiti/Studio Idea II · IT

Pepsi-Cola International
Beverage
1975 · Richard Hess · US

Storno
Radio technology
1966 · Morten Peetz-Schou,
Bent Danielsen · DK

Sielco
Engineering
1982 · R. Nava, D. Soffientini,
A. Ubertazzi · IT

Costa dei Ciclopi
Restart facility
1977 · Armando Milani · IT

Schweizer Kunstzeitschrift
Art magazine
1950s · Roger-Virgile Geiser · CH

Gebrüder Schellenberg Werbeagentur
Advertising
1950s · Gebrüder Schellenberg
Werbeagentur · CH

La Bottega del Vasaio
Ceramics
1977 · R. Nava, D. Soffientini,
A. Ubertazzi · IT

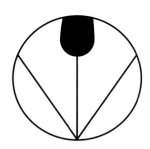

Flora Olomouc
Flower festival
1970s · Jan Rajlich · CZ

Technika
1958 · Jan Rajlich · CZ

Webunion Hohenstein-Ernstthal
Weaving
1965 · Eberhard Richter · DE-GDR

International Telephone and Telegraph Corporation
Telecommunications
1960s · Carl Regehr · US

L'Administration de la Voie Maritime du St. Laurent
Seaway administration
1960s · Gilles Robert · FR

R.W.L. Laidlaw Lumber
1969 · Peter G. Ulmer/
Stewart & Morrison · CA

Fiat Service
Automobile repairs
1962 · Giovanni Brunazzi · IT

Nickelhütte St Egidien
Insulation materials
1965 · Jürgen Henker · DE-GDR

Fundación Compartir
Education
1980 · Dicken Castro · CO

Radio Berlin International
Broadcasting
1965 · Rudolf Grüttner · DE-GDR

Vereinigte Metall-Halbwerkzeuge
Metal tools
1965 · Werner Duda · DE-GDR

Pulex Laboratories
Chemicals
1970s · Robert Hagenhofer · US

Goldschmiede Bausch-Engeln
Goldsmiths
1951 · Walter Breker · DE

Canadian Council on Urban and Regional Research
1963 · Fritz Gottschalk/
Gottschalk+Ash · CA

Fundación Mito Juan Pro-Música
Record label
1969 · Nedo Mion Ferrario · VE

Prices and Incomes Commission
1971 · Rolf Harder/
Design Collaborative · CA

Canadian Film Institute
1962 · Georges Beaupré · CA

Ofen- und Herdbau, Großenhain
Ovens
1965 · Berthold Resch · DE-GDR

Caterplan Services
Food services
1969 · René Demers/
Hiller Rinaldo Associates CA

Brau-und Malz-Union Hadmersleben
Brewing
1965 · Peter Hamann · DE-GDR

Laboratori Cosmochimici
Bandages and ointments
1960s · Walter Ballmer · IT

Pan American Games Society
Sports association
1967 · William Mayrs · CA

Old Mill Towers
Apartment building
1965 · James Donahue/
Cooper & Beatty · CA

Deutsche Medizin-Messe
Medical exhibition
1978 · Michael Herold · DE

Boda Glasbruk Glassworks
1960s · Bertil Andersson-Bertilson · SE

Club de Golf de la Vallée du Richelieu
Golf club
1966 · George Huel · CA

Mount McKinley National Park
1970 · G. Dean Smith · US

Pelican Films
Film production
1960s · S. Neil Fujita · US

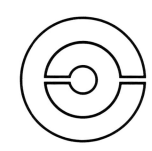

Concordia S.P.R.L.
Insurance
1965 · Antoon de Vijlder · BE

Paseo
Sporting goods
1980 · Reynaldo Da Costa   US

Yosemite National Park
1968 · G. Dean Smith · US

Institute of Art Studies
1950s · Josef Müller-Brockmann · CH

Knitwear Factory
1960s · Willi Sutter · SE

**Hokkaido Nogydantai
Kenkohoken Kumiai**
Insurance
1977 · Katsumi Maetani · JP

AT & T
Telecommunications
1969 · Saul Bass · US

CHIARIFORTI

Chiari & Forti
Foods
1969 · Bob Noorda/
Unimark International · IT

Ota Dental Clinic
1974 · Koichi Watanabe · JP

Car Factory
1960s · Bob Noorda/
Unimark International · IT

Ohio Center
Banquet hall
1975 · Chermayeff & Geismar · US

Drogheria Neri
Pharmacy
1943 · Carlo L. Vivarelli · CH

Color Research Center
1968 · Nakade Teijiro · JP

Tourism Association
1970 · Tomás Vellvé · ES

Institute for Export Control
1960s · Ludvík Feller · CZ

Worldport Corporation
Furniture
1958 · Read Viemeister · US

Sardinhas Coqueiro
Tinned sardines
1958 · Alexandre Wollner · BR

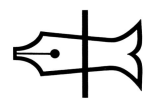

Helmut Fischer
Stationery
1940s · Helmuth Kurtz · CH

Ernst & Co.
Grocery
1940s · Robert Sessler · CH

Zoological Gardens, Asahikawa
1966 · Susumo Endo · JP

Saffa Cartiera
Paper
1966 · Walter Del Frate · IT

The Toledo Museum of Art Bookstore
1978 · Terry Lesniewicz, Al Navarre · US

Internationale Luftfrachtgesellschaft
Air freight
1963 · Erich Unger · DE

Square Grip Reinforcement
Structural steel reinforcement
1960s · Henrion Design Associates · UK

Melli
Gardening equipment
1969 · Veniero Bertolotti/Studio 4 · IT

Aigec
Design
1963 · Aldo Novarese · IT

Sok Cooperative Organization
Furniture fair
1969 · Osmo Omenamäki · FI

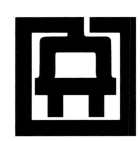

Haushaltstechnik, Berlin
Home appliances
1965 · Dieter Herzschuh · DE-GDR

**Arbeitsgemeinschaft zur Eingliederung
Behinderter in die Volkswirtschaft**
Disabled people's employment training
1960s · Peter Beck · DE

**Schweizerische Zentralstelle
für Flüchtlingshilfe**
Refugee aid agency
1940s · Helmuth Kurtz · CH

Akkumulatorenbau Leipzig
Accumulators
1965 · Horst Hilbert · DE-GDR

Watney Combe Reid & Co.
Brewing
1960s · Milner Gray/
Design Research Unit · UK

L. S. Croth & Co.
Insurance law office
1969 · John S. Brown · CA

Verlag Die Wirtschaft
Publishing
1965 · Herbert Prüget · DE-GDR

Form Mediation International
Design agency
1964 · Pieter Brattinga · NL

Kies- und Kalksandsteinwerk Fahr
Gravel and limestone
1965 · Hans-Dieter Nemitz · DE-GDR

Bouvet Ponsar et Cie
Cement
1966 · Etienne Bucher · FR

Bompiani
Publishing
1965 · Franco M. Ricci · DE

Mar Beach
Watersports club
1960s · Nedo Mion Ferrario · VE

Sigtay
Light-bulbs
1968 · Michel Olyff · BE

Pépiniériste Rosiériste Alfred Etter
Flowers
1960s · Roger-Virgile Geiser CH

Henschel Verlag
Publishing
1965 · Herbert Prüget · DE-GDR

Malik Verlag
Publishing
1925 · George Grosz · DE

Kulturbund Rostock
Cultural alliance
1965 · Helmut-Feliks Büttner · DE-GDR

Ballard, Todd & Snibbe
Architecture
1960s · Rudolph de Harak · US

Associazione Latti Sterilizzati
Association of milk producers
1967 · Sergio Privitera/P&T · IT

Fisons Canada
Insecticides
1965 · Chris Yaneff · CA

Nazareno Gabrielli
Leather goods
1971 · Mimmo Castellano · IT

B. Fischer Buchdruckerei
Printing
1960s · Peter Läderach · CH

Caracas Hilton
Hotel
1968 · Gerd Leufert · VE

Aviso N.V.S.A.
1960s · Benno Wissing · NL

Einkaufszentrum mit vier Geschäften
Shopping center
1984 · Paul Effert · DE

Qualitätssiegel Echt Silber
Silver quality-mark
1974 · Hans Karl Rodenkirchen · DE

La Stabilité
Insurance
1965 · George Huel · CA

European Home Study Council
Distance learning
1966 · Carl Steinherr · NL/SE

Shoe Export
1960s · Per Einar Eggen · NO

**Chemisch-Technische Abteilung
der Bally Schuhfabriken**
Shoe factory technical laboratory
1940s · Celestino Piatti · CH

Hamburger Großdruckerei
Printing
1940s · Gust Hahn · DE

Buchhaus
Bookstore
1965 · Karl Thewalt · DE-GDR

Yoshinofuji
Clothing
1977 · Yasaburo Kuwayama · JP

Olle & Wolter Verlag
Publishing
1978 · Anonymous · DE

Fisons Horticulture
Fertilisers
1960s · Ruth Gill, Roger Philips · UK

**Wasserversorgung und
Abwasserbehandlung**
Water supply and sewage treatment
1965 · Harry Prieß · DE-GDR

National Film Studios of Ireland
1976 · Richard Eckersley · IE

**International Public
Relations Association**
1966 · Hans Kleefeld/
Stewart & Morrison · DE/US

Amfac
Land development
1966 · Clarence Lee · US

Ceramiche Musa
Ceramics
1974 · Alfredo de Santis · IT

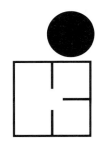

Karol Ike
Photography
1967 · Anonymous · CA

Société Prénatal
Baby products
1966 · Rudi Meyer · FR

Baker Institute
Medical research
1960s · Whale & Emery · AU

Dierig Holding
Textiles
1979 · Rolf Müller · DE

Kuwahara
Automobiles
1981 · Sogen Onishi · JP

Ross Murarka
Publishing
1971 · Sudarshan Dheer · IN

Das Band
Clothing
1960s · M. Rudin · CH

Erfurt-Kfz-Zubehör
Automobile accessories
1965 · Karl-Jürgen Härtel · DE-GDR

Metrocraft
Publishing
1977 · Don Connelly · US

F. & H. Sutcliffe
Construction company
1969 · Gavin Healey/
Healey Mills Associates · UK

The Bellwood Company
Doors
1961 · Joseph Weston · US

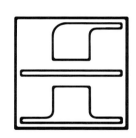

Fristho
Furniture
1960s · Wim Crouwel · NL

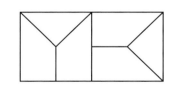

Meerbuscher Künstler
Artists association
1979 · Walter Breker · DE

Spectralite
Signs
1968 · Harry Bowler, Jean Morin/
Girard, Bruce et Associés · CA

Colombian Bags
1978 · Dicken Castro · CO

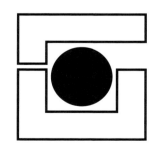

Gudbrandsdalens Uldvarefabrik
Furniture
1960s · Anonymous · NO

A. S. Nicholson & Son
Timber
1965 · Jack Reid/
Hiller Rinaldo Associates · CA

Turnbull Elevator
Elevators
1964 · Bob Anderson/
Hiller Rinaldo Associates · CA

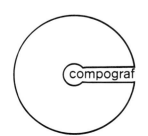

Compograf
Printing
1968 · Giovanni Brunazzi · IT

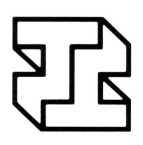

Ikola Design
1979 · Gale William Ikola · US

Nacional de Resinas
Plastics
1978 · Fernando Rión · MX

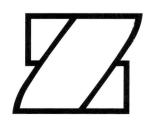

Zinnober Verlag
Publishing
1984 · Jan Buchholz, Peter Albers · DE

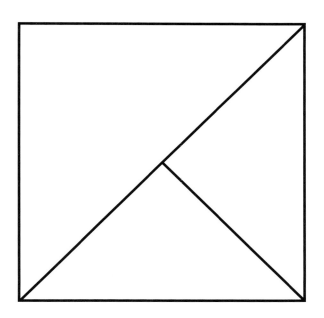

Städtische Kunsthalle Düsseldorf
Art gallery
1967 · Walter Breker · DE

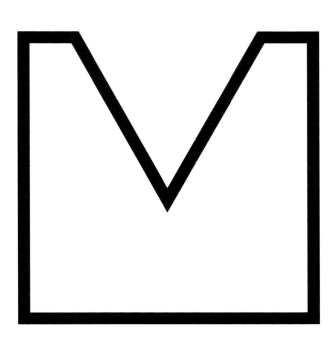

Meplex
Metal goods
1969 · Klaus Hofmann · CH

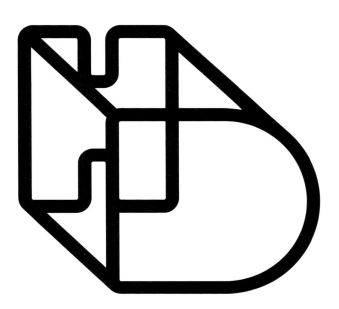

Horacio Durán
Furniture
1971 · Ernesto Lehfeld · MX

Cobat Bautechnik
Engineering
1969 · Sessler & Klein · DE

Rochester Community Savings Bank
1983 · Michael Leidel,
Kathie Burgund · US

Vereinigte Offset-Druckereien
Printing
1966 · Werner Keidel · DE

Centraal Ziekenhuis
Hospital
1966 · Jan Jaring · NL

Collège de Maisonneuve
School
1969 · George Huel,
Pierre-Yves Pelletier · CA

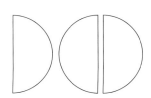

Design Objectives
Product development
1970 · Alan Fletcher/Pentagram · UK

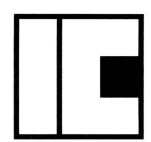

Interchoice Contracting
Construction company
1975 · Angelo Sganzeria · IT

Amorós Hermanos
Advertising film production
1969 · Toni Miserachs,
Mariona Aguirre · ES

Severomoravské
Paper
1983 · Stanislav Kovár · CZ

Yamamoto Balster
1983 · Hiroshi Iseya · JP

Kato Insatu
Printing
1973 · Sumio Hasegawa · JP

Jerome & Norris
Insurance
1966 · David Caplan · UK

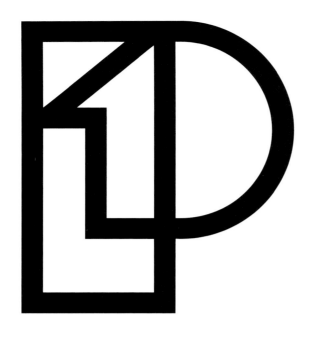

Planning One
Interior design
1979 · Kazuo Kanai · JP

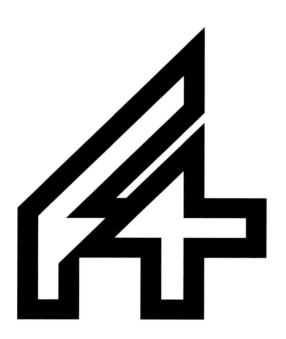

F4 Arquitectos
Architecture
1964 · Joan Pedragosa · ES

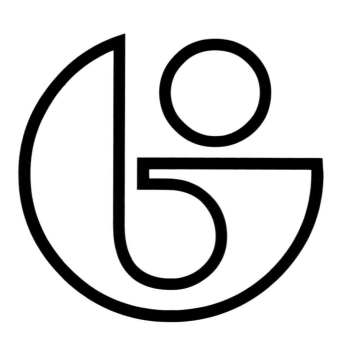

Fundação Bienal de São Paulo
Art foundation
1965 · PVDI · BR

Mowlem
Engineering
1960s · Conran Design Group · UK

Interinca
Design
1978 · Francisco Rendiles Coll · VE

Juracime
Cement
1960s · Paul Bühlmann · CH

Termoraggi
Fuel oil
1968 · Veniero Bertolotti/Studio 4 · IT

Deutscher Arbeiterjugendkongress
Workers youth congress
1965 · Ludwig Bonitz · DE-GDR

Erik Jørgensen Møbelfabrik
Furniture
1960s · Anonymous · DK

Administración Pública
Magazine
1970 · Claude Dietrich · PE

Verde Japan
1983 · Taijiro Nakayama · JP

Anthony Blond
Publishing
1962 · Fletcher, Forbes, Gill · UK

Kuraray
Safety glass
1964 · Tadasu Fukano · JP

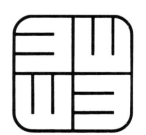

Emme Edizioni
Publishing
1967 · Salvatore Gregorietti/
Unimark International · IT

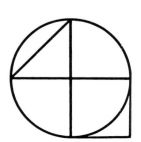

**Technical School of
Advertising and Design**
1965 · Günter Junge · DE-GDR

13th Festival della Moda Maschile
Fashion fair
1963 · Theodoor Manson · IT

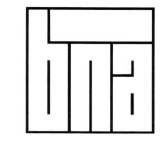

Bond van Nederlandse Architecten
Association of architects
1969 · Otto Treumann · NL

Shipley-Jones Associates
Design
1979 · Richard Wittosch · US

**Eidgenössisches Institut
für Reaktorforschung**
Nuclear research institute
1960s · Walter Bangerter · CH

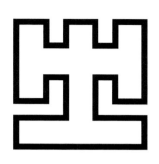

Tamminen & Havaste
Architecture
1969 · Seppo Polameri · FI

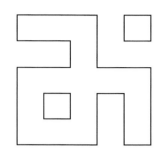

Anivo
Furniture
1967 · Rudolf Verelst · BE

H. Schneider
Ceramics
1969 · Kurt Wirth · CH

Gics Leuchten
Lighting
1969 · Hans Karl Rodenkirchen · DE

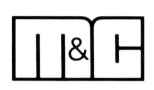

M. & C. Druckerei & Verlag
Printing and publishing
1970s · Ekkehart Rustmeier · DE

Eduard Keller
Import-export
1972 · Hansruedi Scheller · CH

B. Mohamed Badawi
Engineering
1980 · Manfred Wutke · DE

Krimek
CNC machines
1987 · Hans Karl Rodenkirchen · DE

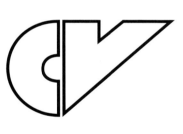

Claudius Verlag
Publishing
1986 · Werner Richter · DE

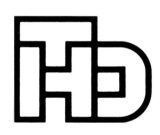

TypeHouse Duragraph
Printing
1982 · Cyril John Schlosser · US

Sye-Hsing
Machinery
1978 · Kao Yu-Lin · TW/JP

Campus Verlag
Publishing
1975 · E. Warminski · DE

Massiv-Heimbau
Construction company
1969 · Peter Riefenstahl · DE

Barbara Farber
Fashion
1971 · Helmut Salden · NL

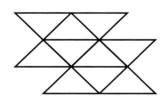

Hong Kong Hilton
Hotel
1960s · Henry Steiner · HK

Lejaby
Clothing
1969 · Charles Roth/
Delpire-Advico · FR

Schweizerische Bodenkreditanstalt
Bank
1962 · Hansruedi Scheller · CH

Oriental System Development
1983 · Kenji Suzuki · JP

Toy Works
Toys
1968 · Ken Garland · UK

Ladan
1973 · Cato Hibberd · AU

Superposition

Überlagerung

Overlay

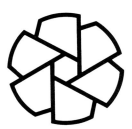

Plüss-Staufer
Chalk
1968 · Hans R. Woodtli · CH

**IUPAC Conference on
Physical Organic Chemistry**
1971 · Gisela Buomberger · CH

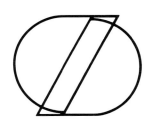

**Instituto de
Orientación en Arte, Caracas**
Art academy
1969 · Nedo Mion Ferrario · VE

Naturkundemuseum Bielefeld
Natural history museum
1967 · Heinz Beier · DE

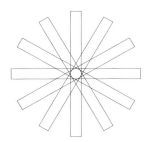

L. Speich
Printing
1957 · Heini Fischer · CH

Unione Mondiale dello Sci Nautico
Sports association
1968 · Giancarlo Iliprandi · IT

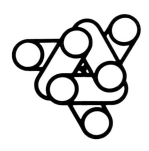

IPI
Prefabricated building parts
1973 · Mimmo Castellano · IT

Systema Leasing
1978 · Manfred Korten · DE

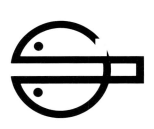

Fischerei Cürten
Fishing
1960s · Klaus Winterhager · DE

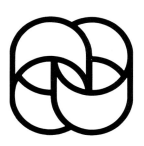

United Paper Mills
1960s · Carl Swann · UK

Swedish Union
1960s · Bertil Andersson-Bertilson · SE

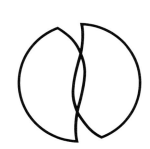

Birrificio Angelo Poretti
Brewing
1960s · Michele Provinciali · IT

Luce Servici Sap
Lighting
1973 · Paola Trucco/Fantastici 4 · IT

Union
Political party
1950s · Heinz Schwabe · DE

Compesca
Fishery
1966 · Alexandre Wollner · BR

Broadbents of Southport
Clothing
1967 · Tony Forster · UK

Japan Six Cities Trade
Exhibition
1971 · Tomoichi Nishiwaki,
Akisato Ueda · JP

Panam Propaganda
Advertising
1959 · Alexandre Wollner · BR

Sierracin Corporation
Aircraft parts
1971 · Thomas Ohmer,
Lou Frimkess · US

Verzekerings Maatschappij
Insurance
1968 · Hartmut Kowalke,
Christine Witt/Total Design · NL

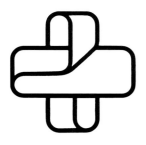

Tosama Domžale
Hygiene products
1977 · Ivan Dvoršak · YU

Iron Trade International
1978 · Luigi Milani · IT

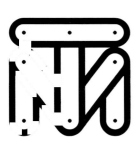

Mobiltecnica
Metal furniture
1967 · Piero Sansoni · IT

M&M
Furniture
1960s · Adolf Flückiger · CH

Security Life
Insurance
1978 · Clive Gaey · BR

Brot & Backwarenfabrik Bergen
Bakers
1965 · Klaus Grosche · DE-GDR

Westinghouse Learning Corporation
Education
1967 · Tom Woodward · US

Molden Seewald
Publishing
1982 · Hans Schaumberger · AT

Zen Environmental Design
1974 · Takenobu Igarashi · JP

Elda
Clothing
1971 · Carla Gard/Delpire-Advico · FR

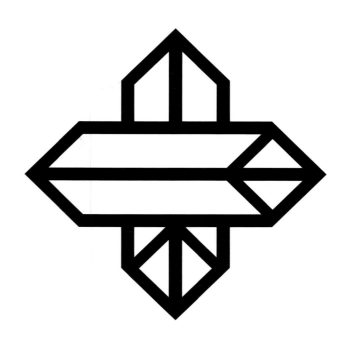

Otto Harberer
Ventilation systems
1940s · Paul Sollberger · CH

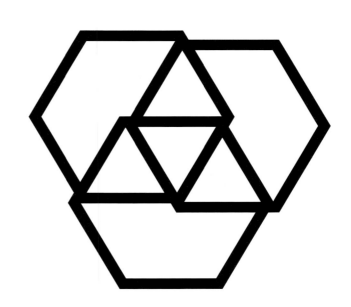

Trelement-Bau
Construction company
1963 · Eberhard G. Rensch · DE

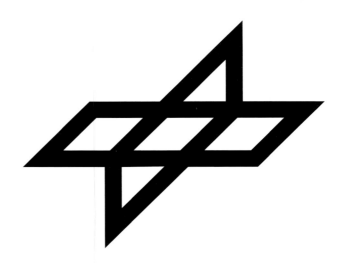

Deutsche Luft und Raumfahrtgesellschaft
German aerospace
1975 · Bruno K. Wiese · DE

Rat des Bezirks Rostock
City council
1965 · Ludwig Bonitz · DE-GDR

Lamper
Metal furniture
1971 · Francesc Guitart · ES

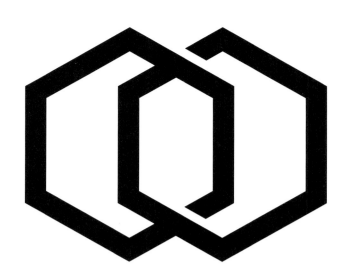

Polska Firma Handlowa
Import-export
1960s · Stephan Śledziński · PL

OKD Konsumverband Solothurn
Foods
1978 · René Bischof · CH

Bunte Stube Ahrenshoop
Ceramics
1965 · Georg Hülsse · DE-GDR

Promociones Immobiliarias
Construction company
1965 · Claude Dietrich · PE

Packaging Design Magazine
1966 · Andrew Kner · US

Metro Sprinkler
Fire extinguishers
1968 · Appelbaum & Curtis · US

Ontario Hydro
Energy supplier
1962 · Allan Robb Fleming · CA

Infor-Información Organizada
Advertising
1970 · Nedo Mion Ferrario · VE

Panorama
Exhibition
1965 · Rudolf Graßmann · DE-GDR

Prospero
Restaurant
1967 · Silvio Coppola · IT

Laboratório Maurício Villela
Pharmaceuticals
1960s · Aloísio Magalhães/PVDI · BR

Deutsches Nährmittelwerk
Foods
1940s · Gust Hahn · DE

Sitos-Werke
Baking powder
1960s · Walter M. Kersting · DE

G. B. Bernini & Figli
Furniture
1965 · Walter Ballmer · CH

Lorenz
Watches
1964 · Piero Ottinetti · IT

Jean-Pierre Lamy
Sunglasses
1967 · Julien van der Wal · CH/FR

Clinica Nuestra Señora de Guadalupe
Hospital
1967 · Gerd Leufert · VE

Werner Quack Verlag
Publishing
1926 · Anonymous · DE

Hermesbank
Bank
1940s · Götz Neuke · DE

Yurdaer Altintaş
Advertising
1960s · Yurdaer Altintaş · TR

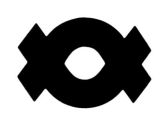

Kansai Electric
Energy supplier
1960s · Shichiro Imatake · JP

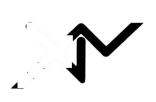

Sala Mendoza
Art gallery
1970 · Manuel Espinoza · VE

Sociedad Bolivariana de Arquitectos
Society of architects
1968 · Gerd Leufert · VE

Petroleum Refinery
1960s · Tadeusz Pietrzyk · PL

Emil Daiber
Picture mounts
1959 · Hanns Lohrer · DE

Cooperativa Central dos Produtores de Açúcar e Alcool do Estado de São Paulo
Sugar and alcohol producers union
1960s · Aloísio Magalhães/PVDI · BR

Valle Alto
Canned foods
1959 · Nedo Mion Ferrario · VE

Blaine Karsten & Deirdre Michael
Wedding commemoration
1976 · Rockford Mjos · US

Stephens Biondi Decicco
Design
1960s · Stephens, Biondi, Decicco · US

Cooperativa Central dos Produtores de Leite do Estado de São Paulo
Milk producers union
1960s · Aloísio Magalhães/PVDI · BR

Westel
Television recording systems
1966 · G. Dean Smith · US

Editorial Arte
Printing
1967 · John Lange · VE

Instituto Nacional de Cultura y Bellas Artes
Cultural institute
1965 · Gerd Leufert · VE

Laplante et Langevin
Printing
1968 · Pierre-Yves Pelletier · CA

Suomen Akateeminen Urheiluliitto
Sports association
1969 · Jukka Veistola, Tapio Korpisaari, Antti Laiho/Sok · FI

Vaccari Zincografica
Printing
1970 · Ivan Vaccari · IT

Osuuskunta Villakunta
Textiles
1965 · Jukka Pellinen · FI

Suomen Säästöpankkiliitto
Bank
1968 · Matti Viherjuuri/
Markkinointi Viherjuuri · FI

Chiswell Wire Company
Wire products
1960s · Peter Wildbur · UK

F. Lorenz Handweberei und Textilien
Textiles
1940s · Kurt Wirth · CH

Swedish Consumers Cooperative
1967 · Björn Petersson, Paul
Persson/Annonsbyrån Svea · SE

Animex
Import-export
1962 · Leon Urbanski · PL

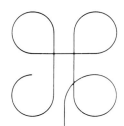

Club Hanataba
Nightclub
1956 · Takeshi Otaka · JP

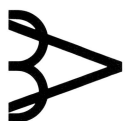

Ateneo de Bocoró
Cultural association
1963 · Nedo Mion Ferrario · VE

Burlington Industries
Textiles
1964 · Chermayeff & Geismar · US

Theodor Blitz Wäschefabrik
Lingerie
1965 · Fritz Bonß · DE-GDR

Tikkaustuote
Textiles
1966 · Rolf Christianscn · FI

H. O. Persiehl
Printing
1932 · Anonymous · DE

Goldmann Cegos
Trading center
1969 · Carlo Bruni · IT

Telespazio
Space technology
1967 · Sergio Ruffolo · IT

KMC
Publishing
1969 · Jiří Rathouský · CZ

Armaturenwerk
Fittings
1965 · Henry Siebert · DE-GDR

Pramassolwerk
Chemicals
1965 · Walter Seifert · DE-GDR

The Empire Life Assurance Company
Insurance
1968 · James D. Taylor/
Rous & Mann Press · CA

Olivetti Elea 9003
Electronics
1960s · Ettore Sottsass · IT

Vie Design Studios
1950 · Read Viemeister,
J. Budd Steinhilber · US

Bank of Yokohama
1956 · Yoshio Hayashi · JP

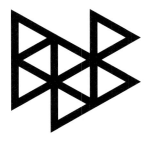

Burkhardt Buchdruck
Printing
1962 · Hans Hartmann · CH

Arthur Jäger
Clothing
1965 · Karl-Jürgen Härtel · DE-GDR

**Ministerium für Handel
und Versorgung Arkalaine**
Trade association
1965 · Ingo Arnold · DE-GDR

Unión de Centros de la Edificación
Urban engineering
1968 · José Baqués · ES

Werres & Geuertz
Rental cars
1954 · Hans Karl Rodenkirchen · DE

Henry S. Miller
Real estate
1967 · Crawford Dunn · US

The East Ohio Gas Company
Gas supplier
1960s · Lester Beall · US

Unibanco
Bank
1964 · PVDI · BR

Wilhelm Schröder Buchdruckerei
Printing
1954 · Hans Karl Rodenkirchen · DE

**Association Grands et
Jeunes d'Aujourd'hui**
Artists association
1971 · Pham Ngoc Tuan · FR

Prolansa
Wire products
1969 · Claude Dietrich · PE

Wirkmaschinenbau Apolda
Engineering
1965 · Fritz Deutschendorf · DE-GDR

Wel-tex
Textiles
1970 · Franciszek Winiarski · PL

Administración y Proyectos
Investment
1969 · Ribas & Creus · ES

Toyo Rayon
Synthetic fibers
1960s · Yoshitaro Isaka,
Keiko Takemura · JP

International Geomarine Corporation
Offshore mining
1967 · Detlef Hallerbach · US

Architekturbüro Hans Bosshard
Architecture
1977 · Odermatt+Tissi · CH

Wacoal Corporation
1977 · Landor Associates · US

Casa de la Amistad
Social organization
1978 · Félix Beltrán · CU

PGH Harzer
Clothing
1965 · Horst Jacob · DE-GDR

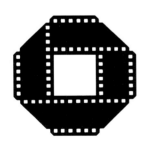

Cinema of the University of California
1971 · Harry Murphy, Bud Thon/
Harry Murphy & Friends · US

Percy Haynes & Co.
Stationery
1960s · Fletcher, Forbes, Gill · UK

National Arts Centre, Ottawa
1967 · Ernst Roch/
Design Collaborative · CA

**Empetur Empresa de
Turismo de Pernambuco**
Travel agency
1968 · Joaquim Redig · BR

Cooperative Kopernik
Metalworks
1965 · Wladyslaw Brykczynski · PL

International Leather Workers Union
1971 · Ann Crews · US

Perfect Bindery
Bookbinding
1960s · Aero Press · US

Stella-Meta Filters
Water filtration
1972 · Tor A. Pettersen/
Lock Pettersen · UK

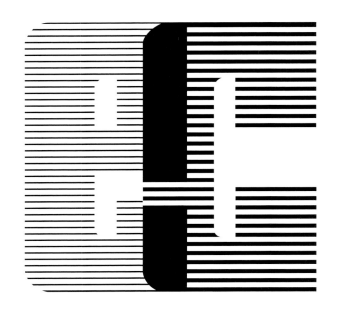

Eurocheque
Banking
1968 · Heinz Schwabe · DE

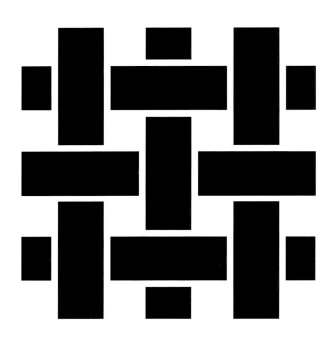

Jack Lenor Larsen
Textiles
1962 · James S. Ward, Arnold Saks · US

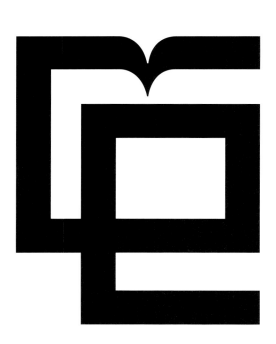

National Economics Editions
Publishing
1966 · Franciszek Winiarski · PL

Lausitzglas Weißwasser
Glass
1965 · Gretel Salomo · DE-GDR

Österreichischer Gewerbeverlag
Publishing
1948 · Anonymous · AT

Sørliemøbler
Furniture
1960s · Anonymous · NO

Studio per Industria Tessuti
Textile design
1960s · M. Schneider/Studio Boggeri · IT

**Industrial and Commercial
Property Construction**
1976 · Charlotte Potts · US

Hanf- und Leinenverkaufsgesellschaft
Hemp and linen
1940s · Hermann Eidenbenz · CH

KUED Channel 7 PBS, Utah
Broadcasting
1976 · Michael Richards,
Allen Loyborg · US

Nakladatelstvi Svoboda
Publishing
1968 · Jiří Rathouský · CZ

Colecciones Venezolanas
Art exhibition
1969 · Manuel Espinoza · VE

Cooperative Walter
Textiles
1968 · Wladyslaw Brykczynski · PL

Società Pubblicità Editoriale
Advertising
1982 · Giancarlo Iliprandi · IT

Diseñadores Comerciales
Design
1963 · Amand Domènech · ES

Transport Handelsgesellschaft
Transportation
1965 · Herbert Prüget · DE-GDR

Weißensee Maschinenbau
Engineering
1965 · Horst Jacob · DE-GDR

Tapeten-Ring
Wallpaper manufacturers
trade association
1972 · Siegfried W. Küchler · DE

Tekniska Verken
Electronics
1970 · Ove Engström · SE

GB
Vinyl production
1960s · Jiří Rathouský · CZ

Editions René Julliard
Publishing
1957 · Marcel Jacno · FR

Pattloch Verlag
Publishing
1976 · Klaus Imhoff · DE

Pentamarmi
Marble quarries
1972 · Mimmo Castellano · IT

GS Eisengießerei
Iron foundry
1970s · Heiko Groschke · DE

Kristjan Kristjansson
Design
1960 · Kristjan Kristjansson · IS

Urbanistico Territoriale
Urban development
1970 · Michele Spera · IT

C.O.N.I.
National Olympic committee
1970 · Mimmo Castellano · IT

Toninelli
Art gallery
1960s · Erberto Carboni · IT

Argo Lumber
Building materials
1968 · Ron Richards · CA

Aldus Books
Publishing
1966 · Romek Marber · UK

Boffi
Interior fittings
1971 · Mimmo Castellano · IT

Centre National des Arts
Theater
1969 · Raymond Bellemare · CA

Robin Tuff Associates
Security services
1970 · Leslie Smart · CA

British Aluminium
1959 · Abram Games · UK

Shearson Hammill
Investment
1963 · Philip Gips/Gips & Danne · US

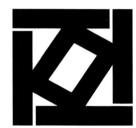

Hotel Ambasador, Opatija
1965 · Grega Košak · YU

Lucassen
Furniture
1967 · Tel Design Associated · NL

Canada Wire and Cable Company
Cabling
1969 · René Demers/
Hiller Rinaldo Associates · CA

Crédit Agricole
Bank
1969 · Raymond Gid · FR

Positiv/
Negatif

Positiv/
Negativ

Positive/
Negative

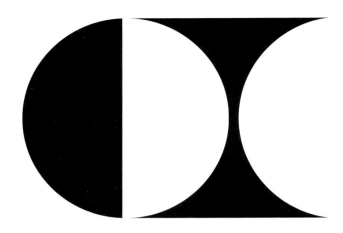

Polar International Brokerage
Investment
1962 · Eckstein-Stone · US

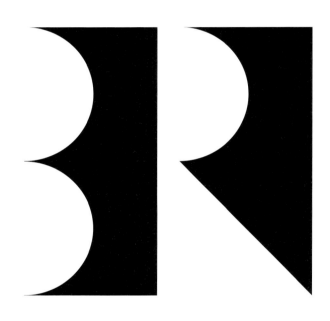

Bayerischer Rundfunk
Broadcasting
1962 · Richard Roth · DE

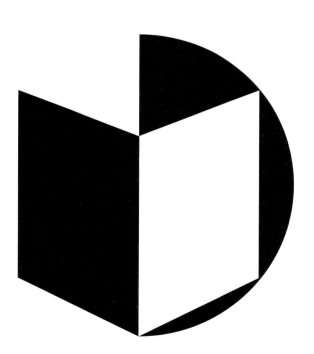

Openbare Bibliotheek
Public library
1958 · Ralph Prins · NL

Promociones Pando
Construction company
1981 · Elías García Benavides · ES

Yamamura Senkaku
Leather dyeing
1980 · Kuniharu Masubuchi,
Ikuo Masubuchi · JP

Untergrundbahn
Public transport (proposed design)
1960s · Hans Weckerle · DE

Ditta Commerciale
1960s · Aldo Novarese · IT

Nihon LCA
Management consultancy
1983 · Akira Hirata, Koji Mori,
Namiko Nishida · JP

Plattenspielerwerk Delphin
Turntables
1965 · Wolfgang Kroh · DE-GDR

Fritz Steck
1950s · Eugen & Max Lenz · CH

Xerca
Publishing
1969 · Rémy Peignot · FR

Mantelbeton-Isolierschalung
Cement
1960s · Hans-Joachim Brauer · DE

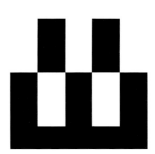

Wallace & Hess Studio
Design
1962 · Hess & Antupit · US

DIMAC
Mexican designers association
1972 · Ernesto Lehfeld · MX

François Engel
Photography
1968 · Philippe Gentil · FR

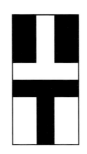

Truninger Kopiermaschinen
Photocopiers
1966 · Gisela Buomberger · CH

ID
Office furniture
1964 · Ina Kershen · US

Centrade Bank
1970 · Eugen & Max Lenz · CH

Autogarage Anderegg
Automobile garage
1950s · Karl J. Weiss · CH

F.lli Dioguardi
Construction company
1963 · Mimmo Castellano · IT

Pflanzenfettkombinat Velten
Foods
1965 · Conrad Priem · DE-GDR

Bero-Kaffee & Extrakt
Coffee
1965 · Otto Kietzmann · DE-GDR

Chance Vought Aircraft
Aircraft technology
1960s · Lester Beall · US

Galería 22
Art gallery
1968 · Gerd Leufert · VE

Davis Delany
Printing
1960s · A. Ross, B. Thompson · US

Neckermann
Mail-order (proposed design)
1960s · Robert Berndt · DE

Fiedler Fabrics
1960s · Anonymous · DK

Fairfield & Dubois
Architecture
1971 · Hans Kleefeld/
Stewart & Morrison · CA

IW
1960s · M. Schneider/
Studio Boggeri · IT

Western Gypsum
Building materials
1960s · Lester Beall · US

Nieswand Verlag
Publishing
1986 · Anonymous · DE

Kartonagefabrik
Packaging materials
1950s · Gust Hahn · DE

CKG
Real estate
1975 · Masatoshi Shimokawa · JP

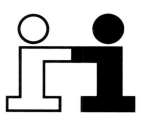

Ideal Lebensversicherung
Insurance
1963 · Erich Unger · DE

Schiffini
Kitchens
1964 · Ennio Lucini · IT

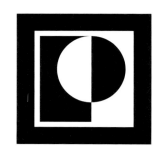

Primistères
Grocery
1970 · Lonsdale Design · FR

Stahl für die Welt von Morgen
Steel congress
1965 · Anonymous · DE

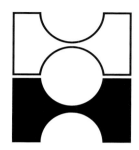

Hans Hesse
Architecture
1968 · M. van Winsen · NL

Novamedical
Pharmacy
1964 · Piero Sansoni · IT

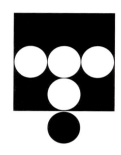

Tosho
Printing
1968 · Mitsuo Katsui · JP

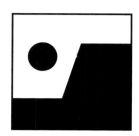

Tekstil-Opplysning
Textiles
1967 · Per Einar Eggen/
Alfsen, Becker & Bates · NO

Batterien- und Elementefabrik Tabarz
Batteries
1965 · Martin Rosette · DE-GDR

Fiol-Biblioteket
Book series
1966 · Morten Peetz-Schou,
Bent Danielsen · DK

Melnor Industries
Gardening equipment
1964 · Stanley Eisenman,
David Enock · US

Inco International Consultants
Advertising
1968 · Hans Lambach · DE

**Mecklenburgische
Getränke- und Konservenfabrik**
Beverages and canning
1965 · Heinz Kippnick · DE-GDR

Escuela de Diseño, Mexico
Design school
1970 · Lance Wyman · US

Holzgroßhandel Stenicka
Wholesalers
1960 · Hans-Joachim Brauer · DE

Staff & Schwarz Leuchtenwerk
Lighting
1965 · Anonymous · DE

FG Papiergroßhandlung
Paper
1950 · Heinz Hadem · DE

Foire Internationale de Bruxelles
Trade fair
1965 · Luc Van Malderen · BE

Arkana-Verlag
Publishing
1970 · Rolf Arnold · DE

**Vereinigung Selbstständiger
Augenoptikermeister**
Opticians association
1970s · Anonymous · DE

Packungswerk Hamburg
Packaging
1963 · Philipp Karl Seitz · DE

Minnesota Mutual Life
Insurance
1977 · Peter Seitz, Hideki Yamamoto · US

Osang Verlag
Publishing
1979 · Hugo Ballon · DE

Express Forwarding and Storage
Postal services
1957 · Fischer-Nosbisch · DE

Reynaldo Da Costa
Design
1966 · Reynaldo Da Costa · VE

Vär-Sas
Plastics
1979 · István Szekeres · HU

Hasegawa Interior
Interior design
1974 · Akisato Ueda · JP

Ferrero Süsswaren
Confectionery (proposed design)
1960s · Eugen & Max Lenz · CH

Axel Juncker Verlag
Publishing
1958 · Herbert Stengel · DE

Kollar Heinz
Brokers
1975 · James Lienhart · US

**Asociación de
Industriales de Artes Gráficas**
Printers union
1968 · Gerd Leufert · VE

Harrison Wholesale Company
1967 · H. B. Smith, Franz Altschuler · US

Peninsula Brokers
Real estate
1982 · Alvin Joe · US

Jakob Lauri
Photo supplies
1960 · Therese Aeschberger-Sollberg/
Atelier Eduard Weber · CH

Canada Trust
Bank
1971 · Manfred Gotthans,
Chris Yaneff · CA

Kurt Peyer
Real estate
1976 · Jost Hochuli · CH

Svensk Bilprovning
Automobile safety tests
1966 · Lars Bramberg · SE

Tokyo Central Museum
1971 · Kazumasa Nagai · JP

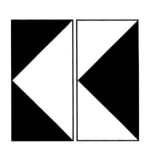

Kossuth Könykiadó
Publishing
1969 · Judit Erdélyi · HU

Petrochemia
Chemicals
1960s · Wladyslaw Brykczynski · PL

Bill Rolle & Associates
Public relations
1978 · Pat Taylor · US

Hala Mirowska
Department store
1964 · Roman Duszek · PL

Pour une entreprise, une institution, une exposition ou un événement, un bon insigne peut devenir un signe de reconnaissance très efficace qui rend superflue toute autre forme d'explication écrite. Seule condition : l'insigne doit être simple, il doit porter en lui le symbole évident du sujet ou de l'objet, et sa forme doit être facile à lire et à retenir.
Josef Müller-Brockmann

Ein gutes Signet kann für eine Firma, Institution, Ausstellung oder Veranstaltung ein sehr wirkungsvolles Kennzeichen sein, das jede weitere textliche Erklärung überflüssig macht. Einzige Voraussetzung: Das Signet muss einfach sein, das zwingende Sinnbild des Themas oder Gegenstandes in sich tragen und seine Form muss leicht zu erfassen und einprägsam sein.
Josef Müller-Brockmann

A good logo can be a very effective trademark for a company, institution, exhibition or event, making any further written explanation superfluous. The logo must be simple and must embody a forceful representation of the subject or object, and its shape must be memorable and easy to understand.
Josef Müller-Brockmann

Notec
Linen
1966 · Emilia Nozka-Paprocka · PL

Lindell
Art supplies
1959 · Inkeri Vallioja · FI

Old
Photolithography
1969 · Walter Del Frate · IT

Aerlod Teoranta
Airline
1960s · Richard Geiger/Signa · IE

Dřevokombinát
Timber
1969 · František Bobáň · CZ

Stadt Neuhausen am Rheinfall
City identity
1971 · Peter G. Ulmer · CH

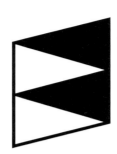

Wirtschaft und Werbung
Publishing
1950s · Anonymous · DE

Antonio Corona
Photocopiers
1964 · Carmelc Cremonesi/
Stile-Advertising · IT

Jugoslovenski Institut za Urbanizam
Urban planning
1969 · Nenad Novakov · YU

Asturquimica
Chemicals
1974 · José Santamarina/
Elias & Santamarina · ES

Mobília Contemporanea
Furniture
1964 · Willys de Castro · BR

Petrochemia
Petroleum refinery
1960s · Jerzy Cherka · PL

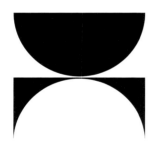

Vega
Optical products
1964 · Meta Vrhunc · YU

Nichi Foods
Restaurant
1979 · Kazumasa Nagai · JP

Union des Moulins à Huile de Provence
Vegetable oil manufacturers union
1964 · Design Groupe Viaud · FR

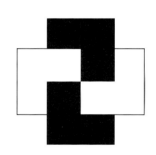

Tage Poulsens Møbelsnedkeri
Furniture
1960s · Anonymous · DK

Interplan
Interior design
1964 · James Lienhart/RVI Corp. · US

Konishiroku Photo Industry
Photographic equipment
1973 · Kazumasa Nagai · JP

Kurt Versen
Lighting
1963 · Rudolph de Harak · US

Mitsui Knowledge Industry
Communications
1971 · Gan Hosoya · JP

**Venezuelan Pavilion,
Expo '64-'65, New York**
World's fair stand
1964 · Gerd Leufert · VE

Maebara Coating
1983 · Yasaburo Kuwayama · JP

Montarbo Elettronica
Acoustic devices
1970 · Walter Hergenröther · CH

Werkzeugmaschinenwerke, Chemntz
Machine tools
1965 · Wolfgang Hoepfner · DE-3DR

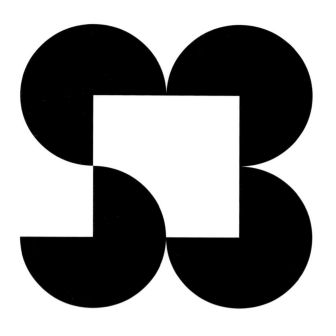

Sandra Berler
Photography gallery
1970s · Lance Wyman · US

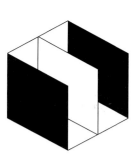

Ed Toyda
Real estate
1972 · Francesc Guitart · ES

Republika
Foods
1960s · Dotscho Dotschev · BG

Gebrüder Sulzer
Metal casting
1960s · H. Spiegelberg · CH

Union of Oil and Soap Industries
Trade union
1960s · Kantcho Kanev · BG

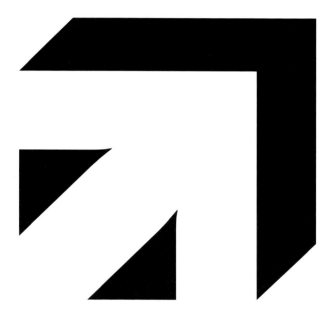

Berlin Display Studios
Interior design
1970 · Jürgen Naurath, Ulrich Rechner · DE

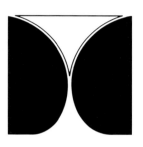

Cafeteria
1969 · José Santamarina/
Elias & Santamarina · ES

Khourie & Lawrence Associates
Interior design
1968 · Bill Hyde · US

Schnitt- & Formenbau Berlin
Construction company
1965 · Rudolf Graßmann · DE-GDR

Pacesetter Bank
1970 · James Lienhart · US

Bay State Abrasives
Bonded abrasive products
1960s · Malcolm Grear · US

Enric Graells
Architecture
1971 · Francesc Guitart · ES

Circolo Nautico Imperia
Yacht club
1972 · Giovanni Brunazzi · IT

Comsip Automation
Electronics
1969 · Jacques Nathan-Garamond · FR

Japanese Film Festival
1960s · Gerd Leufert · VE

Boris Fehrmann
Photography
1960s · Jaska Hänninen · FI

**Vyzkumny Ustav
Agrochemickej Technologie**
Chemicals
1968 · František Bobáň · CZ

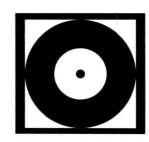

Deutscher Schallplattenclub
Record label
1961 · Wolf D. Zimmermann · DE

Women's Magazine
1969 · Shigeo Fukuda · JP

K. Thienemanns
Publishing
1973 · Ernst Strom · DE

Leipziger Wollkämmerei
Weaving
1965 · Ruth Weber · DE-GDR

Galanteria Drewna
Toys
1967 · Emilia Nozka-Paprocka · PL

Isofarm
Pharmacy
1969 · G. & R. Associati · IT

Staatsbad Bad Elster
Health resort
1965 · Karl Thewalt · DE-GDR

Kaanapali Beach
Whale-spotting
1964 · Ken Parkhurst · US

Opolanka
Clothing
1965 · Roman Duszek · PL

Nurmen Konepaja
Metal goods
1968 · Kyösti Varis · FI

Lanificio di Somma
Wool
1963 · Aldo Calabresi/Studio Boggeri · IT

Zenhanren
Agriculture
1967 · Yoshio Hayashi · JP

Magyar Munkásmozgalmi Múzeum
Museum
1969 · Gábor Papp · HU

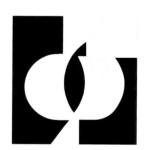

Jiří Rathouský
Design
1960s · Jiří Rathouský · CZ

Refolit
Printing
1970 · Gerd Leufert · VE

First National City Bank
1970 · Studio González Ruiz &
Shakespear · AR

Melka
Clothing
1958 · Olle Eksell · SE

Gulf States Chemicals
1980 · Tracy Turner · US

Early Bird
1983 · Shigo Suzuki, Shigo
Yamaguchi, Masaki Furuta · JP

Richard Hühnerkopf
Liquors
1973 · Heinz Schwabe · DE

Central Lutheran Church
1988 · Peter Seitz · US

Eidgenössisches Sängerfest 1973
Music festival
1959 · Odermatt+Tissi · CH

**Ausstellung Internationale
Gebrauchsgraphik 1948**
Design exhibition
1948 · Jupp Ernst · DE

Lebensversicherungen
Insurance
1950s · Heinz Schwabe · DE

Forschervereinigung
Researchers association
1950 · Walther Bergmann · DE

**Nahrungs- und
Genußmittelbetrieb, Halberstadt**
Foods
1965 · Peter Hamann · DE-GDR

Nederlandse Stichting voor Statistiek
Statistics office
1969 · Tel Design Associated · NL

Møbelprodusentenes Landsforening
Furniture
1968 · Paul Brand · NO

Universidad Provincial de Mar del Plata
University
1968 · Ricardo Blanco · AR

Girl Scouts of the USA
1978 · Saul Bass, Art Goodman/
Bass-Yager Associates · US

High Park Physiotherapy Clinic
1968 · Carl Brett/
Hiller Rinaldo Associates · CA

PGH Wasseraufbereitung
Water treatment
1965 · Johannes Brase · DE-GDR

Werbeagentur Maier
Advertising
1965 · Anonymous · CH

**Canadian Association
for Retarded Childen**
1960s · Rolf Harder · CA

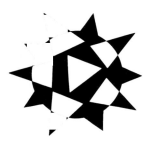

Goldene Kastanie
Packaging design
1965 · Jan Hollender · PL

The Canadian Conference of the Arts
1968 · Carl Brett/
Hiller Rinaldo Associates · CA

Pacifica Foundation
Broadcasting
1964 · James Cross · US

Fischverarbeitungsmaschinenbau
Fish processing machinery
1965 · Georg Hülsse · DE-GDR

Russell & Hinrichs
Design
1966 · Tony Russell, Kit Hinrichs · US

Ingram
Paper
1967 · James Cross · US

Dolphin
Book series
1960s · George Giusti · US

Sukuwall Kojimachi
Hotel
1988 · Shigeo Fukuda · JP

Yokota
Silk products
1967 · Takeshi Otaka · JP

Thomas & Kurzberg
Printing
1950s · Jupp Ernst · DE

Katsuyama Bowling Center
1971 · Gan Hosoya · JP

Ind Coope
Brewing
1950s · Abram Games · UK

De Ploeg

1964 · Teun Teunissen van Manen · NL

Teun Teunissen van Manen
(1918–2001) was a Dutch
industrial and graphic designer.
His earliest success came in
the 1950s with his designs
for the homeware manufacturers
Mepal. From 1964 onwards
he was in-house designer for
the textile producer De Ploeg.
He spent much of his later
career teaching and headed the
department of applied graphic
communication at the Dusseldorf
School of Art. He also lectured
at the polytechnic in the same
German city and at the Gerrit
Rietveld Academie in Amsterdam.

Teun Teunissen van Manen
(1918–2001) war ein niederlän-
discher Industrie- und Grafikdesigner. Seine ersten Erfolge
feierte er in den 1950er-Jahren
mit Entwürfen für den Haushalts-
warenhersteller Mepal. Von 1964
an war er der Hausgrafiker des
Stoffeherstellers De Ploeg. Seine
spätere Karriere ist vor allem von
Lehrtätigkeiten geprägt, so leitete
er die Klasse für angewandte
Grafik an der Kunstakademie
Düsseldorf und war an der Fachhochschule Düsseldorf sowie an
der Gerrit Rietveld Academie
in Amsterdam als Dozent tätig.

Teun Teunissen van Manen
(1918–2001) était un graphiste
et designer industriel hollandais.
Il connaît ses premiers succès
dans les années 1950 avec les
projets qu'il réalise pour le producteur d'articles domestiques Mepal.
À partir de 1964, il est le graphiste
attitré du fabricant de tissus De
Ploeg. Sa carrière tardive a surtout
été marquée par son activité
d'enseignant : il a dirigé un cours
de graphisme appliqué à l'École
des Beaux-Arts de Düsseldorf et
enseigné à la Fachhochschule de
Düsseldorf – ainsi qu'à la Gerrit
Rietveld Academie, à Amsterdam.

The textile manufacturer De Ploeg (which
means "the community") was founded in 1923
in the Dutch town of Bergeijk. In the early years
it produced towels and other household textiles.
After World War II, curtain and upholstery
fabrics became the firm's most successful products. The designer Teun Teunissen van Manen
was appointed in the late 1950s to create a top-
quality corporate image for De Ploeg. He produced a highly appropriate trademark that could
be the focal point of any kind of communication.
In 1968 he published a manual explaining his
whole design concept and describing in detail his
use of color and typography in his work for the
textile company. For decades afterwards, the book
became required reading for new generations
of designers.

Bereits 1923 wurde unter dem Namen De Ploeg
(übersetzt: „Die Gemeinschaft") im niederländischen Bergeijk eine Weberei gegründet, die in
den Anfangsjahren vor allem Handtücher und
andere Gebrauchsstoffe herstellte. Nach dem
Krieg wurden dekorative Entwürfe für Vorhänge
und Möbelbezüge zum Erfolgsprodukt des
Unternehmens. Der Gestalter Teun Teunissen
van Manen wurde Ende der 1950er-Jahre
engagiert, um für das Unternehmen einen
professionellen visuellen Auftritt zu entwickeln.
Er entwarf ein wohldurchdachtes Markenzeichen,
das im Mittelpunkt sämtlicher Medien stehen
sollte. In einem umfangreichen Manual mani-
festierte er 1968 das gesamte Designkonzept
für den Stoffhersteller und definierte Farb- und
Typografieanwendungen im Detail. Das Buch
diente zahlreichen nachfolgenden Gestaltern
über Jahrzehnte als Richtlinie.

Dès 1923, un tissage était fondé sous le nom
De Ploeg (« La Communauté ») à Bergeijk,
aux Pays-Bas. Pendant ses premières années
d'activités, l'entreprise produisit principalement
des serviettes et autres tissus utilitaires. Après
la guerre, des créations de rideaux et de tissus
d'ameublement décoratifs devinrent ses produits
phares. À la fin des années 1950, le créateur
Teun Teunissen van Manen fut chargé de développer une identité visuelle professionnelle
pour l'entreprise. Il conçut un logo soigneusement pensé qui devait être au centre de tous les
médias. En 1968, il exposa l'intégralité du graphisme conçu pour le producteur de tissu dans
un volumineux manuel décrivant en détail l'utilisation des couleurs et de la typo. Pendant des
décennies, ce livre servira de ligne directrice
à de nombreux créateurs.

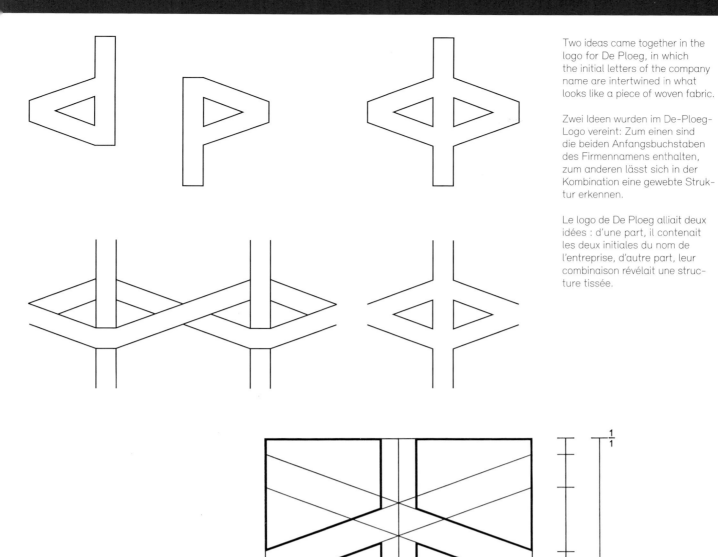

Two ideas came together in the logo for De Ploeg, in which the initial letters of the company name are intertwined in what looks like a piece of woven fabric.

Zwei Ideen wurden im De-Ploeg-Logo vereint: Zum einen sind die beiden Anfangsbuchstaben des Firmennamens enthalten, zum anderen lässt sich in der Kombination eine gewebte Struktur erkennen.

Le logo de De Ploeg alliait deux idées : d'une part, il contenait les deux initiales du nom de l'entreprise, d'autre part, leur combinaison révélait une structure tissée.

As the logo multiplies, the woven effect is strengthened. The pattern became an important part of the company's visual image.

Der Effekt einer gewebten Struktur wird durch die Vervielfachung des Logos noch einmal verstärkt. Das Muster wurde zu einem wichtigen Gestaltungselement im visuellen Auftritt des Stoffeherstellers.

L'effet de structure tissée est encore renforcé par la multiplication du logo. Ce motif devint un élément graphique important de l'identité visuelle du fabricant textile.

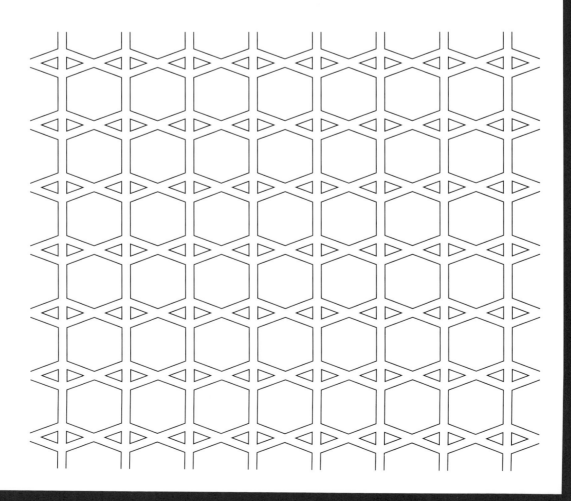

The pattern created by combining the logo with bright colors
became a predominant feature
of all De Ploeg's communications.
It was crucial for the company
to have a strong brand image since
the design was used to advertise
a wide range of textiles.

Ein Muster, das sich aus der
Kombination von Logo und
klaren Farben ergab, wurde zum
dominierenden Element in der
Unternehmenskommunikation
von De Ploeg. Da das Design oft
in Verbindung mit unterschied-
lichsten Stoffmustern eingesetzt
wurde, war eine derart markante
Präsenz wichtig.

Le logo associé à des couleurs
franches et utilisé comme motif
a été l'élément prédominant
des présentations de De Ploeg.
Le design étant souvent utilisé
avec les motifs textiles les plus
divers, sa forte prépondérance
a joué un rôle de premier plan.

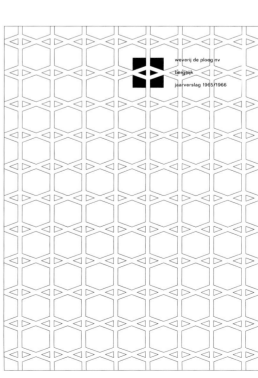

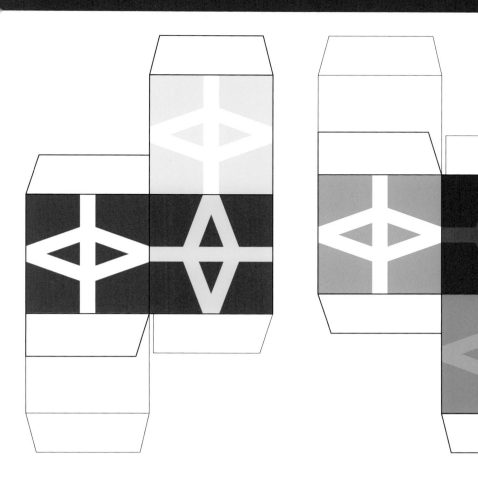

ploegstoffen
projektstoffen

Stokke & Blindheim Möbelfabrikk
Furniture
1965 · Paul Brand · NO

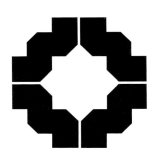

Minerali e Metalli
Import-export
1969 · Renato Romiti/Studio Idea II · IT

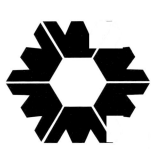

Stadt Wulfen
City identity
1970s · Hanns Lohrer · DE

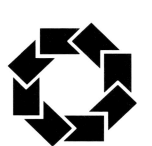

Furness Holding
1968 · Ben Bos · NL

Precision Tools
1970 · Ernst Roch/
Design Collaborative · CA

Marché International de Rungis
Market halls
1967 · André Chante/
Hollenstein Création · FR

Klöckner
Metal
1954 · Jupp Ernst · DE

ISLO
Aluminum foundry
1978 · Ernesto Lehfeld · MX

Traders International
1979 · Azar Khosrovi-Ivorsohk · US

Honeywell Europe
Electronics
1983 · Gavin Healey · UK

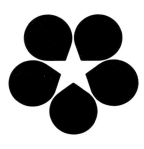

**United States Air Force
Office of Information**
1969 · G. Dean Smith · US

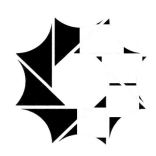

Ontario Pavilion, Expo '67, Montreal
World's fair stand
1967 · Hans Kleefeld/
Stewart & Morrison · CA

Art Council, San Diego State University
1979 · Allan W. Miller · US

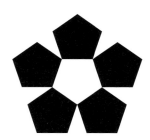

Mas
Cosmetics
1969 · Pérez Sánchez · ES

Kamas Industri
Agricultural machinery
1964 · Allan Jungbeck · SE

Europa Lack
Paint
1970s · J. A. Schürmann · DE

Saitama Bank
1973 · Kazumasa Nagai · JP

Torin Corporation
Metal-forming machinery
1968 · Heiner Hegemann/
Chermayeff & Geismar · US

Le Nordet
Theater
1971 · Raymond Bellemare · CA

Chase Manhattan Bank
1960s · Tom Geismar/
Chermayeff & Geismar · US

Concretex Engenharia de Concreto
Concrete
1973 · João Carlos Cauduro,
Ludovico Antonio Martino · BR

Psychographic Marketing Panels
Research institute
1971 · Donald Crews · US

Ready Rent-All Systems
Rental services
1968 · Arnold Saks · US

Italian Association for Family Therapy
1980 · Sandra Holt · IT

Mochiya
Bakery
1960s · Susumu Kimura · JP

Superband
Engineering
1973 · R. Nava, D. Soffientini,
G. Romani, A. Ubertazzi · IT

Agrisystem
Agriculture
1979 · R. Nava, D. Soffientini,
G. Romani, A. Ubertazzi · IT

Vetreria di Vernante
Glass
1964 · Till Neuburg · IT/CH

Transammonia
Chemicals
1969 · Arnold Saks · US

Bankers Trust of Columbia
1980s · Michael Vanderbyl · US

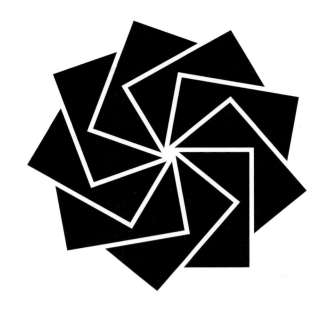

Gooische Glas- en Verfhandel
Craft supplies
1967 · Ben Bos/Total Design · NL

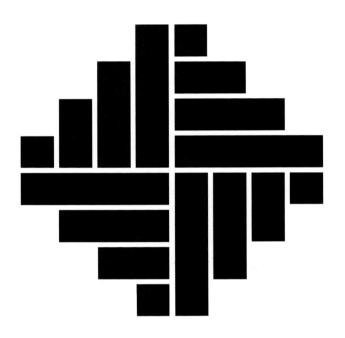

Royfund
Investment
1969 · Rolf Harder/Design Collaborative · CA

Olympic Games, Munich 1972
1972 · Coordt von Mannstein/
Graphicteam Köln · DE

Gardena
Gardening tools
1970 · Hannes Schober,
Wolfram Reinhardt · DE

Precisa
Technical instruments
1976 · Manuel Sanchez · MX

Consorcio Mexicano de Exportadores
Trade association
1974 · Ernesto Lehfeld · MX

Horst Slesina Werbegesellschaft
Advertising
1962 · Horst Slesina · DE

Asahi Mutual
Insurance
1972 · Ikko Tanaka · JP

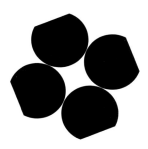

Osaka Art Festival
1960s · Takeshi Otaka · JP

Oakland Fishing Company
1979 · Anonymous · US

Fotolabor
Photography and printing
1970 · Luisa Moser/Studio Bruni · IT

Pharmacraft
Pharmacy
1966 · Patricia Turnbull · CA

Woodward Cape & Associates
Architecture and engineering
1964 · Crawford Dunn · US

Mover
1960s · Franz Wagner · US

Galería Espiral
Art gallery
1958 · Nedo Mion Ferrario · VE

Südfrüchte-Importhaus
Foods
1963 · Franz Hermann Wills · DE

**Transpress -
Verlag für Verkehrswesen**
Publishing
1965 · Günter Henkel · DE-GDR

Suomen Sähköteknikkojen Liitto
Electronics
1961 · Tapio Vallioja · FI

Shinko Electric
Electronics
1959 · Kenichi Yoshioka · JP

Accurate Diamond Tools
Cutting tools
1976 · Ronald Cutro · US

Stichting Rijnmond-Nordzeekanal
Transportation
1960s · H. P. Doebele · NL

Proof Press Magazine
Student magazine
1968 · Paul M. Levy · US

Point Press
Printing
1975 · Burt Smith · US

Fashion Canada
Domestic fashion promotion
1970 · Fritz Gottschalk/
Gottschalk+Ash · CA

Suomen Auto
Automobile industry union
1962 · Olof Eriksson · FI

Machelor Maintenance Services
Property management
1966 · Gerald Westby · US

Controls Company
1960s · John Massey · US

Salon de Escultura y Obra Grafica
Design exhibition
1977 · Jorge Sposari · AR/MX

**American Institute
of Interior Designers**
1980 · Michael Vanderbyl · US

Saim Solar
Heating systems
1972 · Silvio Coppola · IT

Sintemex
Management consultancy
1974 · Ernesto Lehfeld · MX

Toyo Rayon
Synthetic fibers
1964 · Takeshi Otaka · JP

Stadsschouwburg Haarlem
Theater
1969 · Jaap Frank · NL

Fiat – Divisione Mare
Turbines
1971 · C.G.S.S. Creativi Associati · IT

Karnabaer
Textiles
1967 · Thröstur Magnusson, Hilmar
Sigurdsson/Argus Advertising · IS

Valtur
Tourism
1966 · Hazy Osterwalder/
Studio Boggeri · IT

Banco do Estado de São Paulo
Bank
1970s · Aloísio Magalhães/PVDI · BR

Kaufman Astoria Studios
Film studios
1982 · Saul Bass, G. Dean Smith · US

Brown & Company
Road construction
1969 · Herbert Meyers · CA

Bruckmann Verlag
Publishing
1970 · Dieter Urban · DE

German Pavilion, Expo '70, Osaka
World's fair stand
1969 · Coordt von Mannstein · DE

Ontario Arts Council
1983 · Debbie Adams · CA

Tanzschule Hadrich
Dance school
1965 · Ernst Lauenroth · DE-GDR

Hydropump
Swimming pools
1966 · Donald H. Tartak · US

Asada
Ironworks
1960s · Tetsuo Katayama · JP

ICSID Congress
Design congress
1978 · Ernesto Lehfeld · MX

Sunstar Foods
1973 · Dave Bartells,
Gale William Ikola · US

Brooks Resources
Foundation
1982 · Michael Vanderbyl · US

Museo de Ciencias Naturales
Natural history museum
1970 · Gerd Leufert · VE

Istituto per il Commercio Estero
Foreign trade institute
1971 · Pino Tovaglia · IT

Joe Dieter
Design
1971 · Joe Dieter · US

Oerlikoner Eloid-Verzahnung
Machine tools
1940s · Paul Aschwanden · CH

Instituto Peruano del Desarrollo
National development office
1967 · Claude Dietrich · PE

Ralin Productions
Film production
1960s · Wallace Walker · US

Historisches Museum Frankfurt am Main
Historical museum
1970 · Herbert W. Kapitzki · DE

Diateknikk
Audio-visual systems
1967 · Paul Brand · NO

Sociedade Amigos de Imirin-Açu
Tourism
1966 · João Carlos Cauduro · BR

British Leyland
Automobile manufacturer
1978 · Henrion Design Associates · UK

Fathers of Confederation Centre
Cultural center
1964 · Fritz Gottschalk/
Gottschalk+Ash · CA

Kjell Karlsen Entertainment
Concert promotion
1970 · Paul Brand · NO

Canadian Crafts Council
1970s · Anonymous · CA

Edizioni del Diaframma
Publishing
1963 · Giancarlo Iliprandi · IT

Control Center
1960s · Gerd Leufert · VE

**Arbeitsgemeinschaft
des Kunsthandwerks NRW**
Arts and crafts association
1950 · Walter Breker · DE

Cogis
Import-export
1969 · Bob Noorda/
Unimark International · IT

Ginza Shashinko-sha
Photographic supplies
1962 · Nakajo Masayoshi · JP

De Bortoli
Furniture
1958 · Bruno Monguzzi/
Studio Boggeri · IT

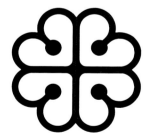

City of Montreal
City identity
1981 · George Huel · CA

Turbocompresores
Air-conditioning
1981 · Monica Morales · MX

Ferraniacolor
Film materials
1961 · Piero Sansoni · IT

Furukawa Sansui Kai
Trading
1969 · Kazumasa Nagai/
Nippon Design Center · JP

ZEWAS Staaken
Electronics
1965 · Conrad Priem · DE-GDR

Tischer
Real estate
1974 · Michael Vanderbyl · US

Sankyo Kohki
Optical industry
1967 · Tadashi Masuda · JP

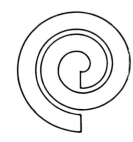

Inventum Staff Personnel
1973 · Graphic Concept · AU

Fedeindustria
Industry association
1974 · Armando Ferraro Senior · VE

Slinger Group
Printing
1961 · June Fraser/
Design Research Unit · UK

Wagen-Shuzo
Brewing
1958 · Takeshi Otaka · JP

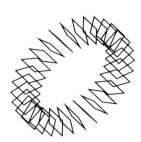

Polygon Pictures
Film production
1970s · Takenobu Igarashi · JP

**Werkzeugmaschinen
Oerlikon, Bührle & Co.**
Machine tools
1940s · Balthasar Rauch · CH

Mec-Mor
Knitting machines
1960s · Hanns Lohrer · DE

Rotation
Theater
1960s · Olaf Gaumer, Peter Maus · DE

Interactive Data Services
Computer rentals
1968 · Heiner Hegemann/
Chermayeff & Geismar · US

Tozai Bunka Koryu Center
International cultural exchange
1960s · Yoshio Amaya · JP

Ediciones Hormé
Publishing
1960 · Lala Méndez Mosquera · AR

Sobre Ondas
Motorcycles
1969 · Willys de Castro · BR

Pirelli Seawings
Plastics
1965 · Pino Tovaglia · IT

Serfontana
Shopping center
1972 · Alfred Weiss · CH

Banco Mexicano Somex
Bank
1979 · Joe Vera, Francisco Tellez · MX

Aco
Machinery
1970 · Gerd Leufert · VE

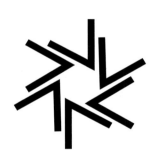

Alfredo Vidal
Travel agency
1965 · Robert P. Gersin · US

K. Siegrist Pflanzenzucht
Plant breeding
1960s · Walter Ballmer · CH

Carborundum
Abrasive
1966 · Richard De Natale · US

I.O.S.
Art association
1969 · Michel Martina · FR

Psychiatric Facility
1950s · Paul Jacopin · CH

Elektrotekchnický Ústav
Electronic machines
1974 · František Bobáň · CZ

Caliumi F.lli
Clothing
1960 · Walter Ballmer · IT

Japan Pearl Promotion Association
1965 · Takashi Kono · JP

PC Photo
Publishing
1960 · Gan Hosoya · JP

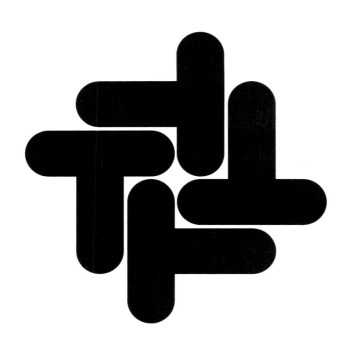

Titan Fasteners
Fittings and washers
1968 · Appelbaum & Curtis · US

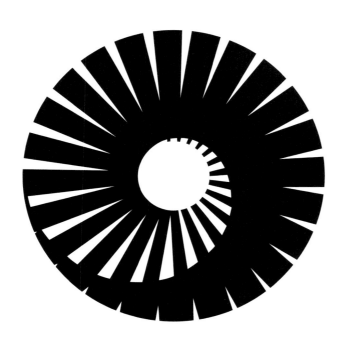

Ontario Ministry of Labour
Government office
1978 · Roslyn Eskind, David Gibson · CA

Falcinelli Ceramiche
Wall and floor tiles
1973 · Franco Grignani · IT

Fordprint Lithography
Printing
1965 · Carl Brett/
Hiller Rinaldo Associates · CA

Duzan
Ceiling and roof building
1960s · Lars Bramberg · SE

Arti Grafiche Fantoni
Design
1960s · Pier Vico Cortesi · IT

Impresa Carlo Frigerio
Construction company
1968 · Massimo Dradi · IT

Stieger Siebdruck
Printing
1960s · Elias Stieger · DE

Roland von Siebenthal
Photo studio
1960s · Anonymous · CH

Saratoga Performing Arts Center
1966 · Charles Fuhrman · US

Walter Mantegazza
Punch cards
1965 · Armando Milani · IT

Finnkino Oy
Movie rentals
1965 · Kyösti Varis · FI

Servissystems
Cleaning systems
1969 · Kyösti Varis · FI

Idea Books
Publishing
1969 · Roberto Innocenti · IT

Royal Architectural Institute of Canada
1969 · Ken Patton · CA

Musées Nationaux du Canada
Museums association
1970 · Georges Beaupré · CA

Offset-Druck Lausanne
Printing
1950s · Roger-Virgile Geiser · CH

Kolín Oil Refinery
1950s · Oldřich Kopecký · CZ

Maschinenbau W. Ratsch
Engineering
1965 · Karl Amann · DE-GDR

Sundt & Company
1969 · Bruno Oldani · NO

Fabrik für Kosmetische Artikel
Cosmetics
1940s · Gust Hahn · DE

Toys Corporation
1950s · Emil O. Biemann · US

**National Institute
of Industrial Research**
1964 · Eduardo A. Cánovas · AR

**State of Minnesota
Agricultural Products**
1983 · Peter Seitz · US

Ogilvie
Haircare products
1970s · Dominik L. Burckhardt · US

Kona Surf Resort
Hotel
1970 · Clarence Lee · US

Bank of Tokyo
1967 · Ikko Tanaka · JP

Cedfi Film
Film production
1972 · Niklaus Troxler · CH

Feria del Pacífico
Tourist festival
1966 · Claude Dietrich · PE

Marine Accessory Company
Boat fittings
1960s · Michael Tucker · UK

Prose Recycling
1983 · Peter G. Ulmer · CH

D. W. Graham and Associates
Landscape architecture
1966 · Jacques E. Charette · CA

Julien et Mège
Industrial pumps
1964 · Jean-Marie Chourgnoz/
Chourgnoz Publicité · FR

Islander Inn
Hotel
1970 · Clarence Lee · US

Norm Scudellari
Photography
1970 · Leslie Smart · CA

Ippodo Gallery
Art gallery
1970 · Shigeo Fukuda · JP

Floron
Artificial flowers
1960s · Gerd Leufert · VE

Kauai Surf Resort
Hotel
1970 · Clarence Lee · US

Olivetti
Office machines
1960s · Giovanni Pintori · IT

Three-dimensional

Dreidimensional

Tridimensionnel

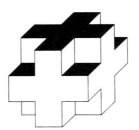

University of Chicago
Hospitals and Clinics
1971 · Edward Hughes · US

Instituto Nacional de Industria
Organization for national industries
1979 · Tomás Vellvé · ES

Kassenbouw Broeiramen
Boxes
1961 · Ralph Prins · NL

Dresdner Packungsbetrieb
Packaging
1965 · Fritz Panndorf · DE-GDR

Cooperativa Consumo
Consumers association
1969 · Francesc Guitart · ES

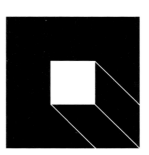

Quadrant
Construction company
1974 · Scott Engen · US

Takeuchi Iin
Healthcare
1978 · Tadamasa Katsube,
Kenji Sakamoto · JP

Architectural Research Center
1974 · Ernesto Lehfeld · MX

Avant Cards
Publishing
1977 · Marty Neumeier · US

Museo Nacional
Museum
1970 · Félix Beltrán · CU/MX

Instituto del Libro Cubano
Cuban book institute
1971 · Félix Beltrán · CU

Vargas
Construction company
1978 · Félix Beltrán · CU/MX

Institute of Urban Planning
1960s · Shigeo Fukuda · JP

State Secretary for Urban Development
and Ecology
1983 · Manuel Sanchez · MX

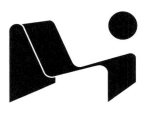

Le Mobilier International
Furniture
1971 · Claude A. Simard · CA

Aannemingsbedrijf van Heeswijk
Construction company
1969 · Ben Bos/Total Design · NL

Hino Architect & Engineering
1975 · Tadamasa Katsube · JP

Daiichi Zoen Doboku
Landscape architecture
1981 · Akira Hirata, Hiroshi Mori · JP

Immobiliare Erba
Real estate
1973 · Rinaldo Cutini · IT

Nowea Ausstellungsgesellschaft
Exhibitions (proposed design)
1970 · Walter Breker · DE

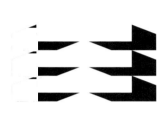

SCAB
Insurance
1972 · Jean Delaunay/Look · FR

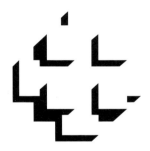

Banco Central do Brasil
Bank
1975 · PVDI · BR

Facility Technology & Management
Computer systems
1969 · Eskil Ohlsson · US

Steel Properties
1960s · Ward & Saks · US

Arpa
1972 · Silvio Coppola · IT

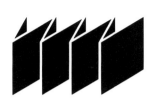

Wolfgang Mann Verlag
Publishing
1986 · Anonymous · DE

Staubar Maribor and Dos
Construction company
1974 · Matjaz Bertonceli · YU

Peter Green
1975 · Gavin Healey · UK

New Left Books
Publishing
1970 · Ken Garland · UK

Malmö Exhibition Center
1980 · Gun Larson, Kerstin Larson · SE

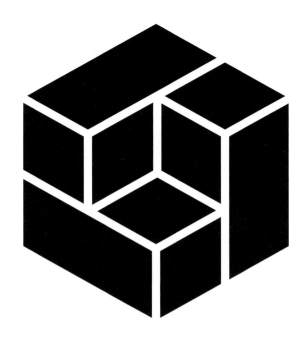

Haraldssøn
Office furniture
1968 · Paul Brand · NO

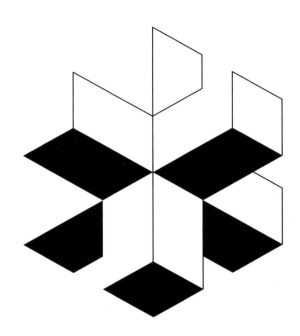

Francisco Soler
Construction company
1972 · Francesc Guitart · ES

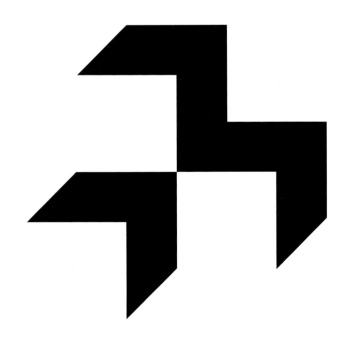

British Organisation for the Development of Exports
1968 · John Gibbs/Unit Five Design · UK

Architecture 70
Architectural congress
1969 · Gerd Leufert · VE

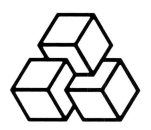

Banco do Estado do Rio Grande
Bank
1965 · Aloísio Magalhães/PVDI · BR

Tanigawa Jitsugyo
Nightclub
1974 · Teruo Fujishige · JP

American Federation of Arts
Traveling exhibition
1967 · Rudolph de Harak · US

Italstat
Bank
1973 · Mimmo Castellano · IT

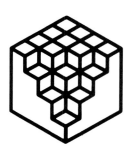

L'Escalier
Clothing
1970 · Michele Spera · IT

Pictogramma
Art gallery
1971 · Michele Spera · IT

Habitat Ufficio
Interior design
1981 · R. Nava, D. Soffientini,
A. Ubertazzi · IT

Japan Typography Association
1978 · Takenobu Igarashi · JP

Berger Türenbau
Doors
1971 · Walter Bosshardt · CH

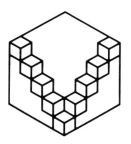

Vedior Investments
1976 · Ben Bos · NL

Compagnie Italiana Vendite
Import-export
1973 · Egidio Bonfante,
Theodoor Manson · IT

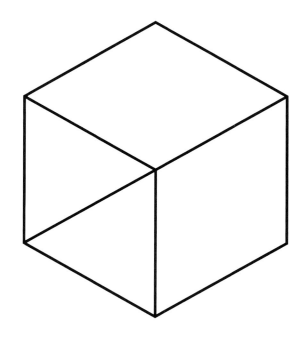

Otto Zapf Möbel
Furniture
1965 · Wolfgang Schmidt · DE

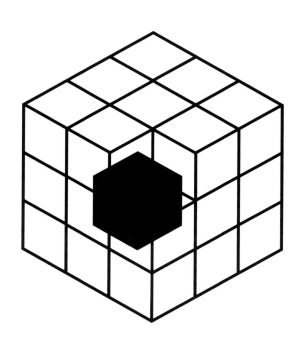

Marion Shop
Toys
1971 · Luciano Francesconi · IT

Colegio de Arquitectos
School of architecture
1977 · Álvaro Sotillo · VE

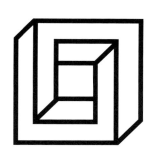

Perfect Film &
Chemical Corporation
1968 · Hess & Antupit · US

Se.Co.A.
Management consultancy
1973 · Da Centro Disegno · IT

Montedison
Chemicals
1972 · Landor Associates · US

Minnesota Social Services
1974 · Peter Seitz · US

American Can Company
Can manufacturer
1967 · George Tscherny · US

York Centre
1973 · Stuart Ash/
Gottschalk+Ash · CA

Socialstyrelsen
Social services
1968 · Lars Ringholm · SE

Unione Nazionale Costruttori Serramenti
Alluminio Acciaio Leghe
Building workers union
1973 · Studio GSZ · IT

Canaco Monterrey
Chamber of commerce
1982 · Jorge Sposari · AR

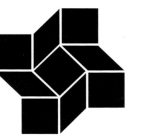

Jörn Jörgensen
Design
1967 · Paul Brand · NO

Arcan Eastern
Shelving
1970 · Savage Sloan · CA

Associazione Pittura Pavia
Art association
1972 · Pietro Galli · IT

Budaprint
Textiles
1965 · Gábor Papp · HU

Kunstverein Biel
Art association
1958 · René Brotbeck · CH

Idea Muebles
Furniture
1971 · Pérez Sánchez · ES

Orfebreria Colonial
Art exhibition
1970 · Manuel Espinoza · VE

Rade Šupić
Wooden products
1973 · Dalibor Martinis · YU

Univerza v Mariboru P. A.
University
1980 · Ivan Dvoršak · YU

Hair Care Treatments
by Avon Cosmetics
1971 · Vance Jonson · US

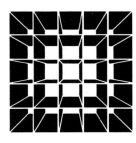

Hewitt Associates
Management consultancy
1982 · Jack Weiss, Randi Robin · US

Taro Product
Architecture
1970 · Mitsuhiko Sasao/
McCann Erickson-Hakuhodo · JP

Messe für Inneneinrichtung
Trade fair
1974 · Michael Herold · DE

Verlagsgruppe
Publishing
1953 · Heinz Schwabe · DE

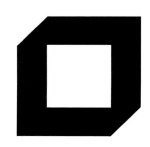

SHV Bouwsector
Construction company
1967 · Benno Wissing, Pieter van Delft/
Total Design · NL

**Community Builders
and Building Materials**
1960s · Franciszek Winiarski · PL

Centro Commerciale Americano
Exhibition of plastic products
1967 · Carlo Bruni · IT

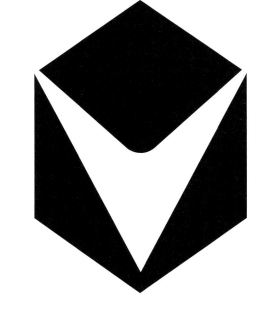

Vita Farmac
Pharmaceuticals
1955 · Ryszard Sidorowski · PL

American Housing Guild
Home building
1971 · Jay Hanson · US

Central Office of Information
Marketing and communications
1972 · Cecil Bourchier, Carl Wilson/
COI Design Unit · UK

New York Times Books
Publishing
1970 · Edward Marson · US

Commercial Industrial Systems
1981 · Thomas Ohmer, Koji Takei · US

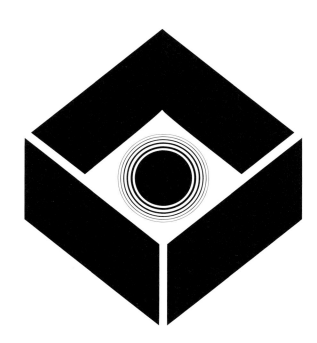

The California State Exposition
Exhibitions
1966 · Saul Bass & Associates · US

The Icehouse, San Francisco
1975 · Michael Vanderbyl · US

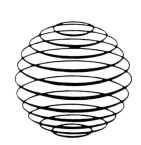

Hemisphere Club
Lunch club
1970 · George Nelson · US

Clawges Associates
Advertising
1967 · Hess & Antupit · US

Hattori
Watches
1970 · Shigeo Fukuda · JP

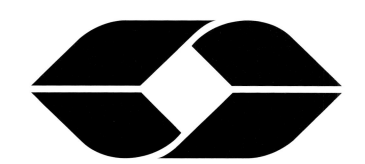

Equity Funding Corporation of America
Insurance
1969 · Gary Hinsche/Robert Miles Runyan · US

G. Jantsch Druckerei
Printing
1980 · Hermann Zapf · DE

Hazelden Treatment Center
1989 · Peter Seitz · US

Lukas Beddy
Furniture
1970 · Emanuele Centazzo/Sitcap · IT

Mitsui Home
Grocery
1977 · Iwao Miyanaga,
Yasaburo Kuwayama · JP

Linguaglossa
Steel
1976 · Francesco Burcini · IT

Seiho-Sha
Art gallery
1976 · Shigeo Fukuda · JP

Cromotip
Printing
1968 · Nedo Mion Ferrario · VE

Irish Steel Limited
1978 · Damien Harrington · IE

Matthaes Verlag
Publishing
1986 · Anonymous · DE

Tecnotec
Metals
1980 · Félix Beltrán · CU

Consolidated Mutual Insurance Company
1960s · Philip Franznick · US

Kuresa
Adhesive films and papers
1980 · Claude Dietrich · PE

Meyster
Publishing
1977 · Anonymous · DE

Tenicaña
Foods
1978 · Dicken Castro · CO

R. W. Buelow Architects
1981 · Gale William Ikola · US

Miyamaru
Bookstore
1978 · Osamu Ogawa,
Junzo Yamamoto · JP

Ranno Book
Publishing
1975 · Ronald Cutro · US

Georgia Bankers Association
State banks organization
1980 · Don Connelly · US

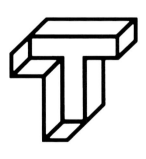

Tornaghi Mobiliere
Furniture
1979 · R. Nava, D. Soffientini,
G. Romani, A. Ubertazzi · IT

Schreinerei Wüst
Carpentry
1970 · Atelier Stadelmann Bisig · CH

Siderurgica del Pacifico-Sidelpa
Ironworks
1976 · Dicken Castro · CO

Quinpool Centre Developments
1977 · Rick Cartledge · CA

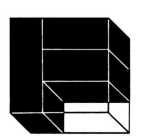

Alberto Ferrari
Construction company
1971 · Emanuele Centazzo/Sitcap · IT

Interexport
Import-export
1983 · Félix Beltrán,
Mónica Reyes · CU/MX

Solfer
Metals
1978 · Francesco Burcini · IT

Proda
Electronic data-processing
1969 · Claude Dietrich · PE

The Income Fund of America
Investment
1973 · Thomas Ohmer, Carl Seltzer · US

Standard Show Services
Exhibitions
1968 · Ernst Roch/
Design Collaborative · CA

Guérin
Construction company
1969 · Alain Pontecorvo, Daniel Maurel/
Chourgnoz Publicité · FR

International Design Center
Furniture
1966 · Gordon Salchow · US

Promusel
Haulier
1983 · José Santamarina/
Elias & Santamarina · ES

Interco Container
1970s · R. Nava, D. Soffientini,
G. Romani, A. Ubertazzi · IT

Himes
Printing
1975 · Lanny Sommese · US

Matui Architectural Office
Planning office
1977 · Akisato Ueda · JP

Empaques de Cartón Titán
Packaging
1970s · Lance Wyman · US/MX

Eskil Ohlsson Associates
Design
1970 · Eskil Ohlsson · US

Techint
Engineering
1969 · Bob Noorda/
Unimark International · IT

Lopes Galerie für Konkrete Kunst
Art gallery
1976 · Odermatt+Tissi · CH

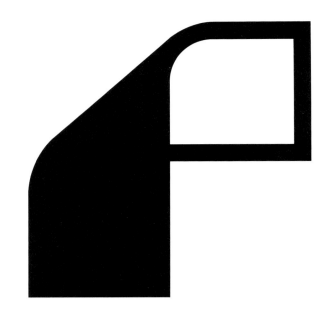

Fotoklub Maribor
Photographers club
1975 · Ivan Dvoršak · YU

Harmonic Groupement
Industrial investment
1973 · Jean Delaunay/Look · FR

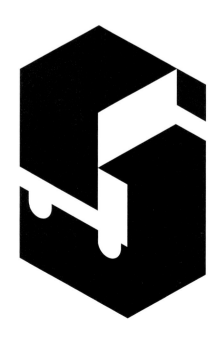

Sabco
Trucks
1967 · Jay Hanson · US

238

Policicomer
Import-export
1971 · Enric Huguet · ES

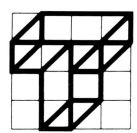

Takenobu Igarashi
Design
1975 · Takenobu Igarashi · JP

Nordiska
Investment
1968 · Hess & Antupit · US

Riva & Mariani
Thermoacoustic insulation
1969 · Alfredo Troisi · IT

Tercoma
1971 · Pal Horváth/H Design · BE

Ulshore
Pharmaceuticals
1981 · Maurizio Milani · IT

Delta Books
Publishing
1969 · Jiří Rathouský · CZ

**American Foundation on
Automation and Employment**
1970 · S. Neil Fujita · US

Structural Softwoods
Timber
1982 · Damien Harrington · IE

Tilysa Construcciones
Construction company
1980 · Morfos Diseño · MX

Telimena
Textiles
1965 · Witold Surowiecki · PL

City College
1969 · Pieter van Delft/
Unimark International · US

Investors Diversified Services
Financial management
1977 · Gale William Ikola · US

Peter Paulsen
Real estate
1978 · Harry Murphy, Stanton Klose · US

Nuratex
Timber
1965 · Bob Noorda/
Unimark International · IT

Creative Parks & Playgrounds
1965 · Lance Wyman · US

Triverse
Exhibition systems
1965 · Stephen Dunne/
Unimark International · US

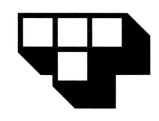

Toyofuku-Kensetsu
Construction company
1981 · Shigenobu Nagaishi · JP

Teledyne
Broadcasting
1964 · Maurice Yanez/
Robert Miles Runyan · US

Architecture of Mexico
Magazine
1970 · Lance Wyman · US

Universa v Mariboru
University
1977 · Ivan Dvoršak · YU

Zinc Development Association
Zinc
1969 · Crosby, Fletcher, Forbes · UK

Shrenuj & Co.
Jeweler
1976 · Sudarshan Dheer · IN

System Creates
Planning office
1978 · Takao Yoguchi · JP

Service Editions S.E.D.E.C.
Publishing
1970 · Jacques Nathan-Garamond · FR

H. Wesselo en J.J. van Voorst
Architecture
1970 · Jan Jaring · NL

Cartiera di Tolmezzo
Paper
1959 · Giulio Confalonieri, Ilio Negri · IT

Vetreria Angelana
Glass
1981 · Francesco Burcini · IT

Tetsuya Ohta
Design
1980 · Tetsuya Ohta · JP

Toshi Kenchiku Kenkyusho
Planning office
1981 · Akiyoshi Kuwahara · JP

Zinc Development
Association Conference 1966
1969 · Crosby, Fletcher, Forbes · UK

Pavatex Garantien
Guarantees
1982 · Marc Burckhalter,
Peter Christensen · CH

Cashmart Wholesale Grocers
1968 · Negus & Negus · UK

Hawker Siddeley
Aircraft production
1963 · Minale, Tattersfield, Provinciali · UK

Bruno Manetti
Insurance
1970 · Massimo Dradi · IT

Banque Nationale de Paris
Bank
1967 · A. Baier/Delpire-Advico · FR

Luís López y Guillermo Sáez
Architecture
1968 · Ribas & Creus · ES

Geigy Pharmazie
Pharmaceuticals
1967 · Markus Löw · CH

Slovenija Ceste Tehnika
Construction company
1979 · Ivan Dvoršak · YU

Vereinigung Karster Künstler
Artists association
1984 · Paul Effert · DE

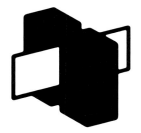

Internazionale Marmo Macchine
Trade fair
1980 · Sergio Salaroli,
Michele Spera · IT

NEC Corporation Engineering Center
1978 · Koichi Mizuno · JP

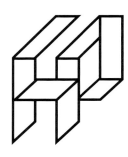

Hotel La Pedregosa
1969 · Nedo Mion Ferrario · VE

Estructuras Activas
Industrial design
1970 · Nedo Mion Ferrario · VE

Michael Novak
Architecture
1975 · Lanny Sommese · US

Tairumento
Construction company
1983 · Yukihisa Nakayama · JP

Fapasa
Road construction
1958 · Enric Huguet · ES

Theissen
Roofer
1980 · Michael Herold · DE

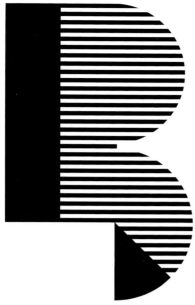

Leonblu
Furniture
1971 · Silvio Coppola · IT

Container Corporation of America
Packaging
1958 · Ralph E. Eckerstrom · US

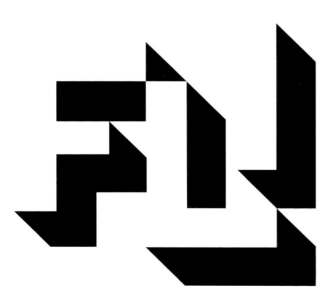

Fairlawn Industries
1970 · David Leigh · US

ESAB
Welding equipment
1974 · Cult Dahlen · SE

Zenex
Construction company
1981 · Tony Forster · UK

Webeg Baugesellschaft
Construction company
1972 · Siegfried W. Küchler · DE

Nobrium
Chemicals
1971 · Mervyn Kurlansky/
Pentagram · UK

Redi-Mix Associates
Construction company
1980 · Richard Wittosch · US

Dimension
Broadcasting
1960s · Franz Wagner · US

Quel que soit l'effet de la couleur ou de la forme, un logo est d'abord convaincant par sa teneur. Un bon logo illustre les prestations et les fonctions de ce qu'il représente. Pendant le processus créatif, il arrive souvent qu'un aspect prédomine, mais dans sa forme définitive, un logo séduit par son équilibre.
Shin Matsunaga

Ein Logo überzeugt trotz prägnanter Farbe oder Form vor allem durch seine Substanz. Ein gutes Logo veranschaulicht die Leistungen und Funktionen dessen, was es repräsentiert. Im kreativen Prozess steht zwar häufig ein Aspekt im Vordergrund, doch in der endgültigen Form besticht ein Logo durch Ausgewogenheit.
Shin Matsunaga

Even when of superior color or form, in the end, what makes a logo work is its substance. Good logos make visible the achievements and actions of the products they represent. Often in the creative process, one aspect dominates, but once completed, balance is the key to making a logo shine.
Shin Matsunaga

Blanc sur noir

Weiß auf Schwarz

White on Black

Montagebau Plannungsgesellschaft
Construction company
1968 · Josefine Fellmer · DE

Ontario Trucking Association
Transportation
1974 · Peter Adam/
Gottschalk+Ash · CA

Ono City Ironware Cooperative
Workers association
1982 · Ikuya Kimura · JP

Elektro-Heikes
Electronics
1969 · Josefine Fellmer · DE

Maglificio Gianluca
Clothing
1968 · Dante Bighi · IT

Visual Communications
Design
1979 · Nagato Kawamoto · JP

**Canadian Government
Pavillion, Expo '70, Osaka**
World's fair stand
1970 · Neville Smith · US

Facit
Furniture
1960s · Anonymous · SE

Air Jamaica
Airline
1969 · Hans Kleefeld/
Stewart & Morrison · CA

Weberei Wängi
Weaving
1968 · Peter Bloch · CH

Hokkaido Takushoku
Bank
1969 · Shigeo Fukuda · JP

René Gigandet
Design
1960s · René Gigandet · CH

Oclesna Galleria
Art gallery
1975 · František Bobáň · CZ

Société Française des Presses Suisses
Printers association
1950s · Georges Wicky · CH

Pirelli Due Palme
Carpets
1967 · Amleto Dalla Costa · IT

The Plessey Company
Electronics
1960s · Norbert Dutton/
Rapier Design · UK

**Schweizerische Zentrale
für Verkehrsförderung**
Transport promotion
1940s · Walter Käch · CH

Hotel Thüringer Tourist Suhl
1965 · Walter Höhne · DE-GDR

Kona Inn
Hotel
1970 · Clarence Lee · US

R. Murray & Son
Construction company
1970 · Raymond Lee · CA

Max
Soap
1980 · Fumio Koyoda · JP

Mitake Yogyo
Landscape gardening
1983 · Yasuhisa Iguchi · JP

Reska
Furniture
1960s · Anonymous · DK

Jigoro Kano Judo Club
Sports
1959 · Giancarlo Iliprandi · IT

Color Communications
Inks
1970 · James Lienhart · US

Bactine
Skin cream
1960s · Morton Goldsholl
Design Associates · US

Medium Publicidad
Advertising
1965 · Rómulo Macció · AR

Tele-Tape Productions
Television studios
1968 · Seldon G. Dix Jr. · US

Suginoko Academy
School
1983 · Yasuhisa Iguchi · JP

TV Tokyo
Broadcasting
1983 · Yasuhisa Iguchi · JP

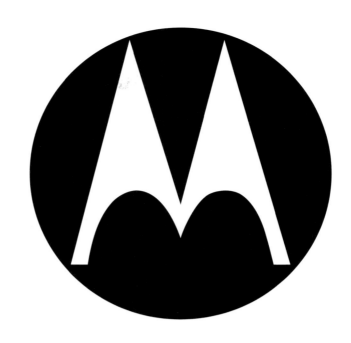

Motorola
Telecommunications
1952 · Morton Goldsholl · US

Marufuku
Ceramics
1979 · Kazuharu Fuji · JP

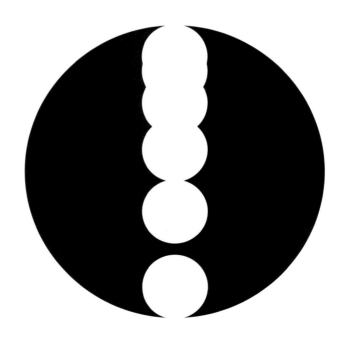

Bank of Iwate
1971 · Shigeo Fukuda · JP

Kokusai International
Travel agency
1969 · Jim Miho · JP

Taiyo Kobe Bank
1973 · Tadashi Ohashi · JP

WE Elementewerke
Machine parts
1970 · Ekkehart Rustmeier · DE

Ontario Film Laboratories
1970 · Leslie Smart · CA

Japan Sporting Goods
1975 · Kazumasa Nagai · JP

Nichimo Prefabrication
Construction company
1973 · Tetsuo Noda · JP

Gremrath
Office supplies
1960s · Wolfgang Schmittel · DE

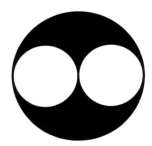

Filotecnica Salmoiraghi
Glass lenses
1957 · Studio Benca · IT

Howard Miller Clock Company
1950 · George Nelson, Irving Harper · US

Kowa Art Printing
1979 · Kimito Ohashira · JP

Kitazawa Distribution Industry
1983 · Tsutomu Shimoyama · JP

Miyanami Engineering
1980 · Shunji Ninomi · JP

Kyowa Bank
1968 · Tadashi Ohashi · JP

Honmachi Print
Printing
1976 · Michio Ogura · JP

United Semiconductor
Electronics
1967 · Carl Seltzer · US

Gomen
Clothing
1971 · Takeshi Otaka · JP

Meiji
Chocolate
1967 · Tadashi Ohashi · JP

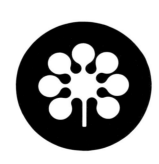

Leiv Engelschiön
Cosmetics
1969 · Bruno Oldani · NO

Sanford Marine
Marine services
1967 · Philip Seefeld · US

Kyoho
Textiles
1969 · Tomoichi Nishiwaki,
Akisato Ueda · JP

Toilet Laundries
Cleaners
1960s · Ernst Roch · CA

AX
1970s · Ekkehart Rustmeier · DE

Prestigio Linoleum
Flooring
1958 · Roberto Sambonet · IT

Rosati Club
1969 · Pino Tovaglia · IT

Seiwa Electric
Electronics
1982 · Akisato Ueda · JP

Stilnovo
Lamps
1969 · Giancarlo Iliprandi · IT

Metal Association
1965 · Paul Bühlmann · CH

Hansruedi Scheller
Design
1966 · Hansruedi Scheller · CH

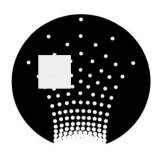

Miss Universe Contest
Beauty pageant
1978 · Joe Vera, Francisco Tellez · MX

Nakajima Hozando
Household items
1980 · Tadashi Ishikawa,
Hideko Sakado · JP

Oakville Transit
Public transport
1973 · Stuart Ash/
Gottschalk+Ash · CA

Action for Right to Life
Social campaign
1976 · Dieter Urban · DE

Nuhold American Corporation
Waterproofing
1970s · Franz Wagner · US

Nihon Racquetball Renmei
Sports association
1981 · Yukio Kanise · JP

Ernst Pollak Verlag
Publishing
1926 · Anonymous · DE

Eastern Airlines
1960s · Lippincott & Margulies · US

Franco Ranchetti
Photocopiers
1960 · Heinz Waibl · IT

Ichiko
Advertising
1983 · Tadamasa Katsube · JP

Silkrom
Pigments and dyes
1957 · Ilio Negri · IT

Ishihara Studio
Photography
1979 · Yoshihiro Kishimoto · JP

H. Te Laake
Watches
1967 · Bruno K. Wiese · DE

Paracom
Sporting goods
1977 · Mike Quon, Chris Zoulamis · US

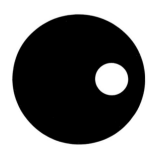

Rees-Hough
Tunnel construction
1968 · John Gibbs, Garth Bell/
Unit Five Design · UK

Daiwa Manekin Company
Window mannequins
1960s · Takashi Kono · JP

Neukirchener Verlagsgesellschaft
Publishing
1974 · Kurt Wolff · DE

Miyazaki Hoso
Broadcasting
1975 · Eita Shinohara · JP

Ram Ridge Corporate Park
Industrial park
1975 · Robert A. Gale · US

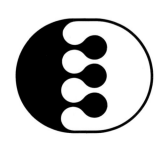

Dr. Wander
Pharmaceuticals
1967 · Peter Megert · CH

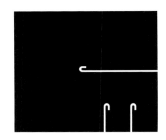

MILA - Costruzioni Milano
Construction company
1970 · Nino Capsoni · IT

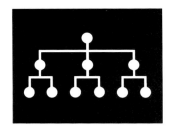

Spencer Stuart & Associates
Management consultancy
1960 · Morton Goldsholl · US

Bertelsmann Buchclub
Book club
1952 · Siegfried Kortemeier · DE

Edelweiss
Paper
1966 · Ribas & Creus · ES

Georg Boesch
Horticulture
1950s · Franz Fässler · CH

**Kimberly-Clark Corporation
Munising Paper Division**
1957 · Morton Goldsholl · US

Sacoim
Construction company
1966 · Bob Noorda/
Unimark International · IT

Erzeugnisgruppe Beleuchtungsglas
Lighting systems
1965 · Gretel Salomo · DE-GDR

Sakamoto Printing
Printing
1977 · Kazuharu Fuji · JP

Künstlergruppe Junger Westen
Artists association
1950s · Jupp Ernst · DE

Sonika
Tape recorders
1960s · Bob Noorda · NL

**Vereinigung zur Werbung
für Schweizer Papier**
Paper industry promotion
1960s · Anton Schutzbach · CH

Cinémathèque Suisse
Cinema
1960s · Roger-Virgile Geiser · CH

Ramco
1977 · Diana Graham · US

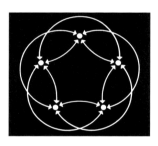

Institut Pédagogique National
Education
1969 · René Ponot · FR

Vitamine
Gardening equipment
1970 · Velizar Petrov · BG

Schweizer Druckerei
Printing
1960s · Roger-Virgile Geiser · CH

Heiwa
Paper
1970 · Hiroshi Ohchi · JP

Ledebur Fliesen
Tiling
1970 · Oanh Pham Phu · DE

Trade Fair for Silk Products
1960s · Jun Tabohashi · JP

Ankerfarm
Pharmacy
1963 · Giancarlo Iliprandi · IT

York Gymnastic Club
1970 · Richard Janis · CA

Dai-ichi Kangyo
Bank
1971 · Reman · JP

Advertising Photographers Association
1967 · Tadashi Masuda · JP

ZDF/Zweites Deutsches Fernsehen
Broadcasting
1961 · G. W. Hörnig · DE

J. Sephiha
Optician
1966 · André van der Beken · BE

Miloš Ćirić
Design
1979 · Miloš Ćirić · YU

Oelmühle Hamburg
Oil mill
1974 · Studio Freudenthal · DE

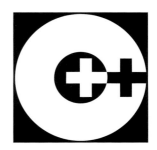

Red Cross Blood Donation
1960s · Hans Hartmann · CH

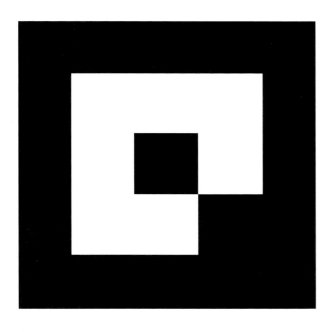

Rochester Institute of Technology
University
1966 · R. Roger Remington · US

Heberlein Holding
Textiles
1960s · Hansruedi Widmer/
Devico AG · CH

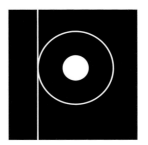

Photo Set
1971 · Hans Hurter · CH

Atelier Moderner Beleuchtungskörper
Lighting
1940s · Karl J. Weiss · CH

GTBA Briard
Construction company
1971 · Jean Delaunay/Look · FR

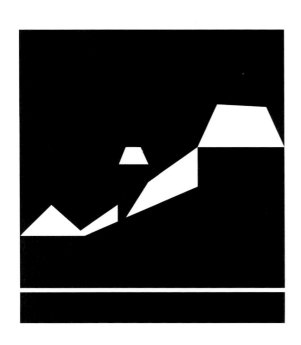

Staatliche Galerie Moritzburg
Art gallery
1965 · Gerhard Voigt · DE-GDR

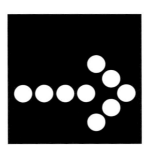

Schweizer Reisekasse
Travel agency
1954 · Kurt Wirth · CH

Teatro la Tertulia
Theater
1972 · Félix Beltrán · CU/MX

Probjeto
Furniture
1964 · Alexandre Wollner · BR

De Wylderbeek
Education
1964 · Marcel Pijpers · NL

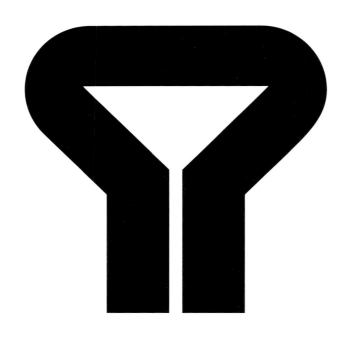

Galleria Peccolo
Art gallery
1971 · Franco Grignani · IT

International Airport Consultants of Montreal
Airport management
1970 · Julien Hébert · CA

La Comète
Film advertising
1960s · Bob Noorda · IT

Pharmaceuticals
1950s · Just Reinhold · DE

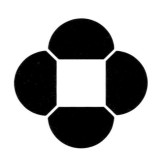

Place Bonaventure
Merchandising
1967 · Fritz Gottschalk/
Gottschalk+Ash · CA

Errebi
Cosmetics
1967 · Franco M. Ricci · IT

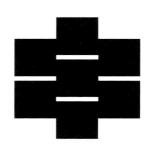

Building Materials
1960s · Gregor Kintzel · DE

Erdölchemie
Chemicals
1968 · Graphicteam Köln · DE

Exposition Belge des Transports
Exhibition committee
1964 · Julian Key · BE

Tarchomin
Pharmaceuticals
1957 · Jerzy Cherka · PL

Archer Daniels Midland
Chemicals
1960s · Charles MacMurray, F. Gomez/
Latham Tyler Jensen · US

Cellulose and Paper Factory
1960s · Ernst Roch · CA

Wako Shoken
Security
1967 · Takeshi Otaka · JP

Ottagono
Publishing
1970 · Pino Tovaglia · IT

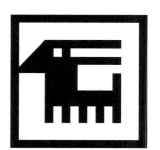

Népművészeti és Háziipari V.
Folk-art trading
1964 · István Szekeres · HU

Gulf Life Holding Company
Insurance
1975 · Jack Evans · US

Torii & Co.
Pharmaceuticals
1983 · Kazuo Tanaka · JP

Knechtel
Grocery wholesaler
1969 · John S. Brown · CA

Marumiya Loan Service
Securities
1983 · Shizuo Yoneda,
Koichi Watanabe · JP

Seilerei Denzler
Ropes
1940s · Pierre Gauchat · CH

Constructora Jamsa
Engineering
1974 · Fernando Rión · MX

Pila
Tourism
1979 · Giovanni Brunazzi · IT

Vega
Clothing
1977 · Raúl Shakespear,
Ronald Shakespear · AR

Bunnosuke Syokuhin
Foods
1978 · Hiroyuki Okuda · JP

Modine Manufacturing
Heating equipment
1956 · Charles MacMurray/
Latham Tyler Jensen · US

Redaelli-Como
1978 · Pietro Galli · IT

Richmond Research Corporation
Film projectors
1961 · Appelbaum & Curtis · US

Marukai Corporation
1981 · Koichi Watanabe · JP

Jinotron
Electronics
1983 · Francesco Burcini · IT

Pirelli Superga
Footwear
1961 · Aldo Calabresi/
Studio Boggeri · IT

Sun Art Printing
1983 · Hiroshi Manzen · JP

Taiheiyo Marine
Fishing accessories
1981 · Koichi Watanabe · JP

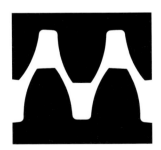

Werkzeugmaschinenfabrik John Scheer
Machine tools
1965 · Wolfgang Hoepfner · DE-GDR

Sesam
Bookstore
1974 · Jost Hochuli · CH

The Whiskey House
Import-export
1960s · Giulio Confalonieri · IT

Ulkomainos
Advertising
1957 · Teuvo Tynkkynen/
Mainos Taucher Reklam · FI

Petronic
Electronics
1979 · Ove Engström,
Torgny Gustavsson · SE

Park Apotheke
Pharmacy
1950s · Eugen & Max Lenz · CH

Franklin Simon
Grocery
1970s · Push Pin Studios · US

Akademie Verlag
Publishing
1947 · Anonymous · DE

Kirjaliike
Bookstore
1961 · Alfons Eder · FI

Dyrlund-Smith
Furniture
1960s · Anonymous · DK

Arndt-Verlag
Publishing
1963 · Anonymous · DE

Maschinenhandel Niederer-Künzle
Machinery
1968 · Eugen & Max Lenz · CH

Egon Guenther Gallery
Art gallery
1958 · Peter B. Eliastam · SA

FEZN
Public relations
1967 · Crosby, Fletcher, Forbes · UK

Les Assurances Nationales
Insurance
1968 · Pascal Besson · CH

VEB Hydrocarbon
Fuel company
1965 · Horst Müller · DE-GDR

Weaving
1954 · Jupp Ernst · DE

Grupo Juridico OM
Legal office
1977 · Reynaldo Da Costa · VE

Elektrochemie und Plaste Halle
Chemicals and plastics
1965 · Gerhard Voigt · DE-GDR

Robapharm Laboratorium
Pharmaceuticals
1940 · Hermann Eidenbenz · CH

MH Investments
1970s · Robert Hagenhofer · US

Aspa-Plast-System
Frames
1977 · Walter Hergenröther · IT

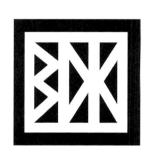

BDK Kulturorganisation
Cultural organization
1950s · Eugen Hotz · CH

Fromageries Bel
Cheese
1968 · Lonsdale Design · FR

Werner Müller
Tailor
1955 · Rudolf Bircher · CH

Olympia Turm Verlag Alfred Wurm
Publishing
1960 · Josef Blaumeiser · DE

Wolfgang Krüger
1965 · Berthold Lindner · DE-GDR

Hunt-Wesson Foods
1967 · Saul Bass, Clarence Sato · US

Cliché Lang
Printing engravers
1969 · Walter Bosshardt · CH

Weather Routing
Weather forecasting
1978 · Bill Bundzak · US

Nederlandse Spoorwegen
Dutch railways
1950s · Gerard Douwe · NL

Bertelsmann Buchclub
Book club
1957 · Sepp Huber · DE

Maritime Telegraph & Telephone
1966 · Hans Kleefeld/
Stewart & Morrison · CA

Savings Institutions
Magazine
1983 · James Lienhart · US

Sartoria Terenghi
Tailor
1967 · Armando Milani · IT

State Bank of Slinger
1970 · James Lienhart · US

Doubinski Frères
Furniture
1965 · Raymond Loewy/CEI · FR

British Petroleum
Oil and gas
1961 · Raymond Loewy/CEI · UK

Technische Hogeschool te Delft
University
1957 · Otto Treumann · NL

Verlag Friedrich Middelhauve
Publishing
1950 · Heinrich Wehmeyer · DE

Carl Koch & Co.
Printing
1958 · Rudolf Bircher · CH

Chesta
Beverage
1970 · Hiroshi Ohchi · JP

22 Dicembre
Film production
1962 · Max Huber · IT

Capper-Neill
Construction company
1967 · Rupert Armstrong, Milner Gray/Design Research Unit · UK

Kuachukov Závod
Footwear
1964 · Sotir Sotirov · BG

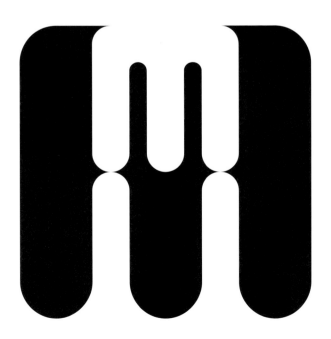

Marcello Masi
Office machines
1973 · Rinaldo Cutini · IT

Typographic   **Typografisch**   **Typographique**

T

Alongside abstract or semi-representational images, lettering and word-marks play a key role in modernist logos. While the meaning of a symbol-based logo can only be deciphered when words of explanation are added, typographic signs are instantly "legible". In addition to popular word-marks, usually showing the full name of the company, single letters or combinations of letters represent a special kind of typographic logo. Following in the age-old tradition of the monogram, one or more single letters stand for a company's complete graphic identity.

Neben den abstrakten oder teilgegenständlichen Zeichen gehört auch die Kategorie der Buchstaben- oder Wortmarke zu den modernistischen Logos. Während symbolbasierte Zeichen oft nur im Zusammenspiel mit erklärender Schrift ihre Bedeutung erhalten, sind typografische Zeichen direkt „lesbar". Ergänzend zur weitverbreiteten Wortmarke, die meist den vollständigen Unternehmensnamen abbildet, stellen Einzelbuchstaben bzw. Buchstabenkombinationen eine besondere Gruppe im Bereich der typografischen Logos dar. Nach der Tradition historischer Monogramme verweisen hier nur einzelne Buchstaben auf den kompletten Wortlaut eines Unternehmens.

À côté des signes abstraits ou partiellement figuratifs, certains logos modernes relèvent encore d'une autre catégorie, celle des sigles et des logotypes. Alors que les signes symboliques prennent tout leur sens dans l'interaction avec l'écrit qui les éclaire, le signe typographique est directement « lisible ». Complétant le logotype largement répandu, qui reproduit généralement le nom complet de l'entreprise, les lettres isolées ou les combinaisons de lettres constituent un groupe particulier dans le domaine du logo typographique. Dans le sillage du monogramme traditionnel, seules des lettres isolées renvoient ici au nom complet de l'entreprise.

A à Z

A bis Z

A to Z

Celfa
Metalworks
1961 · Mimmo Castellano · IT

Ace
Metal fences
1978 · Joseph M. Essex/
Burson-Marsteller · US

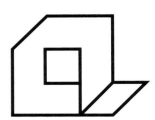

Aval Publicistas
Advertising
1969 · Nedo Mion Ferrario · VE

Abrate Ferruccio
Antiques
1978 · Carlo Malerba · IT

Amerika Haus Berlin
Cultural association
1972 · Norbert & Monika Baum · DE

Ameriways
Airline
1980 · Félix Beltrán · CU/MX

Azuma Drive-In
1975 · Akisato Ueda · JP

RAI Radiotelevisione Italiana
Broadcasting
1969 · Giancarlo Iliprandi · IT

Ajinomoto
Foods
1973 · Saul Bass · US

Fundación José María Aragón
Research institute
1973 · Norberto H. Coppola · AR

Sendan
Textiles
1974 · Yukio Inamoto, Akisato Ueda · JP

Centro Cine Ateneo
Cultural association
1969 · Manuel Espinoza · VE

Associated Rubber
Rubber linings
1981 · Don Connelly · US

**Museo de Arte
Contemporáneo de Caracas**
Art museum
1974 · Nedo Mion Ferrario · VE

Anivdes
Trade association of painters
1968 · Carlo Bruni · IT

Armbruster Manufacturing
Tents
1975 · Don Davis · US

Farmaceutici Midy
Pharmacy
1969 · Armando Milani · IT

Japan Travel Bureau
Travel agency
1970 · Gan Hosoya · JP

**The Certified General
Accountants Association of Canada**
1971 · Manfred Gotthans,
Chris Yaneff · CA

Autophon
Telecommunications
1969 · Paul Bühlmann · CH

Angli AS
Textiles
1964 · Adam Moltke · DK

Aluminum Company of America
1970s · Saul Bass & Associates · US

Amasco
Road construction
1960s · Kenneth Hollick · UK

Architetto Edo Zanaboni
Architecture
1978 · Guido Redaelli · IT

Centro de Arte Actual
Art association
1974 · Dicken Castro · CO

Japan Agricultural Co-op Association
Federation of agricultural cooperatives
1964 · Yoshio Hayashi · JP

Laboratoires Anphar
Pharmaceuticals
1962 · Etienne Bucher · FR

Sundelta
1981 · Ken'ichi Hirose · JP

San Francisco International Airport
1969 · Thomas Laufer & Associates · US

Anniversario Argentina
Commemorative event
1960s · Rómulo Macció · AR

Avery
Label maker
1970s · Saul Bass & Associates · US

Mechanikai Művek
Heating technology
1970 · István Szekeres · HU

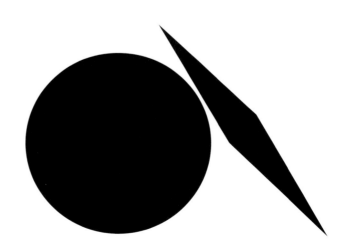

Studio di Architettura
Design and architectural school
1981 · A. G. Fronzoni · IT

Atlas Film

1962 · Fritz Fischer, Klaus Küchler · DE

In 1960 Hanns Eckelkamp founded Atlas Film, a movie distribution company offering new international releases and revivals of screen classics to German cinemas. High-class films needed equally high-class advertising, so the company hired the graphic artist Fritz Fischer as its art director. In collaboration with his colleague Klaus Küchler, Fischer developed the company's memorable logo and for many years was responsible for all the visual materials required to promote the Atlas Film identity. This included creating a unique and carefully considered poster design for each film that the distributors brought to the screen—something almost unheard of in the 1960s. Fischer and his wife Dorothea either designed these themselves or commissioned graphic artist friends to do the job. At the end of the 1960s the distribution company was declared bankrupt. Nevertheless, the name and logo of Atlas Film survives to this day and continues to be used unchanged in the entertainment sector.

Hanns Eckelkamp gründete 1960 den Filmverleih Atlas Film, der aktuelle Werke der internationalen Filmkunst erstmalig sowie hochwertige Klassiker erneut in die deutschen Kinos brachte. Die anspruchsvollen Filme sollten adäquat beworben werden, und so engagierte man den Grafiker Fritz Fischer als Art Director für das Unternehmen. Gemeinsam mit seinem Mitarbeiter Klaus Küchler entwickelte Fischer das einprägsame Markenzeichen des Verleihs und war über Jahre für den gesamten visuellen Auftritt von Atlas Film verantwortlich. Dazu gehörte, dass jeder der ins Kino gebrachten Filme ein individuelles und durchdachtes Erscheinungsbild erhielt – eine Novität in der damaligen Filmlandschaft. Fischer und seine Frau Dorothea setzten die Designs selber um oder beauftragten befreundete Grafiker. Ende der 1960er-Jahre musste der Verleih Insolvenz anmelden. Name und Logo von Atlas Film überlebten jedoch und werden bis heute in nachfolgenden Unternehmenssegmenten in unveränderter Form eingesetzt.

En 1960, Hanns Eckelkamp fondait le distributeur de films Atlas Film, qui fournissait aux salles de cinéma allemandes des œuvres actuelles en exclusivité, mais aussi, à nouveau, les grands classiques du septième art. Les films de qualité devaient bénéficier d'une promotion appropriée, et l'on nomma donc Fritz Fischer directeur artistique de l'entreprise. Avec son collaborateur Klaus Küchler, Fischer développa le logo mémorable du distributeur et assura pendant des années toute la communication visuelle d'Atlas Film. Concrètement, chaque film distribué en salle se voyait doté d'une identité visuelle particulière soigneusement peaufinée, une démarche inédite dans le paysage cinématographique de l'époque. Fischer et sa femme Dorothea créaient eux-mêmes les graphismes ou en confiaient la réalisation à des collègues amis. À la fin des années 1960, le distributeur dut mettre la clef sous la porte, mais le nom et le logo d'Atlas Film survécurent et sont encore utilisés aujourd'hui inchangés par les repreneurs du secteur.

Fischer-Nosbisch was the name of the studio operated jointly by Fritz Fischer (1919–97) and his wife Dorothea Fischer-Nosbisch (1921–2009) in Frankfurt am Main from 1946 until 1967. Together they worked on designs commissioned by clients in the pharmaceutical and industrial industries and in the cultural sector. Their outstanding work for Atlas Film in the 1960s made the partnership famous throughout Germany. After the couple split up, each continued to work separately on assignments, including several special issue stamps for Deutsche Post.

Fischer-Nosbisch hieß in den Jahren 1946 bis 1967 die Ateliergemeinschaft des Gestalterehepaars Fritz Fischer (1919–97) und Dorothea Fischer-Nosbisch (1921–2009) in Frankfurt am Main. Gemeinsam realisierten sie Gestaltungsaufträge für Unternehmen aus der Pharmabranche sowie aus Industrie und Kultur. Die herausragenden Arbeiten für Atlas Film machte die Arbeitsgemeinschaft in den 1960er-Jahren deutschlandweit bekannt. Nach der Trennung arbeitete man separat an Aufträgen, u. a. wurden mehrere Sonderbriefmarken für die Deutsche Post realisiert.

Fischer-Nosbisch, tel est le nom de la communauté d'atelier formée de 1946 à 1967 par le couple Fritz Fischer (1919–97) et Dorothea Fischer-Nosbisch (1921–2009) à Francfort-sur-le-Main. Les deux graphistes réalisent alors des designs pour des laboratoires pharmaceutiques, des entreprises industrielles ou des institutions culturelles. Dans les années 1960, les excellentes créations pour Atlas Film font connaître Fischer-Nosbisch dans toute l'Allemagne. Après leur séparation, les deux graphistes ont travaillé séparément à des commandes, réalisant notamment plusieurs timbres spéciaux pour la Poste allemande.

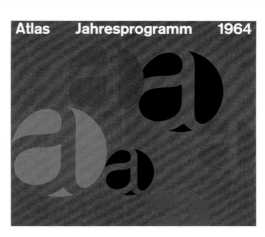

Only the logo remained a constant feature of Atlas Film's corporate image, a common practice for many organizations of the period. By always working with the same design team the company's brand remained consistent, and therefore, from the public's point of view, reliable.

Das Logo war die einzige echte Konstante im Erscheinungsbild von Atlas Film – so wie es zu dieser Zeit noch bei vielen Unternehmen üblich war. Da man mit nur einem Grafikerteam zusammenarbeitete, gelang es dennoch einen einheitlichen Auftritt durchzuhalten.

Le logo d'Atlas Film a été la seule véritable constante de l'identité visuelle du distributeur – ce qui était alors le cas pour beaucoup d'entreprises. Comme on ne travaillait qu'avec une seule équipe de graphistes, une identité visuelle cohérente pouvait malgré tout être assurée.

100 Filmplakate

Wolfgang Schmidt

Atlas Film was famous for its unusual posters created either by the Fischer-Nosbisch team or by a series of great German graphic designers like Hans Hillmann, Karl-Oskar Blase and Wolfgang Schmidt. Every film had its own visual identity, which was also used in all other visual media.

Aushängeschilder des Unternehmens waren die ungewöhnlichen Filmplakate, die vom Team Fischer-Nosbisch sowie einer Reihe der besten deutschen Grafikdesigner wie Hans Hillmann, Karl-Oskar Blase oder Wolfgang Schmidt entworfen wurden. Jeder Film erhielt eine eigene visuelle Identität, die auch in sämtlichen weiteren Medien beibehalten wurde.

Les vitrines publicitaires de l'entreprise étaient les affiches de cinéma inhabituelles conçues par l'équipe Fischer-Nosbisch et par toute une série des meilleurs graphistes allemands comme Hans Hillmann, Karl-Oskar Blase ou Wolfgang Schmidt. Chaque film recevait sa propre identité visuelle, que l'on retrouvait aussi dans tous les autres médias.

According to market research at the time, within only a few years the Atlas Film logo became one of Germany's best-known trademarks. After the company went into administration, rival distributors reworked its logo in an attempt to cash in on its remarkable image.

Nach nur wenigen Jahren war das Logo von Atlas Film, damaliger Marktforschung zufolge, eines der bekanntesten Markenzeichen Deutschlands. Nach der Insolvenz ließen konkurrierende Filmverleiher ihre Logos überarbeiten, um vom herausragenden Image des Unternehmens zu profitieren.

Selon les études de marché de l'époque, après seulement quelques années, le logo d'Atlas Film était un des sigles les plus connus en Allemagne. Après la faillite de l'entreprise, les distributeurs concurrents firent remanier leurs logos pour profiter de l'excellente image de l'entreprise.

Maribor Airport
1976 · Ivan Dvoršak · YU

Lüttgen Versicherungen
Insurance
1981 · Manfred Korten · DE

Adapta Translations
1967 · Fritz Gottschalk/
Gottschalk+Ash · CA

Alain Carrier
Design
1968 · Alain Carrier · FR

Alfa Jewelry
1965 · Félix Beltrán · CU/MX

Ai Planning
Advertising
1983 · Tadamasa Katsube · JP

Annonsbyråernas Förening
Advertising
1967 · Peter G. Ulmer · SE

Region of Aquitaine
Tourism
1970 · Alain Carrier · FR

Aurora
Furniture
1972 · A. G. Fronzoni · IT

Asakura
Real estate
1981 · Shigeo Katsuoka · JP

Academic Aye Computer
1980 · Minoru Takahashi · JP

Hiroshi Awatsuji Design Room
Textiles
1970 · Ikko Tanaka · JP

**Institut pour les Techniques
de Construction**
Technical institute
1971 · Florent Garnier · FR

**Associação dos Usineiros
do Estado de São Paulo**
Workers association
1960s · Rafael Rodrigues · BR

Autobianchi
Automobiles
1968 · Ilio Negri · IT

Antigorio
1962 · Bruno Monguzzi/
Studio Boggeri · IT

Nichigo Times
Publishing
1975 · Shin Matsunaga · JP

Alitalia
Airline
1969 · Landor Associates · US

Ambra Domestic
Electronics
1979 · Armando Milani,
Maurizio Milani · IT

Catholic Church
1981 · Gustavo Gómez-Casallas,
Rodrigo Fernández · CO

Takaoka Royal
Sports club
1980 · Kazuo Tajima · JP

Allegheny Power System
Energy supplier
1960s · Ad Tolhuis · US

Arclight Productions
Film production
1989 · Edward Hughes · US

The Douglas Allred Company
Real estate
1982 · Don Young · US

Asfaltor Oy
Road construction
1959 · Martti A. Mykkänen · FI

Asahi Pentax
Cameras
1968 · Shigeo Fukuda · JP

Ajinomoto
Spices
1960s · Takashi Kono · JP

Antich
Alcoholic beverages
1966 · Tomás Vellvé · ES

Renault Alpine
Automobiles
1971 · Anonymous · FR

Joele Almagiá
Cosmetics
1969 · Vittorio Antinori · IT

Avida Dollars
Art gallery
1984 · A.G. Fronzoni · IT

Aquadrom
Swimming pools
1978 · Werner Weissbrodt · DE

Arval
Cosmetics
1962 · Remo Muratore · IT

Heart Art
1973 · Ikko Tanaka · JP

**Arbeitsgemeinschaft
kultureller Institutionen**
Cultural association
1960 · Walter Breker · DE

Azote
Chemicals
1973 · Selahattin Sönmez · TR

Antonelli Vivai-Pavia
Horticulture
1976 · Pietro Galli · IT

Albitex
Cotton
1960 · Max Huber · IT

Aephus Designs
1986 · Fred E. Denzler · US

Allied Casting
Construction company
1960s · Kramer, Miller, Lomden,
Glassman Inc. · US

Asahi Culture Center
1974 · Shigeo Fukuda · JP

Industrial Adhesives
1960s · Peter Gauld/Lintas · UK

Praga Kulturalna
Cultural center
1965 · Zdeněk Ziegler · CZ

Abbott
Pharmaceuticals
1960s · Don Ervin/
George Nelson & Co. · US

American Savings Bank
1969 · Tom Woodward · US

Ali Reza Group
Oil industry services
1970 · Tor A. Pettersen · UK

**Almer-Société Algérienne
du Méthanol et des Résines**
1972 · Michel Waxman/
Waxman Design · BE

Argus Press
Printing
1976 · Fred E. Denzler · US

Asama Motor Lodge
Parking lot
1962 · Nakajo Masayoshi · JP

Asko Möbel Helsinki
Furniture
1966 · Michel Olyff · BE

10th Internationaler Archiv-Konress
Archiving congress (proposed design)
1984 · Erwin Poell · DE

Efibanca Bank
1977 · Ettore Vitale · IT

Alvit
1973 · Nicola Russo · IT

Autopistas
Road construction
1967 · Enric Huguet · ES

Auleama International Group
1970s · Robert Hagenhofer · US/UK

Gas und Wasserwerke
Energy technology
1980 · Othmar Motter · AT

Arterior
Textiles
1965 · Graphicteam Köln · DE

Centro de Coleccionadores de Arte
Art center
1968 · Willys de Castro,
Hércules Barsotti · BR

Admiral Corp.
Electronics
1960s · Morton Goldsholl
Design Associates · US

Budimex
Import-export
1960s · Jolanta Baracz · PL

Artothek
Art gallery
1982 · Paul Effert · DE

Arce Editrice
Publishing
1967 · Claudio Platania · IT

Admiral Corp.
Electronics
1960s · Morton Goldsholl
Design Associates · US

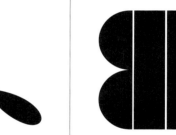

Vertriebsagentur Berlin
Import-export
1970 · Ludvík Feller · DE

Asturias Savings Bank
1983 · Elías García Benavides · ES

Alecta
Wood shavings
1954 · Albe Steiner · IT

Altdorfer Samen
Seeds
1950s · Fred Stolle · DE

Bächtold + Brodmann
Printing
1978 · Roland Hirter · CH

Josef Armellini
1973 · Othmar Motter · AT

Acfis Kompact
Refrigerators
1973 · Walter Hergenröther · CH

Industriezweig Armaturen
Fittings
1965 · Herbert Prüget · DE-GDR

Industrial Bolsera
Packaging
1974 · Tomás Vellvé · ES

BBB Furniture
1968 · Italo Lupi · IT

Big
Publishing
1980 · Yasaburo Kuwayama · JP

Houtoku
Furniture
1980 · Shunji Ninomi · JP

Bates Brothers
Engineering
1963 · Woudhuysen Inc. · UK

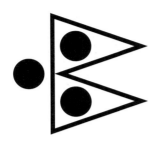

**Staatliche Akademie
für Grafik, Druck und Werbung**
Design school
1950s · Franz Hermann Wills · DE

Borgogna Art Gallery
1970 · Angelo Sganzeria · IT

Bagel Druck
Printing
1971 · Walter Breker · DE

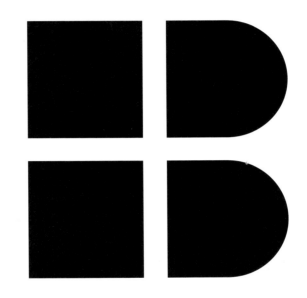

Bunka Hyoronsha
Publishing
1982 · Makoto Yoshida · JP

British International Paper
1969 · Michael Burgess · UK

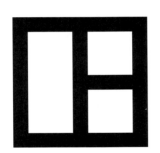

Walter Bangerter
Design
1960s · Walter Bangerter · CH

Bank vom Linthgebiet, Uznach
1969 · Peter Hablützel · CH

Bateau Lavoir
Art gallery
1970 · Michele Spera · IT

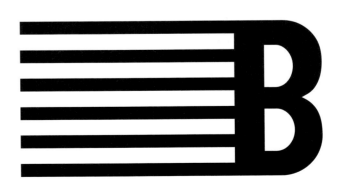

E. Breuninger
Textiles
1948 · Hanns Lohrer · DE

Bicentenario Simón Bolívar
Commemorative occasion
1979 · Gerd Leufert · VE

Tre B
Design
1975 · Armando Milani · IT

Verkehrsverein Basel
Tourism
1968 · Armin Hofmann · CH

Reginald Bennett
Import-export
1968 · Stuart Ash/
Gottschalk+Ash · CA

Bill Bantey & Associates
Management consultancy
1969 · Fritz Gottschalk/
Gottschalk+Ash · CA

B Galerie 33
Art gallery
1950s · Marcel Wyss · CH

A. Bagel Grafische Anstalt
Printing (proposed design)
1950s · Heinrich Wehmeyer · DE

A. Bertelli
Pharmacy
1964 · Albe Steiner · IT

Bäckerei Burkhardt, Volketswil
Bakery
1973 · Odermatt+Tissi · CH

**Bienal Internacional del Deporte en las
Bellas Artes, Barcelona**
Sports festival
1971 · Julián Santamaría · ES

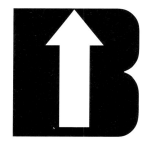

Bostleman Corporation
Construction company
1973 · Terry Lesniewicz, Al Navarre · US

Magasins du Printemps Brummell
Clothing
1970 · Jean Widmer · FR

Brno Balance
Art exhibition
1970s · Jan Rajlich · CZ

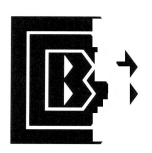

Bolli
Construction company
1977 · Peter G. Ulmer · CH

Birkhäuser Verlag
Publishing
1979 · K. Bruckmann · CH

Baumechanik Barleben
Engineering
1965 · Rudolf Purke · DE-GDR

Buffet Badischer Bahnhof
Restaurant
1960s · Ferdi Afflerbach · CH

Svensk bil Batterifabrik
Automobile batteries
1960s · Tom Huttgren · SE

Brandeis University Women's Committee
1965 · Joe Selame · US

Briefing
Postal services
1966 · Kyösti Varis · FI

Becky Bisoulis
Clothing
1970s · James Lienhart · US

Ostthüringer Brauereien, Pößneck
Brewing
1965 · Fritz Deutschendorf · DE-GDR

Boles Aero
Caravans
1960s · Jerry Braude · US

Banner Printing
1960s · Jerry Braude · US

Stowarzyszenie Bojownik
Social organization
1962 · Jarosław Jasiński · PL

Bellfeed
Textiles
1980 · Akira Hirata, Yoshiharu Saito · JP

Battery & Electric Service
1970 · Peter Hablützel/
Gazette Printing Company · CA

Bautechnik Seibert-Stinnes
Engineering
1973 · Heinz Schwabe · DE

Barazzoni Fratelli
Advertising
1969 · Ennio Lucini/
Promotion Pubblicità · IT

Hermann Baldauf
Goldsmith
1965 · Karl-Heinz Lötzsch · DE-GDR

Félix Beltrán
Design
1960 · Félix Beltrán · CU

Bras
Food technology
1966 · Titti Fabiani/Studio B · IT

Blanc
Industrial design
1971 · Pérez Sánchez · ES

Breuer Uhren
Watches
1960 · Hans-Joachim Brauer · DE

Bernische Lokalbank
Bank
1960s · Hans Hartmann · CH

Ernst Brucker
Road construction
1956 · Hanns Lohrer · DE

Werbedienst Berlin
Advertising
1965 · Anonymous · DE

Berlin-Kosmetik
Cosmetics
1965 · Ingo Arnold · DE-GDR

Beta Heating Systems
1970 · Ernst Roch/
Design Collaborative · CA

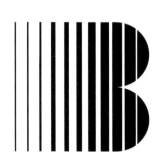

Bilumen
Furniture
1969 · G. & R. Associati · IT

Benzinger
Publishing
1953 · Eugen & Max Lenz · CH

Chemische Werke Buna, Schkopau
Chemicals
1965 · Gerhard Voigt · DE-GDR

Bacci
Art dealer
1970 · G. & R. Associati · IT

**Beauté-Centre Thérapeutique
d'Esthétique, Paris**
Massage salon
1969 · Daniel Maurel/
Chourgnoz Publicité · FR

Bonded Services
Film and tape storage
1966 · Arnold Roston · US

P. Bork Scandinavia
Furniture
1960s · Anonymous · DK

Bertuzzi
Food-processing machinery
1971 · Guido Redaelli · IT

A. Bertelli
Pharmacy
1964 · Albe Steiner · IT

Borrallo
Furniture
1969 · Ribas & Creus · ES

Industrial Blueprinting and Supply
Technical drawing
1966 · Richard Janis · CA

Druckerei Bund Pochon-Jent
Printing
1966 · Werner Mühlemann · CH

Buttmann
Building cleaning
1970 · Peter Riefenstahl · DE

Saint John Harbour Bridge Authority
Bridge maintenance
1966 · J.C. Stackhouse Studios · CA

Bonifatius Druck Buch Verlag
Publishing
1960 · Gerhard Böhle · DE

Berliner Verkehrsbetriebe
Public transport
1960 · Hace Frey · DE

Stork Seriepompen
Water pumps
1964 · M. van Winsen · NL

Biocell
Biochemicals
1971 · Andrea Rossi · IT

Boilot
Cranes
1971 · Erich Brenzinger/
Recherche et Design · FR

Beba Beton
Cement
1962 · Klaus Grözinger, Dieter Heil · DE

Bank für Tirol und Vorarlberg
1982 · Othmar Motter · AT

Barbour Index
Information service
1963 · Ken Garland · UK

Blechpackungswerk Staßfurt
Metalworks
1965 · Rudolf Purke · DE-GDR

Bio Decision Laboratories
Clinical research
1971 · Francis R. Esteban · US

Frischbetonwerk, St. Stephan
Cement
1960s · Hans Thöni · CH

Boffi
Kitchens
1960 · Giulio Confalonieri · IT

Bonfantini Service
Computer services
1971 · Emanuele Centazzo/Sitcap · IT

R. L. Banks & Associates
Railroad freight logistics
1972 · George Tscherny · US

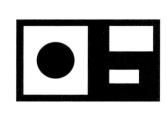

Papierwarenhandlung
Stationery
1950s · Franz Olivier Trog · CH

Bess & Associates
1967 · Michael Reid · US

A. Bertelli
Pharmacy
1964 · Albe Steiner · IT

Bilia
Trade fair
1960s · Lars Bramberg · SE

R. Brockhaus
1957 · Ralf Rudolph · DE

Conrad Bailey
Photography
1966 · James Lienhart/RVI Corp. · US

Bergelectric Corporation
Electrics
1960s · Don Weller · US

Cirla
Granite
1968 · Dante Bighi · IT

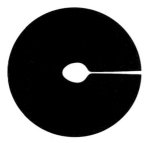

Speisegaststätte Casino
Restaurant
1965 · Heinz Kippnick · DE-GDR

Crea-Filmi
Film production
1966 · Kyösti Varis · FI

Pratt Institute
Design school
1960s · Lance Wyman · US

Cidesco International
Education (proposed design)
1961 · Georges Beaupré · CH

Commerzbau Bauträgergesellschaft
Property development
1970s · Hanns Lohrer · DE

Cimet
Freeze-drying machinery
1967 · Salvatore Gregorietti/
Unimark International · IT

Capitol Records
Record label
1960s · Rod Dyer · US

Chimetal
Chemicals
1962 · Massimo Dradi · IT

Commerce Bank
1973 · Richard Yeager · US

Clark Technologies
Mechanical engineering
1975 · R. Roger Remington · US

Centro de Convenciones Gonzalo Jiménez de Quesada
Congress center
1979 · Dicken Castro · CO

Continental Can
Canning and packaging
1972 · Anspach Grossman Portugal · US

Cayena
1978 · Hugo Arapé · FR

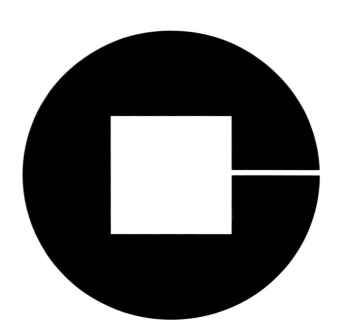

Carl Christiansen
Construction company
1961 · Werner Hartz · DE

Ihara Chemical Industry
1983 · Tsuneo Arima · JP

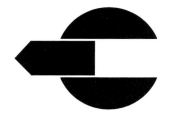

Carcaba
Haulier
1982 · José Santamarina /
Elias & Santamarina · ES

Canadian Pacific, Montreal
Haulier
1968 · Lippincott & Margulies · US

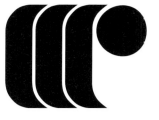

**Camden Committee
for Community Relations**
Social work
1966 · Ken Garland · UK

Nippon Computer
1971 · Yuji Baba · JP

Consolidated Foods Corporation
1972 · Landor Associates · US

A. Carbo
Jeweler
1973 · Enric Huguet · ES

Colin Hochstin Company
Investment
1977 · Mike Quon, David Rubin · US

Colmers
Grocery
1966 · Kenneth Hollick · UK

Cook's Travel Service
Travel agency
1964 · Gerald Rosso · US

Caprotti Manifattura
Textiles
1959 · Max Huber · IT

Coplay Cement
1979 · Bill Bundzak · US

Conte
Accountancy
1969 · Claude Dietrich · PE

Coletti
Furniture
1968 · Franco M. Ricci · IT

Equipmag
Interior design
1970 · Jean Delaunay/Look · FR

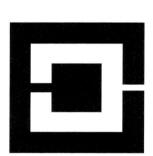

Clipho Cliché
Typesetting
1962 · Morten Peetz-Schou · DK

Commodore
Computer systems
1965 · Chris Yaneff · CA

Complett
Knitting machines
1964 · Montaini+Neuburg · IT

Casagrande Impianti
Hydraulic systems
1983 · Alfredo de Santis · IT

Corsair
Heating technology
1965 · Anthony Smith, Roger Turpin · UK

Credit Cart
Bank
1978 · Guillermo Gonzáles Ruiz · AR

Československé Státní Dráhy
Czechoslovakian state railway
1974 · Jiří Rathouský · CZ

Bonairia Casu
Advertising
1974 · Rinaldo Cutini · IT

Cooper
Construction company
1969 · Chris Yaneff · CA

Carlo Cisventi
Photography
1970 · Carlo Bruni · IT

Cavazzoni
Carpets
1969 · Franco M. Ricci · DE

Le Canne
Hotel
1972 · A. G. Fronzoni · IT

Ceteco
Paper
1960s · Heinz Waibl · IT

Association for Solidarity with Cuba
Political campaign group
1969 · Félix Beltrán · CU

Command
Travel agency
1978 · D. Bruce Zahor · US

Visibilia Caracas
Design exhibition
1968 · Gerd Leufert · VE

KM Associates
Exhibition equipment
1968 · William Newton · CA

Cyrmac Plastics
1970 · Raymond Bellemare · CA

Continentale Versicherungen
Insurance
1970 · Ulrich Schürmann · DE

Calwer Passage
Shopping center
1978 · Hanns Lohrer · DE

Koyo Shigyo
Printing
1964 · Takeshi Otaka · JP

Caterpillar Tractor
Construction equipment
1967 · Lester Beall · US

Cord Chemical Company
1968 · Raymond E. Meylan · UK

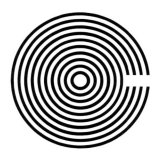

Cometa
Photo technology
1968 · Gérard Guerre/Technés · FR

Condor Records
Record label
1962 · John Denison-Hunt · UK

Presses Centrales de Lausanne
Printing
1970 · Pierre Bataillard · CH

Canon
Office machines
1983 · Minoru Takahashi · JP

Chemi
Chemicals
1973 · Franco Grignani · IT

Canto-Kuoro
Choir
1967 · Jaska Hänninen · FI

Chemometall
Metalworks
1978 · Badian & Weinblatt · AT

Circoli Repubblicani
Political party
1972 · Michele Spera · IT

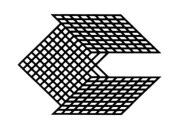

Galería Conkright
Art gallery
1973 · Gerd Leufert · VE

Gibson Kelite
Chemicals
1960s · Heinz Grunwald · AU

Continental Savings & Loan
Bank
1960s · Chuck Rhoades · US

Centrum-Warenhaus
Department store
1965 · Herbert Prüget · DE-GDR

VEB Chemieausrüstungen
Chemistry equipment
1965 · Fritz Deutschendorf · DE-GDR

Creative Photography
1963 · Ernst Roch/
Design Collaborative · CA

Cochrane Photographic Studio
1960s · Anonymous · US

C-Film
Film distributor
1970 · Ekkehart Rustmeier · DE

Cassina
Furniture
1953 · Giancarlo Pozzi · IT

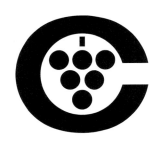

Consorzio Vini di Carema
Wine association
1959 · Walter Ballmer · IT

W. Bertschi & Sohn
Bakery
1940s · Alfons Grimm · CH

Jeunesses Musicales du Canada, Montreal
Music association
1968 · George Huel,
Pierre-Yves Pelletier · CA

Cygnet
1973 · John Nash/
Richard, Nash & Friends · UK

Caleta Hotel, Mexico
1970 · Lance Wyman · US

Diblo Holding
Import-export
1979 · Joe Vera, Francisco Tellez · MX

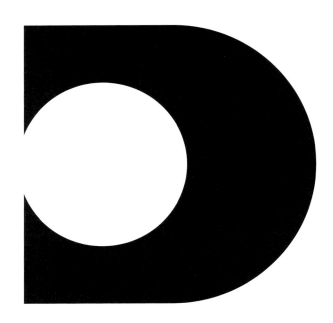

Delta Tooling
Machinery
1960s · Mort Walsh · CA

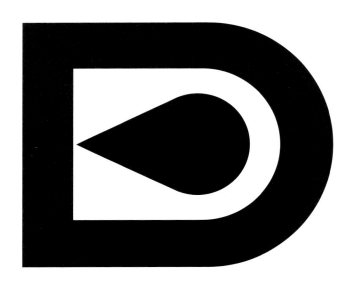

Clichy Distugil
Plastics
1967 · Jacques Nathan-Garamond · FR

Design Team
1969 · Antoon de Vijlder · BE

**Przedsie Biorstwo Budowy
Dróg i Mostów**
Architecture
1976 · Tytus Walczak · PL

KD Shoes
Footwear
1960s · Sotir Sotirov · BG

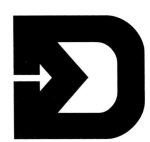

Dired
1979 · Silvio Gayton · US

Derbyshire County Council
Regional administration
1975 · Kenneth Hollick · UK

Défilé Foires
Exhibition
1970s · Jan Rajlich · CZ

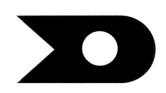

Deutsche Dunlop
Tires
1950s · Hanns Lohrer · DE

David Osbourne
Engineering
1980 · Denise Spaulding · US

Ducommun
Engineering services
1970s · Saul Bass & Associates · US

D. I.
Design and development
1972 · Stuart Ash/Gottschalk+Ash · CA

Studio de Création Roger Druet
Design
1966 · Roger Druet · FR

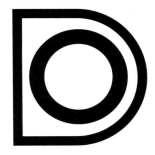

Ring Design
1961 · Knut Yran · SE

Durham Regional Government
1974 · Ron Richards · CA

Daimaru Shokuhin
Foods
1982 · Hideki Aoki · JP

Open Design
Industrial design
1978 · Carlo Malerba · IT

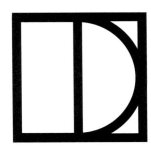

Design Center Österreich
Design association
1965 · Anonymous · AT

**21st Century Association
Design Festival**
1982 · Akisato Ueda · JP

Fonderies E. Desbeck
Ironworks
1968 · Gilles Fiszman · BE

International Design and Woodcraft
1978 · Rolf Harder · CA

Devi Productions
Film production
1971 · Mike Quon · US

Dicomed
Color film recorders
1990 · Peter Seitz · US

DuPage Power Wash
Pressure washing
1980 · Richard Wittosch · US

Dimelo Construções e Empreendimentos
Steel construction
1976 · PVDI · BR

LD Birdseed
1961 · Rolf Harder/
Design Collaborative · CA

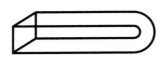

Imposibilia
Design exhibition
1968 · Gerd Leufert · VE

Richard Doerfel
Heating systems
1965 · Paul-Helmut Becker · DE-GDR

Yugocryl Liubliana
Chemicals
1972 · Matjaz Bertonceli · YU

Dupan Sogefor
Fiberglass
1964 · Yvon Laroche · CA

Landbrugets Afsaetningsudvalg
Foods
1958 · Olle Eksell · SE/DK

De Coene
Furniture
1964 · Michel Olyff · BE

Fotoaktiv 57
Photography fair
1965 · Georg Hülsse · DE-GDR

Charles Jourdan & Fils
Footwear
1970 · Roland Jourdan · FR

Dansk Droge Import
Pharmaceuticals
1968 · Morten Peetz-Schou · DK

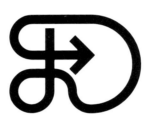

Dentsu Driving Club
1960s · Jun Tabohashi · JP

Designeering
Technical drawings
1960 · Leslie Smart · CA

Lakeshore Data Services
1968 · Leslie Smart · CA

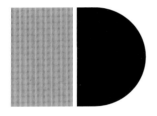

House of Denmark
Furniture
1967 · Raymond Lee · CA

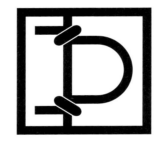

Drawag Glattbrugg
Wires
1960s · Franz Fässler · CH

Danesi
Coffee
1969 · Sergio Salaroli · IT

Donald Duncan
Transportation
1960s · Rolf Harder · CA

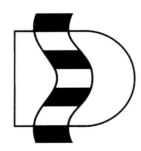

Stadt Düsseldorf
City identity (proposed design)
1984 · Paul Effert · DE

Stadt Düsseldorf
City identity (proposed design)
1978 · Walter Breker · DE

Collezione Delta
Furniture
1971 · Sergio Salaroli · IT

Dril de Mexico
Drilling
1971 · Ernesto Lehfeld · MX

Reese-Gesellschaft Hameln
Foods
1950 · Heinrich Wehmeyer · DE

Dismero
Textiles
1983 · Oanh Pham Phu · DE

Société Dennery
Shop systems
1970 · Pham Ngoc Tuan · FR

Dariosecq
Furniture
1969 · Michel Quennessen · FR

Alfred Ehrlin
Furniture
1960s · Anonymous · SE

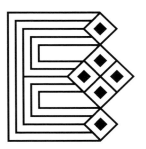

E-Marke
Crayons
1960s · Walter Breker · DE

PGH Elektro
Electronics
1965 · Horst Wenzel · DE-GDR

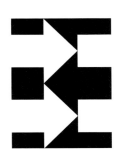

E. Eversen
Air-conditioning
1966 · Per Einar Eggen/
Alfsen, Becker & Bates · NO

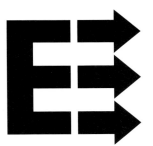

Emhart Corporation
Machinery
1957 · Lester Beall · US

Euromar
Import-export
1968 · Armando Milani · IT

Torii & Co.
Pharmaceuticals
1977 · Kazuo Tanaka · JP

Elliot's Books
Publishing
1960s · William Wondriska · US

Europaper
1970 · Knut Yran · NO

Elite Circuits
Electronics
1978 · Don Young · US

Ergometrix Office Systems
1978 · Tracy Turner · US

Weinkellerei Eckert
Wines
1950s · Gust Hahn · DE

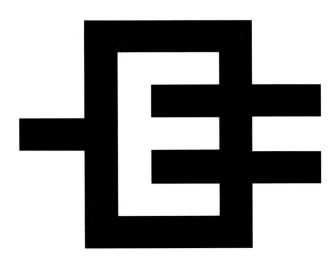

Electrolux
Domestic appliances
1962 · Marcel Wyss · CH

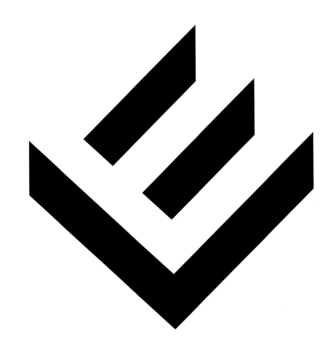

Edwin Vogt & Partner
Printing
1982 · Armin Vogt · CH

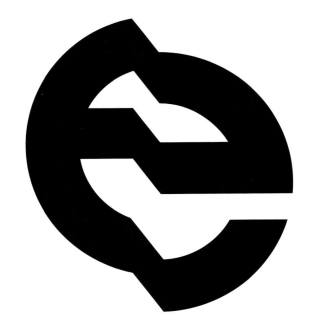

Ediltur
Travel agency
1975 · Alfredo de Santis · IT

Ceco
Steelworks
1960s · Dickens Design Group · US

Ecopex
1977 · Hugo Arapé · FR

CE Gärtnereibetrieb
Gardening
1970 · Ekkehart Rustmeier · DE

Interhotel Erfurter Hof
Hotel
1965 · Fritz Deutschendorf · DE-GDR

Engineering Concepts
1975 · Jack Evans · US

US Energy Research and Development
1978 · George Jadowski · US

Eliograf Artigrafiche
Typesetting
1968 · Sergio Salaroli · IT

Estonian Girl Gymnasts
Sports team
1968 · Vello Hubel · CA

Econ Technologies
Digital systems integration
1975 · R. Roger Remington · US

Etinor AS
Adhesives
1970 · Ove Engström · SE

Ensamblaje
Assembly workshop
1969 · Gerd Leufert · VE

Izerusha
Publishing
1972 · Sumio Hasegawa · JP

Espacio
Furniture
1968 · Félix Beltrán · CU/MX

Everon
Opticals
1960s · Magalhães,
Noronha & Pontual · BR

H. B. Seilling Holzgroßhandel
Timber
1969 · Josefine Fellmer · DE

Europharma Karlsruhe
Pharmaceutical trade fair
1959 · Hace Frey · DE

Encuentro de Escultores
Artists association
1978 · Félix Beltrán · CU/MX

Société d'Electro-Chimie d'Ugine
Chemicals
1966 · Paul Gabor · FR

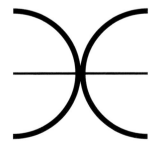

Electa Editrice
Publishing
1967 · Giancarlo Iliprandi · IT

Firma für Elektrotechnik
Electronics
1960s · Hans Wydler · CH

Eastern Lithographing
Printing
1966 · Leslie Smart · CA

Chimica Etra, Canavese
Chemicals
1959 · Walter Ballmer · IT

Hotel Le Reine Elizabeth, Montreal
1968 · Jean Morin · CA

Firma für Elektrotechnik
Electronics
1960s · Hansruedi Widmer · CH

Editeur
Publishing
1970 · Jean Delaunay/Look · FR

Eason's Advertising Service
1960s · Eason's Advertising Service · IE

Eltz
Ship windows
1965 · Alfred Mähler · DE-GDR

VVB Plast-Elast-Verarbeitung
Plastics
1965 · Christoph Hülsenberg · DE-GDR

VEB Kraftfahrzeug Instandsetzung
Automobile repair
1965 · Fritz Deutschendorf · DE-GDR

L'Echoppe
Gift shop
1965 · Albert Hollenstein/
Hollenstein Création · FR

Ellerman Companies
Insurance
1975 · James Lienhart · US

Estexa
Textiles
1964 · Carlos Alberto
Méndez Mosquera · AR

Kenya Exploration Society
Geographical society
1972 · Walter Plata, Hemant Patel · KE

Anzen Kogaku Kenkyujo
Research institute
1975 · Shigeo Katsuoka · JP

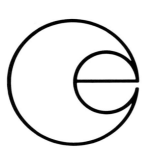

Edition Leipzig
Publishing
1975 · Sonja Wunderlich · DE-GDR

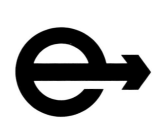

DIA Maschinen Export
Machinery
1965 · Klaus Lempke · DE-GDR

Ets Elco
Tools
1964 · Raymond Loewy/CEI · FR

Esrolko Gewürz Givaudan
Spices
1970 · Hans Hurter · CH

East Cleveland
Metalworks
1960s · A. Norman Law · US

East River Savings Bank
1970 · David Leigh · US

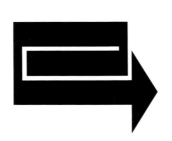

Executronics
Management consultancy
1969 · J. & A. Breukelman
Design Associates · CA

New Rochelle
City identity
1976 · Thomas Starr · US

Les marques commerciales les plus efficaces sont souvent celles qui ne cherchent pas vraiment à décrire précisément un produit ou un processus. C'est plutôt par leur forme qu'elles évoquent une certaine qualité qui, par la répétition, finit par traduire exactement l'intention initiale.
Alvin Lustig

Die erfolgreichsten Markenzeichen sind häufig solche, die das Produkt oder den Prozess gar nicht genau zu beschreiben versuchen. Vielmehr beschwören sie durch ihre Form eine bestimmte Qualität, die durch Wiederholung schließlich genau das ursprünglich Beabsichtigte bedeutet.
Alvin Lustig

Actually the most successful marks are quite often those that make no effort to describe accurately a product or process. Rather, by selection of the forms they attempt to evoke a certain quality that by repetition will come to mean everything originally desired.
Alvin Lustig

Entenkombinat
Foods
1965 · Horst Müller · DE-GDR

Edition Leipzig
Publishing
1975 · Gert Wunderlich · DE-GDR

Famos
Textiles
1976 · R. Nava, D. Soffientini, G. Romani, A. Ubertazzi · IT

State University of New York
1973 · Don Nichols · US

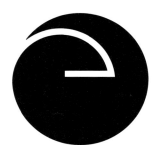

Emhart Offsetdruckerei
Printing
1960s · Herbert Wenn · DE

Deltec Electronics
1973 · Emanuele Centazzo/Sitcap · IT

Bureau d'Etude d'Esthétique Industrielle
Industrial design
1965 · Jacques Nathan-Garamond · FR

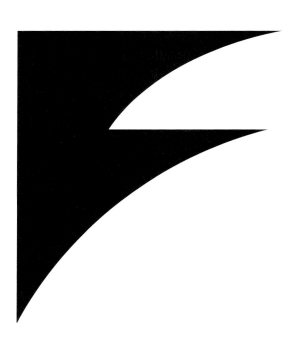

Fuji Kyuso
Haulier
1978 · Shinichi Takahara · JP

Equipesca
Fishing equipment
1957 · Alexandre Wollner · BR

EZ Enterprises
1981 · Steve Sheldon · US

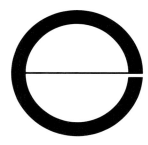

Electrolux
Electronics (proposed design)
1960s · Kurt Wirth · CH

Erfachrome
Photographic services
1972 · Michel Rubens · BE

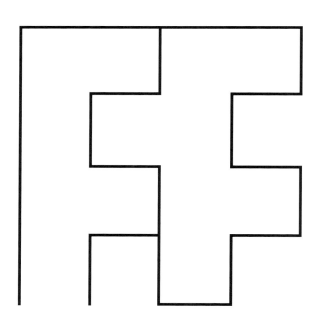

Formation Furniture
1965 · Fletcher, Forbes, Gill · UK

Parfümerie Exquisit
Perfumery
1965 · Renate Wenzel · DE-GDR

Environmental Products
Furniture
1972 · Harry Murphy · US

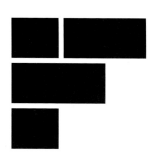

Gebrüder Feierle
Construction company
1982 · Othmar Motter · AT

Finlayson
Textiles
1970s · Anonymous · FI

Friesland Bank
1973 · Wim Crouwel · NL

Eidgenössisches Turnfest 1963
Sports festival
1962 · Blaise Bron · CH

Fidelity Group of Funds
Investment
1979 · George Tscherny · US

Franco Cristaldi & Federico Fellini
Film production
1972 · Michele Spera · IT

Ernst Fischer
Steelworks
1961 · Fridolin Müller/Erwin Halpern · CH

Fjellberg Grafisk
Design
1967 · Erik & Klaus Fjellberg · NO

Fujiwara Hisato
Gardening equipment
1971 · João Carlos Cauduro,
Ludovico Antonio Martino · MX/JP

Finaldi
Electronics
1965 · A. G. Fronzoni · IT

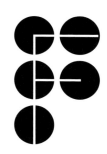

Fukuoka Kagaku Kogyo
Chemicals
1970 · Uehara Masashi/
Nippon Design Center · JP

Finnish Export Furniture
1950s · Kosti A. Antikainen · FI

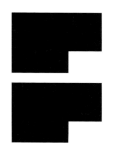

Donald Forrest
Architecture
1969 · David J. Plumb · UK

Chemische Fabrik
Chemicals
1946 · Walter Breker · DE

Frölunda Torg
Shopping center
1965 · Olle Eksell · SE

Spedition Fritz
Transportation
1960s · Hanns Lohrer · DE

Ferrero
Foods (proposed design)
1975 · Aldo Novarese · IT

Galway Foundry & Engineering
Metalworking
1960s · Brandon Matthews · IE

Fravemøllen
Paint
1969 · Claus Rostrup · DK

FIDIMI
Investment
1970 · Sergio Salaroli · IT

N. V. Fokkens-Arnhem
Engineering
1969 · Frits W. van Ooststroom · NL

Atrium
Construction company
1960s · Oanh Pham Phu · DE

**Fédération Internationale
pour l'Education Artistique, Basel**
Art schools association
1958 · Emil Ruder · CH

Fabrimetal
Metalworks
1966 · Jacques Richez · BE

Oy Aero Finnair
Airline
1966 · Kyösti Varis · FI

C. Fullá
Mechanic
1965 · Tomás Vellvé · ES

Frick Ingénieur
Heating technology
1950s · Otto Krämer · CH

Goppion Caffè
Restaurant
1970 · Umberto Facchini · IT

Fuji Seiko
Precision technology
1981 · Makoto Yoshida · JP

Funktio
Furniture
1968 · Eero Syvänoja/
Markkinointi Viherjuuri · FI

Frankfort Fuels
1964 · Carl Brett/
Hiller Rinaldo Associates · CA

Giorgi
Advertising
1965 · Giorgi · FR

Frontier Airlines
1977 · Saul Bass & Associates · US

Federal Cei
Machinery
1976 · Carlo Malerba · IT

Ferrafalti
Road construction
1973 · Emanuele Centazzo/Sitcap · IT

Einkaufszentrum Glatt
Shopping center
1964 · Moritz S. Jaggi · CH

Finlevy
Record label
1966 · Jukka Pellinen · FI

Fuji Landscape
Landscape architecture
1983 · Hiro Terao · JP

Falken Verlag
Publishing
1973 · Peter Schultze/
Schultze und Zimmermann · DE

Getex Consult
Engineering
1969 · Werner Hartz · DE/CH

Schweizer Filmarchiv
Film archive
1950 · Hermann Eidenbenz · CH

Nippon Family Book
Bookstore
1978 · Koichi Mizuno · JP

Furuya Seika
Toys
1966 · Kenji Ito · JP

Graphic Center
Printing
1968 · Robert Geisser · CH

Futatsuka Jidosha
Automobile repair
1982 · Atsutaka Chono,
Hideshi Takahashi · JP

Fábrica de Plástico
Plastics
1965 · Félix Beltrán · CU/MX

Franke-Wärmegeräte
Heating technology
1965 · Herbert Prüget · DE-GDR

Stadt Gelsenkirchen
City identity
1970s · Eberhard Hippler · DE

Radio Glasgow
Broadcasting
1973 · Ralph Semmence, David Stanfield/
Daily Mirror Design Group · UK

Giardini
Synthetic materials
1973 · G. & R. Associati · IT

George Gärtner
Advertising
1971 · G. W. Hörnig · DE

H. Gertsch & Co.
Cleaning machines
1965 · Hans R. Woodtli · CH

Global Marine Products
1981 · Rick Cartledge · CA

A. & M. Giuliani
Chemicals
1971 · Ilio Negri · IT

J. R. Geigy
Pharmaceuticals (proposed design)
1960s · Toshihiro Katayama · JP

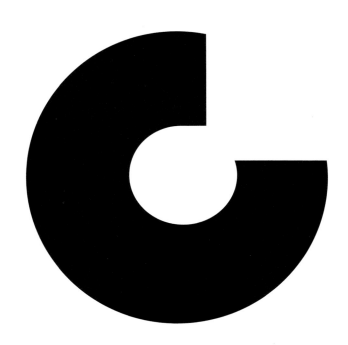

Rex Granby Studios
Artist's agent
1968 · Tony Forster · UK

Société Générale de Banque
Bank
1966 · Jacques Richez · BE

Girad
Bank
1960s · Emil O. Biemann · US

Gilligan Election Campaign
1970 · Stan Brod · US

Nederlandse Gasunie
Energy supplier
1965 · Otto Treumann · NL

Grúas Guanipa
Leasing services
1979 · Reynaldo Da Costa · US

Girec
Engineering
1964 · Luc Van Malderen · BE

Georg Jensen Sølvsmedie
Product design
1969 · Morten Peetz-Schou, Ulla Heegaard · DK

Giro 4
Measuring instruments
1971 · Reynaldo Da Costa · VE

Printing Services
1960s · Félix Beltrán · CU

Grobermann
Carpets
1978 · Colin Knaud/
Pacific Rim Design & Direction · CA

Orient-Occident
Textiles
1963 · Jukka Pellinen · FI

**22nd International Geographical
Congress, Ottawa**
1969 · Fritz Gottschalk, Ian Valentine/
Gottschalk+Ash · CA

General Telephone and Electronics
1960s · Emil O. Biemann · US

Grath
Property management
1983 · Manfred Korten · DE

Five G Marketing
Advertising
1966 · John B. Castle/
Castle, Chappell and Partners · UK

Kingston Gifts
Promotional gifts
1968 · Eurographics · UK

Ghia
Automobiles
1960s · Giovanni Brunazzi · IT

Gordon Grant
1979 · Terry Lesniewicz, Al Navarre · US

Matsushita Electric Works
1981 · Nobuyuki Hagiwara,
Fumio Koyoda · JP

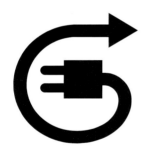

Imatran Voima
Electronics
1968 · Olof Eriksson · FI

Golden Guernsey Dairy
1975 · Ken Eichenbaum,
Doris Stein · US

Gary National Bank
1970s · James Lienhart · US

J. R. Geigy
Pharmaceuticals
1956 · Jörg Hamburger · CH

Bernhard Gieseke
Road construction
1963 · Josefine Fellmer · DE

Glyvenol
Chemicals
1968 · A. G. Fronzoni · IT

Laboratoires Goupil
Pharmaceuticals
1966 · Lonsdale Design · FR

Verkehrsverein Grindelwald
Tourism
1969 · Hans Hartmann · CH

Ed. Gerlach
Chemicals
1963 · Ulrich Maass · DE

The National Giro Post Office
1969 · Henrion Design Associates · UK

Gilcodan
Textiles
1970 · Adam Moltke · DK

Siedlung Gäbelbach, Bern
Shopping center
1970 · Hans Hartmann · CH

Green Chemical
Plastic bags
1974 · Katsumi Nagata, Yasaburo
Kuwayama, Ikuo Masubuchi · JP

Hans-Joachim Gericke
Architecture
1966 · Klaus Grözinger,
Peter Riefenstahl · DE

Giuliani
Pharmacy
1965 · Ribas & Creus · ES

Graphic Designers Association
1979 · Kazuo Kishimoto · JP

Grantham Rainwear
1960s · Julian Swift/Dolphin Design
Associates · UK

Gerdau Grupo Siderúrgico
Steelworks
1977 · PVDI · BR

Stanley A. Grant
Embroidery
1966 · E. J. Morrison/
Stewart & Morrison · CA

Taeppefabrik
Carpets
1960s · Anonymous · DK

Gipron
Skates and skiing equipment
1971 · Studio GSZ · IT

VEB Gölzaplast
Plastics
1965 · Gerhard Voigt · DE-GDR

McGee Fuels
1969 · Frank Lieberman · US

Goertz Mantelhaus
Textiles
1967 · Hans Ulrich Allemann/
Erwin Halpern Werbeagentur · DE

Gerber Werbeagentur
Advertising
1950s · Marcel Wyss · CH

George Vries
Musical instruments
1957 · Franz Hermann Wills · DE

VEB Gießereianlagen
Foundry
1965 · Manfred Kloppert · DE-GDR

Mechanic
1980 · Walter Hergenröther · IT

Centre de Création Industrielle
Industrial design association
1969 · Jean Widmer · FR

Gaston-Cognac Edeka Großkellerei
Wines
1960s · Ingo & Christine Friel · DE

Canada Golf Shokai
Sporting goods
1960s · Kenji Ito · JP

Goto Kogei
Industrial design
1966 · Nakajo Masayoshi · JP

Grafispania
Design exhibition
1966 · Tomás Vellvé · ES

The Guinness Record Group
Publishing
1979 · Silvio Gayton · US

Genthiner Brauhaus
Brewing
1965 · Peter Hamann · DE-GDR

Goldkreis Verkaufsorganisation
Import-export
1950s · Karl-Heinz Jagals · DE

Hermann Geiling
Advertising
1950s · Geiling Werbegesellschaft · DE

Gretag
Electronics
1982 · Peter Christensen,
Marc Burckhalter · CH

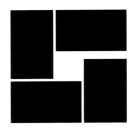

Golden Harvest
Film production
1970 · Anonymous · HK

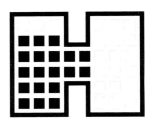

Hobis Telephone Systems
1983 · Don Connelly · US

VVG
Design association
1960s · Anonymous · BE

Gelco Corporation
Transportation
1979 · Peter Seitz,
Hideki Yamamoto · US

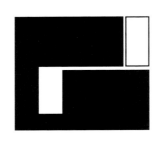

Federico Grau
Printing
1968 · Tomás Vellvé · ES

Horsa Hotéis Reunidos
Hotel chain
1970 · S. R. Alvim · BR

W. Girardet Buchverlag
Publishing
1973 · Anonymous · DE

Gasparotto
Footwear
1958 · Heinz Waibl · IT

J. R. Geigy
Pharmaceuticals (proposed design)
1960s · Toshihiro Katayama · JP

Hotel
1956 · Félix Beltrán · CU/MX

Prince Motor Sales
1960s · Jun Tabohashi · JP

Gamabus
Automobile engineering
1981 · R. Nava, D. Soffientini,
A. Ubertazzi · IT

Granite State Credit Union
Bank
1983 · Charles M. Mosco · US

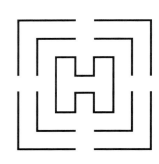

Huvag Handel
Import–export
1970 · Hans Hurter · CH

Gower
Cosmetics
1969 · Enzo Careccia/
Opit Pubblicità · IT

GTO Skiing Equipment
1975 · Yuji Kawarabayashi,
Akisato Ueda · JP

Globe Verlag
Publishing
1950s · Josef Autherid · AT

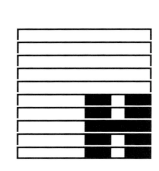

Gesellschaft für Holzstoffbereitung
Timber
1960s · Walter Bosshardt · CH

J. R. Geigy
Pharmaceuticals (proposed design)
1960s · Toshihiro Katayama · JP

J. R. Geigy
Pharmaceuticals (proposed design)
1960s · Toshihiro Katayama · JP

Garciet
Canning
1967 · Leen Averink/Mafia · FR

Hotel Metropole, Geneva
1982 · Julien van der Wal · CH

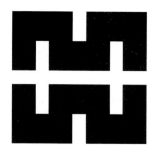

Deutsche Stahllamelle, Hünnebeck
Steelworks
1950s · Anonymous · DE

Hackensack Medical Center
Hospital
1982 · Robert P. Gersin,
Abner Gutierrez · US

Hershey Trust
Investment
1969 · David L. Burke · US

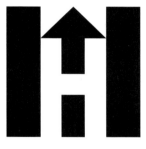

Jalo Haapala
Construction company
1962 · Martti A. Mykkänen · FI

Hong Kong Land
Property development
1970 · Henry Steiner · US

Spanplattenwerk Fideris
Chipboard
1955 · Peter Ruedi · CH

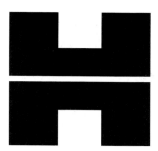

Wilhelm Hoffmann
Carpentry
1966 · Klaus Grözinger,
Peter Riefenstahl · DE

Halifax Transit
Haulier
1969 · Fritz Gottschalk,
Ian Valentine/Gottschalk+Ash · CA

Hechinger Company
Home-improvement stores
1975 · Chermayeff & Geismar · US

Hotel Limmathaus
1960s · Rudolf Bircher · CH

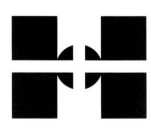

Health Careers of Ohio
Medical employment
1975 · Monica Brown, Stan Brod · US

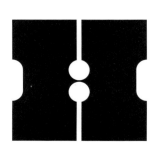

Hojer Taeppefabrik
Carpets
1960s · Anonymous · DK

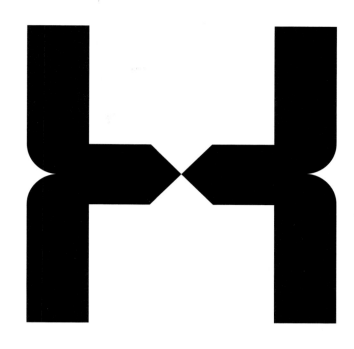

Halifax Shopping Center
1961 · Ernst Roch/Design Collaborative · CA

Hunziker Transporte Rüschlikon
Haulier
1960s · Hansruedi Scheller · CH

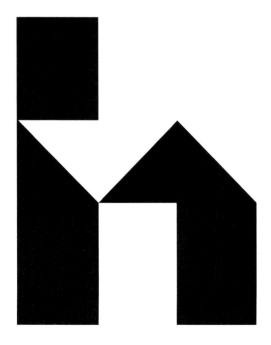

Haslett Warehouse & Transportation
1964 · Robert Pease · US

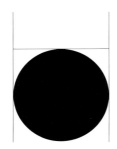

Richard Helland
Design
1966 · Richard Helland · US

Hudson's Bay Oil and Gas
1967 · Chris Yaneff · CA

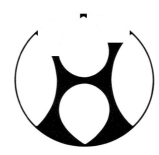

Hinds Cosmetics
1964 · Dominik L. Burckhardt · US

Hilton
Hotel chain
1964 · Anonymous · US

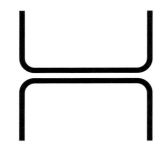

L. Holzer & Co.
Tables
1968 · Ken Garland · UK

Hiraki
Beverages
1982 · Takao Sasaki, Yutaka Mitani · JP

Hoesch
Steelworks
1960s · Heinz Schwabe · DE

Hart Manufacturing
1960s · Emil O. Biemann · US

Halpern Werbeagentur
Advertising
1960s · Erwin Halpern · CH

Felix Handschin
Ceramics
1960 · GGK · CH

Godfred H. Petersens Møbelvaerksteder
Furniture
1960s · Anonymous · DK

Hipertonicks
Electronics
1975 · Robert Hagenhofer · US

Agroinform
Agriculture
1976 · István Szekeres · HU

Hawaiian Airlines
1970 · Clarence Lee · US

Hojer Tæppefabrik
Carpets
1960s · Anonymous · DK

Hotel Tateshina
1967 · Takashi Kono · JP

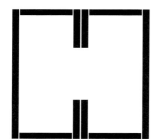

Christian Holzäpfel
Furniture
1960 · Karl Gerstner · CH

Hotel Sogo Palace, Takayama
1982 · Hidemichi Yamao · JP

Bernard Harris
Import-export
1964 · James Cross · US

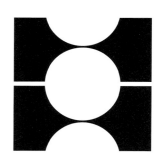

Honkarakenne Oy
Construction company
1970 · Seppo Polameri · FI

Walter Herzog
Advertising
1960 · Walter Herzog · CH

The Hong Kong Hyatt Hotel
1960s · Henry Steiner · HK

Harbel
Cosmetics
1972 · G. & R. Associati · IT

Hayashi Industry
1967 · Yoshio Hayashi · JP

Hans Schaub
Printing
1962 · Hans Knöpfli · CH

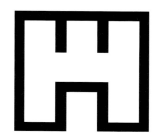

Stadt Hamburg
City identity (proposed design)
1960s · Uli Schierle · DE

Hooper
Construction company
1965 · Jerry Dahm/
Vie Design Studios · US

Hirota
Refrigerators
1976 · Koichi Watanabe · JP

Héliographia Arts Graphiques
Printing
1960s · Roger-Virgile Geiser · CH

Pequeño Teatro de Ensayo
Theater
1970s · Emiro Lobo · VE

**Hessen-Nassauische
Versicherungsanstalt**
Insurance
1981 · Dieter Urban · DE

Hormicuba
Concrete
1972 · Félix Beltrán · CU

Häberli Möbel
Furniture
1950s · Marcel Wyss · CH

Heidolph
Electronics
1960s · Mendell & Oberer · DE

Holzhandel
Wood
1960s · Hansruedi Scheller · CH

Holzwaren
Wood products
1950s · Kurt Sieth · DE

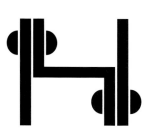

Henderson Steel Construction
1974 · Ernst Roch · CA

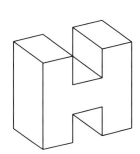

Brian Harvey
Architecture
1968 · Bob Gill · US/UK

Hans Hemmi
Advertising
1960 · Hans Hemmi · CH

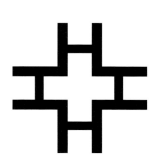

Helanca Heberlein
Elastic materials
1950s · Otto Krämer · CH

Vesijohtoliike Huber
Air-conditioning
1963 · Matti Ojanen · FI

Honda Curtain
Interior design
1977 · Yoneo Jinbo · JP

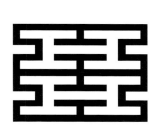

Hong Kong Hilton
Hotel
1960s · Henry Steiner · HK

Richard Hemingway & Partners
Construction company
1982 · Keith Murgatroyd,
Tony Forster · UK

Hindermann
Furniture
1974 · István Morócz, Sára Ernő · HU

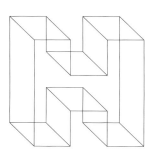

Hammerplast Manchester
Glass
1975 · Keith Murgatroyd,
Tony Forster · UK

Hokushin
Printing
1982 · Soichi Saito · JP

HH Hotels
Hotel chain
1960s · Hiroshi Ohchi · JP

Herbst et Cie
Audio technology
1964 · Jacques Nathan-Garamond · FR

Galerie 33 15, Siedlung Halen
Art gallery
1950s · Marcel Wyss · CH

Hadeka
1970s · Anonymous · DE

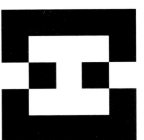

Ianua
Design
1977 · Guillermo Gonzáles Ruiz · AR

Concertgebouw Haarlem
Concert hall
1969 · Jaap Frank · NL

Frankfurter Handelsbank
Bank
1972 · Götz Neuke · DE

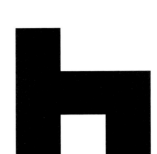

Hans Huber Metallbau
Metal construction
1950s · Peter Kräuchi · CH

Istanbul Carpet Center
1981 · Selahattin Sönmez · TR

Hire's Red Hearth
Restaurant chain
1965 · Eiko Pech/Stewart & Morrison · CA

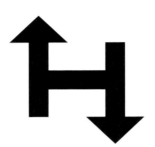

Hess Hoch- und Tiefbau
Construction company
1950s · Marcel Wyss · CH

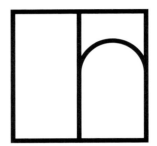

Hörnemann Verlag
Publishing
1980 · Rolf Bürnmann · DE

**Impol Slovenske Bistrica &
Dos Ljubljana**
Metal-processing industry
1975 · Ivan Dvoršak · YU

Messwerkzeugfabrik H. Hommel
Measuring instruments
1940s · Oskar Spitzer · AT

Percy Haynes
Paper
1963 · Fletcher, Forbes, Gill · UK

Honma Interior
Interior design
1983 · Yasaburo Kuwayama · JP

Imagenetics
Exhibition design
1964 · Appelbaum & Curtis · US

Heco Envelope Company
1964 · Hayward R. Blake · US

Dr. Hegemann Werbeagentur
Advertising
1956 · Ulrich Maass · DE

Hart Press
Printing
1971 · Cyril John Schlosser · US

Imagen
Design studio
1969 · Claude Dietrich · PE

Höganäs
Furniture
1960s · Anonymous · SE

Th. Hartwig Druckerei
Printing
1960 · Johann Will Münch · DE

Leonard Heicklen Studios
Photography
1968 · Peter K. Good · US

Tokyo Illustrators Club
1966 · Makoto Wada · JP

I.S.V.E.T.
Institute for economic development
1962 · Mimmo Castellano · IT

Impuls
Interior design
1968 · Paul Brand · NO

Karkula Iittala
Tableware and kitchen items
1960s · Timo Sarpaneva · FI

Galvanite
Electroplating
1960s · Herbert Auchli · CH

Institut für Industrielle Isoliertechnik
Piping and insulation
1965 · Werner Rudolph · DE-GDR

Inducal
Heating technology
1965 · Herbert Prüget · DE-GDR

Infrarot-Anlagen
Infra-red technology
1965 · Herbert Prüget · DE-GDR

Interchim
Industrial organization
1965 · Gerhard Voigt · DE-GDR

Indumar
Furniture
1972 · Ricardo Blanco · AR

Iwatani Sangyo
Propane products
1970 · Ikko Tanaka · JP

Illva
Distillery
1963 · Walter Del Frate · IT

Hotel International, Košice
1968 · František Bobáň · CZ

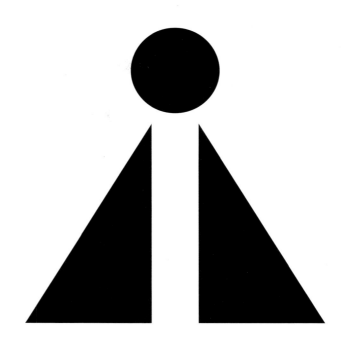

Kempinform
Campsite
1983 · István Szekeres · HU

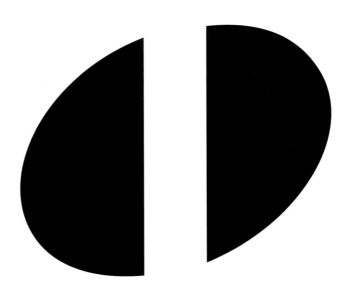

Ishigami Nikko
Gems
1982 · Harukata Yano, Hiro Terao · JP

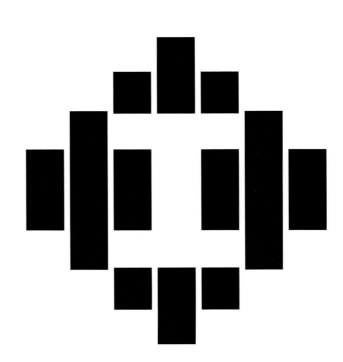

Intersport
Sporting goods
1962 · David J. Goodman/Porter & Goodman Design · US

Jagdish J. Chavda
Design
1975 · Jagdish J. Chavda · US

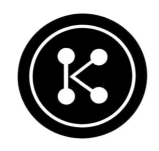

Georg Keck & Cie
Textiles
1960s · René Schmid, Bruno Kümin · CH

Agence Ker
Advertising
1970 · Claude-Marc Perrot,
Jean-Claude Müller · US

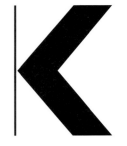

Jules Kielholz
Textiles
1940s · Gottfried Honegger · CH

Apparatebau Jentsch
Machinery
1950s · Sepp Huber · DE

Knaur Buchverlag
Publishing
1951 · Anonymous · DE

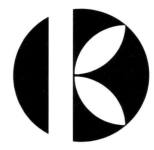

OK Foods
1982 · Akira Hirata,
Koji Mori · JP

Rolf Koller
Advertising
1967 · Michael Freisager · CH

Jugenddienst Verlag
Publishing
1969 · Peter-Torsten Schulz · DE

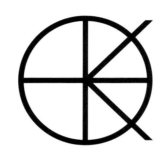

Keskus
Finnish sauna
1970 · Gorm Larsen/Lund & Lommer · FI

Kopp Bauunternehmung
Construction company
1960s · Hansruedi Scheller · CH

Képzömüvészeti Kiadó
Publishing
1980 · László Puskás, Sára Ernö · HU

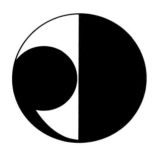

Družstvo Javorina
Grocery
1967 · František Bobáň · CZ

Mineralölwerk Klaffenbach
Fuel oil
1965 · Norbert Wientzowski · DE-GDR

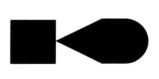

Kuhn & Drake
Architecture
1961 · James S. Ward, Arnold Saks · US

Lauritz Kloster
Shipping services
1965 · Knut Yran · NO

Jochan Regenschirme
Umbrellas
1982 · Hans-Peter Frantz · DE

Konsum Genossenschaft
Consumer cooperative
1965 · Herbert Prüget · DE-GDR

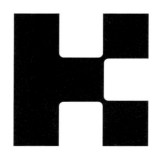

Kanbun
Tools
1978 · Nagato Kawamoto · JP

Kicken Investments
1979 · Herbert Wenn · DE

Bombay Tools Supplying Agency
1979 · Ajit S. Chavan, Raju D. Bind · IN

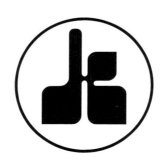

I.F.E.
Cosmetics
1971 · Mirella Romeo/Studio Idea II · IT

Krestmark Aluminum
1975 · Jack Evans · US

Kreuz Verlag
Publishing
1978 · Hans Hug · DE

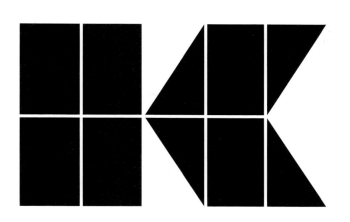

Kartografický
Cartography
1968 · Zdeněk Ziegler · CZ

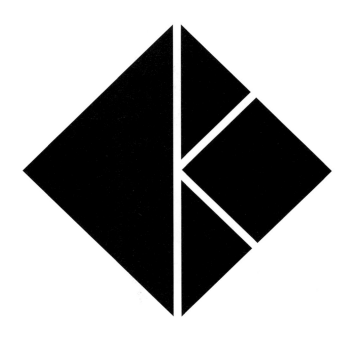

Keller & Co.
Printing
1967 · Anonymous · CH

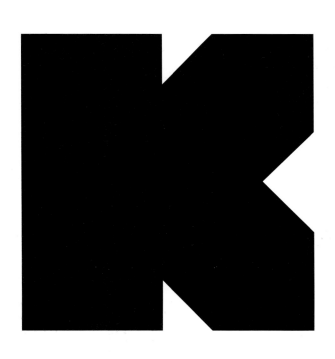

Kälin & Co.
Carpentry
1969 · Ruedi Peter · CH

Kohner Toy Company
1971 · Vance Jonson · US

Atelier Küchler
Design
1972 · Siegfried W. Küchler · DE

Kismet
Gas station fittings
1968 · Crosby, Fletcher, Forbes · UK

Karolton Envelope Company
1960 · Morton Goldsholl · US

Kantonbank Appenzell
Bank
1977 · Othmar Motter · AT

Kinney Service Corporation
1960s · Ed Lukas · US

Kunststoffgesellschaft Luzern
Plastics
1964 · Hans Hurter · CH

Kieffer Pacific
Furniture
1975 · Harry Murphy · US

Kleiber
Plastics
1981 · Othmar Motter · AT

William Kreysler Association
Composite manufacturing
1982 · Harry Murphy · US

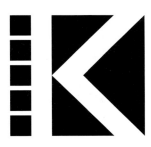

Studio Kaminski
Film production
1971 · Harry Murphy, Eileen Lavelle/
Harry Murphy & Friends · US

Bŭlgarska Televiziya
Broadcasting
1977 · Nikola Nikolov · BG

Kroma Lithographers
Printing
1969 · Eskil Ohlsson · US

Könyvértékesitö Vállalat
Bookstore
1978 · István Szekeres · HU

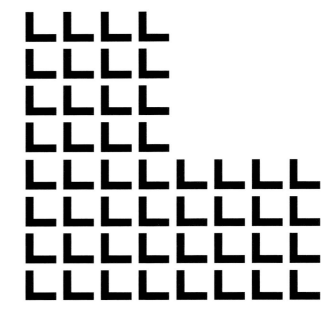

Letra y Linea
Printing
1982 · Félix Beltrán · CU/MX

Victor Kemp Company
Floor coverings
1980 · Ed Penniman · US

Yashiro Kuwayama
Engineering
1978 · Yasaburo Kuwayama · JP

John Kirkham & Associates
Art services
1964 · H. B. Smith · US

The Kuhne
1975 · Dawn Gustus · US

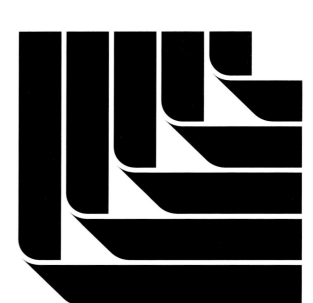

Leona Textiles
1970s · Lance Wyman · US

F. W. Kampmann
Tools
1965 · Walter Seifert · DE-GDR

Keil Verlag
Publishing
1979 · Anonymous · DE

Konsum-Produktionsbetriebe
Beverages
1965 · Karl Thewalt · DE-GDR

Källemo
Furniture
1960s · Anonymous · DK

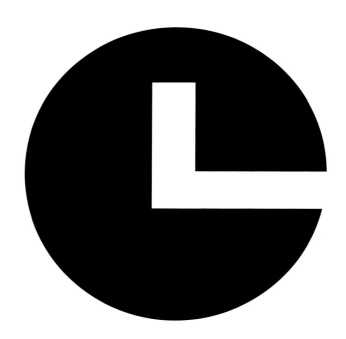

Corporate Lithographing
Printing
1960 · Carl Brett/Hiller Rinaldo Associates · CA

Konsum-Produktionsbetriebe
Foods
1965 · Karl Thewalt · DE-GDR

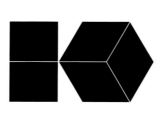

Albert Krafczyk
Industrial photography
1968 · Stuart Ash/Gottschalk+Ash · CA

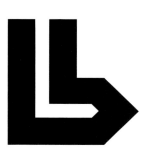

Ravuron
Tennis Club
1975 · Teruo Fujishige · JP

Lembo
Silverware
1982 · Alfredo de Santis · IT

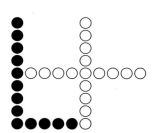

R. Lüscher
Electronics
1968 · Peter Schaufelberger · CH

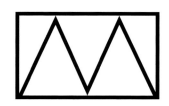

Schilthornbahn
Public transport
1962 · Walter Amstutz · CH

Ivica Lovincic
Packing and freight
1978 · Ivan Dvoršak · YU

Lutheran Brotherhood
1977 · Peter Seitz,
Hideki Yamamoto · US/JP

Ralph Licastro
1979 · Lanny Sommese · US

MM Flachglasfabrik
Glass
1950s · Gust Hahn · DE

Hans Looser
Advertising
1965 · Hans Looser · CH

Lockwood Company
Harvesting equipment
1969 · James Cross · US

Photo+Lithoanstalt Weiss
Photography and lithography
1973 · Hans E. Scheur · DE

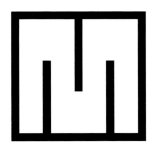

E. Merck
Pharmaceuticals
1968 · Kurt Wirth · CH

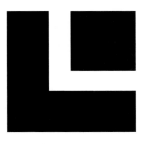

Lloyd Consulting Research
Management consultancy
1965 · Appelbaum & Curtis · US

Lawry's Foods
1959 · Saul Bass & Associates · US

Limburgse Akademie voor Kunst
Art school
1971 · Wim Simons · NL

Mountaingate
Real estate
1975 · John Follis, Wayne Hunt · US

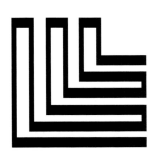

Loomloft
Weaving
1969 · Jean Morin, Karen Bulow · CA

Bertelsmann Verlag
Publishing (proposed design)
1940s · Joseph Binder · AT

Lucas Industries
Automobile and aerospace components
1975 · Pentagram · UK

Magnus Olesen
Furniture
1960s · Anonymous · DK

Studio Lobo
Advertising
1990 · A. G. Fronzoni · IT

Lanza
Machine components
1968 · Renato Borsoni/Studio A. S. · IT

Leslie Salt Company
Salt production
1963 · Landor Associates · US

Stevens Meubel Fabriek
Furniture
1967 · Charles Jongejans · NL

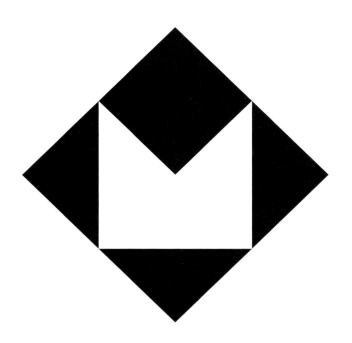

R. Müller & Cie.
Textiles
1963 · Paul Bühlmann · CH

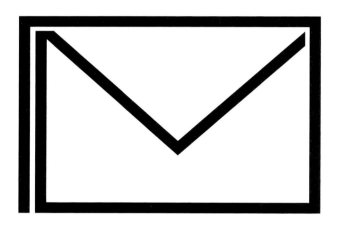

Mailer
Direct mail services
1966 · Rolf Christianson · FI

Merck
Pharmaceuticals
1950s · Enzo Rösli · CH

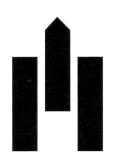

Patronato Joan Miró
Art foundation
1970 · Pedro Ariño · ES

Martex
Roof construction
1965 · Félix Beltrán · CU

Market Technicians Association
Investment analysis
1980 · Joseph Boggs · US

Tessitura di Mompiano
Textiles
1970 · Silvio Coppola · IT

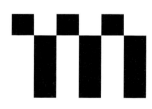

Telco Marketing Services
Investment information
1970 · David L. Burke · US

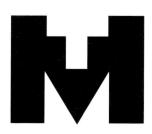

Machine Technology
Metalworks
1968 · Michel Dattel · US

Magellan
Film production
1969 · James Marrin · US

Mecort Meccanica Pesante
Industrial machinery
1979 · Armando Milani,
Maurizio Milani · IT

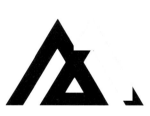

Gifu-Ken Kani-Gun Mitake-Cho
Administration
1976 · Tadahiko Ogawa · JP

Mexico City Metro
Public transport
1969 · Lance Wyman · US

Meisterschule für Buchdrucker
Printing school
1960s · Hermann Virl · DE

Anyagmozgatási
Haulier
1981 · István Szekeres · HU

Mony Corporation
Lighters
1958 · Yasuhiro Kojima · JP

Confiserie Meyer
Foods
1963 · Hans Knöpfli · CH

Maison Blanche
Department stores
1969 · Bruno Ruegg/
Unimark International · US

Madin
Insurance
1960 · José Santamarina/
Elias & Santamarina · ES

Productos Metálicos
Metalworks
1980 · Jorge Sposari · AR/MX

Midland Industries
Plastics
1966 · Leslie Smart · CA

CIBA
Pharmaceuticals
1960s · Elfriede Anderegg · CH

Munising Paper
1960 · Morton Goldsholl
Design Associates · US

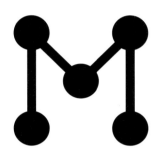

Messe München
Trade fair
1983 · Dieter Urban · DE

Taipei Miramar Hotel
1979 · Kao Yu-Lin · TW

Modine Manufacturing
Heat transfer equipment
1960s · Charles MacMurray · US

Marum International
Stockings
1960s · Hanns Lohrer · DE

Robert Morse
Industrial services
1963 · Frank Lipari/
Gazette Printing Company · CA

Murayama
1982 · Ken'ichi Hirose · JP

Madison Laboratories
Pharmaceuticals
1966 · Herman & Lees Associates · US

Merrill Manufacturing
Wells
1960s · Hudson-Wolter &
Associates · US

Martello Plastics
1982 · Damien Harrington · IE

Manthey Klavianos
Musical instruments
1963 · Erich Unger · DE

Miyoshigasu
Air-conditioning
1973 · Makoto Yoshida · JP

Mipolam Teppichboden
Carpets
1969 · Coordt von Mannstein · DE

McRobert Spring
Automobile parts
1963 · Allan Harrison · CA

Medical Information Network Service
1980 · Minoru Takahashi · JP

Dr. Madaus & Co.
Pharmaceuticals
1960s · Anonymous · DE

Martin Marietta
Electronics
1960s · Lester Beall · US

C. Martínez
Engineering
1964 · Félix Beltrán · CU

M Products
Construction materials
1969 · Arthur Cole · UK

Erin Mills Development Corp.
Real estate
1960s · Allan Robb Fleming,
James Donahue · CA

Midpac Trucking
Transportation
1970 · Clarence Lee, Ryo Urano · US

Manhattan School of Music
1969 · Appelbaum & Curtis · US

Metro Savings & Loan Bank
1983 · Cliff Chandler, Melanie Bass · US

Kenchiku Mode Kenkyujo
Architecture
1962 · Gan Hosoya · JP

Bank of Montreal
1966 · Hans Kleefeld/
Stewart & Morrison · CA

Drogerie Muff
Pharmacy
1966 · Atelier Stadelmann Bisig · CH

Laboratoires Roland-Marie
Research laboratory
1960s · Bucher-Crémières · FR

Scei
Electric radiators
1945 · Max Huber/Studio Boggeri · IT

Mitchell Travel Service
Travel agency
1960s · Robert R. Overby · US

Mundici Arredamenti
Furniture
1968 · Rolando Baldini,
Vania Vecchi/Studio Zot · IT

Ted Mahieu
Photography
1965 · Michel Dattel · US

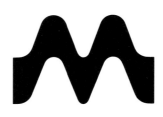

DH Foods
Restaurant
1974 · Mitsuo Ishida, Tamami Sato · JP

Japan Electrical Appliances
1960s · Toru Otsuka · JP

Marxer Laboratori
Pharmaceuticals
1949 · Walter Ballmer/Studio Boggeri · IT

Liverpool Metalling
Metalworks
1968 · Crosby, Fletcher, Forbes · UK

Instructional Media Systems
Audio-visual equipment
1969 · Paul M. Levy · US

Modan
Textiles
1973 · Kazuo Ono · JP

Arcadi Moradell Bosch
Design
1968 · Arcadi Moradell Bosch · ES

Montecatini
Chemicals
1960 · Carlo Dradi · IT

Mohon Realty
Real estate
1974 · Terry Lesniewicz, Al Navarre · US

Mechanisierung Oschersleben
Engineering
1965 · Rudolf Purke · DE-GDR

Magius
Publishing
1967 · Ribas & Creus · ES

Moldes Industriales
Industrial molds
1982 · Fernando Rión · MX

Mutual Oil
Fuel oil
1972 · Joe Selame · US

Morishige Dolls
1974 · Kazuho Yamamoto · JP

Midwest Nuclear
1970s · Bob Swisher · US

Vab Mobili di Tumidei Alceo
Furniture
1971 · Marisa Tumidei · IT

Nortrabulk
Transportation
1960 · Knut Yran · NO

NI
Import-export
1970s · Félix Beltrán · CU

National Property Development
1974 · Stuart Ash/Gottschalk+Ash · CA

Northern States Power
Energy supplier
1977 · Gale William Ikola · US

Neiman
Construction company
1960s · Itsu McFarland,
Gerry Rosentswieg · US

Newman Steel
Steelworks
1974 · Chris Yaneff,
Manfred Gotthans · CA

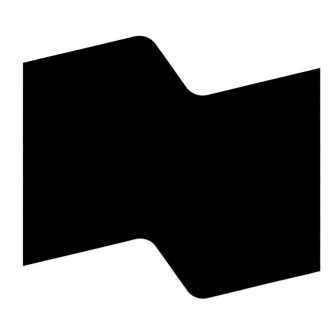

National Bank of Canada
1979 · Vasco Ceccon · CA

Neckermann
Mail-order (proposed design)
1960 · Walter Sauer · DE

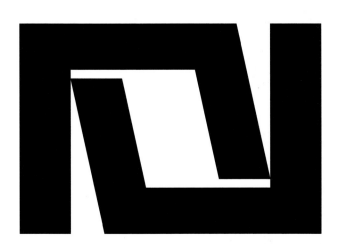

H. Folkmar Naske
Architecture
1971 · Peter Riefenstahl · DE

Nyffeler
Construction company
1962 · Kurt Wirth · CH

Neuköllner Ölmühle
Oil mill
1950s · Heinz Schwabe · DE

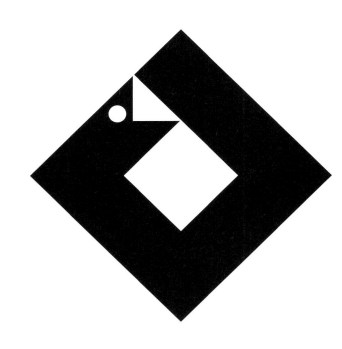

Delta
Pharmaceuticals (proposed design)
1967 · Bruno K. Wiese · DE

NAF
Real estate
1980 · Shigeo Katsuoka · JP

Footwear
1963 · Ernst Ruchay · DE

Roy Nicholls
Photography
1968 · Carl Brett/
Hiller Rinaldo Associates · CA

Nankodo
Bookstore
1980 · Tetsuya Ota · JP

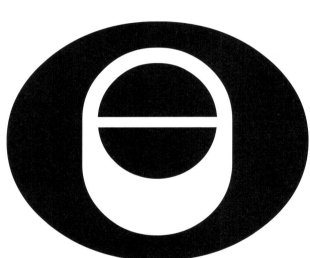

International Coffee Organization
1969 · PVDI · BR

Norfact
Glassware
1960s · Anonymous · NO

Novaroad
Road construction
1980 · Rolf Harder · CA

Holz Naumburg
Wood
1965 · Bernhard Wille · DE-GDR

Netra
Haulier
1971 · Asher Kalderon · IL

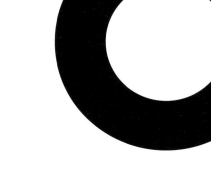

County Transport Company
1982 · Ove Engström, Ingvar Johansson · SE

Viskosefaser-Werke
Fiber processing
1950s · Walther Bergmann · DE

Nippon Oil
Fuel oil
1975 · Kageyoshi Morishita,
Kimio Oike · JP

Omega Construction
1970 · Jacques Bellemare · CA

Gruppo Sportivo
Sports club
1974 · Giovanni Brunazzi · IT

Porsche
Automobiles (proposed design)
1960s · Hanns Lohrer · DE

Polygraph-Export
Printing machinery
1965 · Dieter Lehmann · DE-GDR

Olzog Verlag
Publishing
1972 · Hugo Ballon · DE

Plumbing Contractors Association
1960s · Robert Pease,
Peter Kramer · US

Pitori Pikori
Engineering
1975 · Sadao Sugaya · JP

Plüss Drück
Printing
1958 · Hans Neuburg · CH

Fate
Tires
1964 · Ricardo Blanco · AR

Polydiamants
Diamond trade
1971 · Giovanni Brunazzi · IT

Presspau
Construction company
1970 · Giovanni Brunazzi · IT

Ropraz
Plastics
1960s · Adolf Flückiger · CH

Foto Ottica Randazzo
Photography accessories
1960 · Roberto Sambonet · IT

**Den Danske Presses
Faellesindkøbs Forening**
Publishers association
1970 · Morten Peetz-Schou · DK

Probst Film Tricktechnik
Film animation
1960s · Hans Knöpfli · CH

Peterson Productions
Film production
1960s · Theo Dimson · CA

Petroleum
1960s · Marcello Minale,
Brian Tattersfield/Minale, Tattersfield,
Provinciali · UK

Peres Sports
Sporting goods
1967 · José Baqués · ES

Ponpizoo
Restaurant chain
1970s · D. Bruce Zahor, Joel Mitnick · US

Playcenter
1973 · João Carlos Cauduro,
Ludovico Antonio Martino · BR

Öffentliche Bausparkassen Deutschland
Building societies
1960s · Joseph Binder · AT

Pakkasakku
Batteries
1965 · Eka Lainio/
Markkinointi Viherjuuri · FI

Café Palheta
Coffee
1962 · PVDI · BR

The Pacific Hotel
1972 · Fred O. Bechlen/
Koide Advertising Art · JP

Platicone
Engineering
1975 · Pietro Galli · IT

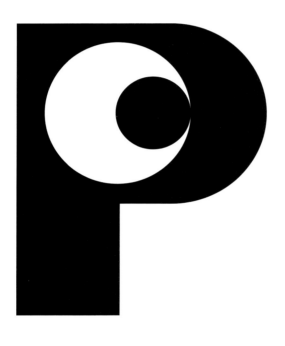

Pfauen Mode
Textiles
1964 · Armin Hofmann · CH

Pinckard Realty
Real estate
1965 · Peter Seitz · US

Polyclair
Office machines
1960 · Pino Tovaglia · IT

Palace Shipping Leasing Service
1973 · Katsumi Nagata,
Yasaburo Kuwayama · JP

Perukmakaren
Parking lot
1967 · Rune Monö · SE

Pierrel
Pharmacy
1957 · Albe Steiner · IT

Perkins Paper Products
1968 · Laurent Marquart/
Jacques Guillon Designers · CA

Théâtre des Prairies
Theater
1966 · Yvon Laroche · CA

Petrag
Human resources
1975 · Peter G. Ulmer · CH

Papeteries de Pont-Sainte-Maxence
Paper
1965 · Jacques Nathan-Garamond · FR

Matti Pietinen
Photography
1968 · Kyösti Varis · FI

Progil
Chemicals
1968 · Raymond Loewy/CEI · FR

Panom
Engineering
1980 · Shigeo Katsuoka · JP

Messrs Paolantoni
Artists materials
1973 · Alfredo de Santis · IT

Pyteco
Construction company
1972 · Joe Vera, José Luis Ortiz · ES

Tipo Print
Printing
1988 · Max Huber · IT

**Association Internationale
des Fibres Polynosic**
Synthetic fibers
1966 · Gilles Fiszman · BE

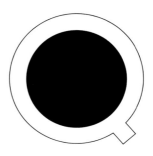

Cue Line Sound
Electronics
1964 · Fletcher, Forbes, Gill · UK

Colleen Pencils
1962 · Tadashi Masuda · JP

Polygal
Medical services
1960s · Carl B. Graf · CH

W. F. Purser
Carpentry
1964 · Crosby, Fletcher, Forbes · UK

Finer Company
Telecommunications
1969 · A. G. Fronzoni · IT

Precinor
Foundry
1967 · Daniel Maurel/
Chourgnoz Publicité · FR

Packaging Corporation of America
1960s · Robert Sidney Dickens · US

Promécam Sisson Lehmann
Aerospace component manufacture
1965 · Design Groupe Viaud · FR

Quirra
Textiles
1969 · Patrizia Pataccini/
Studio Cortesi · IT

Krawiectwo Spółdzielni
Textiles
1965 · Jan Hollender · PL

Pulvitec Mining
1982 · Félix Beltrán · CU/MX

Parma-ovo
Foods
1970 · Silvio Coppola · IT

QuickMaid Rental Service
Vending machines
1973 · Ken Garland · UK

Pronit
Record label
1960s · Jan Hollender · US

Partheil-Bauschlosserei
Metal-working
1965 · Heide Hattebuhr · DE-GDR

Tratamiento y Orientación
Education
1975 · Dicken Castro · CO

Quadriga Verlagsgesellschaft
Publishing
1986 · Manfred Manke · DE

Randox EPD
Computer services
1967 · Roy Walker · UK

Boutique Paco Ruiz
Textiles
1968 · Pedro Ariño · ES

Palestro
Typesetting
1978 · Carlo Calligaris · IT

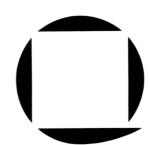

Quad Typographers
Typesetting
1964 · Mo Lebowitz · US

Jeff Quon
Pharmacy
1982 · Mike Quon · US

Reliance Steel
Metal processing
1971 · Ray Engle, Jerome Jensik · US

Reflex Design
1981 · Armando Milani · IT

Reich Verlag
Publishing
1974 · Rainer Fuhrmann · CH

Quintus International
1973 · Dwight Frazier, Paul Hauge/
Newmarket Design Associates · US

Rhodiatoce
Synthetic fibers
1969 · Bob Noorda/
Unimark International · IT

Doris Reinemann Fotostudio
Photography
1983 · Manfred Korten · DE

Rodinco
Engineering
1968 · Ove Engström · SE

Quartet Books
Publishing
1973 · Michael Jarvis · UK

Rug Tuffers
1976 · Peter Adam/Gottschalk+Ash · CA

R+R Raffinerie
Fuel oil
1960s · Roger-Virgile Geiser · CH

Rencontre de Jeune Talent
Textiles
1982 · Jost Hochuli · CH

**Zentralstelle für Werbung
der Lebensmittelindustrie**
Silver quality-mark (design system)
1965 · Gerhard Voigt · DE-GDR

Royal Dental Office
1977 · Yukio Kanise · JP

RPR Relazioni Pubbliche
Public relations
1964 · Mimmo Castellano · IT

Rougier
Pharmaceuticals
1960s · Rolf Harder · CA

**Zentralstelle für Werbung
der Lebensmittelindustrie**
Silver quality-mark (design system)
1965 · Gerhard Voigt · DE-GDR

Rehmann & Co.
Packaging
1950s · Hans Weber · CH

The Argentine Chamber of Realtors
Real estate
1960s · Alejandro May · AR

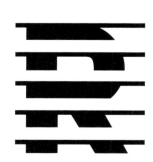

R 71 International
Trade fair for shutters manufacturers
1971 · Peter Wehr · DE

BioQuest
Pharmaceuticals
1969 · Vance Jonson · US

Rhönkunstschnitzerei Empfertshausen
Artist carving
1965 · Herbert Prüget · DE-GDR

Rossipaul Kommunikation
Publishing
1975 · Michael Neugebauer · DE

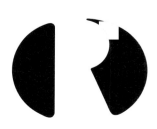

Ravensburger Versicherung
Insurance
1980 · Oanh Pham Phu · DE

Racine Press
Printing
1964 · Rudolph de Harak · US

Rockford Screw Supply Company
1965 · Bruce Beck/
The Design Partnership · US

Ruch Verlag
Publishing
1965 · Jan Hollender · PL

VEB Radebeuler Schuhfabrik
Footwear
1965 · Johannes Brase · DE-GDR

R. A. Consultants
Management consultancy
1982 · Rick Cartledge · CA

Refratechnik
Steelworks
1950 · Walter Breker · DE

Ditta Piriv
1960s · Giulio Confalonieri · IT

Frederic Ryder Company
Typesetting
1970 · David L. Burke · US

Premio Fotografico G. Ratti
Photography award
1971 · Giovanni Brunazzi · IT

William R. Rundle
Import-export
1950s · Theo Dimson · CA

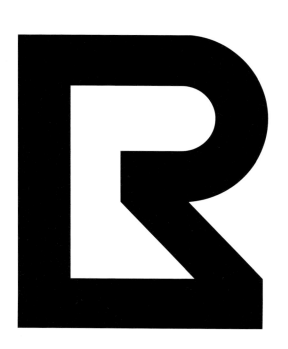

Reilly Lock Corporation
Locksmith
1972 · Stuart Ash/Gottschalk+Ash · CA

Road Constructors
1973 · Don Goodwin, John Spatchurst/
Nielsen Design Associates · AU

Rogers Brothers Company
Agriculture
1960s · Raymond Loewy,
William Snaith · US

Reconsa
Automobile repairs
1979 · Fernando Rión · MX

Real Typographers
Typesetting
1953 · Bob Gill · US/UK

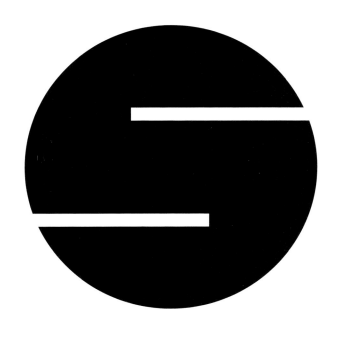

Sparkasse Berlin
Bank
1960 · Hans Adolf Albitz · DE

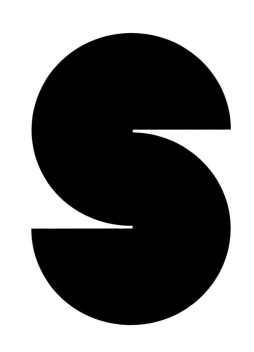

Sitcap
Advertising
1956 · Emanuele Centazzo, Sitcap · IT

Spezialbeton
Cement
1960s · Martz+Bühlmann · CH

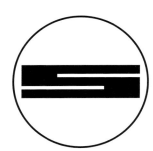

Fachverlag Schiele & Schön
Publishing
1970 · Anonymous · DE

Ed. Suter
Foods
1969 · Pascal Besson · CH

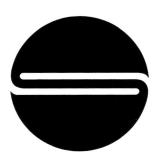

Sarvis
Plastics
1967 · Rolf Christianson · FI

Style Asia
1980 · Sudarshan Dheer · IN

P. N. Stein
Mattresses
1965 · Jürgen Förster · DE-GDR

Däniken
Cables
1960s · Armin Hofmann · CH

Sylvapen
Pens
1965 · Carlos Alberto
Méndez Mosquera · AR

Spinner Hi-Fi
Record label
1958 · Peter Megert · CH

Schwann-Druck
Printing
1960s · Niko Müller · DE

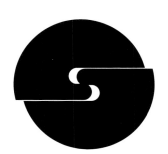

Western-art
Communication services
1970 · Jan Jaring · NL

RFT Rundfunk und Fernsehen
Electronics
1965 · Erhard Müller · DE-GDR

Société Electro-Navale
Ship electronics
1969 · Jacques Nathan-Garamond · FR

**Secretariat for Technical Cooperation
with Developing Countries**
Aid agency
1969 · Børge Nebel · DK

Max Sandherr
Packaging
1965 · Peter G. Ulmer · CH

Saratoga Performing Arts Center
1970s · Charles Fuhrman · US

Bathing Facilities
1980 · Bror B. Zetterborg · FI

Sachsenring
Racing track
1965 · Herbert Prüget · DE-GDR

Von Siebenthal
Photography
1950s · Marcel Wyss · CH

Spectra-Physics
Lasers and optics
1963 · G. Dean Smith · US

Sumino
Machinery
1968 · Takeshi Otaka · JP

Stäubli Buchdruck Offset
Printing
1971 · Hansruedi Scheller · CH

Surveyor Fund
Investment
1968 · Tony Russell · US

Max
Soap
1983 · Fumio Koyoda · JP

**South Shore Mental
Health Center**
1970s · Robert Hagenhofer · US

Segor
Leather
1977 · Hans E. Scheur · DE

Stange
Foods
1963 · Randall R. Roth · US

Schöller-Gruppe
Weaving
1976 · Othmar Motter · AT

The Spencer Foundation
Education research and funding
1973 · Edward Hughes · US

Scenika PJT
Theater
1982 · István Szekeres · HU

H. Schiellerup
Coffee
1968 · Lund & Lommer · DK

Ernst Schamong
Textiles
1972 · Oanh Pham Phu · DE

Schröckel
1950s · Otto Krämer · CH

Schoenberg & Schoenberg
Buttons
1965 · Walter Seifert · DE-GDR

Staatsverlag
Publishing
1965 · Herbert Prüget · DE-GDR

Signum
Publishing
1970s · Mark & Nevosad · AT

Sannwald Decken
Roofer
1982 · Othmar Motter · AT

Schiersner
Steel pipe bending
1960s · Mendell & Oberer · DE

Süßstoff-Vertriebsgesellschaft
Foods
1940s · Gust Hahn · DE

Spagnoli Gallery
Art gallery
1983 · Angelo Sganzeria · IT

Sagdos
Printing
1962 · Piero Sansoni · IT

Schade und Füllgrabe
Supermarket chain
1971 · Atelier Stadelmann Bisig · CH

Banca del Sud
Bank
1980 · Carlo Malerba · IT

Johann Schwärzler
Textiles
1979 · Othmar Motter · AT

F. Somaini Straßenbau
Road construction
1940s · Robert Sessler · CH

Key Sabinal
Construction company
1970 · Chermayeff & Geismar · US

Rank Xerox Copy Department
Photocopiers
1963 · Marcello Minale,
Brian Tattersfield · UK

Salvador Serra
Photography accessories
1967 · Josep Pla-Narbona · ES

Schaffhauser Watte
Cotton
1940s · Robert Sessler · CH

Scubapro
Diving equipment
1960 · Frank R. Cheatham/
Porter & Goodman Design · US

Sanistål
Tool supplies
1981 · Adam Moltke · DK

**Congress on Traffic
Problems in Europe**
1983 · Velizar Petrov · BG

Seiberling Tire and Rubber
1960s · Scherr & McDermott · US

Edwin H. Stuart
Typesetting
1965 · Francis R. Esteban · US

Sibolt
1962 · Bruno Monguzzi/
Studio Boggeri · IT

F. A. Slaney & Co.
Agriculture
1965 · Friedrich Peter · CA

Simtec
Measuring instruments
1964 · Ernst Roch/
Design Collaborative · CA

Signer Metzgerei
Butcher's shop
1968 · Robert Geisser · CH

Silver Real Estate
1963 · Robert Pease · US

Sansom Equipment
Pumps
1965 · J.C. Stackhouse Studios · CA

Software International
Computer software
1978 · Morfos Diseño · MX

Stagni Visual Communications
Design
1964 · Albe Steiner · IT

Systems Professional
Civil engineering
1968 · Usher & Follis Design · US

State Testing Laboratories
1961 · Ted Trinkaus/
Aron & Wayman · US

Shimamura Shuppan
Publishing
1973 · Makoto Yoshida · JP

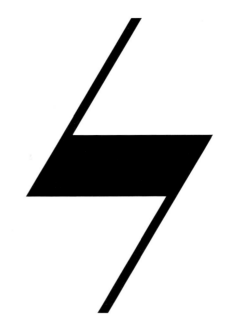

Standard Electric
1961 · Ernst Roch/Design Collaborative · CA

Satoturve
Agriculture
1967 · Teuvo Tynkkynen · FI

South Shore Plaza
Shopping center
1955 · Frederick A. Usher · US

Selig J. Smith
Display apparatus
1964 · Tom Woodward · US

Stierlin & Co.
Construction and engineering
1960s · Peter G. Ulmer · CH

België Energy
Energy supplier
1960s · Michel Waxman · BE

Shimobe Denshi
Electronics
1973 · Makoto Yoshida · JP

**Stadtgeschichtliches
Museum, Wittenberg**
Museum
1965 · Karl Thewalt · DE-GDR

Fred Sands Realty
Real estate
1976 · Thomas Ohmer, Tom Wilson · US

Scott Paper
1962 · George Nelson, Hiram Hash · US

New Style Industry
1979 · Kao Yu-Lin · TW

British Steel Corporation
1968 · David Gentleman · UK

Shankey Steel Supply
1970 · Victor Dicristo · US

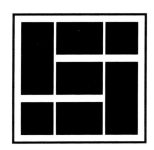

Arthur Sanders
Civil engineering
1961 · Henrion Design Associates · UK

Hotel Sepias
1983 · Katsumi Maetani · JP

Sankei Ad Monthly
Publishing
1963 · Shigeo Fukuda · JP

Seilon
Industrial services
1969 · James Cross · US

Speedrack
Shelving
1966 · Randall R. Roth · US

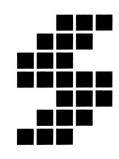

Serit
Printing
1977 · Carlo Malerba · IT

Stancor
Furniture
1967 · Hans Kleefeld/
Stewart & Morrison · CA

P. L. Spagnolo
Furniture
1980 · Marcello d'Andrea · IT

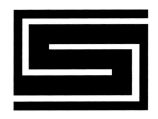

E. Schulz & Co.
Laboratory equipment
1965 · Harry Prieß · DE-GDR

Stäfa
Printing
1972 · Hans Hurter · CH

Stenval
Dairy products
1966 · Raymond Loewy/CEI · FR

Sella Nevea
Ski resort
1978 · Alfredo de Santis · IT

Schöneck
Dressings
1960s · Uli Schierle · DE

Seiyu
Department stores
1973 · Koichiro Inagaki · JP

Ets Recapet
Foods
1966 · Raymond Loewy/CEI · FR

Stimo
Typesetting
1978 · Carlo Calligaris · IT

Moinho Santista
Textiles
1964 · Alexandre Wollner · BR

Simplex Piling
Forklift trucks
1962 · Henrion Design Associates · UK

Summerhill Apartments
1969 · James Donahue/
Cooper & Beatty · CA

Security Pacific National Bank
1966 · Saul Bass & Associates · US

Showa Technical Institute
Dental technology
1975 · Toshiaki Takahashi · JP

ARO
Welding machinery
1977 · Abram Games · UK

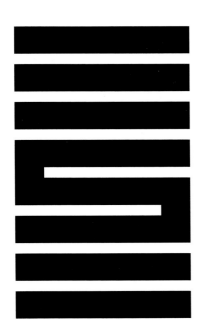

G. F. Smith & Son
Security technology
1965 · Eurographics · UK

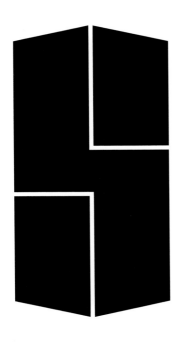

Simon Enterprises
Real estate
1963 · Charles Fuhrman/Robert P. Gersin Associates · US

Schweppes
Beverages
1963 · Leen Averink · FR/UK

Tina-Messerfabrik
Knives
1957 · Klaus Grözinger · DE/CH

Tel Design Associated
Design
1967 · Tel Design Associated · NL

Tate
Advertising
1982 · Shizuo Yoneda,
Koichi Watanabe · JP

Trenco
Textiles
1968 · Louis Swart · NL

Tokyo Tomin Bank
1976 · Shigeo Fukuda · JP

Tenguya
Textiles
1979 · Yasaburo Kuwayama · JP

Terninoss Acciai Inossidabili
Steel plates
1963 · Sergio Salaroli · IT

Hong Kong Telephone Company
Telecommunications
1978 · Henry Steiner · HK

Tero Corvette
Racing cars
1968 · James Lienhart/RVI Corp. · US

Taiping Chemical Industry
1960s · Kenji Ito · JP

Transexpress
Haulier
1969 · Walter Hergenröther · IT

Bestime
Watches
1983 · Ove Engström, Kurt Karlsson · SE

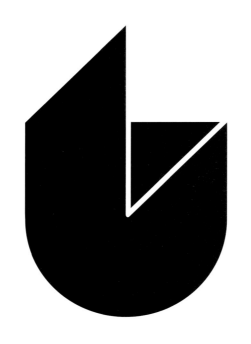

Tigamma
Lighting technology
1969 · Silvio Coppola · IT

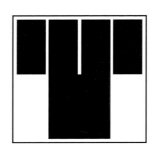

Amigos del Arte
Art collectors
1969 · Ribas & Creus · ES

Stowarzyszenie Tłumaczy Polskich
Polish translators association
1979 · Tytus Walczak · PL

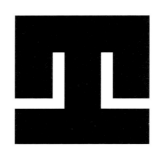

Thermopac
Industrial boilers
1978 · Eduardo A. Cánovas · AR

Tecnes
Excavation and drilling
1964 · Bruno Monguzzi/
Studio Boggeri · IT

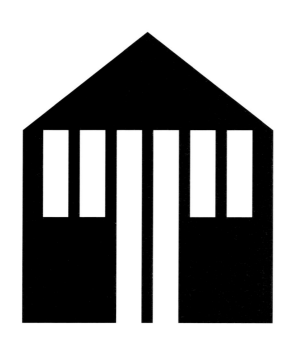

Takusa
Real estate
1980 · Sumio Hasegawa · JP

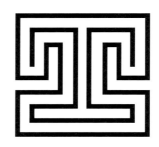

Kustannus Oy Tammi
Publishing
1968 · Martti A. Mykkänen · FI

Tom Green
1982 · Keith Murgatroyd · UK

Tilgmann
Printing
1968 · Alfons Eder · FI

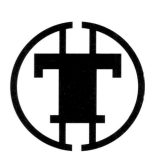

Iron Foundry
1960s · Selcuk Oenal · TR

Tecno
Furniture
1954 · Roberto Mango,
Osvaldo Borsani · IT

Grupo Financeiro TAA
Investment
1967 · Fernando A. T. Rodrigues · BR

Texital
Decoration materials
1966 · Giulio Confalonieri · IT

Top Export
1981 · Armando Milani,
Maurizio Milani · IT

Titeflex
Fluid management solutions
1960s · Lester Beall · US

R. & D. Thiel
Carpentry
1970 · David L. Burke · US

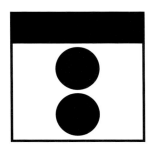

Trinkaus Bank
1974 · Walter Breker · DE

Thomson International
Harvesting equipment
1969 · James Cross · US

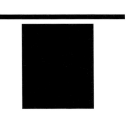

Trivas
Furniture
1982 · Ove Engström,
Eva-Lotta Fuhoff · SE

Transinvest
Road construction
1982 · Léderer Károly, Sára Ernő · HU

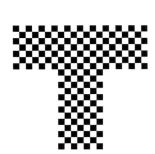

Taxis Nacionales
Ministerio de Transportes
Taxis
1973 · Félix Beltrán · CU/MX

Tranås Pälsvarukompani
Furs
1967 · Ove Engström · SE

Toluian
Carpets
1971 · Silvio Coppola · IT

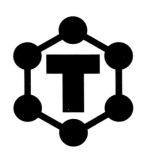

Tecnoresina
Plastics
1953 · Nello Diana/Ferri Pubblicità · IT

Kurt Thurnher
Office supplies
1970 · Othmar Motter · AT

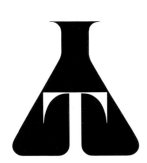

Chemicals
1960s · Wojciech Zamecznik · PL

Treffpunkt Heute
Publishing
1965 · Gerhard Voigt · DE-GDR

Office of Energy Coordination
University of Utah department
1974 · Michael Richards · US

Urbatique Quebec
Urban engineering
1969 · Yvon Laroche · CA

Unitank Storage Company
1976 · Kenneth Hollick · UK

Taikoo Shing
Real estate
1980 · Henry Steiner · HK

United Satellite Communications
Broadcasting
1983 · Philip Gips, Gina Stone · US

Comune di Urbino
City council
1968 · Bert Aureli · IT

United Airlines
1974 · Saul Bass & Associates · US

Uyttenhove
Textiles
1967 · Julian Key · BE

Unione Fornitori Cancelleria
Association of stationery suppliers
1980 · Armando Milani,
Maurizio Milani · IT

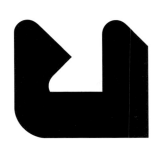

Unial
Aluminum
1979 · Ivan Dvoršak · YU

Carnival
1971 · Félix Beltrán · CU

Colasit
Electroplating
1960s · René Althaus · CH

Van Hospital
1974 · Giovanni Martirossi · IT

Trenes Vertebrados
Public transport
1974 · Elías García Benavides · ES

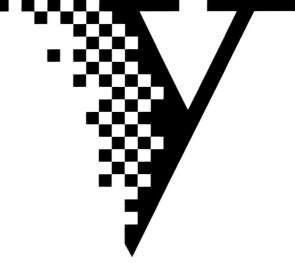

Verlaine
Furniture
1983 · George Delany · US

Ets Vitouy
Textiles
1967 · Raymond Loewy/CEI · FR

Vito's Italian Cars
Imported automobiles
1976 · Conrad E. Angone · US

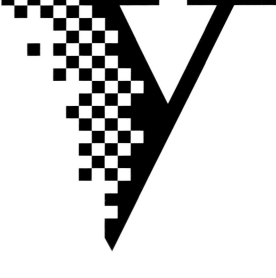

Boutique Veronika
Textiles
1980 · Othmar Motter · AT

Indústrias Villares
Elevators and electric motors
1970 · João Carlos Cauduro,
Ludovico Antonio Martino · BR

Valwood Park
1975 · Jack Evans · US

Peintures Vachon
1971 · Florent Garnier · FR

Veto
Electronics
1968 · Veniero Bertolotti/Studio 4 · IT

Veterinaria
Pharmaceuticals
1940s · Ernst Keller · CH

Vendorafa
Jeweler
1970 · Alfredo Troisi · IT

Vaporette Chemical
Insect extermination
1963 · Jerald O. Page · US

Agencia Vengut
Customs office
1966 · Ribas & Creus · ES

Victoria
Electricity
1967 · Félix Beltrán · CU

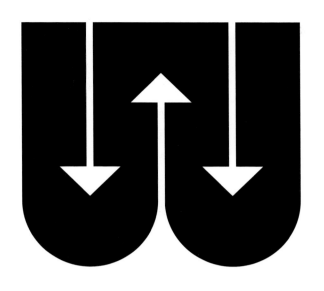

G. Wegele
Elevator technology
1963 · Peter Steiner · DE

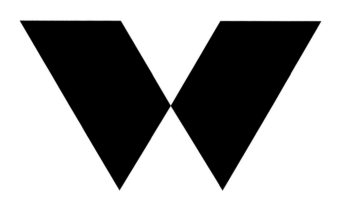

The Wickes Company
Kitchens
1970 · John Greiner/Unimark International · US

Warner Communications
Entertainment group
1972 · Saul Bass & Associates · US

Walde
Automobile parts
1960s · Mario Trüb · CH

Westnofa
Furniture
1960s · Anonymous · NO

Weir Group of Companies
Engineering
1963 · Ken Garland · UK

Wilkin Service
1973 · Don Goodwin, John Spatchurst/
Nielsen Design Associates · AU

Wellmart
Grocery chain
1982 · Hiromi Kuginuki,
Akira Hirata, Koji Mori · JP

Smalteria Metalurgica
Metalworks
1973 · Heinz Waibl · IT

Wamsley Construction
Construction company
1975 · Conrad E. Angone · US

Advertising
1950s · Gust Hahn · DE

C. P. Wakefield
Advertising
1964 · Marcello Minale,
Brian Tattersfield · UK

Weatherford International
Oil and gas
1980s · Kenneth R. Cooke,
Robert Wolf · US

Wanner
Excavators
1981 · Peter G. Ulmer · CH

Grand Union Company
Grocery stores
1979 · Milton Glaser · US

Wima-Produkte
Naturopathy
1967 · Robert Geisser · CH

Royale Belge
Insurance
1968 · Julian Key · BE

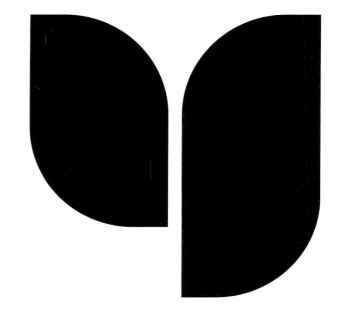

Yuasa Beauty Parlor
Cosmetics
1977 · Masaaki Ishii · JP

Wings Shirts
Clothing
1982 · Diana Graham · US

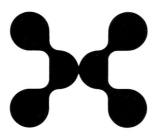

Ken'ichi Hirose's Design Office
1974 · Ken'ichi Hirose · JP

West Racing Cars
Racing team
1983 · Sogen Onishi · JP

Xpos
Exhibition
1970 · Félix Beltrán · CU

Yonex
Sports equipment
1975 · Takahisa Kamijyo · JP

Warwick
Chemicals
1965 · Théodore Stamatakis/
Créations Stama · FR

Xerox Educational Center
Education for printing technology
1971 · PVDI · BR

Ralph Whitehead & Associates
Engineering
1975 · Joe Sonderman · US

Art Hall
1971 · Pal Horváth · BE

Kenneth Yost
Industrial design
1970 · David L. Burke · US

Trident Research & Development
1968 · Leslie Smart · CA

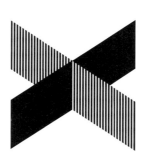

Design Built Exhibits
1975 · George Tscherny · US

Yasuda Trust Bank
1974 · Kazumasa Nagai · JP

Volker Zahm Werbeagentur
Advertising
1960s · Volker Zahm · DE

Zodiak Hospitals
1984 · Brijen Thakkar · IN

**The Young Men's Christian
Association of Chicago**
1967 · H.B. Smith · US

Zerowatt
Electronics
1977 · Armando Milani,
Maurizio Milani · IT

Zimmermann Violinen
Musical instruments
1966 · Kurt Wirth · CH

Yomiuri Times
Publishing
1966 · Yoshio Hayashi · JP

Zürcher Ziegeleien
Bricks
1963 · Jörg Hamburger · CH

Zindler Rotationsdruck
Printing
1940s · Paul E. Weise · DE

Yhtyneet Kuvalehdet
Publishing
1966 · Kyösti Varis · FI

Zubler Annoncen
Advertising
1951 · Armin Hofmann · CH

Zaklady Przem Zapalczanego
Matches
1960 · Ryszard Sidorowski · PL

Yamachan Planning
Engineering
1979 · Iwao Yamaguchi · JP

Zingg
Furniture
1962 · Werner Mühlemann · CH

Ring Railway
Transportation
1980 · S.M. Shah · IN

Yanagi
1976 · Koichi Watanabe,
Ichiro Okada · JP

Zyma Medizin
Pharmaceuticals
1970 · Hansruedi Widmer/
Devico AG · CH

Zentral-Wäscherei
Laundry
1962 · Donald Brun · CH

Le travail sur l'écriture exige une confrontation permanente avec les formes abstraites des lettres. Lorsqu'il doit dessiner un insigne, celui qui travaille avec le signe « lettre » relève un défi particulier dans la mesure où les marques commerciales sont souvent basées sur des formes de lettres.
Adrian Frutiger

Die Beschäftigung mit Schrift bedingt eine ständige Auseinandersetzung mit den ungegenständlichen Buchstabenformen. Wer mit dem Zeichen »Buchstabe« umgeht, fühlt sich herausgefordert, wenn er ein Signet zeichnen soll, sind doch Markenzeichen oft auf Buchstabenformen aufgebaut.
Adrian Frutiger

Working with typefaces requires constant involvement with non-representational fonts. When asked to design a logo, anyone who deals with letters of the alphabet faces a challenge, because trademarks are often built on letters of one shape or another.
Adrian Frutiger

Lettres ouvertes

Offene Buchstaben

Opened-up Letters

Alesia Schweizer
Automobiles
1961 · Amand Domènech · ES

Dimati France
Office supplies
1960s · Ruut van den Hoed · US

Felix Hungerbühler
Bookstore
1962 · Robert Geisser · CH

Barazzoni F.lli
Kitchens
1968 · Ennio Lucini · IT

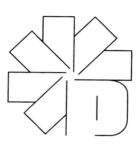

H. Dold & Co.
Paints
1970s · Christian Lang · CH

Gehkens Electrotechniek
Electronics
1978 · Hans Hartzheim · NL

European International Banks
1973 · Heinz Schwabe · DE

Banque Epargne Croissance
Bank
1971 · Hans Troxler/
Delpire-Advico · CH

Walter Horn Architekten
Architecture
1977 · Herbert Wenn · DE

Concord Films
Film production
1977 · Fernando Rión · MX

Element
Construction company
1960s · Marcel Wyss · CH

Hotel Henequen
1975 · Félix Beltrán · CU/MX

Kulturmarkt Dillingen
Cultural association
1980 · Dieter Urban · DE

Franz Fässter
Electronics
1965 · Kurt Stadelmann · CH

Helaby
Import-export
1975 · Chermayeff & Geismar · US

Duquette Plumbing
1977 · Terry Lesniewicz,
Al Navarre · US

Flughafen-Restaurant Zürich
Airport restaurant
1967 · Jörg Hamburger · CH

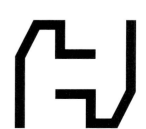

Construction Company
1976 · Bruno K. Wiese · DE

Hutzler
Packaging
1974 · Ruut van den Hoed · US

Museum für Naturgeschichte, St. Gallen
Natural history museum
1976 · Jost Hochuli · CH

Policlínica Geral do Rio de Janeiro
Healthcare
1960s · Aloísio Magalhães/PVDI · BR

Thornton
Drawing instruments
1964 · Norman Stevenson,
Harry Ward · UK

Koller Werbeagentur
Advertising
1960s · Rolf Koller · CH

Neográfica
Printing
1978 · Reynaldo Da Costa · VE

Le Panneau Magnétique
Magnetic advertising panels
1967 · Jacques Nathan-Garamond · FR

Sinuhe
Travel agency
1972 · Manfred Wutke · DE

Marzari Artegrafica
Printing
1970 · Walter Ballmer · IT

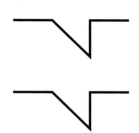

Nishiki Printing
1967 · Hiroshi Ohchi · JP

Construction Company
1970 · Ekkehart Rustmeier · DE

Nuevo Teatro Ofelia Woloshin
Theater
1967 · Claude Dietrich · PE

Max
Towels
1978 · Fumio Koyoda · JP

Ovidio Moro
Construction company
1975 · José Santamarina /
Elias & Santamarina · ES

Rakuzanso
Sporting goods
1983 · Masakazu Tanabe · JP

Architecture Concept
Magazine
1968 · Jean Morin · CA

Nishida Seisakusho
Ceramics
1983 · Kazuharu Fuji · JP

Tyryggue System
1982 · Hans Kündig · SE

Ministerio del Trabajo
Ministry of labor
1979 · Félix Beltrán · CU/MX

Abraham & Straus
Department store
1979 · Tom Geismar/
Chermayeff & Geismar · US

Newton Publishing
1968 · William Newton · CA

Clichy Plastugil
Plastics
1965 · Jacques Nathan-Garamond · FR

Totani Insasu
Printing
1979 · Yukishia Takakita · JP

Associazione Agenzie Italiane Pubblicità
Association of advertising agencies
1966 · Amleto Dalla Costa · IT

Findex
Computer systems
1978 · Jean-Claude Müller · US

A.N.D.A.
Administrators association
1972 · Walter Ballmer · IT

Conicit
Council for technical research
1970 · Gerd Leufert · VE

Aero Revue
Magazine
1969 · Igildo Biesele · CH

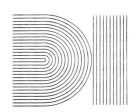

Cable Review
Magazine
1971 · Crosby, Fletcher, Forbes · UK

Ahmedabad Municipal Transport Service
1960s · Girish R. Patel/
National Institute of Design · IN

Dionisio Ielli
Audio equipment
1969 · Riccardo Voglino/Studio B · IT

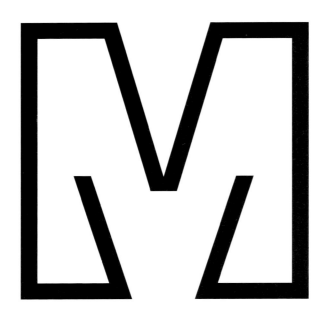

Mensch & Company
Paints
1960s · Armin Hofmann · CH

British Tissues
1976 · Kenneth Hollick · UK

Ecolco
Environmental consulting
1973 · Massimo Dradi · IT

Banco de Italia y Río de la Plata
Bank
1970s · Chermayeff & Geismar · US

Eurocartera
Finance
1971 · Julián Santamaría · ES

Grupo Renovación
Institute of sociology
1970 · Álvaro Sotillo · VE

CP
Broadcasting
1976 · Nikola Nikolov · BG

Flexform
Furniture
1969 · Pino Tovaglia · IT

Financial Times
Newspaper
1969 · Henrion Design Associates · UK

Maison du Jardin-Day
Textiles
1972 · Michel Rubens · BE

Toyota Publica
Automobile
1961 · Ikko Tanaka · JP

Abcisa Barcelona
Electronics
1969 · Arcadi Moradell Bosch · ES

Fitness America Books
Publishing
1975 · Lanny Sommese · US

Longmans, Green Group
Publishing
1969 · Henrion Design Associates · UK

Technicum
Art school
1974 · Jean-Claude Müller · US

Vallesusa
Textiles
1970 · Silvio Coppola · IT

Gerald E. Thomas
1973 · David Leigh · US

Maria Borucki
Travel agency
1968 · Oanh Pham Phu · DE

Toby E. Rodes Consultants
Business consultancy
1960s · Humbert+Vogt · CH

Westminster Press
Publishing
1969 · Henrion Design Associates · UK

Great Western Racing
Racing team
1979 · Thomas Ohmer,
Bruce Dobson · US

Marui
Department stores
1974 · Tetsuo Miyahara · JP

Tequipment
Education
1976 · Keith Murgatroyd,
Tony Forster · UK

Wolters-Noordhoff
Publishing
1967 · Otto Treumann · NL

Hjamar Pettersson
1975 · Hans Kündig · SE

Paul Binder
Goldsmith
1950s · Otto Krämer · CH

Vallecchi Editore
Publishing
1973 · Mimmo Castellano · IT

Zavod Za Ekonomske
Institute for economic research
1981 · Miloš Ćirić · YU

Von Holzen und Hügin
Air-conditioning
1970 · Atelier Stadelmann Bisig · CH

Legler
Textiles
1960s · Jörg Hamburger · CH

Trade Promotion Services
Exhibition management
1971 · John Gibbs, Ben John/
Unit Five Design · UK

Zaegel Held
Heating technologies
1979 · Rudi Meyer · FR

London Electricity Board

1970 · Henrion Design Associates · UK

The London Electricity Board was a public-sector company founded in 1948 to supply power to the British capital. At the same time, the LEB became one of the leading suppliers of electrical goods, which it retailed in its own 76 shops. In 1969 Henrion Design Associates was contracted to produce a study of the government organization's corporate identity and came up with two possible ways to revamp the LEB's outdated and inconsistent public image. A new logo and an integrated corporate design system were introduced in 1970. The system was documented in a manual of 100-plus pages, which was also a comprehensive guide on how it could be applied to everything from neon signs to electricity bills. In the wave of privatization that swept across the United Kingdom in the 1990s, the LEB was broken up and sold to an international corporation.

Der London Electricity Board wurde 1948 als staatliche Einrichtung für die Stromversorgung der britischen Hauptstadt gegründet. Daneben entwickelte sich LEB auch zum größten Anbieter von Elektrogeräten, die in 76 eigenen Läden verkauft wurden. Das Büro Henrion Design Associates erhielt 1969 den Auftrag zu einer Studie über das äußere Erscheinungsbild des Staatsunternehmens und präsentierte zwei Lösungswege zur Erneuerung des veralteten und uneinheitlichen Auftritts. Schließlich wurden 1970 ein neues Logo sowie ein integrales Corporate-Design-System eingeführt. Ein mehr als 100 Seiten starkes Manual diente der Dokumentation und enthielt detaillierte Regeln zur Umsetzung sämtlicher Anwendungsbereiche – von der Leuchtreklame bis hin zum Layout der Stromrechnungen. In den 1990er-Jahren wurde im Zuge der britischen Privatisierungswelle der LEB aufgelöst und an internationale Unternehmen verkauft.

Le London Electricity Board fut fondé en 1948 comme établissement public pour la fourniture d'électricité de la capitale anglaise. Parallèlement, LEB devint aussi le premier fabricant d'appareils électroménagers vendus dans 76 boutiques de la marque. En 1969, le bureau Henrion Design Associates fut chargé de réaliser une étude sur l'identité visuelle extérieure de l'entreprise nationale, et deux solutions possibles furent proposées pour renouveler l'image obsolète et peu homogène de l'entreprise. En 1970 fut finalement introduit un nouveau logo et un système complet de corporate design. Un manuel de plus de cent pages servait de documentation détaillant les règles à suivre pour le transposer dans tous les domaines d'application – de la réclame lumineuse à la mise en page des factures d'électricité. LEB fut dissout dans le sillage de la vague de privatisations britanniques des années 1990 et vendu à différentes entreprises internationales.

FHK Henrion (1914–1990) was one of the most important British designers. Born in Germany, in 1936 he moved to London where he first attracted attention for his work for the magazine *Harper's Bazaar*. From the 1950s onwards he became increasingly involved in the field of corporate design and took on commissions from companies including the Dutch airline KLM. Henrion was an active member of international design associations such as the International Council of Graphic Design Associations (ICOGRADA) and Alliance Graphique Internationale (AGI).

FHK Henrion (1914–1990) war einer der bedeutendsten britischen Grafikdesigner. Der gebürtige Deutsche zog 1936 nach London und erregte mit seinen Arbeiten für das Magazin *Harper's Bazaar* erste Aufmerksamkeit. Ab den 1950er-Jahren arbeitete er verstärkt im Bereich Corporate Design und prägte u. a. über Jahrzehnte das Design der niederländischen Airline KLM. Henrion engagierte sich aktiv in internationalen Design-Verbänden wie ICOGRADA (International Council of Graphic Design Associations) und AGI (Alliance Graphique Internationale).

FHK Henrion (1914–1990) a été un des plus importants designers britanniques. D'origine allemande, il s'installe à Londres en 1936 et se fait d'abord remarquer par son travail pour le magazine *Harper's Bazaar*. À partir des années 1950, il recentre son activité principale sur le corporate design et marquera notamment pendant plusieurs décennies le design de la compagnie aérienne hollandaise KLM. Henrion s'est investi activement dans des associations internationales de design comme ICOGRADA (International Council of Graphic Design Associations) et AGI (Alliance Graphique Internationale).

Henrion and his team replaced the LEB's inconsistent and less-than-inspiring logo with a new, clear-cut image, about which he wrote: "As distinct from the present LEB logotype, which is extremely static, the new logotype has been designed to give an impression of movement and hence dynamism and modernity. It has been tried out experimentally in a great number of applications of all sizes and, wherever it has been used, it retains its characteristic impact."

Den uneinheitlichen und wenig prägnanten Auftritt von LEB ersetzten Henrion und sein Team durch das konstruierte Logo. Er schrieb dazu: „Der neue Schriftzug, der sich von dem äußerst statischen bisherigen unterscheidet, sollte den Eindruck der Bewegung und damit des Dynamischen und Modernen vermitteln. Er wurde experimentell bei zahllosen Anwendungen und in allen Größen getestet und hat dabei nie seine Wirkung verfehlt."

Henrion et son équipe remplacèrent l'image peu homogène et insignifiante de LEB par ce logo construit, à propos duquel le designer écrivit : « Ce nouveau logotype, qui se distingue de l'ancien logotype extrêmement statique, a été conçu pour communiquer une impression de mouvement et donc de dynamisme et de modernité. Il a été testé dans toutes sortes d'applications de tout format sans rien perdre de son impact partout où il a été utilisé. »

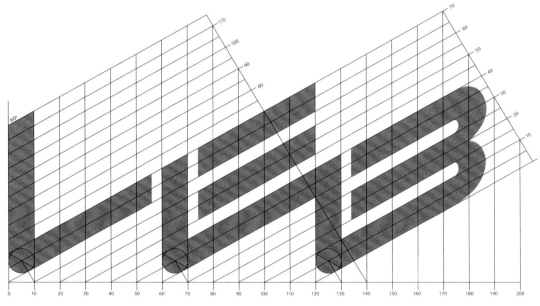

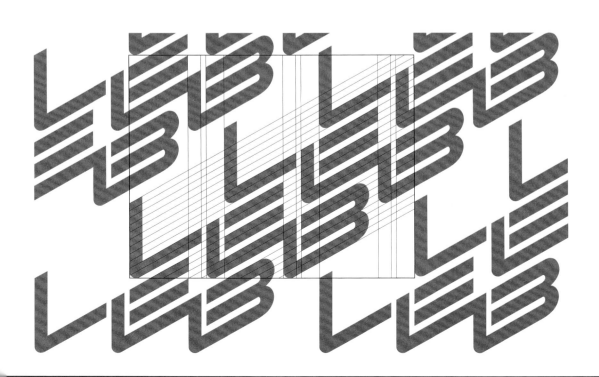

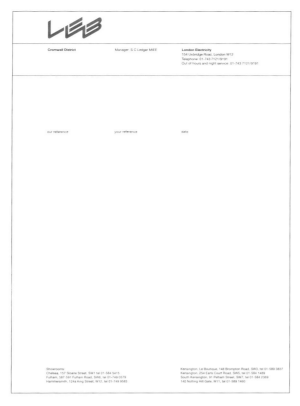

A central feature of the LEB design was the use of the color orange to distinguish it from the blue used by the national-ized gas and water companies. Such a bright color was delib-erately chosen to contrast with the "gray" city of London, and the logo on LEB service vehicles and shop-fronts went on to become an eye-catching feat-ure of the cityscape.

Zentrales Element des LEB-Designs war die Verwendung der Farbe Orange, die in Abgren-zung zu dem Blau der städti-schen Gas- und Wasserwerke ausgewählt wurde. Bewusst hat man für die Anwendung in der „grauen" Stadt London zu einer derart kräftigen Farbe gegriffen, die auf Servicefahrzeugen sowie bei den Ladenbeschriftungen im Stadtbild sofort auffiel.

L'élément central du design réalisé pour LEB était l'utilisation de l'orangé, qui fut préconisée pour le démarquer du bleu des centrales à gaz ou hydrauliques de la ville. Dans la «grise» ville de Londres, on fit très délibé-rément appel à une couleur aussi vive qui sautait immédia-tement aux yeux dans l'image urbaine – sur les véhicules de service et les enseignes des agences.

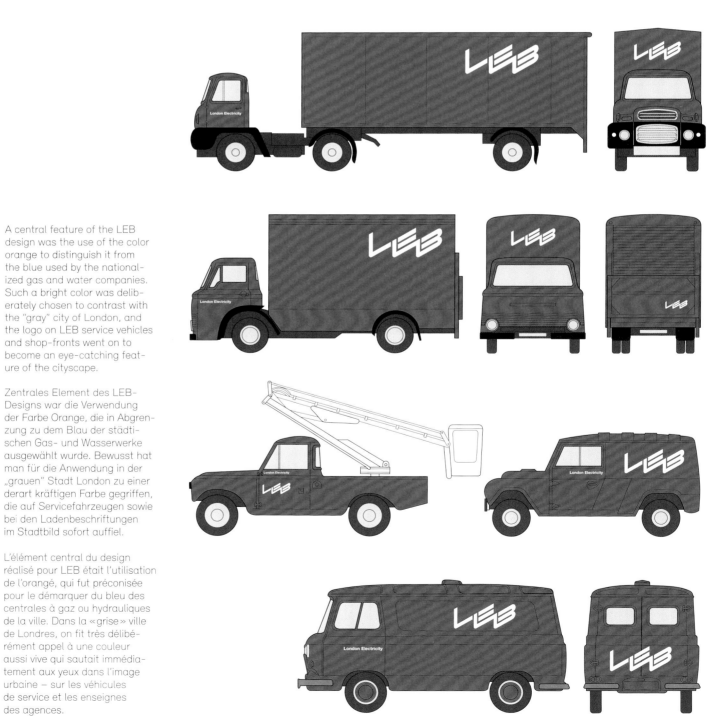

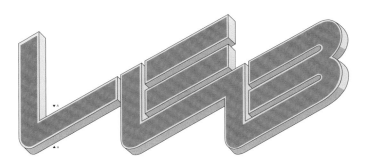

A quick look at the signs above the doors of LEB shops reveals the attention to detail in Henrion Design Associates' work. With the help of an expert lighting engineer they developed a special technique that enabled LEB shop fronts to shine forth in company colors, even at night.

Wie detailliert man in der Aus-arbeitung des Erscheinungsbildes bei Henrion Design Associates vorging, zeigt ein Blick auf die Beschriftungen der Geschäfts-stellen. Gemeinsam mit einem Experten entwickelte das Büro hierzu eine spezielle Leucht-technik, die es ermöglichte, die Fassaden der LEB-Läden auch nachts in der Unternehmens-farbe erstrahlen zu lassen.

Un simple regard sur les inscrip-tions des agences éclaire la précision de détail avec laquelle on définissait une identité visuelle chez Henrion Design Associates. En collaboration avec un expert, le bureau développa une tech-nique d'illumination permettant de faire luire les façades des boutiques LEB aux couleurs de l'entreprise – même la nuit.

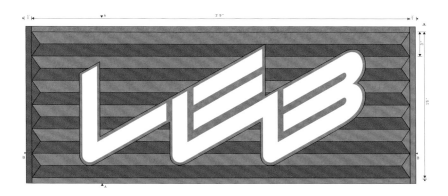

section A-A (not to scale)
These measure are constant for all sizes of sign.

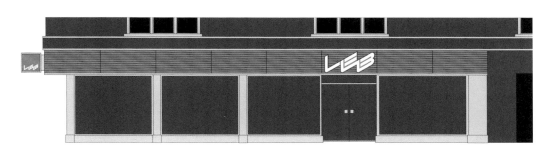

Deux
lettres

Zwei
Buchstaben

Two
Letters

Brescianino
Textiles
1961 · Veniero Bertolotti/Studio 4 · IT

Gomér & Andersson
Real estate
1967 · Ove Engström · SE

Mueller Enterprises
1970s · Jack M. Stricker · US

Anton Kildebergs Møbelfabrik
Furniture
1960s · Anonymous · DK

Fleischkombinat Erfurt
Foods
1965 · Dietrich & Antje Kniffka · DE-GDR

Edizioni della Voce
Publishing
1970 · Michele Spera · IT

Varian and Associates
Electronics
1966 · Giulio Citatto · US

Toyo Kogyo Mazda
Engines
1958 · Hiroshi Ohchi · JP

David Edmunds
1986 · Anonymous · CA

Ing. Joseph Peppler
Thermoplastics
1965 · Fritz Deutschendorf · DE-GDR

Dalmine
Steel tubing
1947 · Remo Muratore/Studio Boggeri · IT

Laboratorios Kramer
Dental laboratory
1966 · José Santamarina/
Elias & Santamarina · ES

Spezialnähmaschinenwerke Limbach
Sewing machines
1965 · Fritz Deutschendorf · DE-GDR

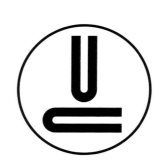

Institut für Meß- und Prüftechnik
Measuring technologies
1965 · Herbert Prüget · DE-GDR

Growth Fund of America
Investment
1969 · Carl Seltzer, James Marrin · US

Time Life Records
Record label
1969 · Matthew Leibowitz · US

Uitgeverij Contact Verlag
Publishing
1958 · Helmut Salden · NL

City-Druck
Printing
1940s · Walter Käch · CH

Feldballes Møbelfabrik
Furniture
1960s · Anonymous · DK

DIA Maschinen Export
Machinery
1965 · Klaus Lempke · DE-GDR

Steuben Verlag
Publishing
1950s · Ernst Rudolf Vogenauer · DE

Bepi Koelliker
Automobiles
1965 · Alfredo Troisi · IT

JK Industriekontor
Industrial trading
1940s · Heinrich Steding · DE

Canada Packers
Foods
1956 · Claire Stewart/
Stewart & Morrison · CA

Technical Center for Aluminum
1966 · Pál Szücs · HU

Nichimo
Real estate
1979 · Akira Hirata, Hiroshi Tada · JP

Leipziger Kommissions- und Buchhandel
Booksellers association
1971 · Sonja Wunderlich · DE-GDR

Markkinointi Viherjuuri
Advertising
1955 · Matti Viherjuuri/
Markkinointi Viherjuuri · FI

Wassersportgemeinschaft Wittenberg
Water-sports club
1965 · Karl Thewalt · DE-GDR

Hermann Rülke
Toys
1965 · Horst Süß · DE-GDR

Cape Universal
Construction materials
1968 · Crosby, Fletcher, Forbes · UK

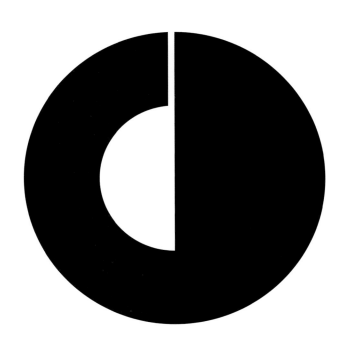

Consolidated Credits & Discounts Bank
1967 · Romek Marber · UK

Intercity-Züge
Public transport
1969 · Coordt von Mannstein · DE

Canadian National Railway
Transportation
1959 · Allan Robb Fleming · CA

Alfieri & Lacroix
Printing
1952 · Franco Grignani · IT

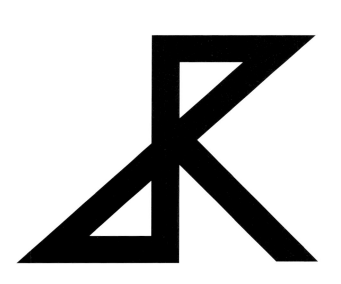

Alfred Ramel
Advertising
1960s · Alfred Ramel · CH

Verlag für Demoskopie
Publishing
1950s · Heinz Schwabe · DE

Ready Steady Go!
Television program
1963 · Arnold Schwartzmann · UK

**Canadian University
Football Championship**
1982 · Ron Richards · CA

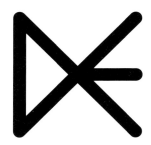

Dassen Elektrotechniek
Electronics
1968 · Marcel Pijpers · NL

Dresdner Packungsbetrieb
Packaging
1965 · Fritz Panndorf · DE-GDR

**Companhia de
Indústrias Químicas do Nordeste**
Chemicals
1968 · Rafael Rodrigues · BR

Manchester Polytechnic
Education
1978 · Hans & Pat Schleger · US

Nippon Research Center
1961 · Kazumasa Nagai/
Nippon Design Center · JP

Edizioni Il Polifilo
Publishing
1969 · Bob Noorda/
Unimark International · IT

State University of New York
1971 · Don Nichols · US

Seraphin Pümpel & Söhne
Windows
1973 · Othmar Motter · AT

Byrge Sorensen & Co.
Chemicals
1966 · Adam Moltke · DK

PGH Einheit Lauchhammer
Electronics
1965 · Manfred Müller · DE-GDR

Furniply
Furniture
1959 · Max Huber · IT

Ascoli Bottoni
Buttons
1968 · Silvio Coppola · IT

Dietrich Kaufmann
Design
1965 · Dietrich Kaufmann · DE-GDR

Gierre
Textiles
1968 · Armando Milani · IT

Fukuda Design
1981 · Masaki Fukuda · JP

ML
1950s · Raoul A. Brink · DE

A. Tarlisio
Furniture
1968 · Silvio Coppola · IT

Central Wagon
Steel products
1965 · David Caplan · UK

Sigfr. Andersson El
Electronics
1969 · Ove Engström · SE

Defa-Gruppe 67
Film production
1967 · Heinz Bormann · DE-GDR

Lanificio Giovanni Tonella
Textiles
1956 · Giulio Confalonieri · IT

Plastic Omnium
Plastics
1965 · Raymond Loewy/CEI · FR

Lunnevads Folkhögskola
Education
1968 · Ove Engström · SE

Interior Forma
Furniture
1963 · Stephen Dunne/
Unimark International · US

Specialty Graphics
Design
1977 · Don Connelly · US

Nobel Bozel
Chemicals
1964 · Raymond Loewy/CEI · FR

Arthur Proudfit
Oil
1960s · Nedo Mion Ferrario · VE

Dancer & Hearne
Furniture
1963 · Ken Garland · UK

The Karosen Company
Fuel oil
1968 · Rod Dyer, Roland Young · US

Integrated Plastics
1967 · Vello Hubel · CA

Dorey Design Group
1960s · Dorey Design · UK

Alpine Meadows of Lake Tahoe
Tourism
1970s · Kate Keating Associates · US

Sobrero
Textiles
1964 · A. G. Fronzoni · IT

Gloweave Shirts
Clothing
1960s · Lee Mason · AU

Kastrup Holmegaard
Glass
1969 · Adam Moltke · DK

G. W. Furniture
1970 · Jean Morin, Denis L'Allier · CA

Eastman Associates
1960s · Primo Angeli · US

Planungsgruppe Untere Rems
Engineering
1970s · Hanns Lohrer · DE

Verkehrsverein Düsseldorf
Tourism
1950s · Jacques Nathan-Garamond · FR

Royle Murgatroyd Design Associates
1980 · Keith Murgatroyd,
Tony Forster · UK

Rhodes & Jamieson
Ready-mix concrete
1970 · Primo Angeli · US

Odermark
Clothing
1970s · Anonymous · DE

Seitsenpainos
Printing
1963 · Kosti A. Antikainen · FI

Hans Kaufeld Polstermöbelfabrik
Furniture
1966 · Anonymous · DE

Morgan Press
Printing
1968 · John Alcorn · US

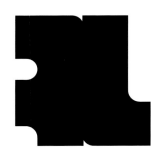

Franco Leoni
Photography
1972 · Luca Apostolo · IT

Field Work
Marketing consultancy
1969 · Piero Barca · IT

Patronato Municipal de la Vivienda
Housing
1966 · José Baqués · ES

Television Corporation of Japan
Broadcasting
1972 · Fred O. Bechlen · US/JP

Deutscher Ingenieur Verlag
Publishing
1957 · Walther Bergmann · DE

Moelven Brug
Prefabricated houses
1968 · Paul Brand · NO

Jorge R.
1960s · Douglas Carr/
Tilds & Cantz Advertising · US

Banco Regional
Bank
1964 · João Carlos Cauduro,
Ludovico Antonio Martino · BR

Maccagno Carlo
Printing
1968 · Carlo Ciarli · IT

Museo de Artes Visuales de Chacabuco
Art museum
1973 · Norberto H. Coppola · AR

Pellicceria Vitale
Textiles
1972 · Silvio Coppola · IT

Lippincott and Margulies
Advertising
1950s · Freeman Craw · US

Didaktica
Language school
1977 · Carlo Marchionni · IT

Palais Wittgenstein
Cultural space
1985 · Paul Effert · DE

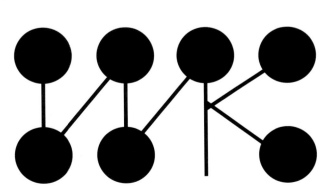

Werner Klapproth Werbung
Advertising
1960s · Werner Klapproth · CH

Studio Del Frate
Design
1968 · Walter Del Frate · IT

Standard Engravers
1959 · A. E. Eddenden · CA

Thorpe Insulation
Thermal insulation
1958 · Hy Farber · US

Offsetdruckerei Emil Grätzer
Printing
1960s · Rudolf Bircher · CH

AC Ediciones
Publishing
1960s · Jordi Fornas · ES

Il Moderno d'Autore
Exhibition of contemporary furniture
1990 · A. G. Fronzoni · IT

Modenantiquaria
Antiques exhibition
1990 · A. G. Fronzoni · IT

Jet-Tours
Travel agency
1982 · Jacques Nathan-Garamond · FR

Cremona Nuova
Typesetting
1969 · Franco Grignani · IT

Technical Publicity International
1965 · Gavin Healey/
Healey Mills Associates · UK

Artemis Verlag
Publishing
1940s · Gottfried Honegger · CH

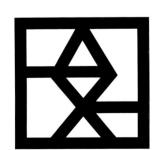

Autovox
1944 · Max Huber · IT

Benziger Verlag
Publishing
1950 · Eugen & Max Lenz · CH

Internationale Musikbibliothek
Music library
1965 · Herbert Prüget · DE-GDR

Macdonald Downie
Printing
1965 · Leslie Smart, Judith Fralick · CA

Erhard & Asociados
Advertising
1972 · Carlos R. Erhard/
Erhard & Asociados · MX

Lead Development Association
Lead industry public relations
1968 · Crosby, Fletcher, Forbes · UK

C. J. Bucher
Printing
1940s · Imre Reiner · CH

Heinz Otto Dessauer
Interior design
1965 · Otto Thiemann · DE-GDR

Szolidaritás
Solidarity movement
1983 · Tamás Ernő · HU

VEB Lacke und Farben
Paints and coatings
1965 · Peter Nietzsche · DE-GDR

Slovakian Print Industry
1981 · Jiří Rathouský · CZ

Deutsche Bank
(proposed design)
1960s · Hermann Virl · DE

Euro Survey
1968 · Philippe Gentil · FR

Noren & Aust Associates
Real estate
1978 · Ed Penniman · US

Barton Realty
Real estate
1963 · Peter Seitz · US

Termica
Air-conditioning
1960s · Heinz Waibl · IT

Getränkekombinat Potsdam
Brewing
1965 · Herbert Prüget · DE-GDR

Thorn Parsons
Electronics
1967 · Peter Rea · UK

G&F
Construction company
1979 · Steve Sheldon · US

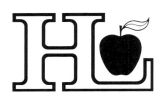

Challenger Sales
1965 · Lance Wyman/
Schmidt Associates · US

Hi-Line Growers
Fruit-growers cooperative
1964 · Sam Payne · US

Sutton & Bell
Interior design
1969 · Allan D. Rae · CA

Leisure Press
Publishing
1975 · Lanny Sommese · US

Solingen
Stainless steel
1969 · Klaus Winterhager · DE

Cinetechnica Madrid
Film production services
1981 · Fernando Medina · ES

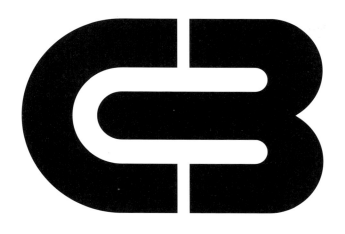

Custom Builders
Construction company
1970s · Bob Swisher · US

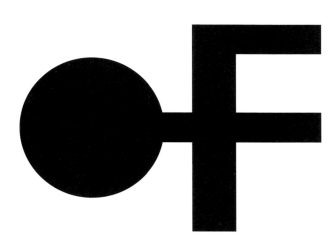

Centro Forme
Furniture
1975 · Heinz Waibl · IT

Transnoel
Haulier
1969 · Tomás Vellvé · ES

Wilhide Interiors
Furniture
1968 · Crawford Dunn · US

Nicoloso Carmelo
Towel dispensers
1973 · Elio Dammicco · IT

Cunard Queen Elizabeth
Cruise ship
1960s · Nick Butterworth · UK

H. + N. Bildgießerei
Fine art foundry
1940s · Ernst Böhm · DE

Insel Taschenbuch
Publishing
1974 · Anonymous · DE

C. F. Christensen
Furniture
1960s · Anonymous · DK

**Zavod za Zdravstveno
in Tehnično Varnost**
Institute for health and technical safety
1960 · Albert Kastelec · SI

AR Antibiotics
Pharmacy
1962 · Dotscho Dotschev · BG

Hotel Aranyhomok
1962 · Árpád Darvas · HU

Allami Gazdaságok
Agriculture
1969 · István Szekeres · HU

Leon Paking
Weaving
1965 · Roman Duszek · PL

Documentary Film Studio
1969 · Jarosław Jasiński · PL

Canadian Premier Life
Insurance
1964 · Richard Janis · CA

Richard Brack Stereo
Audio equipment store
1964 · Imre Koroknay · CA

Ing. Franco Crespi
Machinery
1966 · Salvatore Gregorietti/
Unimark International · IT

Livenza Viaggi
Travel agency
1981 · Alfredo de Santis · IT

Copp Clark
Publishing
1965 · Hans Kleefeld/
Stewart & Morrison · CA

**Reklame Tjenesten for
Danske Andelsselskab**
Advertising
1961 · Adam Moltke · DK

Yusing Y. Jung
Architecture
1965 · Manfred Gotthans,
Chris Yaneff · CA

Janet Rosenblum
Furniture
1966 · Appelbaum & Curtis · US

Unique Marine Hardware
1962 · Edward Oliver · US

Tito Piccoli
Photography
1961 · Theodoor Manson · IT

Johannes Hydraulique
Hydraulic pumps
1969 · Jean Delaunay/Look · FR

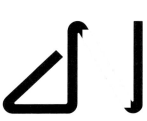

Data Network Corporation
Computer services
1965 · Appelbaum & Curtis · US

Hans Schulz
1974 · Oanh Pham Phu · DE

Ramon Reig Cabanas
Textiles
1966 · Ribas & Creus · ES

Euroceramica
Ceramics
1970 · Walter Ballmer · IT

Farma Lépori
Pharmacy
1969 · José Baqués · ES

SP Chemicals
1960s · Jacques Richez · BE

Said & Maden
Advertising
1960s · Said & Maden · TR

Maglificio Tirelli
Textiles
1971 · Walter Ballmer · IT

Ricerca Quadri
1979 · Centro per il
Disegno Ambientale · IT

Galerie P5
Art gallery
1970s · Hannes Schober,
Wolfram Reinhardt · DE

Churchill Falls Corporation
Energy supplier
1967 · Savage Sloan · CA

Galeria Novas Tendências
Art gallery
1963 · Willys de Castro,
Hércules Barsotti · BR

Longato Arredamenti
Furniture
1965 · Annamaria Coslin · IT

J. R. Geigy Quality + Safety
Pharmaceuticals
1969 · Markus Löw · US

BG
Brewing
1960s · Jacques Richez · BE

Tele Vision
Broadcasting (proposed design)
1950s · Heinz Schwabe · DE

Handwerkerbank Basel
Bank
1950 · Cioma Schönhaus · CH

SD-Druck
Printing
1972 · Hans E. Scheur · DE

Mangiarotti & Morassutti Architetti
Architecture
1955 · Albe Steiner · IT

Stow & Davis
Furniture
1968 · William Tobias/
Robert Miles Runyan · US

Dziewiarska Spółdzielnia Pracy
Knitting factory
1960s · Maria Turkowska · PL

David Foundries
Engineering
1966 · Roy Walker · UK

Skandia Art
Art gallery
1965 · Knut Yran · NO

Architektenverband
Architects association
1965 · Zdeněk Ziegler · CZ

United Dominion
Investment
1961 · Chris Yaneff,
Manfred Gotthans · CA

Technos Progetti
Accountancy
1969 · Michele Spera · IT

Henry Robertz
Design
1965 · Henry Robertz · US

Executive Systems + Programming
Computing services
1972 · Mike Quon · US

TaxShield
Accountancy
1970 · Robert Pease · US

Meijeriteollisuuden Tiedotustoimisto
Dairy products
1965 · Osmo Omenamäki · FI

Companhia Seguradora Brasileira
Insurance
1960s · Aloísio Magalhães/PVDI · BR

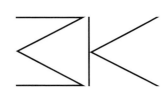

MK Production
Film production
1966 · Gérard Guerre/Technés · FR

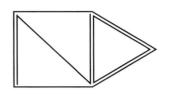

Nippon Design Center
1960 · Kazumasa Nagai · JP

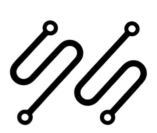

Sound Systems
1966 · Peter Wildbur/
BDMW Associates · UK

Boy Scouts Yokohama '89
Scouts jamboree
1983 · Shigo Yamaguchi · JP

J. P. Weiss Mess-Systeme
Measuring technology
1970 · Alfred Weiss · CH

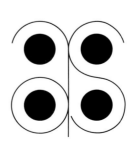

As-Plan
Architecture
1977 · Hanns Lohrer · DE

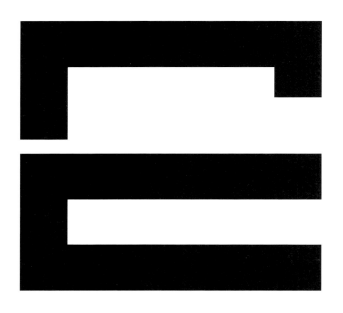

Robert Campiche
Advertising
1960s · Robert Campiche · CH

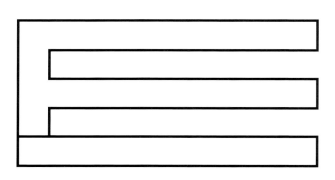

Fideg Elettronica
Electronics
1969 · A. G. Fronzoni · IT

Moldenhauer-Wantikow Baumschule
Tree nursery
1969 · Ulrich Maass · DE

Wilhelm Mimm
Ties
1950 · Walter Breker · DE

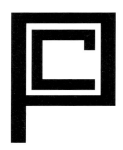

La Carbonique Française
Production of carbon dioxide
1968 · Etienne Bucher · FR

Herbert Chervet
Advertising
1960s · Herbert Chervet · CH

Lan Ron
Construction company
1966 · Frank R. Cheatham/
Porter & Goodman Design · US

Fahrzeugbau Erfurt
Automobiles
1965 · Dietrich Bauer · DE-GDR

Fundación Empresarial
Business initiatives
1960s · Armando Paez Torres · AR

Société Suisse de Ciment Portland
Cement
1962 · Paul Bühlmann · CH

P. Simonsen Specialmøbler
Furniture
1960s · Anonymous · DK

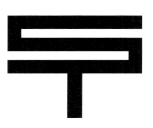

Suomen Tupakka
Tobacco
1950s · Kosti A. Antikainen · FI

Revit
Real estate
1960s · Adolf Flückiger · CH

Electrochimie Ugine
Chemicals
1965 · Philippe Gentil · FR

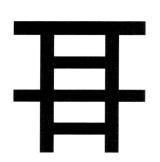

Unika Væv
Furniture
1960s · Anonymous · DK

Fischer Advertising
1970 · Oanh Pham Phu · DE

Eric Johann
Interior design
1961 · Jukka Pellinen · FI

Galeria Bonino
Art gallery
1960 · Beatriz Feitler · BR

Stuermer Architects
1966 · Randall R. Roth · US

Eduard Franke, Erfurt
Machinery
1965 · Martin Rosette · DE-GDR

IP Dekordruckerei
Printing
1970s · Ekkehart Rustmeier · DE

Bröderna Larsson
Textiles
1960s · Ove Engström · SE

Schraubenwerk Heiligenstadt
Screws
1965 · Dietrich Bauer · DE-GDR

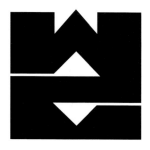

Wohnbau Gröbenzell
Real estate
1970s · Hannes Schober,
Wolfram Reinhardt · DE

Robinson Excavating
1980 · Denise Spaulding · US

Elie Harver
Construction materials
1960s · Jacques Nathan-Garamond · FR

Banco de Crédito Territorial
Bank
1960s · Aloísio Magalhães/PVDI · BR

Urania Bank
1964 · Hans Weber · CH

Irrigation Company
1960s · Anthony Smith, Roger Turpin · UK

Asahi Kasei
Leather products
1983 · Yasunori Suzumori,
Shigo Yamaguchi · JP

Banco Itaú América
Bank
1965 · Aloísio Magalhães/PVDI · BR

Julien et Mège
Industrial heat pumps
1969 · Technés · FR

Cross and Trecker
Machinery
1981 · Mark Topczewski, Frances
Ullenberg, Ken Eichenbaum · US

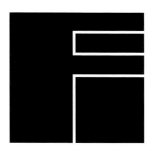

Fiação Indiana
Cotton
1964 · Alexandre Wollner · BR

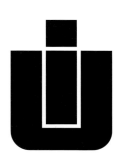

Unione Industriale Torino
Business union
1964 · Aldo Novarese · IT

Time Life
Publishing (proposed design)
1969 · Arnold Saks · US

Straßen- und Tiefbaukombinat Erfurt
Road construction
1965 · Herbert Vogel · DE-GDR

Union Tiefbau
Construction company
1970s · Oanh Pham Phu · DE

Atelier 3D
Design
1960s · Jacques Richez · BE

Franz Stocker
Construction company
1969 · Donald Brun · CH

Bau- und Montagekombinat Erfurt
Construction company
1965 · Karlheinz Herke · DE-GDR

Carte Bleue
Bank
1967 · Daniel Maurel/Chourgnoz Publicité · FR

Tommy Matusi
1977 · William Carson,
Douglas Williams · US

Nippon Chromat Laboratory
1960s · Kenji Ito · JP

Owens-Illinois
Glass bottles
1970s · Chermayeff & Geismar · US

Daido Interior
Department store
1960s · Kenji Ito · JP

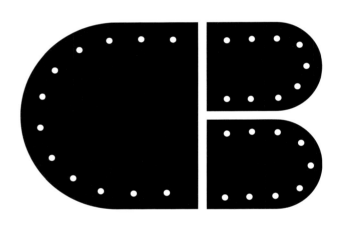

Cobbler's Bench
Footwear
1983 · Mo Lebowitz · US

Kuwait National Petroleum Company
1968 · Crosby, Fletcher, Forbes · UK

Tower Hill Apartments
1965 · John Kobold/
Hiller Rinaldo Associates · CA

Golf Equipment
1970s · David B. Gray/Pierre
Kleykamp Design Association · US

Namiki Camera Shop
1959 · Hiroshi Ohchi · JP

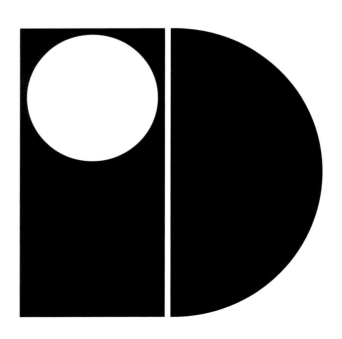

Drevo Industries
Construction materials
1973 · František Bobáň · CZ

Landesstelle für Betriebsschutz
Occupational safety
1977 · Michael Herold · DE

Alcoholism Information Center
1976 · Thomas Ohmer · US

Lorilleux International
Inks
1971 · Alain Carrier · FR

Finitaliana
1974 · Luigi Miani,
Guido Redaelli · IT

Adaptive Test
Machinery
1983 · Jack Evans · US

Morris Graphics
Printing
1966 · Leslie Smart · CA

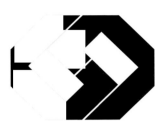

**Society of Graphic
Designers of Canada**
1968 · Jacques E. Charette · CA

Mikimoto
Publishing
1981 · Kuniharu Masubuchi,
Hiroshi Iseya · JP

Adhesive Materials
1969 · Abram Games · UK

Merlin Gerin
Electronics
1966 · Gérard Guerre/Technés · FR

Cook & Shanosky Associates
Design
1960s · Cook & Shanosky
Associates · US

Etta e Giovanni Brunazzi
Design
1966 · Giovanni Brunazzi · IT

Works Management Magazine
1963 · Gavin Healey/
Healey Mills Associates · UK

Grupo Domit
Footwear
1979 · Fernando Rión · MX

3 Suisses
Mail-order
1970 · Mario Cresci/Mafia · FR

Dinamica Umbra
Haulier
1974 · Francesco Burcini · IT

Deutsche Metallmesse
Metals trade fair
1977 · Michael Herold · DE

Arvo Westerlund
Construction company
1966 · Teuvo Tynkkynen/
Mainos Taucher Reklam · FI

Typogabor
Typesetting
1971 · Paul Gabor · FR

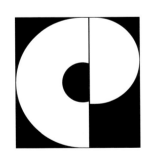

C. Paakkinen
Bakery
1963 · Rolf Christianson · FI

Sunayama Productions
Advertising films
1960s · Mitsuo Katsui · JP

Officine Calabrese
Industrial vehicles
1963 · Heinz Waibl · IT

GraphikArt
Design
1966 · Yvon Laroche · CA

Parking Services
1977 · Scott Engen · US

Studio AX
Interior design
1979 · Othmar Motter · AT

Amitalia Fund Company
Investment
1972 · Charles Rohonyi · BE

Turri Casa
Furniture
1963 · Armando Milani · IT

**Education and Architecture
in the 20th Century**
Design workshop
1968 · William Newton · CA

Radiotelevisione Italiana
Broadcasting
1950 · Erberto Carboni · IT

Angelo Valaguzza
Luggage
1968 · Salvatore Gregorietti/
Unimark International · IT

3M
Multi-technology products
1978 · Siegel & Gale · US

bit
Magazine
1967 · Till Neuburg · CH

Camera di Commercio I.A.A. di Milano
Chamber of commerce
1971 · Mimmo Castellano · IT

Society of Physical Therapists
1969 · Jay Hanson · US

Hans Neuburg
Advertising
1940s · Hans Neuburg · CH

C & B Italia
Furniture
1967 · Bob Noorda/
Unimark International · IT

Carlo Tiscornia
Management consultancy
1967 · Carlo Cattaneo · IT

Post & Telegraphs
1968 · Damien Harrington/
Kilkenny Design Workshops · IE

New Haven
Transportation
1954 · Herbert Matter · US

Odermatt+Tissi
Design
1970s · Odermatt+Tissi · CH

**6th Inter-American
Banking Conference**
1960s · S. Neil Fujita · US

Umemura Stainless
Steelworks
1964 · Yoshio Hayashi · JP

Silkeborg Møbelfabrik
Furniture
1960s · Anonymous · DK

Antiques & Things
1965 · Arnaud Benvenuti Maggs · CA

**Unione Produttori di
Sintetico per Calzature**
Association of shoe manufacturers
1973 · G. & R. Associati · IT

Greenwich Joinery
Carpentry
1973 · Kenneth Hollick · UK

Gelatinewerk Stadtilm
Gelatin
1965 · Dietrich Bauer · DE-GDR

Sapac
Department store
1965 · Leen Averink · FR

Advertising & Sales Club of Toronto
1966 · Manfred Gotthans,
Chris Yaneff · CA

Tokyo Boat Show
1960 · Gan Hosoya · JP

E. M. Miller
Bank
1967 · Vance Jonson · US

Arnoldo Mondadori
Publishing
1969 · Bob Noorda/
Unimark International · IT

Salient Records
Record label
1969 · Rod Dyer · US

Huebner & Henneberg
Architecture
1957 · Randall R. Roth · US

Electronic Memory
Computer systems
1966 · Ken Parkhurst & Associates · US

Tokyo Young Brothers
Textiles
1979 · Michio Ogura · JP

Jornal do Brasil
Newspaper
1973 · PVDI · BR

Orive Laboratorios Perfumes
1968 · Ribas & Creus · ES

Lenzinger Antennenbau
Broadcasting antennae
1950s · Otto Krämer · CH

Japan Design Council
1958 · Hiroshi Ohchi · JP

Voogelaar & Smulders
Financial trading
1969 · A. G. Schillemans · NL

2+1
Television program
1967 · Pierre-Yves Pelletier · CA

Finland Designland
Quality-mark
1968 · Eka Lainio/
Markkinointi Viherjuuri · FI

Goma Shobo
Magazine
1978 · Tetsuya Ota · JP

Compagnie Financière
Bank
1973 · Heinz Schwabe · DE

Textima
Cable insulation
1960s · Josef P. Grabner · CH

Smalteria Viterbese
Enamel
1961 · Italo Lupi · IT

Besana Mobili
Furniture
1960 · Valeriano Piozzi/Piozzi & Cima · IT

Amnesty International
Human rights organization
1972 · Robert Sessler · CH

Vickers & Benson
Advertising
1969 · Hans Kleefeld/
Stewart & Morrison · CA

Amici di Brera
Conservation trust
1969 · Bruno Monguzzi/
Studio Boggeri · IT

Schweizerische Rückversicherung
Insurance
1960s · Walter Reichen, Max Lenz · CH

MM Enclosures
Metal containers
1960s · Ladislav Sutnar · US

Josef Grabner
Design
1960s · Josef P. Grabner · CH

A. C. Distribuidora
1983 · Morfos Diseño · MX

Three Mast
Broadcasting
1977 · Eita Shinohara · JP

Atelier Yran
Design
1958 · Knut Yran · NO

**Research
Institute for Construction**
1982 · Mitsuo Ishida, Toshiro Abe · JP

Banco Comercial Brasil
Bank
1967 · Aloísio Magalhães/PVDI · BR

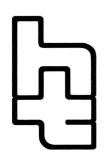

Hoch- und Tiefbau
Construction company
1940s · Walter Sigg · CH

Wilson Walton International
Signs
1970 · Alan Fletcher/
Pentagram · UK

Rutsker Verlag
Publishing
1989 · Anonymous · DE

Loyola University
1959 · Bruce Beck · US

Teatro Popolare Italiano
Theater
1959 · Albe Steiner · IT

Juan R. Da Costa Hidromaticos
Automobile parts
1970 · Reynaldo Da Costa · VE

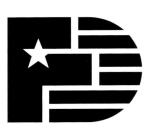

Foote & Davies
Printing
1972 · Critt Graham/
Visual Persuasion · US

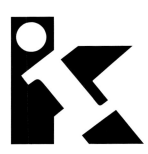

Impresos Œlonia
Packaging
1983 · Morfos Diseño · MX

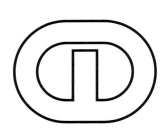

G. D. Allestimenti
Advertising
1969 · Studio GBR · IT

Mason & Mcintosh
Sales agents
1968 · Roger O. Denning · UK

Glass and Ceramics
1965 · Zdeněk Ziegler · CZ

Western Medical
Pharmaceuticals
1975 · Marty Neumeier · US

Vesdre-Escaut
Textiles
1965 · Luc Van Malderen · BE

Physica Verlag
Publishing
1976 · Hans-Günter Diehl · DE

Norrland Center
Exhibition space
1967 · Lars Bramberg · SE

Ringbau Bauunternehmen
Construction company
1975 · Oanh Pham Phu · DE

Swiss TV
Broadcasting
1958 · Carlo L. Vivarelli · CH

United Glass
Glass containers
1963 · David Caplan · UK

Revolution Sound
Recording studio
1969 · James Donahue/
Cooper & Beatty · CA

Ahrend de Cirkel
Office furniture
1962 · Aldo Calabresi/Studio Boggeri · IT

Ahrend Oda
Office furniture
1962 · Aldo Calabresi/Studio Boggeri · IT

Aannemingsbedrijf A.M.J. Bergmans
Construction company
1967 · Bear Cornet · NL

Georges Coslin
Architecture
1965 · Annamaria Coslin · IT

Cemer
Interior design
1970 · Marcello d'Andrea · IT

Groupe Pechiney
Chemicals
1968 · Roger Druet · FR

Albert Einstein Hospital
1961 · Alexandre Wollner · BR

De Pedrini
Photoengraving
1968 · Mimmo Castellano · IT

Dynaflair Corporation
Architecture and engineering
1969 · Peter G. Ulmer/
Stewart & Morrison · CA

**T. Nishiwaki Visual
Design Laboratory**
1955 · Tomoichi Nishiwaki · JP

United Steel Corporation
1964 · Manfred Gotthans,
Chris Yaneff · CA

Metallaufbereitung Erfurt
Metal processing
1965 · Lothar Freund · DE-GDR

Paris Hilton
Hotel
1964 · Raymond Loewy/CEI · FR

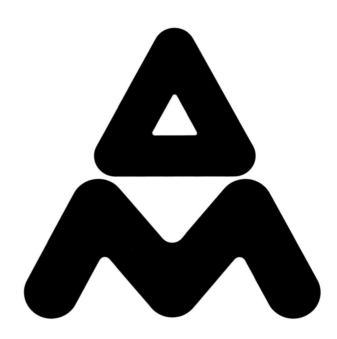

L'Acier Moulé, Paris
Steel
1970 · Albert Boton/Delpire-Advico · FR

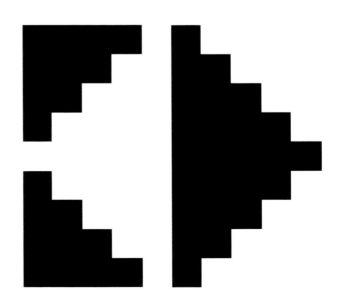

Kuwayama Design Room
1982 · Yasaburo Kuwayama · JP

Trois lettres

Drei Buchstaben

Three Letters

Katholieke Universiteit Nijmegen
University
1960s · Anonymous · NL

Cox of Watford
Furniture
1960 · Henrion Design Associates · UK

Figli di Angelo Bonacina
Furniture
1962 · Ilio Negri · IT

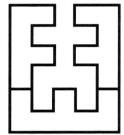
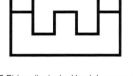

Peter J. Oestergaard
Publishing
1914 · Anonymous · DE

CBM Concrete Company
Construction materials
1970s · Bob Swisher · US

EFF Eidgenössische Versicherungs AG
Insurance
1950s · Helmuth Kurtz · CH

Actualité des Arts Plastiques
Magazine
1970 · René Ponot · FR

Verwaltungs- und
Wirtschaftsakademie, Düsseldorf
Business academy
1986 · Paul Effert · DE

Verlag der Dichtung
Publishing
1920 · Anonymous · DE

SBS Construction Management
1980 · James Lienhart, Al Navarre · US

Electricité de France - Gaz de France
Energy supplier
1963 · Ilio Negri · FR

Istituto Euchimico Milanese
Chemical research
1967 · Armando Milani · IT

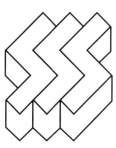
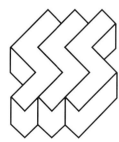

Verlag Michael Winkler
Publishing
1950s · Hermann Kosel · AT

Top Gallery
Art gallery
1970 · John Lange · VE

Sun Sano Sogei-Sha
Design
1982 · Yutaka Sato · JP

IDI Cinematografica
Film production
1972 · Sergio Salaroli · IT

De Swaan Bonnist
Import-export
1960s · Gerard Wernars · NL

Shin Nihon Shokken
Foods
1981 · Tadashi Ishikawa,
Hideko Sakado · JP

International Gold Research
1983 · Hiroshi Fukushima · JP

The McBee Company
Office supplies
1964 · Rudy Eswarin/
Stewart & Morrison · CA

City Investment Trust
1971 · Ken Garland · UK

Latham Tyler Jensen
Industrial design
1963 · Charles MacMurray,
Sherman Mutchnick · US

**International Telephone
& Telegraph Corporation**
1957 · Matthew Leibowitz · US

ECTA-3
Design
1973 · Alberto Isern/ECTA-3 · ES

C. F. Christensen
Furniture
1950s · Anonymous · DK

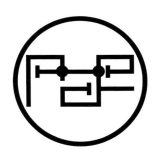

Pirelli
Tires
1960s · Albe Steiner · IT

Farbenfabriken Bayer AG
Paints
1965 · Graphicteam Köln · DE

United States Steel Corporation
1960s · Emil O. Biemann/
Lippincott & Margulies · US

LTZ Lichttechnik
Lighting technology
1950s · Karl J. Weiss · CH

Dai Nippon Printing
1954 · Kenji Ito · JP

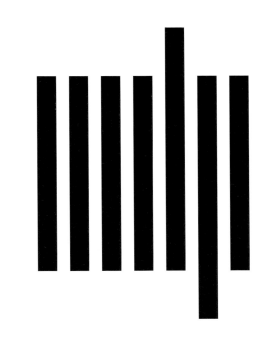

Robert Geisser
Design
1950s · Robert Geisser · CH

M.I.T. Press
Publishing
1962 · Muriel Cooper · US

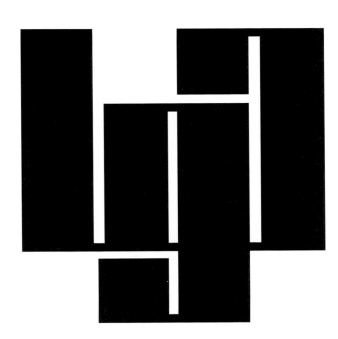

Landesgewerbeamt Baden-Württemberg
Trade supervisory office
1956 · Herbert W. Kapitzki · DE

American Gas & Chemicals
1960s · Stanley Eisenman,
David Enock · US

William M. Rosenbaum
Stockbrokers
1968 · Al Corchia · US

Dr. Te Neuss Großdruckerei
Printing
1950s · Heinz Schwabe · DE

Costruzioni Stradali e Civili
Construction company
1965 · Udo Etzi · CH

Independent Photographers Service
1950s · Allan Robb Fleming · CA

R. J. Reynolds Industries
Tobacco
1969 · Walter P. Margulies/
Lippincott & Margulies · US

**Plumbers & Mechanical Contractors
Association**
1981 · Dennis Pehoski · US

OSC Italia
1979 · Armando Milani,
Maurizio Milani · IT

Cine Club de Valencia
Film club
1950s · Carlos Cruz-Diez · VE

Neue Darmstädter Verlagsanstalt
Publishing
1949 · Helmut Lortz · DE

Aok Kosmetik
Cosmetics
1967 · Anonymous · DE

**Compagnia
Amministratrice Fiduciaria**
Real estate
1970 · Giulio Confalonieri · IT

SIG
1960s · Erik Ellegaard Frederiksen · DK

Mutual Life Assurance Co.
Insurance
1971 · John S. Brown · CA

Ziegelkombinat
Bricks
1965 · Martin Rosette · DE-GDR

I.S.H.
Pharmacy
1963 · Raymond Loewy/CEI · FR

Ente per lo Sviluppo dell'Artigianato
Craft workers agency
1964 · Martin Diethelm · CH

Canadian Industrial Advertisers
1968 · Anonymous · CA

Cheddite Plastic
1970 · Walter Bosshardt · CH

Radio Télévision Scolaire
Broadcasting
1965 · René Ponot · FR

AIB
1965 · Heinz Schwabe · DE

Imprese Turistiche Barziesi
Travel agency
1960s · Cecco Re · IT

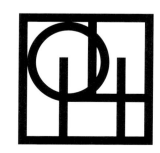

OHL Industrietechnik
Industrial services
1970 · Heinz Schwabe · DE

Associated Irish Menswear
1968 · Eric Patton · UK

School of Social Service Administration
at the University of Chicago
1970 · David L. Burke · US

Stuttgarter Messe und Kongress
Trade fair
1975 · Michael Herold · DE

Instructional Systems Incorporated
Education training
1965 · Lance Wyman · US

General Química Layetana
Chemicals
1968 · José Baqués · ES

Design Projects Center
1960s · Leslie Smart,
Sid Bersucsky · CA

Mac de España
Management consultancy
1972 · Francisco Marco Vilar/
Grupo de Diseño · ES

Van Wijk & Wisser
Import-export
1960s · Jan Jaring · NL

CRL Products and Homewares
Mail-order
1967 · Keith Murgatroyd · UK

Tobu
Department store
1971 · Kakutaro Iimori · JP

Hatsune Industries Co.
Machinery
1979 · Kenji Kaneko · JP

Record Source International
Record label
1959 · S. Neil Fujita · US

Sie
Textiles
1967 · José Baqués · ES

Tri-Arts Press
Printing
1960s · Freeman Craw · US

Les Créations Graphiques
Publishing
1960s · Jacques Nathan-Garamond · FR

CTI Reiseclub
Travel agency
1972 · Siegfried W. Küchler · DE

Association des Designers du Canada
1967 · Claude Gauthier · CA

Sun Spice
Spices
1960s · Koji Kato · JP

Collezione Nai
Interior design
1969 · Massimo Dradi · IT

Compas
Travel agency
1970 · Manuel Espinoza · VE

GMB Associates
Management consultancy
1981 · GMB Associates · US

Istituto Ortopedico Rizzoli
Medical institute
1971 · Walter Hergenröther · IT

Illumination Industries
Lighting
1969 · Primo Angeli · US

ICA Inköpscentralernas
Retail group
1964 · Rune Monö · SE

Einkaufsgenossenschaft
des Autogewerbes
Automobile manufacturers group
1950s · Hans Hartmann · CH

Ticino Vito
1980 · Max Huber · IT

La Gazzetta del Mezzogiorno
Newspaper
1965 · Mimmo Castellano · IT

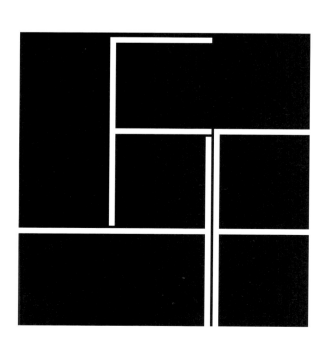

Fonderie Typographique Française
Type foundry
1962 · J. M. L. Richard · FR

Société Financière Européenne
Financial services
1960s · A. Baier/Delpire-Advico · FR

Società Nebiolo
Type foundry
1960 · Aldo Novarese · IT

Ernest J. Swimmer
Toy designer
1968 · Tony Russell · US

Kitanippon Gyogyo
Machinery
1983 · Masaki Fukuda · JP

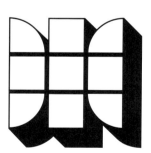

Diffusion Industrielle à Céramique
Ceramics
1968 · Serge Defradat/
Chourgnoz Publicité · FR

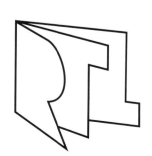

RTL Plus
Broadcasting
1989 · Anonymous · DE

First Los Angeles Bank
1975 · Thomas Ohmer,
Lou Frimkess · US

New Product Management Group
Market research
1979 · Michael J. Russell,
Sylvia Sewell · UK

National Parent
Teacher Association
1977 · Edward Hughes · US

33rd Biennale d'Arte, Venice
Art festival
1966 · Bob Noorda · IT

Integrated Design
Associates
1957 · Allen Porter · US

Foreningen af Danske Civiløkonomer
Association of business economists
1968 · Morten Peetz-Schou · DK

Radio Advertising Representatives
1966 · Tom Woodward · US

ABC Verlag
Publishing
1970 · Anton Schutzbach · CH

General Felt Industries
Textiles
1978 · Philip Gips · US

Diseño Arquitectonico y de Interiores
Interior design
1970 · Pedro Ariño · ES

International Underwater Contractors
Underwater engineering
1970 · Jeanette Koumjian/
Russell & Hinrichs · US

Dent Everyman
Publishing
1960s · John Alcorn · US

Studio Zot
Design and photography
1970 · R. Baldini, D. Ferrari, G. Valbonesi,
V. Vecchi/Studio Zot · IT

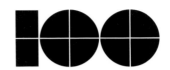

**100th Anniversary of the Printing
Industries of New York**
1963 · Richard Danne/Gips & Danne · US

Tintoria Paolo Barzaghi
Industrial dyeing
1954 · Piero Ottinetti · IT

Lambertus Verlag, Freiburg
Publishing
1961 · Peter Lorenz · DE

**Compagnie Internationale
pour l'Informatique**
Computer science
1968 · Alain Carrier · FR

Fai
Furniture
1970 · Giulio Confalonieri · IT

IPM
Foods
1982 · Francesco Burcini · IT

Club degli Editori
Book club
1960 · Bruno Munari · IT

Desarrollo de Técnicas para Astilleros
Shipyard development
1973 · Alan Fletcher/Pentagram · UK

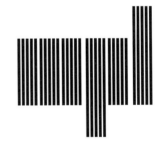

Minneapolis Public Library
1970 · Peter Seitz · US

Illinois National Bank
1975 · Chermayeff & Geismar · US

Dr. Alfred Hüthig Verlag
Publishing
1950 · Anonymous · DE

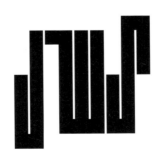

JWS
Machinery
1954 · Carlo L. Vivarelli · CH

CPT Corporation
Word processors
1973 · Peter Seitz · US

Institut Français du Pétrole
Petroleum research
1982 · George McGinnis · US

Löw Schuhfabriken
Footwear
1955 · Leo Gantenbein · CH

Blatter Spieler Sachse Werbeagentur
Advertising
1966 · BSS Werbeagentur · DE

Hammel, Green and Abrahamson
Architecture and engineering
1984 · Peter Seitz · US

Deutscher Studien Verlag
Publishing
1970 · Lily Regehr · DE

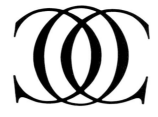

Aktieselskabet C. Olesen
Textiles
1956 · Acton Bjørn · DK

Stop and Save
Trading Stamp Corporation
1962 · Henry Robertz/
The Design Partnership · US

Conditionarento Nord Italia
Climate technology
1973 · R. Nava, D. Soffientini, G. Romani,
A. Ubertazzi · IT

Kentucky Farmers Bank
1980 · Denise Spaulding · US

800 År Jubilæum i Byen København
City anniversary
1967 · Børge Nebel · DK

Smith Kline & French Laboratories
Pharmaceuticals
1968 · Kramer, Miller, Lomden,
Glassman Inc. · US

Radio Corporation of America
Electronics and entertainment
1968 · Walter P. Margulies/
Lippincott & Margulies · US

Impresa Finanza Investimento
Investment
1976 · Giovanni Brunazzi · IT

Dansk Fotografisk Forening
Photographers association
1970 · Morten Peetz-Schou · DK

Art Directors Club (Germany)
Advertising
1964 · Vilim Vasata · DE

Commercial Interiors Corporation
Office design
1966 · Dominick Sarica · US

Uni Design
1971 · Yuji Baba · JP

DDI
Beverages
1969 · Morten Peetz-Schou,
Flemming Hedvard · DK

RAI Radio Italiana
Broadcasting
1960s · Erberto Carboni · IT

Società Generale Semiconduttori
Integrated circuits
1960s · Heinz Waibl · IT

UPS Werbeagentur
Advertising
1965 · UPS Werbeagentur · DE

Linificio e Canapificio Nazionale
Textiles
1966 · Silvio Coppola · IT

Pfälzische Verlagsanstalt
Publishing
1984 · Kurt Weidemann · DE

Pirelli
Tires
1960s · Aldo Calabresi/
Studio Boggeri · IT

Fiorio
Textiles
1959 · Enzo Mari · IT

Calefação Elétrica
Heating technology
1971 · Aristo Rabin · BR

IZI
1970 · Heinz Schwabe · DE

S.I.C. Ceramiche Artistiche
Ceramics
1969 · Carlo Ciarli · IT

Educational Broadcasting Corporation
1960s · Walter Allner · US

La Mercantil Rosarina
Insurance
1960s · Gustavo Balcells · AR

Overseas Containers Ltd.
1975 · Implement · UK

ZIP Zündhölzer
Matches
1960s · Enzo Rösli · CH

Canadian International Paper Company
1965 · Frank Lipari/
Gazette Printing Company · CA

International Record Corporation
Record label
1968 · J. & A. Breukelman
Design Associates · CA

Editions Desclée De Brouwer
Publishing
1953 · Michel Olyff · BE

Géo
Canned foods
1967 · Roman Duszek/
Lonsdale Design · FR

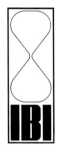

International Bedaux Institute
Workplace efficiency
1967 · Théodore Stamatakis/
Créations Stama · FR

I.S.S.
Information technology
1971 · J. M. L. Richard · FR

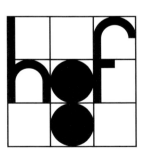

Hygrade Fuels
1968 · Leslie Smart · CA

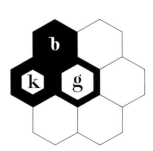

Basler Kulturgemeinschaft
Cultural association
1940s · Hermann Eidenbenz · CH

Cave Carbonato Calcio
Mining
1960s · Marco Del Corno · IT

**Kupferschmiede und
Apparaturen C. Kunze**
Coppersmiths
1965 · Marlene Ramdohr-Bark · DE-GDR

Washington Zoo
1977 · Wyman & Cannan · US

**Großhandelsgesellschaft
Möbel und Kulturwaren**
Wholesale domestic supplier
1965 · Kurt Tuma · DE-GDR

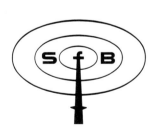

Sender Freies Berlin
Broadcasting
1950s · Heinz Schwabe · DE

**International Minerals &
Chemicals Corporation**
1959 · Morton Goldsholl · US

Les logos sont la forme la plus abstraite du graphisme : l'image et la force d'une organisation ou d'une entreprise, concentrées dans un symbole doté d'une valeur de reconnaissance générale, immédiate. Simplicité et expressivité. Parfois, un logo résulte d'un long processus, de la première idée à la version finale.
Hermann Zapf

Logos sind die abstrakteste Form des Grafikdesigns: das Bild und die Stärke einer Organisation oder Firma, reduziert auf ein Symbol von allgemeinem, sofortigem Wiedererkennungswert. Schlichtheit gepaart mit Ausdruckskraft. Bisweilen steht ein Logo am Ende einer langen Entwicklung von der ersten Idee bis zur endgültigen Ausführung.
Hermann Zapf

The most abstract form of graphic design is logo design. The image and power of an organization or company reduced to a symbol recognized at once by everybody. Simplicity and expression combined in unity by the designer. Sometimes it is the result of a long transformation from the first idea to the final execution.
Hermann Zapf

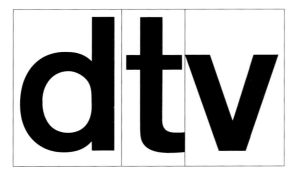

Deutscher Taschenbuch Verlag

1961 · Celestino Piatti · CH/DE

Celestino Piatti (1922–2007) enrolled at the Zurich School of Arts and Crafts in 1937, before serving an apprenticeship in printing and graphic design. In 1948 he set up his own studio in Basel. His illustrations, with their bold, uncomplicated style, earned him success as well as many awards, while the animal books he himself wrote and illustrated made him internationally famous. His work for dtv was the mainstay of his career for over 30 years.

Celestino Piatti (1922–2007) besuchte 1937 die Kunstgewerbeschule Zürich und absolvierte anschließend eine Lehre in Druckerei und Grafik. Ab 1948 war er mit eigenem Atelier in Basel ansässig. Der markante Illustrationsstil bei Büchern und Plakaten verhalf ihm bald zum Erfolg und er erhielt zahlreiche Auszeichnungen. Seine eigenen Publikationen von Tierillustrationen machten ihn auch international bekannt. Die Arbeit für den Deutschen Taschenbuch Verlag bestimmte über 30 Jahre seiner Laufbahn.

Celestino Piatti (1922–2007) fréquente l'École des arts et métiers de Zurich en 1937 avant de suivre une formation d'imprimeur et graphiste. À partir de 1948, il est établi à Bâle, où il fonde son propre atelier. Son style illustratif frappant de livres et d'affiches lui vaut bientôt le succès et de nombreuses distinctions. Ses propres publications d'illustrations animalières l'ont aussi fait connaître internationalement. Le travail qu'il a réalisé pendant plus de 30 ans pour le Deutscher Taschenbuch Verlag a été déterminant pour sa carrière.

In 1961 eleven German-language publishers got together to found a label under which they could all publish their paperback books. The new publishing house confidently branded itself German Paperback Publishers—Deutscher Taschenbuch Verlag, or dtv for short. The Swiss graphic artist Celestino Piatti was chosen to design the logo and the covers for the first dtv titles. Piatti opted for simplicity and understatement. He started by selecting a middle-of-the-road typeface, Akzidenz-Grotesk, as a defining element in the company's first marketing campaign. The combination of its inexpensive paperbacks and simple, modern design perfectly captured the spirit of the 1960s. The firm flourished and, from small beginnings with only a few titles each year, went on to develop a wide-ranging list. Piatti remained dtv's designer for over 30 years and, until the introduction of a whole new design policy, created some 6,300 book covers and a constant stream of advertising material for the Munich-based publishers.

Im Jahr 1961 schlossen sich elf deutschsprachige Verlage mit dem Ziel zusammen, ein gemeinsames Taschenbuch-Label für ihre Werke zu gründen. Den neuen Verlag nannte man selbstbewusst Deutscher Taschenbuch Verlag, kurz dtv. Der Schweizer Grafiker Celestino Piatti wurde als Gestalter des Logos und der ersten dtv-Titel ausgewählt. Piatti setzte auf Reduktion und Understatement. Beginnend beim Logo nutzte er die neutrale Schrift Akzidenz Grotesk als bestimmendes Element im Auftritt des Verlages. Die preisgünstigen Taschenbücher, verbunden mit der reduzierten, modernen Aufmachung, trafen genau den Zeitgeist der 1960er-Jahre. Das Unternehmen florierte, aus anfangs wenigen Titeln pro Jahr entwickelte sich ein umfangreiches Buchprogramm. Piatti blieb über mehr als 30 Jahre der Gestalter des dtv und realisierte bis zur Neuausrichtung des Designs rund 6.300 Buchumschläge sowie unzählige Werbemedien für den Münchner Verlag.

En 1961, onze éditeurs de langue allemande se regroupaient pour fonder une maison d'édition spécialisée dans le livre de poche en vue de publier leurs œuvres. La nouvelle édition fut fièrement appelée Deutscher Taschenbuch Verlag [Le Livre de Poche Allemand], sigle dtv. Le graphiste suisse Celestino Piatti fut choisi pour la création du logo et la conception graphique des premiers titres. Piatti misa sur la réduction et la sobriété. Commençant par le logo, il sélectionna la fonte neutre Akzidenz Grotesk comme élément déterminant pour l'image de l'édition. Les livres de poche bon marché associés à une apparence minimaliste et moderne correspondaient parfaitement à l'esprit des années 1960. L'entreprise prospéra. Les quelques titres édités chaque année se transformèrent en un vaste programme éditorial. Piatti restera le designer de dtv pendant plus de 30 ans. Jusqu'à la redéfinition des orientations graphiques, il a réalisé quelque 6300 couvertures de livres et d'innombrables médias publicitaires pour l'éditeur munichois.

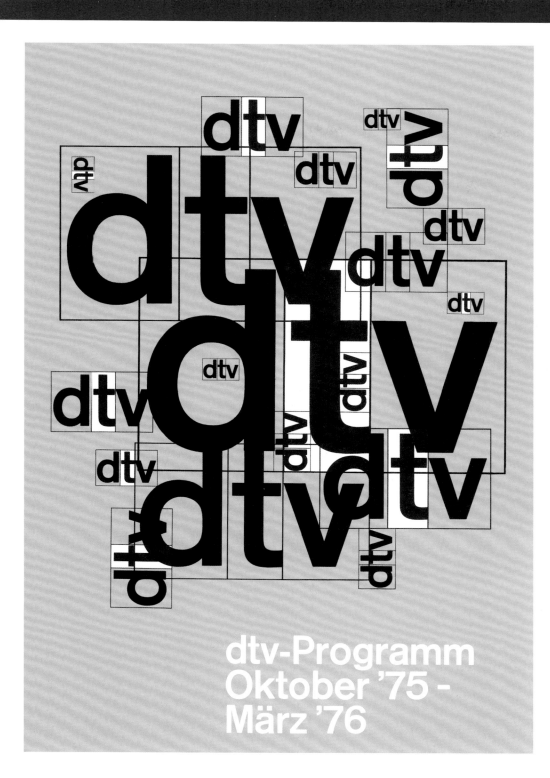

20 Jahre
Deutscher
Taschenbuchverlag
1961–1981

20 Jahre

1961–1981

dtv

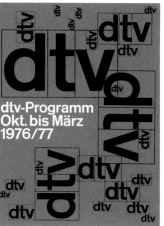

dtv-Programm
Okt. bis März
1976/77

dtv-Programm
Oktober '75 -
März '76

Multi-layering of dtv's muted,
minimalist logo created an
eye-catching brand identity,
which appeared in different
variations on the covers of
the publisher's catalogs.

Durch den Effekt der Verdopplung wurde aus dem reduziert-
kühlen dtv-Logo ein plakatives
Werbemotiv. In unterschiedlichen Spielarten wurde dies bei
Programmheften des Verlages
wiederholt e ngesetzt.

L'effet de redoublement transformait le logo sobre et froid
de dtv en motif d'affiches voyant.
Le procédé fut répété dans
toutes sortes de déclinaisons
sur les plaquettes commerciales de l'éditeur.

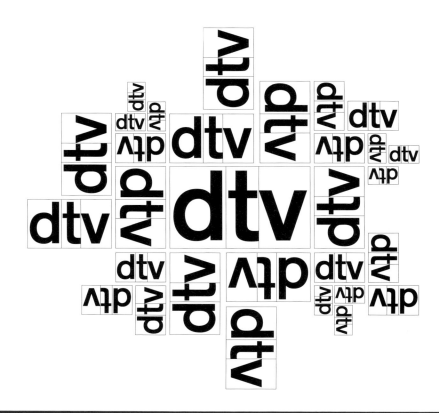

The poster campaigns for dtv
were an opportunity for Piatti
to use his favorite animal images.
As the posters were all his own
work, he was free to design them
with no holds barred. His unmistakable style became instantly
recognizable.

In der Plakatwerbung für den
Verlag konnte Piatti sein bevor-
zugtes Motiv der Tiere unterbrin-
gen. Da sämtliche Arbeiten aus
seiner Hand kamen, konnte er frei
von Einschränkungen gestalten
und erreichte durch seinen unver-
kennbaren Illustrationsstil einen
hohen Wiedererkennungseffekt.

Dans la publicité extérieure de
l'édition, Piatti put faire apparaître son motif de prédilection,
les animaux. Tous les travaux
étant de sa main, il put donner
libre cours à son talent de créateur et parvint à un haut degré
de reconnaissance de la marque
grâce à son style illustratif
incomparable.

White was the predominant color in all dtv's visual imagery. The unchanging typography used on dtv book covers was in stark contrast to the garish graphics used by competitors.

Weiß war die bestimmende Farbe im visuellen Auftritt des Deutschen Taschenbuch Verlags. Die immer nach gleichem typografischem Konzept aufgebauten Buchumschläge standen in krassem Gegensatz zur überladen-bunten Verlagsgrafik der Konkurrenz.

Le blanc est la couleur qui définissait l'identité visuelle du Deutscher Taschenbuch Verlag. Les couvertures de livres, toujours composées sur la base du même concept typographique, étaient en opposition flagrante avec le graphisme éditorial surchargé et chamarré de la concurrence.

dtv

Deutscher
Taschenbuch Verlag
GmbH & Co. KG

Friedrichstraße 1 a
Postfach 4004 22
8000 München 40
Telefon (089) 38 17 06-(0)
Telefax (089) 34 64 28
Telex 5 215 396

Kommanditgesellschaft sD, Sitz München, Registergericht München HRA 16911, persönlich haftender Gesellschafter:
Deutscher Taschenbuch Verlag GmbH, Sitz München, Registergericht München HRB 5 88, Geschäftsführer Dr. Wolfram Göbel

Hugo Bank, München 6360 137 002 BLZ 700 200 01   Deutsche Bank, München 16/ 27749 BLZ 700 700 10
Bankhaus Reuschel, München 1 034 765 BLZ 700 303 00   Postgiro: München 116330-806 BLZ 700 100 60

dtv
ein neuer Typ
des
deutschen
Taschen-
buches

**Ab 1. September
in allen
Buchhandlungen**

---

dtv

Saul Bellow:
Der Regenkönig
Roman

dtv

Walter Jens:
Deutsche Literatur
der Gegenwart

dtv

Mots

Wörter

Words

Seriaal Galerie
Art gallery
1968 · Pieter Brattinga · NL

Speedaprint
Printing
1968 · Robert Davies · UK

Ankit Bombay
1973 · Yeshwant Chaudhary · IN

schwaben bräu

Schwaben Bräu
Brewing
1960s · Nelly Rudin · CH

FILM

Jeremy Lepard Films
Film production
1967 · Rod Dyer · US

expeditie

Hull & Humber Cargo Handling
Haulier
1968 · Eurographics · UK

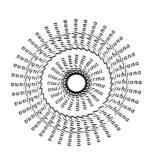

Lumitype Deberny & Peignot
Type foundry
1963 · Rémy Peignot · FR

International Word and Picture Agency
1961 · Gérard Ifert · FR

Comune di Parma
Twinning Parma-Ljubljana
1964 · Franco M. Ricci · IT

readingsystems

Scott, Foresman and Company
Publishing
1969 · Harry Boller/
Unimark International · US

redgreenblue

Red Green Blue
Photographic reproduction
1968 · Rod Dyer, George Osaki,
Roland Young · US

Marketing Strategy Inc.
Statistical research
1960 · Bill Wayman/Aron & Wayman · US

3rd Foratom Congress
British nuclear forum
1967 · Gavin Healey/
Healey Mills Associates · UK

BECH
ELECTRONIC
CENTRE
HCT
TR
RE
O
N
I
C

Bech Electronic Centre
Electronics
1959 · Karl Gerstner · CH

Zanichelli
Engineering
1960s · Walter Hergenröther · IT

FAD
Design association
1962 · Josep Pla-Narbona · ES

Foto Studio 22
Photography
1961 · Albe Steiner · IT

Ritz Italora
Watches
1972 · Da Centro D segno · IT

Graphicus, Progresso Grafico
Magazine
1966 · Giovanni Brunazzi · IT

Ritz Italora
Watches
1968 · Enzo Careccia/Opit Pubblicità · IT

Greater London Secondary Housing Association
1978 · Ken Garland · UK

Marca Tre
Magazine
1966 · Giulio Confalonieri · IT

Beverly Zigaretten
Cigarettes
1967 · Heinz Schwabe · DE

Rasiom
Fuel oil
1968 · Giulio Confalonieri · IT

Patio
Interior design
1974 · Odermatt+Tissi · CH

Svenska Missionsforbundets Union
Missionary union
1960s · Karl Erik Lindgren · SE

CINEM CINEW AA

Cinema
Television program
1966 · Yvon Laroche · CA

Arnold
1950s · Otto Krämer · CH

CANARIS

Canaris
Movie
1962 · Fischer-Nosbisch · DE

BAU AG W.

Bau AG
Engineering
1988 · Odermatt+Tissi · CH

KELVIN

Kelvin Research Corporation
1970s · Robert Hagenhofer · US

Killian

Killian
Department store
1969 · Heinz Waibl/Unimark International · IT/US

Kimo
Furniture
1976 · Odermatt+Tissi · CH

Club de Butxaca
Publishing
1960s · Jordi Fornas · ES

Simon Suds
Car wash
1969 · John Kobold/
Hiller Rinaldo Associates · CA

Van der Vorm's
Construction company
1968 · Geoffrey Gibbons/Allied International Designers · UK

Thomas Bauer
Furniture
1972 · Giulio Confalonieri · IT

Swibar
Watches
1986 · Yeshwant Chaudhary,
Ashok Sood · IN

Frigerio di Desio, Originals
Furniture
1972 · Giulio Confalonieri · IT

Bauer
1950s · Fritz Moeschlin · CH

Will Waller
Packaging
1968 · Edi Doswald · CH

Missoni, Alta Moda
Fashion
1973 · Giulio Confalonieri · IT

Intermedia Vancouver
Arts and sciences institute
1968 · Friedrich Peter · CA

Bikini
Nightclub
1973 · Alberto Isern/ECTA-3 · ES

Galerie Visua
Art gallery
1966 · Pierre-Yves Pelletier · CA

Nido
Ceramics
1960s · Piero Fornasetti · IT

Biennale der Europäischen Grafik
Design festival
1982 · Erwin Poell · DE

Multiplay
Toys
1970 · Ferruccio Soldati · CH

Steiner
Furniture
1953 · Alfred Willimann · CH

Papase
1970s · Franz Wagner · US

Logix Kepner-Tregoe
Education
1970 · Appelbaum & Curtis · US

Tanner
Textiles
1968 · René Brotbeck · CH

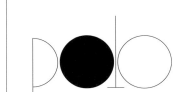

Koyo Office Planning
Computer systems
1983 · Hisahiro Umezawa · JP

United States Polo Association
1968 · James Lienhart/RVI Corp. · US

Hugo Boss
Fashion
1968 · Anonymous · DE

Paul Jost
Real estate
1950s · Lilly Hauser-Baertschi · CH

Interdomo
Industrial design
1973 · Giulio Confalonieri · IT

**Automatic Catering and
Vending Machines**
1974 · Ken Garland · UK

Martignoni Elettrotecnica
Electronics
1965 · Veniero Bertolotti/Studio 4 · IT

Record Magazine
1970 · Peter Hablützel/
Gazette Printing Company · CA

Ocrim
Engineering
1973 · Giulio Confalonieri · IT

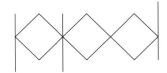

Pier Paolo Delitala
Furniture
1959 · Ilio Negri · IT

Arcus - Tonon Laburthe
Footwear
1973 · J.C. Jouis/Look · FR

Dalmau, Barcelona
Art gallery
1969 · Pérez Sánchez · ES

Asics
Sporting goods
1977 · Herb Lubalin · US

Lignoplast
Plastics
1960s · Alfred Willimann · CH

Cementeria di Merone
Cement
1962 · Paul Bühlmann · CH

Makno
Advertising
1971 · G. & R. Associati · IT

Therma
Household appliances
1958 · Carlo L. Vivarelli · CH

Arpa
Photographic laboratory
1972 · Silvio Coppola · IT

Campus
Furniture
1970 · Pino Tovaglia · IT

Libreria Cortina
Bookstore
1965 · Italo Lupi · IT

Belli Costruzioni Edilizie
Construction company
1969 · Sergio Salaroli · IT

DMS
Publishing
1962 · Wolf D. Zimmermann · DE

Fix & Fertig
Foods
1965 · Gerhard Voigt · DE-GDR

Groupe Design
Industrial design
1959 · Luc Van Malderen · BE

Müller Papeterie
Office supplies
1967 · Hans R. Woodtli · CH

Life
Magazine
1978 · Anonymous · US

Duropal
Kitchen laminates
1970 · Ekkehart Rustmeier · DE

Cities in Crisis
Documentary movie
1967 · Dietmar R. Winkler · US

Jetzer
Furniture
1965 · Anonymous · CH

Venyl
Textiles
1973 · Heinz Schwabe · DE

Iro Bandfournisseure
Machinery
1959 · Hanns Lohrer · DE

TEMI
Freight
1960 · Max Huber · IT

Max Wiener
Textiles
1965 · Karlheinz Herke · DE-GDR

Super Tuft Super Flock
Carpets
1960 · Dietmar Hochstein · DE

Acetat
Chemicals
1957 · Hubert Czermak · DE

Optatron E
Electronics
1960 · Hans-Joachim Brauer · DE

Pluvius
1955 · Uli Huber · DE

Polycon, VVB Baumwolle
Cotton
1965 · Walter Seifert · DE-GDR

B.A.G. Turgi
Lighting
1960s · Gottfried Honegger,
G. Soland · CH

Case
Tractors
1970s · Anonymous · US

Canadian International Comstock
Construction company
1969 · Arthur Irizawa/
Stewart & Morrison · CA

Karl Frech
Bookstore
1965 · Klaus Neumeister · DE-GDR

Polyfor
Textiles
1970 · Rudi Meyer/Publicis · FR

SISFI
Swiss-Italian trade union
1960s · Walter Ballmer · CH

Lawron Industries
Plastics
1969 · René Demers/
Hiller Rinaldo Associates · CA

L'eggs, Hanes Hosiery
Pantyhose
1970 · Roger J. Ferriter/
Lubalin, Smith, Carnase · US

Readak
Reading comprehension systems
1969 · Primo Angeli · US

Gilcodan
Textiles
1970 · Adam Moltke · DK

Pacific
Theater group
1969 · Jerry Braude · US

Dürr
Mechanical engineering
1972 · Werner Hartz · DE

Ditto
Photocopiers
1960s · Morton Goldsholl
Design Associates · US

Levy's
Department stores
1969 · Heinz Waibl/
Unimark International · IT/US

VEB Deko
1965 · Manfred Wolf · DE-GDR

Vêtements de Vacances
Textiles
1962 · Jean Widmer · FR

Tecla Tofano
Art exhibition
1969 · Manuel Espinoza · VE

Dunlop Footwear
1960s · Kenneth Lamble/Clements · UK

ADV Welle Möbelwerke
Furniture
1972 · Max Graf von Pückler,
Norbert Schramp · DE

Stone Container Corporation
Packaging
1959 · Morton Goldsholl · US

KALA
Art gallery
1960s · Juan Carlos Destéfano · AR

Ladybug
Magazine
1969 · Jay Dillon/Hess & Antupit · US

United Supply Company
Plumbing suppliers
1966 · Appelbaum & Curtis · US

boîte à musique

Boîte à Musique
Record store
1957 · Karl Gerstner/GGK · CH

Tout logotype doit être agréable à l'oreille, ne pas susciter d'associations négatives, être prononçable dans une langue étrangère et aussi court que possible. Il est préférable à tout autre type de marque parce qu'il véhicule un contenu informatif direct.
Anton Stankowski

Jede Wortmarke muss phonetisch gut klingen, keine negativen Assoziationen hervorrufen, in einer fremden Sprache aussprechbar und möglichst kurz sein. Sie ist jeder anderen Markenart vorzuziehen, weil sie einen direkten Informationsgehalt hat.
Anton Stankowski

Any word-mark should sound good phonetically, have no negative associations, be easy to pronounce in a foreign language, and be as short as possible. In this way it will be more desirable than other brands because it directly informs the viewer.
Anton Stankowski

Burkhalter & Hufschmid
Electronics
1960s · Atelier Stadelmann Bisig · CH

Ketch Giorgio Confezioni
Textiles
1972 · Giulio Confalonieri · IT

Mobba
Automobiles
1956 · Joan Pedragosa · ES

Woolrich Manufacturing
Cotton
1966 · Kramer, Miller, Lomden,
Glassman Inc. · US

Lever Data Processing System
1969 · Dominick Sarica/
Wallack & Harris · US

Velpan
Carpets
1969 · Enzo Mari · IT

Tecla Sala
Yarns
1963 · Joan Pedragosa · ES

Sica
Textiles
1970 · Mimmo Castellano · IT

Companhia Brasileira de Estruturas
Construction company
1965 · Aloísio Magalhães/PVDI · BR

Spazio Olivetti Arredamenti Metallici
Furniture
1967 · Walter Ballmer · IT

Union Kassenfabrik
Safe manufacturers
1966 · Odermatt+Tissi · CH

Rodo
Toys
1970 · Ken Garland · UK

Pirelli Rivestimenti
Plastics
1958 · Giulio Confalonieri · IT

Targa
Textiles
1969 · Rudi Meyer/Publicis · CH

Anglo Iberica de Construcciones
Construction company
1965 · Ribas & Creus · ES

Lamper
Furniture
1971 · Francesc Guitart · ES/FR

Datalink
Computer systems
1977 · Odermatt+Tissi · CH

Otto
Textiles
1950s · Hanns Lohrer · DE

Cepsa
Magazine
1968 · José Baqués · ES

Arnold Bopp
Sound consultant
1960s · Walter Bangerter · CH

Geldermann & Zone
Textiles
1960s · Klaus Winterhager · DE

Seven Foods
1960s · Hisami Kunitake · JP

Siex
Import-export
1967 · José Baqués · ES

Natur
Foods
1971 · Raymond Bellemare · CA

Buri & Cie
Printing
1964 · Kurt Wirth · CH

Icam
Foods
1967 · Amleto Dalla Costa · IT

Farma Lépori
Pharmaceuticals
1969 · José Baqués · ES

Near East Emergency Donations
1968 · Arnold Saks, Peter Kramer · US

Fanini Fain
Resin manufacturing
1972 · Ennio Lucini · IT

Lyss
Fittings
1960s · Otto Brunner · DE

Lunor
Air filtration systems
1967 · Christian Lang · CH

Sociéte Générale des Drogueries
Trade association
1970 · Jean-Philippe Lenclos,
Georges Lemoine/Delpire-Advico · FR

Elektronische Datenverarbeitung
Data processing
1970 · Rainer Strempel · DE

Austria Club
Social club
1960 · Hans-Joachim Brauer · DE

Vetroflex
Glass fibers
1946 · Hans Neuburg · CH

Budgen
Supermarket chain
1964 · Crosby, Fletcher, Forbes · UK

Riso Kagaku Corporation
Photocopiers
1980 · Anonymous · JP

Mears Caldwell Hacker
Printing
1964 · Fletcher, Forbes, Gill · UK

Zoom
Television program
1967 · Pierre-Yves Pelletier · CA

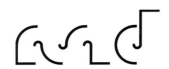

Method Design
Advertising
1971 · Gordon Salchow · US

Race
Furniture
1963 · Ken Garland · UK

Leoba
Stairlifts
1970 · Heinz Schwabe · DE

Bloch
Textiles
1970 · Giulio Confalonieri · IT

Wibor-Modelle
Clothing
1970s · Anonymous · DE

Amoeba
Luggage
1970 · Stanley Eisenman,
David Enock · US

**Manufacturers Association of
Tape & Equipment**
1969 · Dominick Sarica/
Wallack & Harris · US

Elam
Furniture
1960 · Giulio Confalonieri · IT

Aare Verlag
Publishing
1976 · Anonymous · DE

Sofinco Drugstores
1964 · François Dallegret · CA

Mäser
Clothing
1969 · Ruedi Rüegg · CH

Iter Elettronica
Lighting
1972 · Mimmo Castellano · IT

Paular
Chemicals
1966 · Salvatore Gregorietti/
Unimark International · IT

Eucatex
Flooring
1968 · Alexandre Wollner · BR

Telen
Cigarettes
1967 · Heinz Schwabe · DE

Vanita
Magazine
1961 · Ilio Negri · IT

Miwa Pearl
Jewelry
1960s · Takashi Kono · JP

Astarte Cosmetics
1970 · Ernest R. Smith/
Lubalin, Smith, Carnase · US

Alluminio
Aluminum works
1960s · Heinz Waibl · IT

Olivetti
Business machines
1971 · Walter Ballmer · IT

Editrice Mark 3
Publishing
1969 · Danilo Nubioli · IT

Viva Leisure
Leisure center
1978 · Ken Garland · UK

Jowi
Foods
1950s · Franz Olivier Trog · CH

Saridon
Pharmaceuticals
1971 · Giulio Confalonieri · IT

Pierre d'Alby
Fashion
1967 · Jean Widmer · FR

Elna
Sewing machines
1963 · Raymond Loewy/CEI · CH

Addo-x
Calculators
1958 · Ladislav Sutnar · US

Indrofa
Food fair
1966 · Peter Wehr · DE

Cometal
Metalworks
1969 · Franco M. Ricci · IT

Coin
Clothing
1955 · Max Huber · IT

Haute Couture
Fashion
1968 · Yvon Laroche · CA

Cama
Paper
1972 · Studio GSZ · IT

Cooperativa di Consumo
Consumers cooperative
1963 · Italo Lupi · IT

Trix
Clothing
1968 · Michel Coudeyre/Snip · FR

Pagina
Graphics journal
1960s · Heinz Waibl · IT

Doit
Department store
1980 · Katsuhiko Yasuda,
Katsuichi Ito · JP/IT

Cilsa
Ceramics
1968 · Silvio Coppola · IT

Heusgen Krawatten
Ties
1956 · Walter Breker · DE

Officine Riri
Zippers
1960s · Pierre Gauchat · CH

Boffi
Kitchens and bathrooms
1971 · Mimmo Castellano · IT

Sisal-Totip
Betting
1968 · Stefano Simoni · IT

Europistas
Road construction
1968 · José Baqués · ES

Circuit A
Movie rentals
1973 · Jean Delaunay/Look · FR

Signos
Publishing
1972 · Félix Beltrán · CU

Ultimo
Fashion
1969 · James Lienhart/RVI Corp. · US

Elnagh
Motor homes
1970s · Anonymous · IT

Lan Chile 4 Continents
Airline
1970 · Delpire-Advico · FR

Julie T.
Clothing
1969 · Rudi Meyer/Publicis · CH

MONO

Mono
Pencils
1960s · Takashi Kono · JP

ENEL

ENEL
Energy supplier
1960s · Heinz Waibl · IT

Mobil

Mobil
Fuel oil
1964 · Ivan Chermayeff, Tom Geismar/
Chermayeff & Geismar · US

Groba
Foods
1972 · Odermatt+Tissi · CH

Benz
1973 · Odermatt+Tissi · CH

Avant Garde

Avant Garde
Magazine
1960s · Herb Lubalin · US

FIFE FORGE

The Fife Forge
Engineering
1973 · Douglas M. Soeder,
Peter Lloyd/Forth Studios · UK

LEONIAN

Philip Leonian
Photography
1970 · Tony Russell/
Russell & Hinrichs · US

Baric Computing Services
1970 · Marcello Minale,
Brian Tattersfield · UK

Modissa
Fashion
1960s · Ursula Hiestand · CH

Lowe
Film production
1967 · Studio González Ruiz &
Shakespear · AR

magnum

Magnum
Magazine
1954 · Kurt Schwarz · AT

OTTO

Otto
Audio technology
1966 · Tomoichi Nishiwaki · JP

LAN OVER

Lanover
Clothing
1966 · Alexandre Wollner · BR

Navitur
Tourism
1968 · Sergio Salaroli · IT

Gritti
Textiles
1967 · Franco Grignani · IT

Società Elettronucleare Nazionale
Nuclear technology
1960s · Heinz Waibl · IT

Grammo Studio
Record store
1957 · Odermatt+Tissi · CH

National Zeitung

National Zeitung
Newspaper
1960 · Karl Gerstner · CH

Legler Industria Tessile
Textiles
1948 · Eugen & Max Lenz · CH

Raibor
Carpets
1964 · Theodoor Manson · IT

Gowllands
Lenses
1969 · David J. Plumb · UK

**thomas
salter
toys+
sports**

Thomas Salter
Sporting goods and toys
1965 · P. J. McNeil/
Allied International Designers · UK

hecospan

Hecospan
Yarns
1965 · Edi Doswald · CH

CITIBANK

Citibank
1976 · Anspach Grossman Portugal · US

BDF ●●●●
Beiersdorf

Beiersdorf
Consumer products
1978 · Henrion Design Associates · UK

reinh a r d

Reinhard Holzwarenfabrik
Wooden goods
1961 · Odermatt+Tissi · CH

X+TEX

X-Tex
Weaving
1964 · Morten Peetz-Schou · DK

VISTA

Vista
Magazine
1968 · Hess & Antupit · US

ICSID

**International Council of
Societies of Industrial Design**
1968 · Bob Noorda/
Unimark International · IT

arflex

Arflex
Furniture
1966 · Bob Noorda/
Unimark International · IT

CAMINITI

Caminiti
Leather
1952 · Ennio Lucini · IT

**National Aeronautics and
Space Administration**
1976 · Dane & Blackburn · US

es

es
Movie
1966 · Karl-Oskar Blase · DE

PETROBRAS

Petrobrás
Fuel oil
1960s · Aloísio Magalhães, Rafael
Rodrigues, Roberto A. Lanari/PVDI · BR

Eston Confezioni
Clothing
1960s · Antonio Boggeri/
Studio Boggeri · IT

Socodac
Secretarial services
1966 · Gilles Fiszman · BE

Achille Serre
Cleaning services
1968 · Michael Tucker · UK

Leal - La Rinascente UPIM
Quality-mark
1964 · Bob Noorda/
Unimark International · IT

P

The Modernist logos featured in this book were in the main created over a period of about 40 years by graphic designers of varying ages and nationalities. Looking at the logos in this book, it could easily be assumed that none of the designers has an unmistakable style. However, when we explore the work of eight ground-breaking logo designers from different parts of the world and radically different backgrounds, the opposite seems to be true. Furthermore, this selection of works arranged in chronological order also shows how the art of the logo has continued to advance in this Modernist age.

Die meisten der in diesem Buch versammelten modernistischen Logos wurden in einen Zeitraum von etwa 40 Jahren von Gestaltern unterschiedlichen Alters und verschiedener Herkunft entworfen. Betrachtet man die Logos in der in diesem Buch vorliegenden Kategorisierung, entsteht leicht der Eindruck, so etwas wie die individuelle Handschrift eines Gestalters existiere bei diesem Medium gar nicht. Der Blick auf die Arbeiten von acht wegweisenden Logogestaltern, die aus verschiedenen Teilen der Erde stammen und grundverschiedene biografische Hintergründe haben, beweist das Gegenteil. Durch eine chronologische Sortierung der Arbeiten offenbaren sich außerdem visuelle Weiterentwicklungen innerhalb der Ära des modernistischen Logos.

La plupart des logos modernes réunis dans cet ouvrage ont été conçus sur une période d'une quarantaine d'années par des créateurs d'âges et d'origines diverses. En passant en revue les logos classés selon les catégories proposées dans ce livre, le lecteur aura facilement l'impression que quelque chose comme la griffe individuelle d'un designer n'existe pas dans ce médium. Un regard sur les réalisations de huit créateurs de logos issus de différentes régions du monde, avec des biographies très dissemblables, le convaincra du contraire. Le classement chronologique de leurs travaux permet en outre de reconnaître certaines évolutions visuelles pendant l'ère du logo moderne.

Adrian Frutiger

*1928–2015 · CH

Adrian Frutiger was born in 1928 in Unterseen, Switzerland. From 1944 to 1948 he was an apprentice compositor in Interlaken before attending the Zurich School of Arts and Crafts, where Alfred Willimann and Walter Käch were among his teachers. He then started work as a graphic designer in Zurich. His first logotypes, typefaces and woodcuts date from this period. In 1952 Frutiger moved to Paris where he worked for the Deberny & Peignot type foundry. He completed his work on the Univers font in 1957 and in the years that followed it came into use worldwide and remains one of the most popular sans-serif typefaces. In 1962, Frutiger, Bruno Pfäffli and André Gürtler set up their own design studio at Arcueil near Paris. There they produced typefaces for a range of French companies and institutions, including Paris Charles de Gaulle airport, as well as several publishing houses and pharmaceutical firms. At the same time Frutiger taught in Paris at the École Estienne (1952–60) and the École des Arts Décoratifs (1954–68). In 1968 he developed the OCR-B font, which in 1973 was declared a worldwide standard machine-readable font that could also be used for passports and bank statements. Frutiger's 1978 book, *Der Mensch und seine Zeichen* (*Signs and symbols: their design and meaning*, 1989), has become a standard work on design literature and has been translated into seven languages. Published three years later, another book by Frutiger, *Type, Sign, Symbol*, is also hailed as a classic. In the 1970s and '80s, Frutiger produced the font that bears his name—Frutiger—as well as Glypha, Serifa and Avenir. He returned to his native Switzerland in 1992 and lived in Bremgarten near Berne. Until his death in the fall of 2015, he continued to work mainly for the typeface manufacturer Linotype on the digitalization and diversification of his successful fonts.

Europrint
Printing
1960 · Adrian Frutiger · CH/FR

ZEE
1960 · Adrian Frutiger · CH/FR

Imprimerie Hofer
Printing
1960 · Adrian Frutiger · CH/FR

Librairie Hermann, Paris
Bookstore
1961 · Adrian Frutiger · CH/FR

Jacqueline Iribe
Design products
1961 · Adrian Frutiger · CH/FR

Scripta
Toolmaking
1961 · Adrian Frutiger · CH/FR

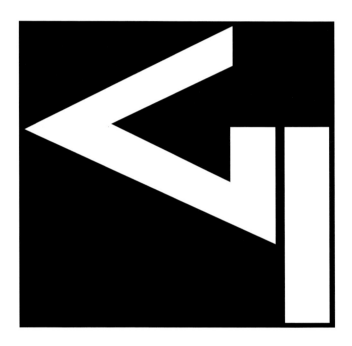

IPREIG
Research institute for industrial design
1960 · Adrian Frutiger · CH/FR

Georges Johannet
Architecture
1960 · Adrian Frutiger · CH/FR

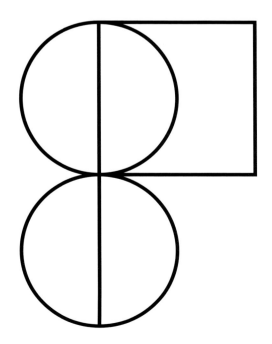

Brancher Frères
Inks
1960 · Adrian Frutiger · CH/FR

Adrian Frutiger wurde 1928 im schweizerischen Unterseen geboren. In Interlaken absolvierte er zwischen 1944 und 1948 eine Schriftsetzerlehre, an der Kunstgewerbeschule Zürich studierte er bei Alfred Willimann und Walter Käch, bevor er schließlich als Grafiker in Zürich zu arbeiten begann. Erste Zeichen, Schriftentwürfe und Holzschnitte entstanden in dieser Zeit. Frutiger zog 1952 nach Paris und wurde Mitarbeiter der Schriftgießerei Deberny & Peignot. Die Arbeiten an der Schriftfamilie Univers schloss er 1957 ab. In den folgenden Jahren verbreitete sich diese international und ist bis heute eine der am meisten genutzten serifenlosen Schriftarten. Gemeinsam mit Bruno Pfäffli und André Gürtler gründete Frutiger 1962 ein eigenes Grafikatelier in Arcueil bei Paris. Erscheinungsbilder für zahlreiche französische Unternehmen und Institutionen wurden realisiert, darunter der Pariser Flughafen, mehrere Verlage und Pharmaunternehmen. Nebenher lehrte Frutiger an der Ecole Estienne (1952–60) sowie an der Ecole des Arts Décoratifs (1954–68) in Paris. Im Jahr 1968 entwickelte er die Schrift OCR-B, die ab 1973 zum weltweiten Standard für maschinenlesbare Schriften erklärt wurde und auch in Ausweisen oder auf Kontoauszügen Anwendung fand. Sein 1978 veröffentlichtes Buch *Der Mensch und seine Zeichen* wurde zum Standardwerk der Designliteratur und erschien in sieben Sprachen. Drei Jahre später legte er mit *Type, Sign, Symbol* eine weitere Publikation zum Thema Zeichen und Logos vor, die heute als Klassiker gilt. In den 1970er- und 1980er-Jahren entstanden Schriften wie die nach ihm benannte Frutiger, zudem Glypha, Serifa oder Avenir. Im Jahr 1992 kehrte er in die Schweiz zurück und lebte in Bremgarten bei Bern. Hier arbeitete er bis zu seinem Tod im Herbst 2015 vor allem für den Schriftenhersteller Linotype an Digitalisierungen und Erweiterungen seiner erfolgreichen Fontentwürfe.

Adrian Frutiger est né en 1928 à Unterseen, en Suisse. De 1944 à 1948, il suit une formation de typographe à Interlaken et étudie à l'École des arts et métiers de Zurich auprès d'Alfred Willimann et de Walter Käch, il commence à travailler comme graphiste à Zurich. À cette époque voient le jour ses premiers projets de fontes, typos et bois gravés. En 1952, Frutiger s'installe à Paris et devient le collaborateur de la fonderie Deberny & Peignot. En 1957, il achève son travail sur la famille de polices de caractères Univers, qui se répand internationalement au cours des années suivantes et qui reste une des linéales les plus utilisées à ce jour. En 1962, Frutiger fonde son propre studio de graphisme avec Bruno Pfäffli et André Gürtler à Arcueil, près de Paris. Il crée les marques commerciales de nombreuses entreprises et institutions françaises, notamment Aéroports de Paris et diverses maisons d'édition et entreprises pharmaceutiques. Parallèlement, il enseigne à l'École Estienne (1952–60) et à l'École nationale des Arts Décoratifs (1954–68) à Paris. En 1968, il développe la police de caractères OCR-B ; à partir de 1973, elle devient le standard international des fontes lisibles par machine et est notamment utilisée pour les pièces d'identité ou les relevés de comptes. Son livre *Der Mensch und seine Zeichen*, paru en 1978 (*L'homme et ses signes*, 2000), est devenu une référence incontournable de la littérature graphique et a été publié en sept langues. Trois ans plus tard, Frutiger propose une autre publication autour des signes et des logos avec *Type, Sign, Symbol*, ouvrage aujourd'hui considéré comme un classique. Dans les années 1970 et 1980 voient le jour des polices comme la Frutiger qui porte son nom, mais aussi les Glypha, Serifa ou Avenir. En 1992, Frutiger rentre en Suisse, vivant désormais à Bremgarten, près de Berne. Jusqu'à sa mort à l'automne 2015, il y travaille à la numérisation et au développement de ses célèbres fontes, essentiellement pour le compte du créateur de polices de caractères Linotype.

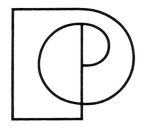

Prache de Franclieu
Commercial bookbinder
1962 · Adrian Frutiger · CH/FR

Heno Watch
Watches
1964 · Adrian Frutiger · CH/FR

ARMA Publicité
Advertising agency
1963 · Adrian Frutiger · CH/FR

Centre International de Généralisation
Industry summits organizer
1965 · Adrian Frutiger · CH/FR

Demy Frères
Cement
1964 · Adrian Frutiger · CH/FR

Hang Druck
Printing
1965 · Adrian Frutiger · CH/FR

Laboratoires Peloille
Pharmaceuticals
1964 · Adrian Frutiger · CH/FR

CNRO
National pension fund
1965 · Adrian Frutiger · CH/FR

Melpomène
Architecture magazine
1964 · Adrian Frutiger · CH/FR

Editions Hermann
Publishing
1960s · Adrian Frutiger · CH/FR

Information et Entreprise
· Public relations
1964 · Adrian Frutiger · CH/FR

Institut Atlantique, Paris
Research institute
1960s · Adrian Frutiger · CH/FR

Laboratoire National d'Essais
Metrological laboratory
1960s · Adrian Frutiger · CH/FR

Sciences
Scientific magazine
1960s · Adrian Frutiger · CH/FR

Winkel Verlag
Publishing
1960s · Adrian Frutiger · CH/FR

CANTADOR

Cantador
Watches
1960s · Adrian Frutiger · CH/FR

Formus
Interior design magazine
1966 · Bruno Pfäffli,
Adrian Frutiger · CH/FR

Alpha & Omega
Religious magazine
1967 · Bruno Pfäffli,
Adrian Frutiger · CH/FR

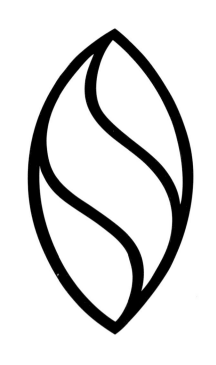

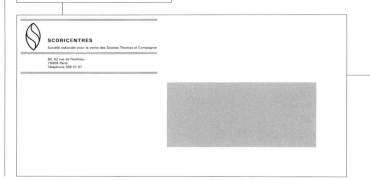

Scoricentres
Steel industry
1970s · Adrian Frutiger · CH

Adrian Frutiger's design for steel producer Scoricentres' logo is a perfect example of his working method. Starting with a sketch, he moved step by step through a series of outlines until he achieved the perfect result. Scoricentres' corporate identity combines a sign designed by Frutiger and typography developed by Bruno Pfäffli.

Anhand seiner Entwürfe für das Zeichen des Stahlhersteller Scoricentres lässt sich Adrian Frutigers Vorgehen bei der Gestaltung beispielhaft nachvollziehen. Ausgehend von einer gezeichneten Form entwickelte er Schritt für Schritt weitere Formen bis zur perfekten Abstraktion. Eingebunden in ein von Bruno Pfäffli entwickeltes Grafiksystem wurde das Zeichen in das Erscheinungsbild eingebunden.

Les projets pour le logo de l'aciériste Scoricentres permet de suivre la démarche créative d'Adrian Frutiger. Partant d'une forme dessinée, il développe pas à pas d'autres formes jusqu'à parvenir à l'abstraction parfaite. Cet insigne fut intégré à l'identité visuelle de l'entreprise dans le cadre d'un système graphique développé par Bruno Pfäffli.

D W D W
D W D W
D W D W
DW DW

Druckerei Winterthur
Printing
1967 · Bruno Pfäffli, Adrian Frutiger · CH/FR

Autoroute Rhone-Alpes
Highway maintenance
1970s · Adrian Frutiger · CH/FR

L'Aéroport de Paris
Airport
1971 · Adrian Frutiger · CH/FR

Pierre Disderot
Lighting
1967 · Bruno Pfäffli,
Adrian Frutiger · CH/FR

Traduction Œcuménique de la Bible
Bible translation
1968 · Adrian Frutiger · CH/FR

Rencontres Lausanne
Christian community
1968 · Adrian Frutiger · CH/FR

Grif
Advertising publisher
1969 · Adrian Frutiger · CH/FR

**Association des Sociétés
Françaises d'Autoroutes**
Highways
1970 · Adrian Frutiger · CH/FR

Brancher
Printing inks
1970 · Adrian Frutiger · CH/FR

Bull General Electric
Electronics
1970s · Adrian Frutiger · CH/FR

Collection Colibiri
Book series
1970s · Adrian Frutiger · CH/FR

Evangelische Gesellschaft, Switzerland
Religious organization
1970s · Adrian Frutiger · CH/FR

Schriftgießerei Haas
Type foundry
1970s · Adrian Frutiger · CH/FR

**National Institute of Design
(Ahmedabad, India)**
1970s · Adrian Frutiger · CH/FR

Philippe Lebaud
Publishing
1970s · Adrian Frutiger · CH/FR

Tissages Normands Réunis
Textiles
1970s · Adrian Frutiger · CH/FR

Autoroute du Sud de la France
Highway
1975 · Adrian Frutiger · CH/FR

CGE Distribution, Paris
Electrical equipment
1977 · Adrian Frutiger · CH/FR

Energies Nouvelles
Publishing
1978 · Adrian Frutiger · CH/FR

icom
Communications
1980 · Adrian Frutiger · CH/FR

Europe
Magazine
1980 · Adrian Frutiger · CH/FR

Musées Nationaux de France
Museums organization
1974 · Adrian Frutiger · CH/FR

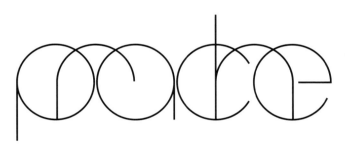

Reliures à Spirales Prache
Spiral bookbinders
1970s · Adrian Frutiger · CH/FR

Musée Rodin
Art museum
1980 · Adrian Frutiger · CH/FR

Du fond d'images vécues et de signes individuels accumulés dans le subconscient tout au long de la vie, des formes émergent, sont pesées, comparées avec d'autres, reliées et superposées (une image en appelant une autre, presque comme dans un rêve). Seul l'essentiel, hésitant, apparaît dans le carnet de croquis, et dans un premier temps seulement comme un aide-mémoire.

Adrian Frutiger

Aus dem Vorrat an erlebten Bildern und erlernten Zeichen, welcher sich im Unterbewusstsein durch das ganze Leben hindurch angesammelt hat, werden Gestalten abgerufen, erwogen, mit anderen verglichen, verbunden und übereinandergelegt (wobei ein Bild das andere ruft, fast wie im Traum). Nur das Wesentliche erscheint auf dem Skizzenblock, zaghaft, zuerst nur als Erinnerungsstütze.

Adrian Frutiger

From the store of images we have seen and symbols we have learned to understand, which accumulate through life in our subconscious, we recall and consider shapes and forms, comparing and connecting them with others and overlaying them, so that one image calls up another in an almost dreamlike way. Only the essential appears tentatively on the sketchpad, at first no more than an aide-mémoire.

Adrian Frutiger

Paul
Ibou
*1939 · BE

Paul Ibou was born in Antwerp in 1939. He studied in his native city from 1954 to 1962, attending first the Royal Academy of Fine Arts and then the Plantin Moretus Institute for Typography. On completing his studies he set up his own studio in the center of Antwerp. Working in every field of graphic design, he became one of Belgium's best-known designers. All his work, whether posters, postage stamps, books or corporate designs, is characterized by his Constructivist approach. He attracted special attention for his logo designs, which featured in many exhibitions and were frequently mentioned in a wide range of publications. Moreover, since the 1960s Ibou has published more than 50 books on art and design. He has acted as an advisor on design issues to the government of Flanders, worked for numerous corporate clients, and been a jury member at design competitions throughout the world. Ibou is renowned not only for his commercial work but also as a freelance artist, who continues to produce paintings and sculptures. These, too, bear his Bauhaus-influenced, experimental, geometric signature. In 1994, in Ostend, he organized the World Symbol Festival, an international exhibition and conference devoted entirely to the logo. Paul Ibou was appointed a Knight of the Order of King Leopold for his services to cultural life over many years. Since 1985 he has lived and worked in a historic castle in the small Belgian town of Zandhoven.

Grafo
Printing
1960 · Paul Ibou · BE

J. Antonissen
Printing
1962 · Paul Ibou · BE

De Rooster
Printing
1962 · Paul Ibou · BE

Scaldia
Paper
1963 · Paul Ibou · BE

Ervé
Printing
1964 · Paul Ibou · BE

Brabo
Toys
1964 · Paul Ibou · BE

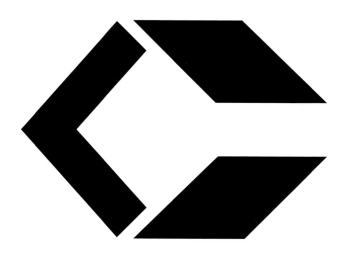

Charlier
Foods
1965 · Paul Ibou · BE

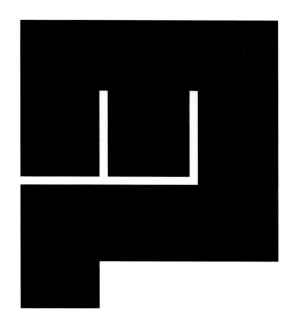

Middelheim Promoters
Cultural organization
1967 · Paul Ibou · BE

Groep 1
Journalists association
1967 · Paul Ibou · BE

Paul Ibou wurde 1939 in Antwerpen geboren. In seiner Geburtsstadt studierte er zwischen 1954 und 1962 an der Koninklijke Academie voor Schone Kunsten und am Plantin Moretus Instituut. Anschließend machte er sich mit einem Büro im Stadtzentrum Antwerpens selbstständig. Hier war er in allen Bereichen des Grafikdesigns aktiv und wurde über die Jahre zu einem der bekanntesten belgischen Gestalter. Ein konstruktivistischer Ansatz ist das durchgängige Element aller seiner Arbeiten – ob Plakate, Briefmarken, Bücher oder Corporate Designs. Besonders seine Logoentwürfe brachten ihm auch internationale Anerkennung ein, die sich in zahlreichen Auszeichnungen sowie Erwähnungen in vielen Publikationen zeigte. Darüber hinaus veröffentlichte Ibou seit den 1960er-Jahren mehr als 50 eigene Bücher rund um Kunst und Design. Er war als Berater in Gestaltungsfragen für die flämische Regierung sowie für zahlreiche Unternehmen tätig und als Jurymitglied bei Designwettbewerben weltweit aktiv. Neben seiner auftragsbezogenen Arbeit wurde er als freischaffender Künstler bekannt und realisiert bis heute Skulpturen und Gemälde. Auch hier ist seine durch das Bauhaus geprägte experimentell-geometrische Handschrift zu finden. In Oostende organisierte er 1994 das „World Symbol Festival", eine internationale Ausstellung und Konferenz, die sich ausschließlich dem Medium Logo widmete. Für seine langjährigen kulturellen Verdienste wurde er mit dem königlichen Kronenorden zum Ritter erhoben. Seit 1985 lebt und arbeitet Paul Ibou in einem historischen Schloss im belgischen Zandhoven.

Paul Ibou est né en 1939 à Anvers. De 1954 à 1962, il étudie dans sa ville natale à la Koninklijke Academie voor Schone unsten et au Plantin Moretus Instituut, puis il prend son indépendance en ouvrant une agence dans le centre d'Anvers. Il y déploie son activité dans tous les domaines graphiques et devient au fil des ans un des plus célèbres graphistes belges. Son approche constructiviste est l'élément constant de toutes ses réalisations – affiches, timbres, livres, corporate design. Ses créations de logos, tout particulièrement, lui valent la reconnaissance internationale, qui se manifeste par de nombreuses distinctions et citations dans des publications. Depuis les années 1960, Ibou a en outre publié plus de 50 livres sur l'art et le design. Il a travaillé comme conseiller en design pour le gouvernement flamand et de nombreuses entreprises et participe à des concours de design en qualité de membre du jury. À côté du travail de commande, ils'est aussi fait connaître comme artiste indépendant et réalise encore aujourd'hui des sculptures et des peintures dans lesquelles on retrouve son écriture personnelle expérimentale et géométrique influencée par le Bauhaus. En 1994, il organise à Ostende le « World Symbol Festival », exposition et symposium exclusivement consacrés au logo. Il a été fait chevalier de l'ordre de la Couronne pour son apport culturel au long cours. Depuis 1985, Paul Ibou vit dans un château historique à Zandhoven, en Belgique.

De Bièvre
Printing
1965 · Paul Ibou · BE

Vécu
Private club
1968 · Paul Ibou · BE

C.N.O.B.S.
Science organization
1966 · Paul Ibou · BE

Sextra
Film editing
1968 · Paul Ibou · BE

Balder
Clothing
1967 · Paul Ibou · BE

CAIB
Railway
1969 · Paul Ibou · BE

Antwerp-Tax
Taxi service
1967 · Paul Ibou · BE

Vandenbranden
Painter
1969 · Paul Ibou · BE

Grisar & Velge
Transportation
1967 · Paul Ibou · BE

Artepik
Cultural center
1970 · Paul Ibou · BE

André Wauters New York
Art gallery
1967 · Paul Ibou · BE

C.G.S.O.
Medical center
1970 · Paul Ibou · BE

Guy Lamoral
Interior design
1970 · Paul Ibou · BE

Soyuznefteexport
Fuel oil
1970 · Paul Ibou · BE

Photocomp Center
Typesetting
1970 · Paul Ibou · BE

Unirep
Graphics production
1970 · Paul Ibou · BE

De Wilde
Accountancy
1970 · Paul Ibou · BE

Leo Struyf
Construction company
1970 · Paul Ibou · BE

Middelheim
Sculpture Biennale
Art festival
1965 · Paul Ibou · BE

In 1949 Antwerp held its first-ever exhibition of sculpture. Over the years, the event in Middelheim Park has grown to become an internationally respected arts festival. In 1965, Paul Ibou, who had only recently started out on his career, was commissioned to create designs for the eighth Biennale. In the years that followed he based his graphics for posters and brochures on a minimalist logo, with variations of shape and detail for each show.

Im Jahr 1949 fand die erste Skulpturenausstellung in Antwerpen statt. Über die Jahre entwickelte sich die Veranstaltung im Middelheim Park zum international beachteten Kunstfestival. Der damals gerade erst ins Berufsleben gestartete Paul Ibou erhielt 1965 den Auftrag für das Design zur achten Biennale. Auf Basis seines reduzierten Logoentwurfs gestaltete er in den folgenden Jahren Plakate und Broschüren für die Veranstaltung, die jeweils mit Form und Details des Markenzeichens spielen.

La première exposition de sculptures fut présentée à Anvers en 1949. Au fil des ans, l'événement du parc Middelheim est devenu un festival d'art au retentissement international. En 1965, Paul Ibou, qui commençait tout juste sa carrière, fut chargé de réaliser le design de la huitième édition de la Biennale. Au cours des années suivantes, sur la base de son logo très sobre, il réalisera pour l'événement des affiches et des brochures qui jouent chaque fois avec la forme et les détails du sigle.

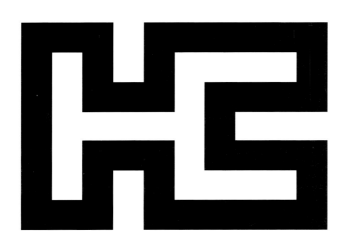

Herman Carpentier
Monogram
1982 · Paul Ibou · BE

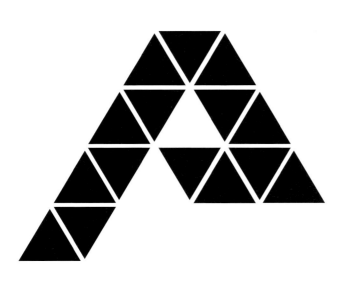

Government of Antwerp
Regional government office
1983 · Paul Ibou · BE

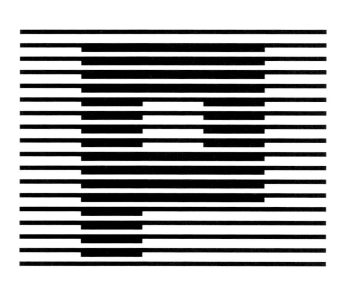

Pittors
Video services
1984 · Paul Ibou · BE

Antwerp Book Fair
1970 · Paul Ibou · BE

Belge Lloyd
Insurance
1970 · Paul Ibou · BE

Kredietbank
Bank
1970 · Paul Ibou · BE

Asco Diamonds
1971 · Paul Ibou · BE

Goyvaerts Gaspard
Accountancy
1971 · Paul Ibou · BE

Suglo
Bakery
1973 · Paul Ibou · BE

Lagotainer
Transportation
1973 · Paul Ibou · BE

Collette
Baking machinery
1974 · Paul Ibou · BE

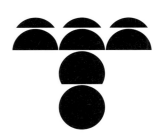

Taché
Jewelry
1974 · Paul Ibou · BE

Mesy Shirts
Clothing
1974 · Paul Ibou · BE

Ibou & Partners
Design studio
1974 · Paul Ibou · BE

Epacar
Paper
1977 · Paul Ibou · BE

Medico Electronic
Medical research
1977 · Paul Ibou · BE

Tolimpex
Customs office
1977 · Paul Ibou · BE

Esco Books
Publishing
1978 · Paul Ibou · BE

Biblo
Publishing
1981 · Paul Ibou · BE

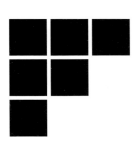

Frisol
Oil
1981 · Paul Ibou · BE

Piessens
Footwear
1981 · Paul Ibou · BE

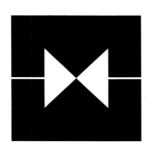

Marc Wouters
Photographer
1982 · Paul Ibou · BE

Medithek
Healthcare
1982 · Paul Ibou · BE

Economic High Institute
Education
1983 · Paul Ibou · BE

Linea
Art & design fair
1983 · Paul Ibou · BE

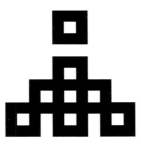

Interecho Press
Publishing
1985 · Paul Ibou · BE

Mercator Press
Printing
1985 · Paul Ibou · BE

Cassochrome
Printing
1985 · Paul Ibou · BE

Cera
Financial services
1986 · Paul Ibou · BE

Furnituregroup
Publishing
1986 · Paul Ibou · BE

Staf Nuyts
Mechanized music
1987 · Paul Ibou · BE

O.V.A.M.
Waste and soil management
1988 · Paul Ibou · BE

Belgian Bankers Association
1989 · Paul Ibou · BE

Contrairement à tous les autres arts graphiques appliqués et techniques publicitaires, qui sont fondamentalement conçus pour une utilisation éphémère, le logo ne vise pas essentiellement à obtenir un succès publicitaire immédiat. Il doit avoir un effet durablement créatif et actif.

Paul Ibou

Im Gegensatz zu allen anderen grafischen Produkten und Werbetechniken, die letztlich recht kurzlebig sind, besteht der Sinn eines Logos oder einer Bildmarke eben genau nicht in einer sofortigen Werbewirksamkeit. Ihr Zweck liegt vielmehr darin, auf Dauer kreativ und ansprechend zu wirken.

Paul Ibou

Contrary to all other applied graphics and advertising techniques, which are basically designed for temporary use, the essential purpose of the logo or picture-mark is not to achieve immediate advertising success—it should have a permanently creative and active effect.

Paul Ibou

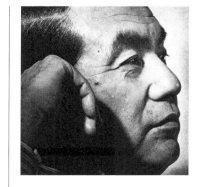

Yusaku Kamekura

1915–1997 · JP

Yusaku Kamekura was born in 1915 in Yoshida (now known as Tsubame). From 1935 to 1938 he studied for a degree in architecture at Tokyo's New Academy of Architecture and Industrial Arts, a private teaching institution modeled on the German Bauhaus. On graduation he worked for various advertising agencies and was also art director of several magazines. In 1951 he became a founder member of the Japan Advertising Arts Club, and in 1960 was one of the founder members of the Nippon Design Center. In 1962 Kamekura set up his own practice, where his work combining Constructivist elements with a traditional Japanese esthetic began to attract attention. In the following years he became one of Japan's best-known graphic designers. His work for the 1964 Tokyo Olympics and Expo '70 in Osaka brought him international recognition. Along with posters and packaging, trademarks were his preferred medium, which he explored in great detail. His book *Trademarks of the World*, published in 1956 and for which he spent five years collecting some 700 logos from across the world, was a standard work for the period. In 1978, he was appointed president of the newly founded Japan Graphic Designers Association and took on more administrative posts in international design organizations. Kamekura continued to work into old age and as late as 1985 created the logo for Nippon Telegraph and Telephone Corporation (NTT), one of the country's most recognizable corporate images. In the same year he launched and edited the magazine *Creation*, which in the space of five years ran to 20 issues charting developments in the world of graphic design. Kamekura died in Tokyo in 1997 aged 82 and is now regarded as one of Japan's most important designers of the 20th century.

Daishowa
Paper
1954 · Yusaku Kamekura · JP

Daishowa (Logo 2)
Paper
1954 · Yusaku Kamekura · JP

**Japan Industrial
Designers Association**
1954 · Yusaku Kamekura · JP

Gendai Geijutsu Kenkyujo
Contemporary art institute
1957 · Yusaku Kamekura · JP

Taiyo Kikai Kogyo Co.
Machinery
1958 · Yusaku Kamekura · JP

Toray Industries
Industrial products
1958 · Yusaku Kamekura · JP

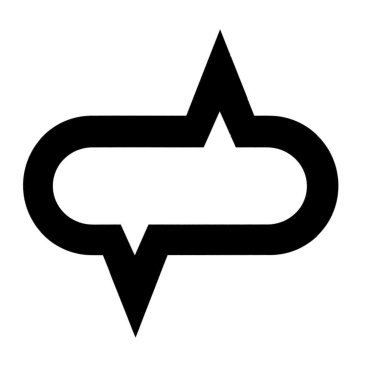

Nippon Broadcasting System
Radio broadcasting
1954 · Yusaku Kamekura · JP

Nikon
Photography
1955 · Yusaku Kamekura · JP

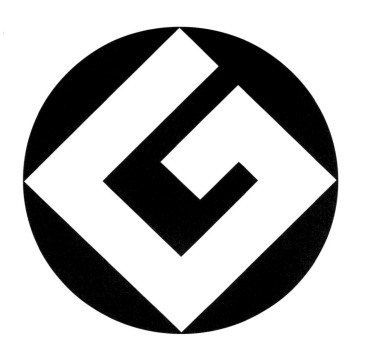

Good Design
Design institute and award
1957 · Yusaku Kamekura · JP

Yusaku Kamekura wurde 1915 in Yoshida (heute: Tsubame) geboren. Von 1935 bis 1938 studierte er mit Schwerpunkt Architektur in Tokio an der Neuen Akademie für Architektur und Industriedesign, einem privaten Institut nach Vorbild des deutschen Bauhauses. Anschließend arbeitete er für Werbeagenturen und als Art Director mehrerer Zeitschriften. Im Jahr 1951 war er Gründungsmitglied des Japan Advertising Arts Clubs und 1960 des Nippon Design Centers. Ab 1962 war Kamekura selbstständig tätig und erregte mit seinen Arbeiten, die Elemente des Konstruktivismus mit traditioneller japanischer Ästhetik verbanden, zunehmend Aufmerksamkeit. In den folgenden Jahren stieg er zu einem der bestbekannten japanischen Grafikdesigner auf. Seine Arbeiten für die Olympischen Spiele in Tokio 1964 sowie für die Expo '70 in Osaka machten ihn auch international bekannt. Neben Plakaten und Verpackungen wurden Markenzeichen zu seinem bevorzugten Medium, mit dem er sich ausführlich beschäftigte. Sein 1956 veröffentlichtes Buch *Trademarks of the World*, für das er in fünf Jahren Arbeit rund 700 internationale Logos zusammentrug, war ein Standardwerk seiner Zeit. Er wurde 1978 Vorsitzender der neu gegründeten Japan Graphic Designers Association und übernahm weitere administrative Aufgaben in internationalen Designorganisationen. Bis ins hohe Alter arbeitete Kamekura an neuen Entwürfen und schuf noch 1985 mit dem Zeichen für das japanische Telekommunikationsunternehmen NTT eines der berühmtesten Markenzeichen des Landes. Im gleichen Jahr initiierte er das Konzept für *Creation*, ein Magazin, das über 20 Ausgaben innerhalb von fünf Jahren Entwicklungen im internationalen Grafikdesign dokumentierte. Kamekura verstarb 1997 im Alter von 82 Jahren in Tokio und gilt heute als einer der wichtigsten japanischen Designer des 20. Jahrhunderts.

Yusaku Kamekura naît en 1915 à Yoshida (aujourd'hui Tsubame). De 1935 à 1938, il suit des études principalement centrées sur l'architecture à la Nouvelle Académie d'Architecture et de Design industriel (Tokyo), une institution privée conçue sur le modèle du Bauhaus. Par la suite, il travaille pour des agences publicitaires et comme directeur artistique de plusieurs revues. En 1951, il devient cofondateur du Japan Advertising Arts Club, et en 1960 du Nippon Design Center. À partir de 1962, Kamekura prend son indépendance et commence à se faire remarquer par des travaux associant éléments constructivistes et esthétique japonaise traditionnelle. Au cours des années suivantes, il devient un des graphistes japonais les plus célèbres. Son travail pour les jeux Olympiques de Tokyo en 1964, puis pour l'Exposition universelle d'Osaka en 1970, lui assurent une renommée internationale. À côté d'affiches et d'emballages, les logos deviennent son médium privilégié et son centre d'intérêt principal. Son livre *Trademarks of the World* publié en 1956, pour lequel il réunira quelque 700 logos internationaux en cinq ans de travail, fut un ouvrage de référence de son époque. À partir de 1978, Kamekura est président de la toute nouvelle Japan Graphic Designers Association et accepte d'autres charges administratives dans des organismes de design internationaux. Kamekura travaillera à de nouveaux projets jusqu'à un âge avancé : en 1985, il crée une des marques commerciales les plus célèbres de son pays avec le logo de l'entreprise de télécommunications japonaise NTT. La même année, il lance le concept de *Creation*, un magazine qui, en cinq ans et 20 éditions, a documenté les évolutions du graphisme international. Kamekura s'éteint à Tokyo en 1997 à l'âge de 82 ans. Il est aujourd'hui considéré comme un des plus grands designers japonais du XXe siècle.

Taiyo Kikai Kogyo Co.
Machinery (Logo 2)
1958 · Yusaku Kamekura · JP

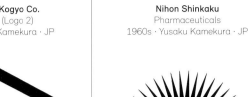

Nihon Shinkaku
Pharmaceuticals
1960s · Yusaku Kamekura · JP

Tonen Petrochemical
Chemicals
1958 · Yusaku Kamekura · JP

World Power Conference
Energy summit
1960s · Yusaku Kamekura · JP

Television Network
1958 · Yusaku Kamekura · JP

DIC
Inks
1961 · Yusaku Kamekura · JP

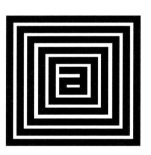

Japan Architects Association
1960 · Yusaku Kamekura · JP

Japan Association for the Advancement of Science
1961 · Yusaku Kamekura · JP

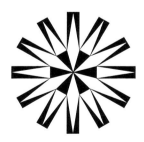

Minami Measuring
Measurement technology
1960 · Yusaku Kamekura · JP

Japan Recruitment Center
Human resources and development
1961 · Yusaku Kamekura · JP

Corona
Automobiles
1960s · Yusaku Kamekura · JP

Tokyu Koku
Airline
1962 · Yusaku Kamekura · JP

Shell
Petroleum
1963 · Yusaku Kamekura · JP

Acro
Business consultancy
1964 · Yusaku Kamekura · JP

Takasaka, Tokyo
Country club
1963 · Yusaku Kamekura · JP

Amagi Highland, Tokyo
Golf course
1965 · Yusaku Kamekura · JP

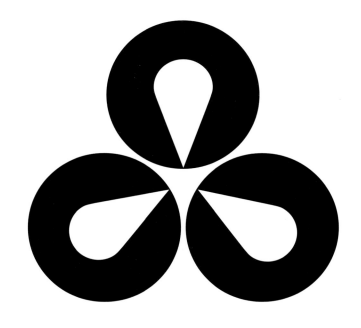

Akane
Ceramics
1965 · Yusaku Kamekura · JP

Yuken Trading
Industrial trading
1963 · Yusaku Kamekura · JP

Nihon Tsushin Kogyo
Telecommunications
1966 · Yusaku Kamekura · JP

Yuken-Boeki
Mail-order
1960s · Yusaku Kamekura · JP

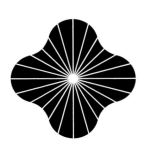

Yamagiwa
Electronics
1966 · Yusaku Kamekura · JP

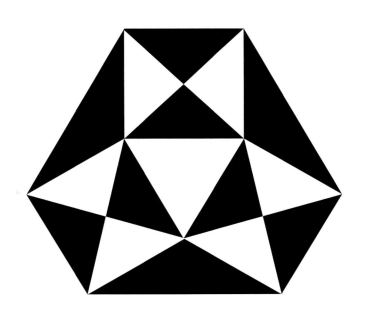

TDK – Tokyo Denki Kagaku Kogyo
Electronics
1966 · Yusaku Kamekura · JP

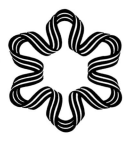

Child Ltd.
Children's clothing
1964 · Yusaku Kamekura · JP

Yamaguchi Bank
1966 · Yusaku Kamekura · JP

Toho Shigyo & Toho Kako
Paper
1964 · Yusaku Kamekura · JP

Ginza Centennial Merchants
Trade organization
1967 · Yusaku Kamekura · JP

Nippon Hoso Kyokai
Broadcasting
1967 · Yusaku Kamekura · JP

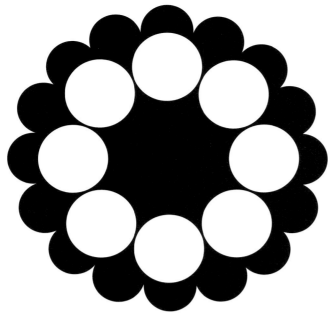
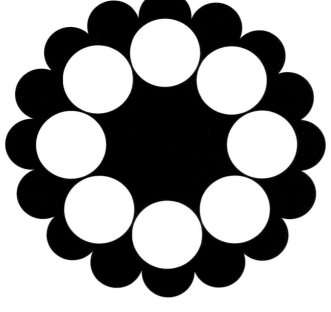

Prince Hotels
1968 · Yusaku Kamekura · JP

Up until 1968, the logo of the Prince Hotels chain was an old family coat of arms with a chrysanthemum in the center. Firstly, Yusaku Kamekura took the flower and transformed it into a symbol, on the white inner circle of which the locations of the hotels were shown. Secondly, he devised a system by which shapes, colors and typefaces could be interchanged to stand for individual hotels. Kamekura described his design as "a combination of Japanese elegance and Western beauty."

Die Hotelkette Prince Hotels verwendete bis 1968 ein altes Familienwappen mit einer Chrysantheme im Zentrum als Logo. Yusaku Kamekura abstrahierte die Blüte zu einem Symbol, bei dem die weißen Innenkreise auf die unterschiedlichen Standorte der Kette verweisen. Im zweiten Schritt wurde ein System konzipiert, das durch unterschiedliche Formen, Farben und Schriften die einzelnen Hotels individuell kennzeichnete. Kamekura beschrieb seine Lösung als „Kombination von japanischer Eleganz und westlicher Schönheit."

Jusqu'en 1968, la chaîne hôtelière Prince Hotels avait eu pour logo un ancien blason familial conçu autour d'un chrysanthème central. Yusaku Kamekura simplifia cette fleur pour en faire un symbole dont les cercles intérieurs renvoient aux différentes implantations de la chaîne. Une deuxième étape conduisit à concevoir un système dans lequel différentes formes, couleurs et écritures caractérisent individuellement les différents hôtels. Kamekura a décrit sa solution comme une « combinaison d'élégance japonaise et de beauté occidentale. »

Kyowa Hakko
Chemicals
1967 · Yusaku Kamekura · JP

Showa Denko
Chemicals
1968 · Yusaku Kamekura · JP

Taiyo Bank
1968 · Yusaku Kamekura · JP

Tokyo Music Institute
1968 · Yusaku Kamekura · JP

Sangetsu
Wallpapers
1969 · Yusaku Kamekura · JP

Tokyo Watch Research Institute
Watch engineering
1969 · Yusaku Kamekura · JP

Tokyu
Advertising agency
1969 · Yusaku Kamekura · JP

Toa Domestic Airlines
1970 · Yusaku Kamekura · JP

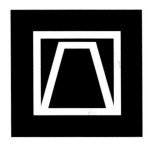

Fuji Bank
1979 · Yusaku Kamekura · JP

Expo '70, Osaka
World's fair
1970 · Yusaku Kamekura · JP

**Quality Label for
Communication Products**
1973 · Yusaku Kamekura · JP

**Nippon Telegraph
& Telephone Corp.**
1985 · Yusaku Kamekura · JP

**The Japan Society of Obstetrics
and Gynecology**
1970 · Yusaku Kamekura · JP

Sports Club
1973 · Yusaku Kamekura · JP

Long-Term Credit Bank of Japan
1986 · Yusaku Kamekura · JP

Yamagiwa
Lighting
1970 · Yusaku Kamekura · JP

Trade Center Building
Commercial skyscraper
1973 · Yusaku Kamekura · JP

Cram School
1986 · Yusaku Kamekura · JP

Takatsuki Resort Lanes, Osaka
Bowling alley
1971 · Yusaku Kamekura · JP

**Association for the Promotion of
Traditional Craftsmanship**
1975 · Yusaku Kamekura · JP

Japan Design Day
Special calendar day
1988 · Yusaku Kamekura · JP

Meiji Seika Kaisha
Chocolate
1971 · Yusaku Kamekura · JP

**East-West Association for
Cultural Exchange**
1978 · Yusaku Kamekura · JP

TAK
Architecture
1992 · Yusaku Kamekura · JP

Les marques sont des moyens importants pour garantir la qualité des produits dans l'esprit du public et lui communiquer une idée du champ d'activité et de l'envergure d'une entreprise. Elles sont donc un facteur tout à fait essentiel pour définir le « visage » d'une firme.
Yusaku Kamekura

Warenzeichen sind wichtige Mittel, um der Öffentlichkeit gegenüber die Qualität von Erzeugnissen zu garantieren und um Menschen eine Vorstellung vom Tätigkeitsbereich und Umfang eines Unternehmens zu geben. Sie sind also ein ganz wesentlicher Faktor für die Prägung des „Gesichts" einer Firma.
Yusaku Kamekura

Trademarks are an important means of guaranteeing to the public the quality of products, while also giving people an idea of the nature and extent of a company's field of activity. They are also a crucial factor in shaping a firm's public image.
Yusaku Kamekura

Stefan Kanchev

1915–2001 · BG

Stefan Kanchev was born in 1915 in Kalofer, Bulgaria. As a child he was taught to draw by his father, an icon painter. From 1933 he studied German philosophy in the capital Sofia. At the same time, he and an artist friend forged identity cards and other documents for anti-Fascists and Jews. In 1940 Kanchev entered the National Academy of Arts to study painting, but gave up his studies when he was hired as art director for a publishing house, so beginning his career as a graphic designer. In 1946, the People's Republic of Bulgaria came into being under Communist rule. In the same year Kanchev received his first commission to design a special stamp for the Bulgarian post office. Many more such assignments were to follow. Five years later he was appointed director of the state committee for graphic design. As such, Kanchev made crucial decisions on the use of graphics in numerous Bulgarian state corporations and institutions. Within a few years, trademark design became his main occupation. His work began to attract the attention of international design magazines and associations such as the International Center for the Typographic Arts and the American Institute of Graphic Arts, and a combination of exhibitions and publications made him one of the best-known and most respected figures on the international design scene. Between 1955 and 1985 Kanchev created around 2,000 trademarks, including logos for Bulgarian state television and the state-owned gas station chain. In the 1970s and '80s, Kanchev won many awards, but with the arrival of computers and the collapse of Communism he sank into oblivion. Only in recent years have several exhibitions and a book been devoted to the designer, who died in 2001, and whose work remains omnipresent in Bulgaria.

Tyutyuneva Promishlenost
Tobacco
1956 · Stefan Kanchev · BG

Applied Arts Center, Sofia
Cultural organization
1957 · Stefan Kanchev · BG

Machinoexport
Machine trade
1957 · Stefan Kanchev · BG

TABSO
Airline
1957 · Stefan Kanchev · BG

Reklama
Advertising agency
1958 · Stefan Kanchev · BG

Avramov
National radio string quartet
1960 · Stefan Kanchev · BG

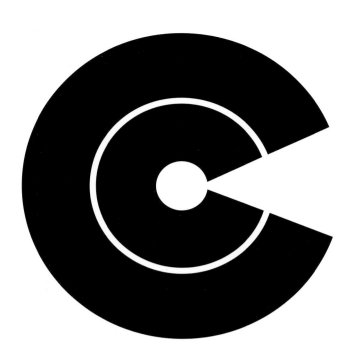

Kino Studio
Film studio
1957 · Stefan Kanchev · BG

Narodna Prosveta
Publishing
1957 · Stefan Kanchev · BG

National Art Gallery, Sofia
1959 · Stefan Kanchev · BG

Stefan Kanchev wurde 1915 im bulgarischen Kalofer geboren. Von seinem Vater, einem Ikonenmaler, erhielt er bereits als Kind Zeichenunterricht. Ab 1933 studierte er zunächst Deutsche Philosophie in der Hauptstadt Sofia. In dieser Zeit fälschte er gemeinsam mit einem befreundeten Künstler auch Ausweise und andere Papiere für Antifaschisten und Juden. An der Nationalen Kunstakademie begann Kanchev 1940 ein Studium der Malerei. Mit Antritt der Position als künstlerischer Leiter eines Verlagshauses gab er sein Studium jedoch auf und begann eine Laufbahn als Grafikdesigner. 1946 wurde die Volksrepublik Bulgarien als kommunistischer Staat neu gegründet. Kanchev erhielt im gleichen Jahr einen ersten Auftrag für die Gestaltung einer Sonderbriefmarke der bulgarischen Post, dem noch viele weitere folgten. Fünf Jahre später berief man ihn zum Vorsitzenden der Staatskommission für Grafikdesign. In dieser Position entschied Kanchev maßgeblich über das Auftreten des bulgarischen Grafikdesigns in zahlreichen staatlichen Unternehmen und Institutionen mit. Der Entwurf von Markenzeichen wurde in den folgenden Jahren zu seiner bestimmenden Tätigkeit. Internationale Designmagazine und Verbände wie das International Center for the Typographic Arts oder das American Institute of Graphic Arts wurden auf seine Arbeiten aufmerksam und machen ihn durch Ausstellungen und Veröffentlichungen zu einer bekannten und respektierten Persönlichkeit der internationalen Designszene. Zwischen 1955 und 1985 entwarf Kanchev rund 2.000 Markenzeichen, darunter das Logo des öffentlich-rechtlichen Fernsehsenders oder der staatlichen Tankstellenkette des Landes. In den 1970er- und 1980er-Jahren erhielt Kanchev zahlreiche Auszeichnungen, geriet jedoch mit Aufkommen des Computers und dem Zerfall des kommunistischen Systems in Vergessenheit. Erst in den vergangenen Jahren wurde das Werk des 2001 verstorbenen Designers, das im heutigen Bulgarien noch immer omnipräsent ist, in mehreren Ausstellungen sowie einem Buchprojekt gewürdigt.

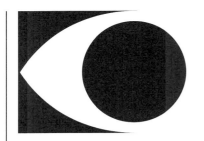

Stefan Kanchev naît en 1915 à Kalofer, en Bulgarie. Dès son enfance, il apprend le dessin avec son père, un peintre d'icônes. À partir de 1933, il commence des études de philosophie allemande à Sofia, la capitale. À la même époque, il fabrique de fausses pièces d'identité avec un ami artiste pour des militants antifascistes et des juifs. En 1940, Kanchev suit des études de peinture à l'École nationale des Beaux-Arts, études qu'il abandonne toutefois lorsqu'il devient directeur artistique d'une maison d'édition et qu'il se lance ainsi dans une carrière de graphiste. En 1946, la Bulgarie est refondée comme État communiste sous le nom de République populaire de Bulgarie. La même année, Kanchev reçoit une commande pour la création d'un timbre spécial de la poste bulgare, première d'une longue série. Cinq ans plus tard, il est nommé président de la Commission nationale de graphisme. C'est à ce poste qu'il devient codécisionnaire de l'identité du graphisme bulgare de nombreuses entreprises et institutions d'État. Au cours des années suivantes, la création de logos devient son activité principale. Des magazines et des institutions de design internationales comme l'International Center for the Typographic Arts ou l'American Institute of Graphic Arts prennent connaissance de son travail – diverses expositions et publications vont faire de lui une des personnalités les plus connues et les plus respectées de la scène du design international. Entre 1955 et 1985, Kanchev a créé environ 2000 logos, notamment celui de la télévision publique ou celui de la chaîne de stations d'essence nationale de Bulgarie. Dans les années 1970 et 1980, Kanchev reçoit de nombreuses distinctions, mais sombre dans l'oubli avec l'arrivée de l'informatique et la chute du régime communiste. C'est seulement au cours de ces dernières années que l'œuvre du designer décédé en 2001, aujourd'hui encore omniprésent en Bulgarie, a été dignement célébré à travers plusieurs expositions et d'un projet de livre.

National Opera, Sofia
1960 · Stefan Kanchev · BG

Central Puppet Theater, Sofia
1963 · Stefan Kanchev · BG

Sadala
Underwater fishing equipment
1960 · Stefan Kanchev · BG

Chimkombinat
Chemicals
1963 · Stefan Kanchev · BG

Vulkan Zement
Cement
1960s · Stefan Kanchev · BG

Dunavia-Rousse
Canned foods
1963 · Stefan Kanchev · BG

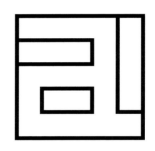

Architectura
Architectural magazine
1961 · Stefan Kanchev · BG

Elektra
Electronics
1963 · Stefan Kanchev · BG

Doso
Diving club
1961 · Stefan Kanchev · BG

Elektroimpex
Electronic devices
1963 · Stefan Kanchev · BG

Union of Bulgarian Artists
1962 · Stefan Kanchev · BG

Fasan
Stockings
1963 · Stefan Kanchev · BG

Mineralni Vodi-Sofia
Mineral water
1963 · Stefan Kanchev · BG

Yagoda-Yambol
Canned foods
1963 · Stefan Kanchev · BG

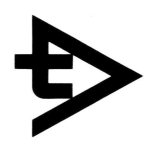

Strasita
Art gallery
1965 · Stefan Kanchev · BG

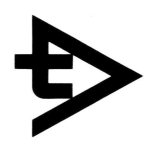

Technoimpex
Patent trading and licensing
1965 · Stefan Kanchev · BG

Slavyanka
Fishery
1963 · Stefan Kanchev · BG

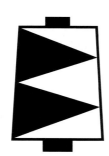

Vreteno Maritza
Textiles
1963 · Stefan Kanchev · BG

Bulgarian Chamber of Commerce
1965 · Stefan Kanchev · BG

Balkancar
Forklift trucks
1966 · Stefan Kanchev · BG

Chimimport
Chemicals
1963 · Stefan Kanchev · BG

Center for Industrial Design, Sofia
1964 · Stefan Kanchev · BG

Bulgarian National Television
Broadcasting
1965 · Stefan Kanchev · BG

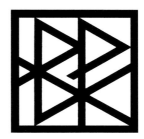

Building Materials
1966 · Stefan Kanchev · BG

Georgi Bakalov
Publishing
1963 · Stefan Kanchev · BG

Elektromedicina
Electronics
1964 · Stefan Kanchev · BG

Frederick Engels
Construction company
1965 · Stefan Kanchev · BG

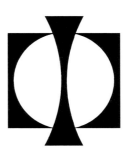

Fotoisdat
Publishing
1966 · Stefan Kanchev · BG

Stomana
Steel production
1963 · Stefan Kanchev · BG

August Popov
Furniture
1964 · Stefan Kanchev · BG

Koprina
Silk
1965 · Stefan Kanchev · BG

Lipa-Silistra
Furniture
1966 · Stefan Kanchev · BG

Vinsavod
Wine
1963 · Stefan Kanchev · BG

Zement Kombinat Wratza
Cement
1964 · Stefan Kanchev · BG

Rodopa
Meat
1965 · Stefan Kanchev · BG

Ribno Stopanstvo
Fishery
1966 · Stefan Kanchev · BG

Petrol
Gas stations
1964 · Stefan Kanchev · BG

For this oil company founded
in 1932 Kanchev designed
a trademark blend of lettering
and imagery which could be
used separately or together.
His preparatory sketches reveal
how he worked, always beginning with endless small drawings. The Petrol AD logos are
still used to signpost nearly 500
gas stations across Bulgaria.

Für das 1932 gegründete
Rohölunternehmen entwarf
Kanchev eine Bild- und eine
Wortmarke, die einzeln oder in
Kombination verwendet werden
konnten. Die dazugehörigen
Skizzen aus dem Entwurfs-
prozess veranschaulichen seine
Arbeitsweise, die immer mit
unzähligen kleinen Zeichnun-
gen begann. Bis heute sind
die Petrol-Logos in Verwendung
und kennzeichnen fast 500
Tankstellen in Bulgarien.

Pour cette entreprise pétro-
lière fondée en 1932, Kanchev
créa un insigne et un logotype
qui pouvaient être utilisés séparément ou combinés entre eux.
Les croquis réalisés pendant le
travail de conception illustrent
la démarche du graphiste, qui
commençait chaque projet par
d'innombrables petits dessins.
L'insigne et le logotype etrol AD
sont encore utilisés aujourd'hui
et signalent presque 500 stations
d'essence en Bulgarie.

Avram Stojanov
Textiles
1967 · Stefan Kanchev · BG

Grashdanski Letischta
Airport maintenance
1967 · Stefan Kanchev · BG

Student Library
Publishing
1967 · Stefan Kanchev · BG

Nauka i Iskustvo
Publishing
1967 · Stefan Kanchev · BG

Sofia Press
National press club
1967 · Stefan Kanchev · BG

Zelulosa i Chartia
Paper
1967 · Stefan Kanchev · BG

Press Center for the World Youth Festival
Festival press office
1968 · Stefan Kanchev · BG

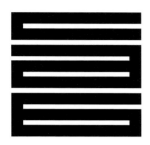

Union of Bulgarian Architects
1968 · Stefan Kanchev · BG

Balkan Litho
Printing
1969 · Stefan Kanchev · BG

State Music Board
National music organization
1969 · Stefan Kanchev · BG

Dimitar Dimitrov
Photographer
1969 · Stefan Kanchev · BG

Communist Party Publishing House
1969 · Stefan Kanchev · BG

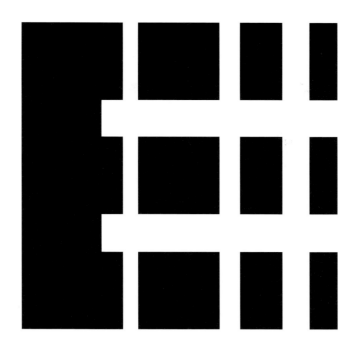

Plant Electronica
Precision machinery
1967 · Stefan Kanchev · BG

State Music Hall, Sofia
Concert hall
1968 · Stefan Kanchev · BG

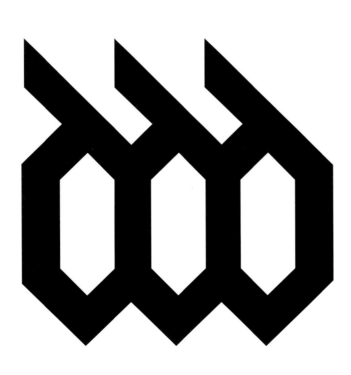

DDD
Chemicals
1970 · Stefan Kanchev · BG

Bulgarian Center for Graphic Design
1970 · Stefan Kanchev · BG

Department of Trademarks and Licensing
Trademarks office
1970 · Stefan Kanchev · BG

Electronic Components
1970 · Stefan Kanchev · BG

Feromagniti
Magnets
1970 · Stefan Kanchev · BG

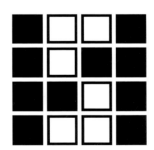

Isida
Tiles
1970 · Stefan Kanchev · BG

Koopturist
Travel agency
1970 · Stefan Kanchev · BG

Rila
Clothing
1970 · Stefan Kanchev · BG

Ministry of Electronics and Electrical Engineering
1971 · Stefan Kanchev · BG

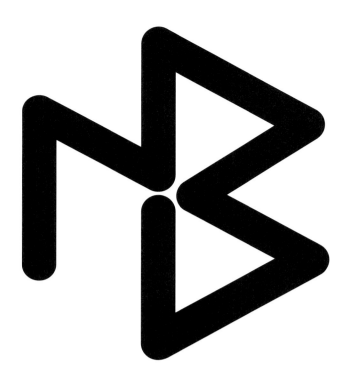

Mladen Wasilev
Construction materials
1972 · Stefan Kanchev · BG

Sofia Film
Film studio
1970 · Stefan Kanchev · BG

Promischleno Stroitelstwo
Construction company
1971 · Stefan Kanchev · BG

Melnitsi
Grain mill
1970 · Stefan Kanchev · BG

Schwann
Mattresses
1971 · Stefan Kanchev · BG

Rahovets
Chemicals
1972 · Stefan Kanchev · BG

Stroitelni Materiali
Construction materials
1970 · Stefan Kanchev · BG

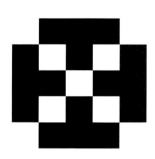

Tonsos
Textiles
1971 · Stefan Kanchev · BG

Allen Mac
Office supplies
1971 · Stefan Kanchev · BG

Central Market, Sofia
Supermarket
1971 · Stefan Kanchev · BG

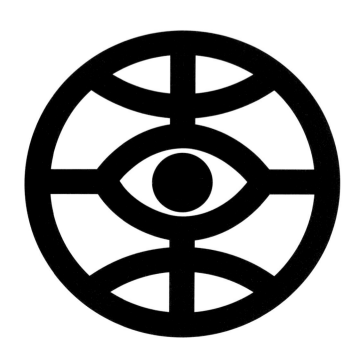

International Biennial of Trademarks
Design exhibition
1979 · Stefan Kanchev · BG

Exhibition of Bulgarian Trademarks
1971 · Stefan Kanchev · BG

Balkantourist
Travel agency
1972 · Stefan Kanchev · BG

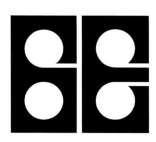

Bitwa Estetica
Interior design
1972 · Stefan Kanchev · BG

Septemvri Industrial Trade
1972 · Stefan Kanchev · BG

Powel Kortchagin
Children's clothing
1974 · Stefan Kanchev · BG

Halli
Supermarket
1972 · Stefan Kanchev · BG

State Press Committee
Media
1972 · Stefan Kanchev · BG

Septemvri
Publishing
1975 · Stefan Kanchev · BG

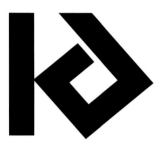

Komsomolgz
Furniture
1972 · Stefan Kanchev · BG

Interior Design
1972 · Stefan Kanchev · BG

Hotel Europa
1976 · Stefan Kanchev · BG

Ludogorska Slava
Metalworks
1972 · Stefan Kanchev · BG

State Puppet Theater, Sofia
1972 · Stefan Kanchev · BG

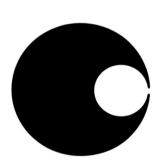

Septemvri
Steel pipes
1979 · Stefan Kanchev · BG

**National Committee for Television
and Radio**
State broadcasting
1972 · Stefan Kanchev · BG

USPEC
Ceramics
1972 · Stefan Kanchev · BG

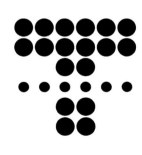

Tehnica
Publishing
1980 · Stefan Kanchev · BG

Preciz-Michai
Metals
1972 · Stefan Kanchev · BG

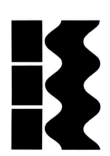

Kamchia
Resort complex
1974 · Stefan Kanchev · BG

CT
Textiles
1982 · Stefan Kanchev · BG

La marque n'est pas censée changer au gré des directions d'entreprise ; c'est un fait dont on doit tenir compte à chaque réorganisation. La tradition a une réelle importance ; elle aide à tenir le cap même quand les grêlons de la concurrence s'abattent sur vous. C'est ce qui fait que je me sens d'une certaine manière impliqué dans le succès des entreprises qui utilisent mes logos.

Stefan Kanchev

Ein Logo sollte sich nicht ändern, sobald die Manager wechseln, und das dürfen wir nicht aus dem Auge verlieren, wenn ein Unternehmen neu aufgestellt wird. Traditionen sind wichtig, sie geben Halt, wenn der Wind der Konkurrenz einem allzu kräftig ins Gesicht weht. Aus dem Grund fühle ich mich zu einem gewissen Grad am Erfolg der Unternehmen beteiligt, deren Logo ich gestaltet habe.

Stefan Kanchev

The trademark should not change when the company's managers do and this is one of the things we should take into account during every reorganization. Certainly tradition counts, which helps you keep your footing even while being buffeted by the winds of competition. For this reason I feel to a certain extent implicated in the success of companies that use my logos.

Stefan Kanchev

Burton Kramer was born in 1932 in
New York's Bronx neighborhood. From 1954
to 1957 he studied at the Institute of Design
in Chicago and at Yale University School of
Arts & Architecture, and also spent a year
at the Royal College of Art in London. Kramer
began his career as an assistant in Will
Burtin's New York studio and as a designer for
various corporate clients including the drug
manufacturer Geigy. In 1961, he moved to
Switzerland to work for the Erwin Halpern
advertising agency, and it was there that he
received the first awards for his work. After
four years in Zurich he joined Paul Arthur
Associates in Toronto, where he worked on
graphics and signage for Expo '67. In 1967
he founded his own studio under the name
of Burton Kramer & Associates—which later
became Kramer Design Associates. Within a
few years it was one of Canada's best-known
design studios, with work mainly focused on
creating complex corporate identities. In the
1970s Kramer developed logos for internationally respected institutions including the
Royal Ontario Museum and the Canadian
Broadcasting Corporation. In 1974 he took
Canadian citizenship and in the same year
became one of the first Canadian members
of the design association Alliance Graphique
Internationale. Between 1980 and 2001 he
taught typography and corporate design at
the Ontario College of Art and Design and was
also a visiting lecturer at several international
universities. In 1993 he turned to painting,
producing work characterized by brightly
colored geometric shapes, and in 2001 he
retired from the design business, handing
the agency over to his son Jeremy. Since then
Kramer has devoted himself exclusively to
abstract painting, continuing to experiment
with the Modernist designs that were the hallmark of many of his commercial commissions.

Burton Kramer

*1932 · CA

American Society of
Magazine Photographers
1958 · Burton Kramer · CA

Ytong
Paper
1961 · Burton Kramer · CA

Canadian Sociology &
Anthropology Association
1965 · Burton Kramer · CA

Interchange
Scholarly magazine
1966 · Burton Kramer · CA

BBR Canada
Concrete construction
1967 · Burton Kramer · CA

clairtone

Clairtone Sound Corporation
Audio electronics
1967 · Burton Kramer · CA

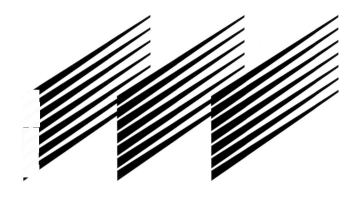

Fiera Milano
Trade fair organizers (proposed design)
1973 · Burton Kramer · CA

Reed Paper Corporation
1975 · Burton Kramer · CA

Hallmark Hotels
Hotel chain
1977 · Burton Kramer · CA

Burton Kramer wurde 1932 im New Yorker Stadtteil Bronx geboren. Er studierte zwischen 1954 und 1957 am Institute of Design in Chicago, an der Yale University School of Arts & Architecture und ein Jahr am Royal College of Art in London. Seine berufliche Laufbahn begann er zunächst als Assistent im Atelier von Will Burtin in New York sowie als Gestalter für verschiedene Unternehmen wie den Medikamentenhersteller Geigy. 1961 zog er in die Schweiz, arbeitete für die Werbeagentur Erwin Halpern und erhielt erste Auszeichnungen für seine Arbeiten. Nach vier Jahren in Zürich ging er nach Toronto, wo er bei Paul Arthur Associates an Designelementen und Leitsystemen für die Expo '67 arbeitete. Unter dem Namen Burton Kramer & Associates (später Kramer Design Associates) gründete er 1967 sein eigenes Studio, das in den folgenden Jahren zu einem der bekanntesten Designbüros des Landes aufstieg. Die Entwicklung von komplexen Erscheinungsbildern wurde zum Schwerpunkt des Studios. In den 1970er-Jahren entwickelte Kramer international beachtete Identitäten für Auftraggeber wie das Royal Ontario Museum oder die Canadian Broadcasting Corporation. Er wurde 1974 kanadischer Staatsbürger und im gleichen Jahr als eines der ersten kanadischen Mitglieder in den renommierten Designverband Alliance Graphique Internationale aufgenommen. Zwischen 1980 und 2001 unterrichtete er Typografie und Corporate Design am Ontario College of Art and Design und war als Gastdozent an mehreren internationalen Hochschulen tätig. Seine Beschäftigung mit freier, auf geometrischen Formen basierenden Malerei begann 1993. Mit dem Jahr 2001 zog er sich ganz aus dem Agenturgeschäft zurück und übergab die Leitung des Designbüros an seinen Sohn Jeremy. Seither beschäftigt er sich ausschließlich mit abstrakter Malerei. Sein modernistischer Gestaltungsansatz, der sich bereits in sämtlichen seiner auftragsgebundenen Arbeiten zeigte, wird hier experimentell fortgeführt.

Burton Kramer est né en 1932 à New York dans le quartier du Bronx. De 1954 à 1957, il étudie à l'Institute of Design à Chicago, à la Yale University School of Arts and Architecture et pendant un an au Royal College of Art à Londres. Il commence sa carrière professionnelle comme assistant dans le studio new-yorkais de Will Burtin et comme designer pour différentes entreprises comme le fabricant de produits pharmaceutiques Geigy. En 1961, il s'installe en Suisse, où il travaille pour le compte de l'agence publicitaire Erwin Halpern et reçoit les premières distinctions pour ses réalisations. Après quatre années passées à Zurich, il s'installe à Toronto et travaille chez Paul Arthur Associates sur des éléments de design et des systèmes signalétiques pour l'Exposition universelle de 1967. En 1967, il fonde son propre studio Burton Kramer & Associates (futur Kramer Design Associates), qui devient au cours des années suivantes un des bureaux de design les plus célèbres du pays. La conception de systèmes visuels complexes devient le cœur de métier du studio. Dans les années 1970, Kramer conçoit les identités visuelles de commanditaires internationalement respectés comme le Musée royal de l'Ontario ou la Canadian Broadcasting Corporation. En 1974, il devient citoyen canadien. La même année, il est un des premiers Canadiens à intégrer la célèbre association de designers Alliance graphique internationale. Entre 1980 et 2001, il enseigne la typographie et le corporate design à l'Ontario College of Art and Design et travaille comme professeur invité dans plusieurs écoles internationales. Son intérêt pour la peinture indépendante basée sur des formes géométrique commence en 1993. En 2001, il se retire des affaires et confie la direction de l'agence de design à son fils Jeremy. Depuis, il se consacre exclusivement à la peinture abstraite. Son approche créative moderniste, déjà visible dans tous ses travaux appliqués, y trouve son prolongement expérimental.

Peter Robinson
Industrial design
1967 · Burton Kramer · CA

Werner Herterich
Exhibition design
1967 · Burton Kramer · CA

Project School-to-School
Educational exchange
1968 · Burton Kramer · CA

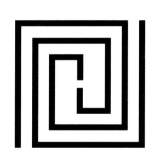

Harbour Square Hotel
1969 · Burton Kramer · CA

Canadian Guild of Crafts
National crafts trust
1969 · Burton Kramer · CA

Children's Playgrounds
Toys
1969 · Burton Kramer · CA

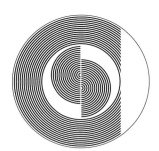

Craft Dimensions Canada
Craft exhibition
1969 · Burton Kramer · CA

Gentil Plastics Lindsay
Plastic goods
1969 · Burton Kramer · CA

Hamilton Hastings
Spark plugs
1969 · Burton Kramer · CA

SCOT
Computers
1969 · Burton Kramer · CA

Ontario Educational Communications Authority
Public education broadcasting
1970 · Burton Kramer · CA

Kuypers Adamson Norton
Industrial design
1971 · Burton Kramer · CA

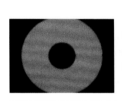

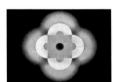
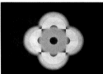

Television Canada

Canadian Broadcasting Company
1974 · Burton Kramer · CA

In the early 1970s, the Canadian state television company was seeking a new corporate identity. In the competition to design a new logo, Burton Kramer's image of radio waves spreading from the central letter "C" was declared the winner. The logo was first used in 1974 as part of an overall visual design strategy. It remained in service, unchanged, until 1992 and is still one of Canada's best-known trademarks.

Das kanadische Staatsfernsehen suchte Anfang der 1970er-Jahre nach einer neuen visuellen Identität. Burton Kramers Konzept des Buchstabens „C" im Zentrum, um den herum sich Sendewellen ausbreiten, setzte sich im internationalen Wettbewerb durch. Eingebettet in ein umfangreiches visuelles Gesamtkonzept wurde es 1974 erstmals verwendet. Das Logo war unverändert bis 1992 im Einsatz und gehört zu den bekanntesten Markenzeichen Kanadas.

Au début des années 1970, la télévision nationale canadienne cherchait une nouvelle identité visuelle. Le concept de Burton Kramer – la lettre «C» centrale autour de laquelle se répandent les ondes radiodiffusées – s'imposa dans le cadre d'un concours international. Inséré dans un vaste concept général, le logo fut utilisé pour la première fois en 1974. Il resta inchangé jusqu'en 1992 et fait partie des sigles les plus connus du Canada.

First Choice! CBC Radio & Télévision

Canadian Broadcasting Corporation · Société Radio-Canada

Canada Systems Group
Computers
1972 · Burton Kramer · CA

York Construction
Construction company
1972 · Burton Kramer · CA

Pinestone Inn and Country Club
Resort and golf club
1972 · Burton Kramer · CA

Surfacing
Annual exhibition
1972 · Burton Kramer · CA

Aerographics
Printing
1975 · Burton Kramer · CA

Ontario Craft Council
Craft promotion and education
1975 · Burton Kramer, Tim Nielsen · CA

Bell Canada
Telecommunications
1978 · Burton Kramer · CA

Glassworks
Art glass
1980 · Burton Kramer · CA

Onex
Packaging
1980 · Burton Kramer · CA

Storwal
Office equipment
1977 · Burton Kramer · CA

Holidays by Wardair
Package holiday airline
1978 · Burton Kramer · CA

Bedford Consulting Group
Management consultancy
1978 · Burton Kramer · CA

Hornepayne Hallmark Town Centre
Shopping center
1978 · Burton Kramer · CA

Trade Typesetting
1978 · Burton Kramer, Joe Gault · CA

Ontario Association of Architects
1979 · Burton Kramer · CA

Tillsonburg Town Centre
Shopping center
1980 · Burton Kramer · CA

Copps Coliseum
Sports arena
1980 · Burton Kramer · CA

Herongate
Shopping center
1981 · Burton Kramer · CA

International Sculpture Symposium
1982 · Burton Kramer · CA

Teknion
Office furniture
1984 · Burton Kramer · CA

Energy Conference
1986 · Burton Kramer · CA

Science North
Museum
1985 · Burton Kramer · CA

North American
Life insurance
1987 · Burton Kramer · CA

St. Lawrence Centre for the Arts
Theater
1987 · Burton Kramer · CA

ZoomIt
Computer software
1988 · Burton Kramer · CA

Amblin Resources
Gold mining
1988 · Burton Kramer · CA

Silver Nightingale Lounge
Bar
1991 · Burton Kramer · CA

Storwal International
Office filing cabinets
1982 · Burton Kramer · CA

Centre Inn
Hotel
1984 · Burton Kramer · CA

Energy Corporation
1990 · Burton Kramer · CA

Un logo efficace doit avoir l'air d'être « fait pour » : il doit projeter l'attitude de l'entreprise, son style et ses aspirations. Le logo conçu pour une banque serait inapproprié s'il devait représenter une agence de voyages, le logo d'une chaîne d'hôtels doit communiquer à la fois confort et efficacité, celui d'une compagnie aérienne vitesse et sécurité.
Burton Kramer

Ein überzeugendes Logo muss einfach „passen", es muss die Einstellung, den Stil und die Zielsetzungen einer Firma widerspiegeln. Das Logo einer Bank wäre nicht das richtige für eine Reiseagentur, das Logo einer Hotelkette sollte Komfort und gleichzeitig Effizienz vermitteln, das einer Fluggesellschaft Geschwindigkeit und Sicherheit.
Burton Kramer

An effective logo must appear to "fit". It must project the corporate attitude, style and aspirations. The logo for a bank would be inappropriate if it appeared to represent a travel agency; the logo for a hotel chain should convey both comfort and efficiency, that of an airline speed and security.
Burton Kramer

Paul Rand

1914–1996 · US

Paul Rand was born in Brooklyn in 1914. From 1929 to 1934 he studied in New York, first at the Pratt Institute, then at the Parsons School of Design, and finally at the Art Students League of New York. He then began his career as an illustrator and art director for magazines, including *Esquire*. Rand first achieved recognition on the design scene between 1938 and 1945 with his extraordinary cover designs for *Direction* magazine. At the same time, he took up his first teaching posts, while also designing book jackets and creating images for advertising campaigns. In 1954 he was named one of New York's ten best art directors. He began designing for IBM in 1956, completely revamping the company's corporate identity, and continued to fine-tune its logos until the early 1990s. Also in 1956 he became professor of graphic design at Yale University, a post he held, apart from some minor interruptions, until 1993. As an educator Rand influenced entire generations of American designers. In the early 1960s he created some of the USA's best-known trademarks, including logos for Westinghouse, ABC and UPS. He published a number of books, some of which are still regarded as standard works, and by participating in countless exhibitions he gradually became one of the 20th century's most important design pioneers. In collaboration with his first wife, Ann, he wrote and illustrated several successful books for children which, like all his other work, were examples of his playful, Modernist style. Developing complex designs and creating eye-catching logos were still his favorite occupations until well into old age. Paul Rand died in 1996 at the age of 82 in Norwalk, Connecticut.

Helbros Watch Company
Watchmaker
1943 · Paul Rand · US

Borzoi Books
Publishing
1945 · Paul Rand · US

Smith, Kline and French
Pharmaceuticals
1945 · Paul Rand · US

Consolidated Cigar Corporation
1959 · Paul Rand · US

Colorforms
Toys
1959 · Paul Rand · US

Cummins
Engines
1962 · Paul Rand · US

Harcourt Brace and Company
Publishing
1957 · Paul Rand · US

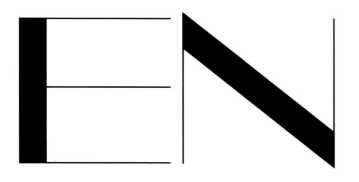

Eliot Noyes & Associates
Architecture and industrial design
1959 · Paul Rand · US

United Parcel Service of America
Courier service
1961 · Paul Rand · US

Paul Rand wurde 1914 im New Yorker Stadtteil Brooklyn geboren. Er studierte zwischen 1929 und 1934 am Pratt Institute, an der Parsons School of Design sowie bei der Art Students League in New York. Im Anschluss begann seine Laufbahn als angestellter Illustrator und Art Director, u. a. für das *Esquire* Magazine. Mit außergewöhnlichen Cover-Entwürfen für das *Direction* Magazine erhielt Rand zwischen 1938 und 1945 erste Aufmerksamkeit in der Designszene. Zur gleichen Zeit trat er erste Lehraufträge an, realisierte Buchumschläge und Werbekampagnen. Im Jahr 1954 wurde er zu einem der zehn besten New Yorker Art Directors gewählt. Seine Arbeit für das Unternehmen IBM begann 1956, dessen visuelle Identität er grundlegend überarbeitete und bis in die frühen 1990er-Jahre bestimmte. Im gleichen Jahr trat er eine Professur an der Yale University an, die er mit kurzer Unterbrechung bis 1993 innehatte. In dieser Funktion prägte Rand ganze Generationen amerikanischer Designer. Anfang der 1960er-Jahre entwarf er einige der bis heute bekanntesten amerikanischen Markenzeichen – darunter die Logos für Westinghouse, ABC und UPS. Durch mehrere Buchveröffentlichungen, von denen viele bis heute als Standardwerke gelten, sowie durch zahlreiche Ausstellungen wurde er über die Jahre zu einer der wegweisenden Gestalterpersönlichkeiten des 20. Jahrhunderts. Gemeinsam mit seiner ersten Frau Ann schrieb und illustrierte Paul Rand mehrere erfolgreiche Kinderbücher, die wie fast alle seine Arbeiten von einem spielerisch-modernistischen Stil geprägt sind. Bis ins hohe Alter blieb die Entwicklung komplexer Designsysteme und der Entwurf prägnanter Zeichen seine bevorzugte Aufgabe. Paul Rand starb 1996 im Alter von 82 Jahren in Norwalk, Connecticut.

American Broadcasting Company
Television network
1962 · Paul Rand · US

Paul Rand naît en 1914 dans le quartier de Brooklyn, à New York. De 1929 à 1934, il étudie au Pratt Institute, à la Parsons School of Design et à l'Art Students League à New York. Après ses études, il se lance dans une carrière d'illustrateur et directeur artistique, notamment pour le magazine *Esquire*. Entre 1938 et 1945, il se fait remarquer par les pages de couverture inhabituelles qu'il crée pour le magazine *Direction*. À la même époque, il accepte ses premiers postes d'enseignement, réalise des couvertures de livres et des campagnes publicitaires. En 1954, il est élu parmi les dix meilleurs directeurs artistiques de New York. C'est en 1956 que Rand commence son travail pour IBM : il redéfinit entièrement l'identité visuelle de l'entreprise et continuera de le faire jusqu'au début des années 1990. Toujours en 1956, il accepte à l'Université Yale une chaire qu'il occupera jusqu'en 1993 avec une courte interruption. C'est à ce poste qu'il marquera des générations entières de designers américains. Au début des années 1960, il conçoit quelques-uns des logos américains les plus célèbres jusqu'à ce jour – notamment ceux de Westinghouse, ABC et UPS. Grâce à plusieurs ouvrages, dont beaucoup font aujourd'hui encore référence, mais aussi a de nombreuses expositions, Rand est devenu au fil des années une des personnalités du monde du design les plus influentes du XXe siècle. En collaboration avec sa première femme Ann, Paul Rand a aussi écrit et illustré plusieurs livres pour enfants couronnés de succès ; comme presque tous ses travaux, ils sont marqués par un style ludique et moderniste. Le développement de systèmes graphiques complexes et la conception de signes marquants sont restés son cœur de métier. Paul Rand s'est éteint en 1996 à Norwalk, Connecticut, à l'âge de 82 ans.

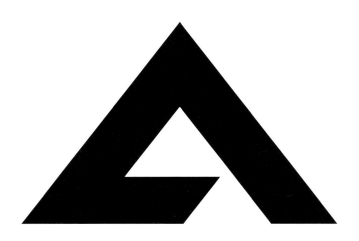

Atlas Corporation
Crankshaft drives
1964 · Paul Rand · US

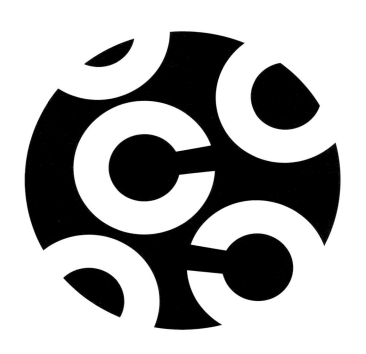

Columbus Indiana Visitors Center
Tourist information
1973 · Paul Rand · US

Westinghouse

abcdefghijklmnopqrstu
vwxyz st ABCDEFGHJKL
MNOPQRSTUVWXYZ&( )
1234567890$¢!?.,:;-""''
abcdefghijklmnopqrstu
vwxyz st ABCDEFGHIJKL
MNOPQRSTUVWXYZ&( )
1234567890$¢!?.,:;-""''

Westinghouse Electric
Energy supplier
1960 · Paul Rand · US

In 1960, Rand designed a new
logo for the Westinghouse
Electric Company, founded in
1886. He played with the initial
"W" to create a design sug-
gesting the interlinked points of
a circuit board. The logo could
be adapted for different applications and Rand demonstrated
how it could even be used
in animations. A year later, he
developed a unique corporate
typeface for Westinghouse which,
like the logo, is still in use.

Für den bereits 1886 gegründeten Elektronikkonzern
Westinghouse entwickelte Rand
1960 ein neues Logo, das den
Anfangsbuchstaben „W" zu einem
abstrahierten Schaltkreis macht.
Das Zeichen war in verschiedenen Anwendungsformen einsetzbar, Rand zeigte sogar Möglichkeiten zum Gebrauch in einer
Animation auf. Ein Jahr später
entwickelte er die Hausschrift
des Unternehmens, die, wie
auch das Logo, bis heute verwendet wird.

En 1960, Rand conçut pour
le groupe d'électrotechnique
Westinghouse – dont la fondation
remonte à 1886 – un nouveau
logo qui présentait l'initiale « W »
comme un circuit électrique abstrait. Ce sigle pouvait être utilisé
sous différentes formes : Rand
montra même des possibilités
de l'utiliser dans une animation.
Un an plus tard, le designer
développait la police de caractères de l'entreprise, qui l'utilise
encore aujourd'hui.

IIT Research Institute
Scientific research
1964 · Paul Rand · US

Ford Motor Company
Automobiles (proposed design)
1966 · Paul Rand · US

US Bureau of Indian Affairs
Office for American Indian welfare
1968 · Paul Rand · US

Tipton Lakes
Community association
1980 · Paul Rand · US

American Institute of Graphic Arts
(proposed design)
1982 · Paul Rand · US

Yale University
1985 · Paul Rand · US

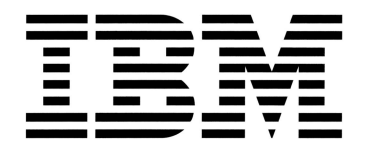

International Business Machines
Technology and
computing solutions
1956/1967 · Paul Rand · US

In 1956, Paul Rand was asked
if he could develop a corporate
identity for the business-machine
developer IBM. Although he had
never before been offered such
a mammoth assignment, he said
he could. He began by designing a new logo and an entire
alphabet in a new, custom-made
typeface. A whole series of other
applications, such as packaging, would follow later. He also
laid down a set of rules for how
the corporation should be represented internationally. The logo
in use today was designed by
Rand in 1967.

Paul Rand wurde 1956 gefragt,
ob er für den Büromaschinen-
hersteller IBM ein Designsystem
entwickeln könne. Obwohl er
einen Auftrag dieser Größe noch
nicht bearbeitet hatte, sagte
er zu und entwickelte zunächst
ein neues Logo samt vollstän-
digem Alphabet. Später folgten
zahlreiche weitere Anwendungs-
möglichkeiten, etwa für Verpackungen, sowie Regeln für das
internationale Auftreten des
Unternehmens. Das Logo in
seiner heute verwendeten Form
gestaltete Rand 1967.

En 1956, on demanda à Paul
Rand s'il pouvait développer un
système graphique pour le fabricant de machines de bureau
IBM. Bien qu'il n'eût encore
jamais traité de commande de
cette envergure, il accepta et
créa d'abord un nouveau logo
et un alphabet complet. Plus
tard suivirent de nombreuses
autres possibilités d'utilisation,
notamment pour des embal-
lages, ainsi que des règles pour
l'identité visuelle internationale
de l'entreprise. Dans sa forme
actuelle, le logo d'IBM a été
développé par Rand en 1967.

IBM *1401 Programming Systems*

P
PR
PRO
PROG
PROGR
PROGRA
PROGRAM
PROGRAMM
PROGRAMMI
PROGRAMMIN
PROGRAMMING

SYSTEMS
YSTEMS
STEMS
TEMS
EMS
MS
S

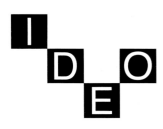

IDEO
Design consultancy
1991 · Paul Rand · US

Morningstar
Investment research
1991 · Paul Rand · US

Creative Media Center
Design
1994 · Paul Rand · US

Gentry Living Color
Foundation
1993 · Paul Rand · US

Computer Impressions
Computers
1995 · Paul Rand · US

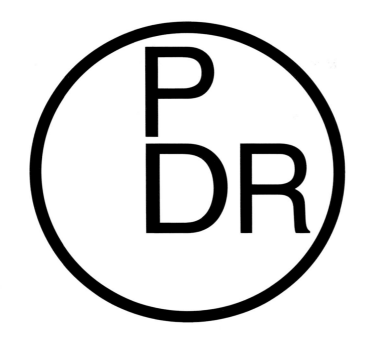

Hub TV
Broadcasting
1995 · Paul Rand · US

Pastore DePamphilis Rampone
Computer graphics
1987 · Paul Rand · US

English First
Language schools
1993 · Paul Rand · US

Enron
Energy supplier
1996 · Paul Rand · US

Le logo est un drapeau, une signature, un blason. Le logo ne fait rien vendre (directement), il identifie. Le logo est rarement la description d'une activité. Le logo tire sa signification de la qualité de ce qu'il symbolise, et non l'inverse. Le logo est moins important que le produit qu'il désigne ; ce qu'il signifie est plus important que son aspect.
Paul Rand

Ein Logo ist eine Flagge, eine Signatur, ein Wappen. Ein Logo verkauft nichts (direkt), es identifiziert. Nur selten beschreibt ein Logo das Unternehmen. Ein Logo erhält seine Bedeutung aus der Qualität dessen, was es symbolisiert, nicht umgekehrt. Ein Logo ist weniger wichtig als das Produkt, für das es steht; sein Gehalt ist wichtiger als seine Optik.
Paul Rand

A logo is a flag, a signature, an escutcheon. A logo doesn't sell (directly), it identifies. A logo is rarely a description of a business. A logo derives its meaning from the quality of the thing it symbolizes, not the other way around. A logo is less important than the product it signifies; what it means is more important than what it looks like.
Paul Rand

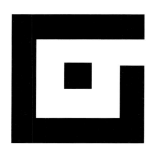

Karol Śliwka was born in 1932 in the village of Harbutowice in Silesia. In 1946, when he was only 14, he began studying painting, sculpture and graphics at night school in the city of Bielsko-Biała. Moving on to the state-run school of art in the early 1950s, he gained a diploma in sculpture and stonemasonry. After completing his studies at the Academy of Fine Arts in Warsaw in 1959, Śliwka decided to make a career in graphic design and opened his own studio in Warsaw. Before long he had successfully completed a large number of assignments. At the same time he competed for and was awarded contracts to create new trademarks. He went on to design postage stamps, posters, packaging and prospectuses for a wide variety of clients in commerce, industry and the cultural sector, and to win awards in national and international competitions. The logo he originally intended for a 1969 poster advertising the Polish bank PKO is still one of the country's best-known trademarks. Śliwka's poster designs won the international competition to design the graphics for the 1980 Moscow Olympics and, four years later, his was also the winning entry in the poster competition for the Olympic Games in Los Angeles. Over the years, he has concentrated more and more on logos. Karol Śliwka lives in Warsaw.

Karol
Śliwka

*1932 · PL

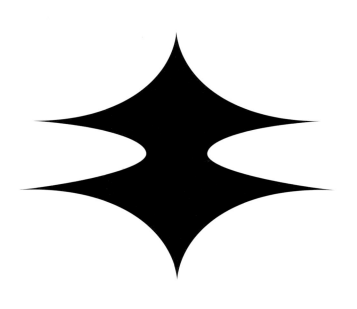

Exhibition of Polish Trademarks
1968 · Karol Śliwka · PL

Ciech
Chemicals
1971 · Karol Śliwka · PL

Mysiadlo
State farm
1971 · Karol Śliwka · PL

Karol Śliwka wurde 1932 in dem schlesischen Dorf Harbutowice geboren. Im Alter von nur 14 Jahren begann er 1946 eine Ausbildung an der Abendschule für Malerei, Bildhauerei und Graphik in Bielsko-Biała. Anfang der 1950er-Jahre wechselte er zur nationalen Kunstschule und erwarb sich dort ein Diplom als Skulpteur und Steinmetz. Schließlich beendete er 1959 sein Studium an der Akademie der Bildenden Künste in Warschau. Śliwka entschloss sich auf dem Feld der angewandten Grafik aktiv zu werden und eröffnete ein eigenes Atelier in Warschau. Bereits nach kurzer Zeit stellte sich der Erfolg ein und zahlreiche Aufträge wurden realisiert. Zudem setzte er sich bei mehreren Wettbewerben durch und gewann zahlreiche Ausschreibungen für neue Markenzeichen. In den folgenden Jahren gestaltete er Briefmarken, Plakate, Verpackungen und Prospekte für unterschiedlichste Auftraggeber aus Wirtschaft, Kultur und Industrie. Auszeichnungen in nationalen und internationalen Wettbewerben folgten. Das eigentlich nur für einen Plakatentwurf angelegte Logo der polnischem Bank PKO entstand 1969 und ist noch heute eines der bekanntesten Signets des Landes. Seine Plakatentwürfe von 1980 setzten sich im internationalen Wettbewerb um Motive für die Olympischen Spiele in Moskau durch, vier Jahre später konnte er diesen Erfolg bei dem Plakatwettbewerb der Spiele von Los Angeles wiederholen. Der Entwurf von Logos blieb über die Jahre Schwerpunkt seines grafischen Schaffens. Karol Śliwka lebt in Warschau.

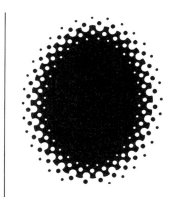

Karol Śliwka est né en 1932 à Harbutowice, un village de Silésie. En 1946, tout juste âgé de quatorze ans, il commence une formation de peintre, sculpteur et graphiste à Bielsko-Biała dans le cadre de cours du soir. Au début des années 1950, il entre à l'École nationale d'Art, d'où il sort avec un diplôme de sculpteur et tailleur de pierre. En 1959, il complète finalement ses études à l'École des Beaux-Arts de Varsovie. Śliwka décide ensuite de travailler dans le domaine du graphisme appliqué et ouvre son propre studio à Varsovie. Il connaît rapidement le succès et reçoit de nombreuses commandes, mais s'impose aussi dans plusieurs concours et gagne de nombreux appels d'offres pour la création de nouveaux logos. Au cours des années suivantes, il réalise des timbres, affiches, emballages et brochures pour différents commanditaires issus de l'économie, de la culture et de l'industrie. Suivent alors des distinctions dans des concours nationaux et internationaux. Le logo de la banque polonaise PKO, initialement conçu pour un projet d'affiche, a vu le jour en 1969 et est aujourd'hui encore un des sigles les plus connus du pays. En 1980, les projets d'affiches de Śliwka se sont imposés dans le cadre du concours international lancé autour de motifs pour les jeux Olympiques de Moscou, succès que le designer réitérera quatre ans plus tard à l'occasion du concours d'affiches des jeux Olympiques de Los Angeles. Pendant toutes ces années, la création de logos n'en est pas moins restée le noyau de son travail graphique. Karol Śliwka vit à Varsovie.

Galux
Glassware
1965 · Karol Śliwka · PL

Z.O.P.Z.
Toys
1966 · Karol Śliwka · PL

Odzież Tarnogórska
Clothing
1965 · Karol Śliwka · PL

Chelmec
Footwear
1967 · Karol Śliwka · PL

Polish Ski Team
Sports team
1965 · Karol Śliwka · PL

Petrolimpex
Fuel oil
1967 · Karol Śliwka · PL

S.P. Powisle
Interior design
1965 · Karol Śliwka · PL

Radoskór
Footwear
1967 · Karol Śliwka · PL

P.S.P.U.W.
Carpentry
1966 · Karol Śliwka · PL

Uroda
Cosmetics
1967 · Karol Śliwka · PL

Reflex
Craft association
1966 · Karol Śliwka · PL

Zakład Obuwniczy Kobra
Footwear
1967 · Karol Śliwka · PL

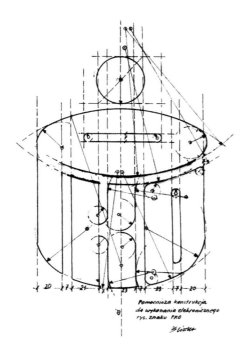

Pomocnicza konstrukcja do wykonania elektronicznego rys. znaku PKO

PKO
Bank
1969 · Karol Śliwka · PL

Every year Poland's PKO bank commissioned a different graphic designer to create a new poster to celebrate World Savings Day in October. Karol Śliwka designed this distinctive poster in 1969 in which he played with the bank's initials to produce a money box into which a coin is being dropped. Awarded the gold medal at the Polish Poster Biennale, the image so delighted PKO management that the bank has used it to this day.

Zum Weltspartag im Oktober gab die polnische Bank PKO jedes Jahr ein neues Werbeplakat bei jeweils einem anderen Grafiker in Auftrag. Karol Śliwka entwarf dieses markante Plakat 1969, bei dem das Buchstabenkürzel der Bank zu einer Spardose wird, in die eine Münze fällt. Die Arbeit erhielt die Goldmedaille der polnischen Plakatbiennale und gefiel auch den Verantwortlichen der Bank so gut, dass daraus das bis heute verwendete Logo des Unternehmens wurde.

Chaque année en octobre, à l'occasion de la Journée mondiale de l'épargne, la banque polonaise PKO commandait une nouvelle affiche publicitaire à un autre graphiste. En 1969, Karol Śliwka dessina cette affiche mémorable qui transformait le sigle de la banque en tirelire. Ce travail reçut la médaille d'or de la Biennale Polonaise de l'Affiche et plut tellement à la direction qu'elle devint le logo de la banque, qui l'a conservé jusqu'à aujourd'hui.

Elektrosprzet
Electronics
1968 · Karol Śliwka · PL

P.I.H.Z. Warsaw
Foreign trade
1968 · Karol Śliwka · PL

Towarzystwo Przyjaciół Warszawy
Friends of Warsaw association
1968 · Karol Śliwka · PL

Wojskowy Hotel Garnizonowy
1968 · Karol Śliwka · PL

Cosmetics
1969 · Karol Śliwka · PL

Liga Kobiet
Women's league
1969 · Karol Śliwka · PL

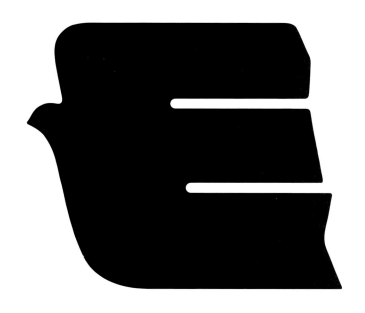

Europejskie Zgromadzenie Studentów
Students association
1974 · Karol Śliwka · PL

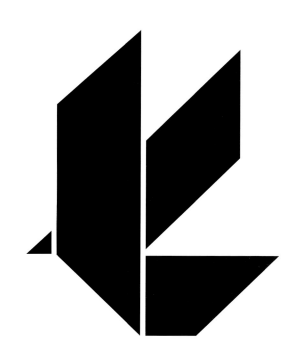

Ministerstwo Komunikacji Polskie
Ministry of communications
1974 · Karol Śliwka · PL

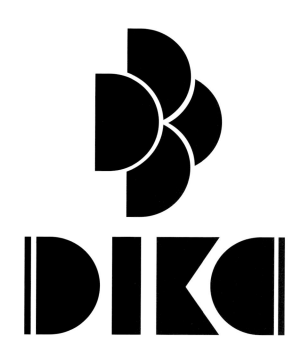

Dika
Import-export
1989 · Karol Śliwka · PL

Walim Fabryka
Textiles
1969 · Karol Śliwka · PL

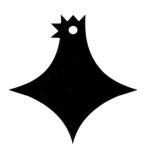

Z.O.P.P.
Souvenir industry trade union
1970 · Karol Śliwka · PL

Technical Institute, Bialystok
Technology research
1970s · Karol Śliwka · PL

Council for Mutual Economic Assistance
Economic organization
1970s · Karol Śliwka · PL

Alina Śliwka
Personal logo
1971 · Karol Śliwka · PL

Zorza
Photographic services
1971 · Karol Śliwka · PL

Zakład Elektronicznej Techniki Obliczeniowej
Computing technology
1972 · Karol Śliwka · PL

Warszawskie Przedsiębiorstwo Geodezyjne
Surveyors
1972 · Karol Śliwka · PL

Pollena
Cosmetics
1973 · Karol Śliwka · PL

Polska Federacja Sportu
Polish sports federation
1973 · Karol Śliwka · PL

Stoleczna Federacja Sportu
Regional sports federation
1974 · Karol Śliwka · PL

Zjednoczenie
Printing
1974 · Karol Śliwka · PL

Aika
Leather
1975 · Karol Śliwka · PL

Uniprod
Community services
1983 · Karol Śliwka · PL

Spółdzielnia Mieszkaniowa
Housing association
1987 · Karol Śliwka · PL

Elektryków Polskich
Electrical engineers association
1976 · Karol Śliwka · PL

Polton
Record label
1984 · Karol Śliwka · PL

Adata
Information technology
1989 · Karol Śliwka · PL

Galeria Plastyka
Art gallery
1977 · Karol Śliwka · PL

Prodex
Polyurethanes
1984 · Karol Śliwka · PL

Hanna Barbera Poland
Animation studio
1989 · Karol Śliwka · PL

Urbanistyki Miasta
Urban planning
1979 · Karol Śliwka · PL

Wydawnictwa Naukowo-Techniczne
Publishing
1984 · Karol Śliwka · PL

Alfa
Chemicals
1990 · Karol Śliwka · PL

Instytut Matki i Dziecka
Medical institute
1980 · Karol Śliwka · PL

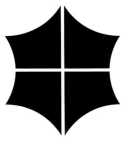

Guild of Leather Craftsmen
1986 · Karol Śliwka · PL

Pacific
Trading
1990 · Karol Śliwka · PL

Polish General Trading Company
1983 · Karol Śliwka · PL

Remed
Medical equipment
1986 · Karol Śliwka · PL

Biocom
Pharmaceuticals
1996 · Karol Śliwka · PL

Je commence par dessiner dans ma tête. Partout où je vais, je me demande : Qu'est-ce que c'est ? Ça se passe où ? Comment aborder la chose ? Quand les idées se cristallisent, je glane des informations sur le sujet sur lequel je travaille. Quand j'arrive à percevoir «l'identité» de l'entreprise, je prends un crayon et du papier.

Karol Śliwka

Meistens fange ich das Zeichnen im Kopf an. Wo immer ich bin, frage ich mich: Was ist es? Wo ist es? Wie mache ich's? Wenn sich die ersten Ideen herauskristallisieren, hole ich aus der Bibliothek ein Nachschlagewerk. Ich sammle Informationen und Material zu meinem Thema. Wenn ich die „Identität" des Unternehmens erfasst habe, greife ich zum Stift.

Karol Śliwka

I usually start from drawing in my mind, and everywhere I am, I think: What is it? Where is it? How can I do this? When a few ideas start to crystallize, I go to the library and get an encyclopedia. I gather information and materials on the subject I am working on. When I've got to know the company's "identity", I take out my pencil and some paper.

Karol Śliwka

AMG Menziken & Gontenschwil
Aluminum
1932 · Anton Stankowski · DE

Sulzer Maschinenfabrik
Machinery
1930s · Anton Stankowski,
Hans Neuburg · DE/CH

Canis Lehrfilme
Educational films
1938 · Anton Stankowski · DE

Klöckner Stahlwerke
Steelworks
1949 · Anton Stankowski · DE

Berga
Curtains
1949 · Anton Stankowski · DE

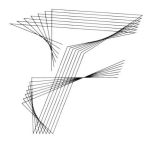

Heinrich Fink Buchdruckerei
Printing
1940s · Anton Stankowski · DE

Anton Stankowski

1906–1998 · DE

Anton Stankowski was born in 1906 in Gelsenkirchen. He served an apprenticeship as a painter of stage sets before becoming a journeyman in a church painter's studio. From 1927 to 1929 he attended the Folkwang School of Art in Essen, where his tutors included Max Burchartz, a pioneer of German graphic design. In 1929 Stankowski moved to Zurich to work in an advertising studio where he first came into contact with Constructivist artists such as Richard Paul Lohse, Herbert Matter and Max Bill. In 1938 he returned to Germany and two years later was drafted for military service, but was soon taken prisoner by Soviet forces and was not released from the PoW camp until 1948. He then spent four years as an editor, graphic artist and photographer for the magazine *Stuttgarter Illustrierte* before finally setting up his own studio in Stuttgart in 1951. He quickly made a name for himself, especially as a designer of trademarks for industrial corporations, and rapidly built up a solid customer base. Within a few years he had to hire more designers and assistants, and his studio became one of Germany's premier addresses for graphic design. Alongside graphic design, Stankowski pursued his interest in Constructivist art, and often the boundaries between his commissioned work and his own artistic projects became blurred. For example, on a number of occasions he used experimental works as illustrations for promotional calendars. He was also commissioned as an interior designer for corporate buildings. His Deutsche Bank logo, designed in 1974 for a competition to create a new brand for the bank, is one of the world's best-known trademarks. When Karl Duschek became a partner in the practice in 1980, Stankowski was able to devote more time to painting. Ever since, the work he did for his own pleasure rather than for clients has been admired in several solo and group exhibitions. Until his death in 1998 Stankowski remained true to his role as an artist who successfully straddled the boundary between working to order and self-expression. His motto continued to be: "Whether it's art or design, it has to be good."

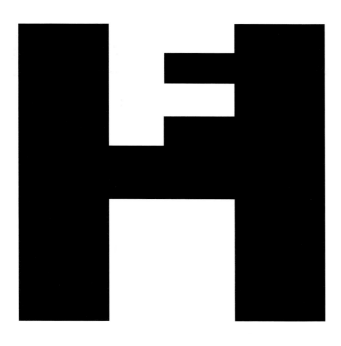

Friedrich Heyking Stahlbau
Steelworks
1953 · Anton Stankowski · DE

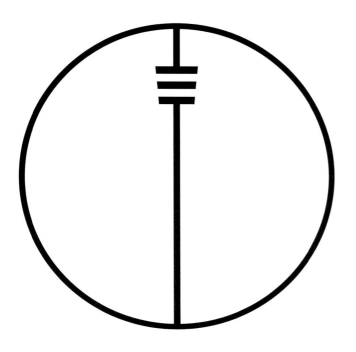

Süddeutscher Rundfunk
Broadcasting
1954 · Anton Stankowski · DE

Dr. O. S. Rechenauer
Management consultancy
1956 · Anton Stankowski · DE

Anton Stankowski wurde 1906 in Gelsenkirchen geboren. Seine Ausbildung begann er bei einem Dekorationsmaler und als Geselle bei einem Atelier für Kirchenkunst. Zwischen 1927 und 1929 studierte er an der Folkwangschule in Essen, u. a. bei Max Burchartz, einem Pionier des deutschen Grafikdesigns. Der Umzug nach Zürich erfolgte 1929, wo er in einem Reklameatelier tätig war und erste Kontakte zu konstruktivistischen Künstlern wie Richard Paul Lohse, Herbert Matter oder Max Bill knüpfen konnte. Er musste 1938 nach Deutschland zurückkehren und wurde zwei Jahre später zum Kriegsdienst eingezogen. Bald darauf geriet Stankowski in russische Kriegsgefangenschaft und kam erst 1948 wieder frei. Danach arbeitete er vier Jahre lang als Schriftleiter, Grafiker und Fotograf bei der *Stuttgarter Illustrierten* und gründete schließlich 1951 ein eigenes Atelier in Stuttgart. Besonders als Entwickler von Markenzeichen für Industrieunternehmen machte er sich schnell einen Namen und konnte einen veritablen Kundenstamm aufbauen. Sein Atelier, in dem er bereits nach wenigen Jahren mehrere Mitarbeiter und Assistenten beschäftigte, wurde zu einer der ersten Adressen für Grafikdesign in Deutschland. Parallel arbeitete Stankowski immer an konstruktivistisch-künstlerischen Arbeiten. Nicht selten war die Grenze zwischen Auftragsarbeit und künstlerischem Projekt fließend. So publizierte er beispielsweise seine experimentellen Arbeiten mehrfach als Werbekalender oder wurde mit künstlerischen Arbeiten für die Gestaltung von Firmengebäuden beauftragt. Mit seinem Logo für die Deutsche Bank, das sich in einem internen Wettbewerb durchsetzte, schuf er 1974 eines der bestbekannten internationalen Markenzeichen. Der Gestalter Karl Duschek wurde 1980 Partner des Ateliers. Stankowski konnte sich nun verstärkt der Malerei widmen. Seine freien Arbeiten wurden spätestens seit dieser Zeit in zahllosen Einzel- und Gruppenausstellungen gewürdigt. Bis zu seinem Tod im Jahr 1998 blieb Stankowski seiner Rolle als Grenzgänger zwischen freien und angewandten Arbeiten treu, gemäß des von ihm selber formulierten Leitspruchs: „Ob Kunst oder Design ist egal – nur gut muss es sein."

Anton Stankowski naît en 1906 à Gelsenkirchen, en Allemagne. Il commence sa formation chez un peintre décorateur, puis comme apprenti dans un atelier d'art d'église. De 1927 à 1929, il suit des études à la Folkwangschule, à Essen, notamment avec Max Burchartz, pionnier du design graphique allemand. En 1929, il s'installe à Zurich, où il travaille dans un atelier de réclames et noue ses premiers liens avec des artistes constructivistes comme Richard Paul Lohse, Herbert Matter ou Max Bill. Contraint de rentrer en Allemagne en 1938, il est mobilisé deux ans plus tard pour le service de guerre. Peu après, il est fait prisonnier de guerre en Russie et ne sera libéré qu'en 1948. À son retour, Stankowski travaille pendant quatre ans comme rédacteur en chef, graphiste et photographe à la *Stuttgarter Illustrierte* avant de fonder finalement son propre atelier en 1951 à Stuttgart. Il se fait rapidement un nom, principalement comme développeur de marques commerciales pour des entreprises industrielles, et parvient à se constituer une véritable clientèle fixe. Son studio, dans lequel il emploie plusieurs collaborateurs et assistants après seulement quelques années, devient une des premières adresses de design graphique en Allemagne. Parallèlement, Stankowski travaille régulièrement à des œuvres artistiques constructivistes, et il n'est pas rare que la frontière entre travail de commande et projet artistique soit perméable : c'est ainsi qu'il publie à plusieurs reprises ses travaux expérimentaux sous forme de calendriers publicitaires ou qu'on lui passe commande d'œuvres artistiques pour décorer des bâtiments industriels. Avec le logo conçu pour la Deutsche Bank, qui s'impose dans le cadre d'un concours interne, il crée en 1974 un des signes les mieux connus au niveau international. En 1980, le graphiste Karl Duschek devient associé de son studio. Stankowski peut alors consacrer davantage de temps à la peinture. Au plus tard à partir de cette époque, son travail indépendant est présenté dans de nombreuses expositions de groupe ou personnelles. Jusqu'à sa mort en 1998, Stankowski est resté fidèle à son rôle de frontalier entre les domaines appliqué et indépendant, conformément à sa devise « Art ou design, peu importe – pourvu que ce soit bon. »

Landwirtschaftlicher Einkauf
Agricultural trade collective
1950 · Anton Stankowski · DE

Haushahn Aufzugfabrik
Elevators
1950s · Anton Stankowski · DE

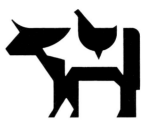

Animal Feed
1950 · Anton Stankowski · DE

Schile
Floor tiler
1955 · Anton Stankowski · DE

Mercedes Zigaretten
Cigarettes
1950s · Anton Stankowski · DE

Pausa
Weaving
1950s · Anton Stankowski · DE

Stolz Werbeplanung
Advertising services
1954 · Anton Stankowski · DE

Spinner
Department store
1953 · Anton Stankowski · DE

Württembergische Bibelanstalt
Publishing
1955 · Anton Stankowski · DE

Gesellschaft für Export und Import
1950s · Anton Stankowski · DE

European Conference of Postal and Telecommunications Administrations
Communications organization
1958 · Anton Stankowski · DE

Iduna Versicherungen
Insurance
1958 · Anton Stankowski · DE

Lührmann Architekten
Architecture
1958 · Anton Stankowski · DE

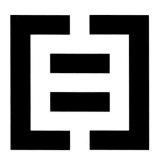

Bürkert Regeltechnik
Control systems engineering
1959 · Anton Stankowski · DE

Deutsche Zeitung, Stuttgart
Newspaper
1959 · Anton Stankowski · DE

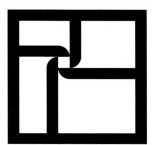

Air-conditioning
1959 · Anton Stankowski · DE

Savag Versicherung
Insurance
1959 · Anton Stankowski · DE

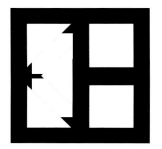

Kornhaus
Textiles
1960s · Anton Stankowski · DE

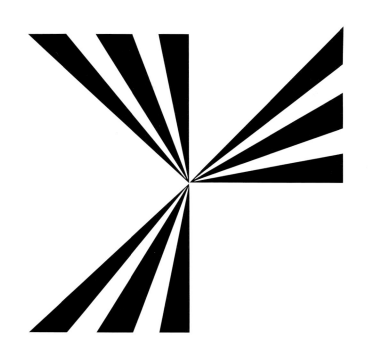

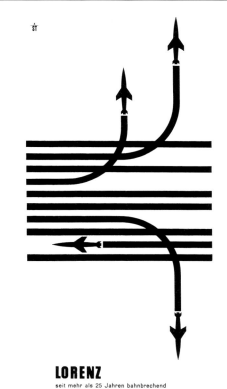

Standard Elektrik Lorenz
Electronics
1955 · Anton Stankowski · DE

Stankowski's 30-year working relationship with SEL made the Stuttgart-based electronics firm his first and most loyal client. In the mid-1950s he designed the company's "starburst" logo, about which he wrote: "The logo expresses the correlation and interaction between sending and receiving. The starting point was a basic symmetrical shape. The result of transforming symmetricality into asymmetricality makes the logo more attention-grabbing and more memorable."

Das Stuttgarter Elektronik-unternehmen SEL war mit einer 30 Jahre anhaltenden Zusammenarbeit einer der ersten und längsten Auftraggeber Stankowskis. Mitte der 1950er-Jahre entstand der sogenannte „Strahlenstern" als Markenzeichen des Unternehmens. Stankowski schrieb dazu: „Das Zeichen drückt die Korrelation und Wechselbeziehung zwischen Senden und Empfangen aus. Ein symmetrisches Grundprinzip war Ausgangspunkt. Die daraus entwickelte asymmetrische Lösung bekommt so einen verstärkten Aufmerksamkeits- und Erinnerungswert."

Avec 30 ans de collaboration suivie, l'entreprise d'électrotechnique SEL sise à Stuttgart a été un des commanditaires de la première heure et les plus constants de Stankowski. Au milieu des années 1950 fut créée « l'étoile branchue », logo de l'entreprise à propos duquel Stankowski a pu écrire : « Ce signe exprime la corrélation et l'interaction entre émission et réception. Au départ, il y a eu un principe fondamentalement symétrique. La solution asymétrique qui en a résulté se charge ainsi d'un effet d'attention et de remémoration accru. »

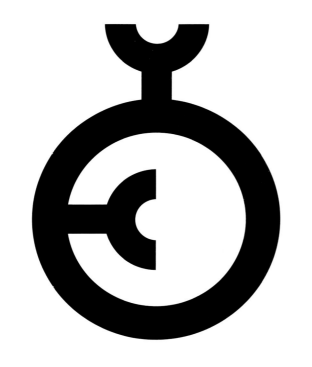

Rat für Formgebung
Design council
1960 · Anton Stankowski · DE

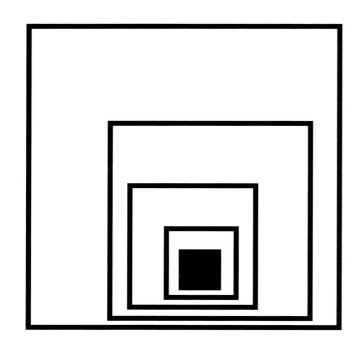

Planen und Wohnen
Interior design
1960s · Anton Stankowski · DE

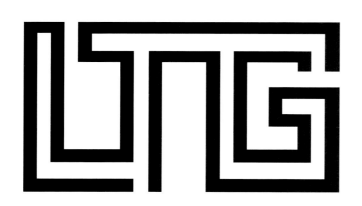

LTG Lufttechnische Gesellschaft
Air-conditioning
1962 · Anton Stankowski · DE

Zweites Deutsches Fernsehen
Broadcasting (proposed design)
1960 · Anton Stankowski · DE

Viessmann
Heating technology
1960 · Anton Stankowski · DE

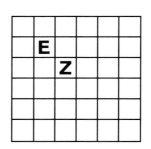

Skol
Liquor
1960 · Anton Stankowski · DE

EZ – Gütezeichen für Fertigbauteile
Prefabricated building materials
1963 · Anton Stankowski · DE

Behr Möbel
Furniture
1963 · Anton Stankowski · DE

Casserole
Food stores
1965 · Anton Stankowski · DE

Walter Beck Meßtechnik
Measuring technology
1965 · Anton Stankowski · DE

Gavas
Injection molding
1965 · Anton Stankowski · DE

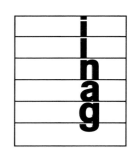

Ilnag
Roller shutters
1965 · Anton Stankowski · DE

Vetega
Trade organization
1966 · Anton Stankowski · DE

Das Bunte Blatt
Magazine
1967 · Anton Stankowski · DE

Reproduktionsmaschinen AG
Reprographics
1960s · Anton Stankowski · DE

werk bund

Deutscher Werkbund
German association
of craftsmen
1963 · Anton Stankowski · DE

The Deutsche Werkbund is an association of artists, architects, designers and industrialists that was founded in 1907. When Stankowski was commissioned to design a new logo in 1963, the organization had 14 independent regional branches. His design solution consisted of the words "Werk" and "Bund," which could be changed through color variations and different positioning of the two syllables. The image reflected the centralized as well as the decentralized nature of the association. The logo is still in use today.

Der Deutsche Werkbund ist eine wirtschaftskulturelle Vereinigung von Künstlern, Architekten, Unternehmern und Sachverständigen, die bereits 1907 gegründet wurde. Als Stankowski 1963 mit dem Entwurf eines neuen Signets beauftragt wurde, hatte der Werkbund 14 unabhängige Landesverbände. Seine Lösung bestand in einer kombinierten Wortmarke, die sich durch unterschiedliche Platzierung und Farbigkeit verändern ließ. Als visuelle Synthese wurde Zentralisation und Dezentralisation des Vereins widergespiegelt. Bis heute ist sein Logo in Verwendung.

Le Deutscher Werkbund, regroupement économique et culturel d'artistes, architectes, entrepreneurs et experts a été fondé dès 1907. En 1963, au moment où Stankowski est chargé d'en concevoir le nouveau signet, le Werkbund compte déjà 14 associations indépendantes œuvrant chacune dans le cadre d'un Land. Sa solution graphique fut une marque combinée pouvant être modulée en termes de disposition et de couleurs. La synthèse visuelle traduisait le caractère centralisé et décentralisé du Werkbund.

Stadt Hamburg
City identity (proposed design)
1968 · Anton Stankowski · DE

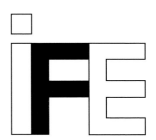

Plus
1967 · Anton Stankowski · DE

IFE Fahrzeugkonstruktion
Automobile design
1968 · Anton Stankowski · DE

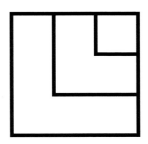

**Rationalisierungskuratorium
der Deutschen Wirtschaft**
Trade organization
1968 · Anton Stankowski · DE

BERLIN

Stadt Berlin
City identity
1969 · Anton Stankowski · DE

Trissl Lift
Ski lift
1969 · Anton Stankowski · DE

Deutscher Ring
Insurance
1969 · Anton Stankowski · DE

Stadt Nellingen
City identity
1969 · Anton Stankowski · DE

Söll
Metalworks
1970 · Anton Stankowski · DE

Stadt Brühl
City identity
1971 · Anton Stankowski · DE

Siedlungswerk Wohnungsbau
House construction
1972 · Anton Stankowski · DE

Flughafen Stuttgart
Airport
1972 · Anton Stankowski · DE

Hüller
Machine tools
1973 · Anton Stankowski · DE

**Internationale Messe für
Sanitär Heizung und Klima**
Heating and sanitation trade fair
1974 · Anton Stankowski · DE

Münchner Rück
Insurance
1974 · Anton Stankowski · DE

Pausa Industriefräsen
Milling machinery
1970s · Anton Stankowski · DE

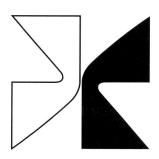

Klinikum Uni Göttingen
University medical institute
1975 · Anton Stankowski · DE

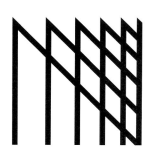

Stahlhochbau RAL-Gütezeichen
Steel engineering
1975 · Anton Stankowski · DE

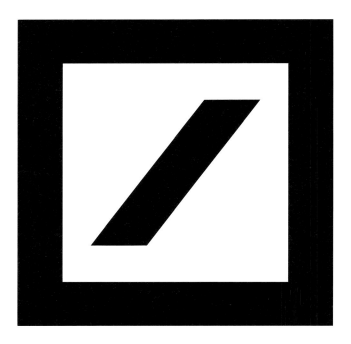

Deutsche Bank
1973 · Anton Stankowski · DE

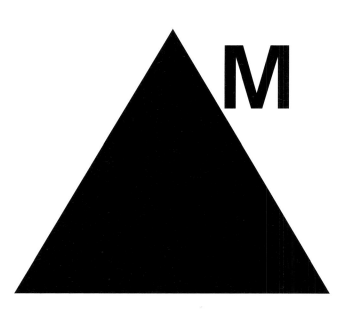

Merkurbergbahn Baden-Baden
Mountain railway
1980 · Anton Stankowski · DE

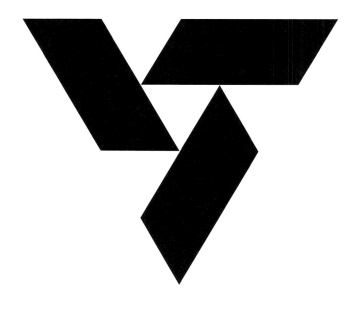

Vereinte Versicherung
Insurance
1986 · Anton Stankowski · DE

Bickenbach Industriebedarf
Industrial supplier
1977 · Anton Stankowski · DE

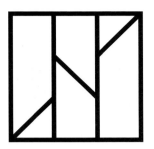

Europalia 77
Arts festival
1977 · Anton Stankowski · DE

Silit
Metal goods
1977 · Anton Stankowski · DE

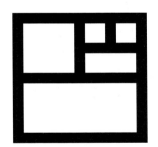

IG Immobiliengesellschaft
Real estate
1979 · Anton Stankowski · DE

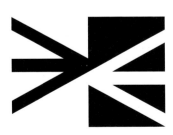

Moeckl Dialog Funkgeräte
Radio equipment
1979 · Anton Stankowski · DE

Kreiskrankenhaus Sigmaringen
Hospital
1980 · Anton Stankowski · DE

Hatje Verlag
Publishing
1980 · Anton Stankowski · DE

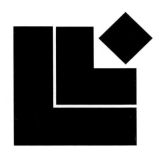

RKW Seminare
Small business workshops
1980 · Anton Stankowski · DE

Treffpunkt Senior
Senior citizens organization
1980 · Anton Stankowski · DE

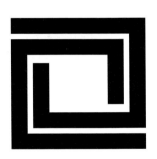

TTW Heizkessel
Heating technology
1980 · Anton Stankowski · DE

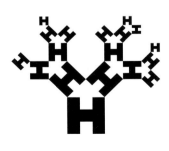

Landesgartenschau Schwäbisch-Hall
Horticultural show
1982 · Anton Stankowski · DE

Basketball Europameisterschaft
European basketball championship
1985 · Anton Stankowski · DE

Deutsches Sportmuseum
Sports museum
1986 · Anton Stankowski · DE

Autohaus Salzmann
Automobile dealer
1987 · Anton Stankowski · DE

BKK Bundesverband der Betriebskrankenkassen
Union of company health insurance funds
1988 · Anton Stankowski · DE

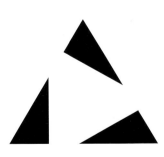

Ingenieurbaupreis Ernst & Sohn
Civil engineering
1988 · Anton Stankowski · DE

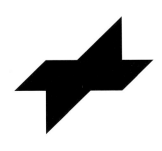

Altana AG
Chemicals
1990 · Anton Stankowski · DE

Eberhard Mayntz
Construction company
1993 · Anton Stankowski · DE

La marque est l'élément le plus important de l'image de l'entreprise. Son caractère prioritaire lui vient notamment du fait qu'en tant que constante publicitaire elle doit avoir un effet intemporel. Elle est à la fois constante visuelle, signal et marqueur.
Anton Stankowski

Die Marke ist das wichtigste Element des Firmenbildes. Sie erhält ihre Priorität auch dadurch, dass sie als Werbe-Konstante zeitlos zu wirken hat. Sie ist visuelle Klammer, Signal und Markierung zugleich.
Anton Stankowski

The brand is the most important element in a company's image. This means that its top priority is its ability to function for all time as a constant promotional tool. It is simultaneously a visual hook, a signal and an identifier.
Anton Stankowski

Créateur Index

Gestalter Index

Designer Index

S

Ackermann, Marion; Rathgeber, Pirkko: *Piktogramme – Die Einsamkeit der Zeichen*; Deutscher Kunstverlag, Stuttgart 2007

Adams, Sean: *Masters of Design.Logos & Identity – A Collection of the Most Inspiring Logo Designers in the World*; Rockport Publishers, Beverly 2008

Aicher, Otl: *The World as Design*; Ernst & Sohn, Berlin 1991

Aicher, Otl; Krampen, Martin: *Zeichensysteme der visuellen Kommunikation – Handbuch für Designer, Architekten, Planer, Organisatoren*; Alexander Koch Verlag, Munich 1980

Amstutz, Walter (ed.): *Who's Who in Graphic Art*; Amstutz & Herdeg Graphis Press, Zurich 1962

Amstutz, Walter (ed.): *Who's Who in Graphic Art, Vol. 2*; Amstutz & Herdeg Graphis Press, Dübendorf 1982

Arcimowicz, Andrzej (ed.): *Karol Śliwka*; Agencja Wydawnicza Agar, Warsaw 2011

Aynsley, Jeremy: *Grafik-Design in Deutschland 1890–1945*; Verlag Hermann Schmidt, Mainz 2000

Baer Capitman, Barbara: *American Trademark Designs*; Dover Publications, Mineola 1976

Baker, Eric; Blik, Tyler (eds.): *American Trademarks – A Compendium*; Chronicle Books, San Francisco 2010

Bakker, Wibo; Kempers, Bram: *Droom van helderheid – huisstijlen, ontwerpbureaus en modernisme in Nederland 1960–1975*; NAi Uitgevers, Rotterdam 2011

Bass, Jennifer; Kirkham, Pat (eds.): *Saul Bass – A Life in Film & Design*; Thames & Hudson, London 2011

Bateman, Steven; Hyland, Angus: *Symbol*; Laurence King Publishing, London 2011

Blauvelt, Andrew; Johnson, Pamela (eds.): *Peter Seitz – Designing a Life*; Minneapolis College of Art & Design, Minneapolis 2007

Blauvelt, Andrew; Lupton, Ellen (eds.): *Graphic Design – Now in Production*; Walker Art Center, Minneapolis 2011

Bos, Ben; Bos, Elly (eds.): *AGI – Graphic Design Since 1950*; Thames & Hudson, London 2007

Bos, Ben; Shaughnessy, Adrian; Brook, Tony (eds.): *TD 63–73 – Total Design and its Pioneering Role in Graphic Design*; Unit Editions, London 2011

Bosoni, Giampiero; Campana, Mara; Moos, Stanislaus von (eds.): *Max Huber*; Phaidon, London 2006

Brändle, Christian; Gimmi, Karin; Junod, Barbara; Reble, Christina; Richter, Bettina: *100 Jahre Schweizer Grafik*; Lars Müller Publishers, Zurich 2014

Braus, Günter; Müller, Rolf (eds.): *HQ – High Quality* (several volumes); Heidelberger Druckmaschinen AG, Heidelberg 1985–98

Bröhan Design Foundation: *Wilhelm Deffke – Pioneer of the Modern Logo*; Scheidegger & Spiess, Zurich 2014

Brüning, Ute (ed.): *Das A und O des Bauhauses – Bauhauswerbung. Schriftbilder, Drucksachen, Ausstellungsdesign*; Bauhaus-Archiv, Leipzig 1995

Bund Deutscher Gebrauchsgraphiker e.V. Landesgruppe Berlin (ed.): *Berliner Gebrauchsgraphiker*; Berlin 1963

Bund Deutscher Gebrauchsgraphiker e.V. Landesgruppe Berlin-Brandenburg (ed.): *XX Eigen-Marken*; Berlin 1921

Bund Deutscher Gebrauchsgraphiker e.V. Landesgruppe Rhein-Main (ed.): *Marken & Zeichen*; Frankfurt am Main 1923

Cabarga, Leslie (ed.): *A Treasury of German Trademarks. Vol. 1 1850–1925*; Art Direction Book Co., New York 1982

Camuffo, Giorgio; Piazza, Mario; Vinti, Carlo (eds.): *TDM5 – Grafica Italiana*; Corraini, Mantua 2012

Chermayeff, Ivan; Geismar, Tom; Geissbuhler, Steff (eds.): *TM – Trademarks Designed by Chermayeff & Geismar*; Lars Müller Publishers, Baden 2000

Chermayeff, Ivan; Geismar, Tom; Geissbuhler, Steff (eds.): *Designing*; Graphis Books, New York 2001

Colizzi, Alessandro; Ossanna Cavadini, Nicoletta: *Heinz Waibl 1931 – Graphic designer, Il viaggio creativo*; Silvana Editoriale, Milan 2014

Conradi, Jan: *Unimark International – The Design of Business and the Business of Design*; Lars Müller Publishers, Baden 2010

Conraths, Hans: *The Creation of the FIAT Logo*; Conraths/Vogt, Basel 2012

Cooper, Al (ed.): *World of Logotypes* (3 volumes); Art Direction Book Co., New York 1976–87

Cotton; Michelle: *Design Research Unit (1942–72)*; Koenig Books, London 2010

Crosby/Fletcher/Forbes (eds.): *A Sign Systems Manual*; Praeger Publishers, New York 1970

Deffke, Wilhelm; Hinkefuss, Carl Ernst: *Handelsmarken und Fabrikzeichen*; Wilhelmswerk, Berlin 1917

Dheer, Sudarshan: *Symbols, Logos and Trademarks – 1500 Outstanding Designs from India*; Dover Publications, Mineola 1998

Diethelm, Walter; Diethelm, Marion; Carmi, Eugenio (eds.): *Signet, Signal, Symbol – Handbuch internationaler Zeichen*; ABC Verlag, Zurich 1984

Dopress Books: *Dynamic Logo*; China Youth Press, Harrow, Middlesex 2013

Durrell, Greg (ed.): *Burton Kramer Identities – A Half Century of Graphic Design (1958–2008)*; Lulu.com 2011

Ehmcke, F.H.: *Wahrzeichen – Warenzeichen*; Verlag Werbedienst, Berlin 1921

Eiber, Rick; Pedersen, B. Martin (eds.): *World Trademarks – An International Collection of Symbol and Logotype Designs of the Last One Hundred Years* (2 volumes); Graphis Press, New York 1996

Effert, Paul: *Paul Effert – Marken-design*; Beineke Dickmanns Druck und Verlag, Kaarst 2000

Evamy, Michael: *Logo*; Laurence King Publishing, London 2007

Evamy, Michael: *Logotype*; Laurence King Publishing, London 2012

Finsterer-Stuber, Gerda (ed.): *Marken und Signete*; Hoffmann Verlag, Stuttgart 1957

Fletcher, Alan; Forbes, Colin; Gill, Bob: *Graphic Design – Visual Comparisons*; Studio Books, London 1963

Friedl, Friedrich; Ott, Nicolaus; Stein, Bernard: *Typographie – Wann Wer Wie*; Könemann, Cologne 1998

Frutiger, Adrian: *Der Mensch und seine Zeichen* (3 volumes); Eidos, Münster 1978–81

Frutiger, Adrian: *Type, Sign, Symbol*; ABC Verlag, Zurich 1980

Frutiger, Adrian: *Nachdenken über Zeichen und Schrift*; Haupt Verlag, Bern 2005

Fukuda, Shigeo (ed.): *Idea Special Issue. Graphic Design in West Germany*; Seibundo Shinkosha, Tokyo 1976

Gauss, Ulrike (ed.): *Anton Stankowski 06 – Aspekte des Gesamtwerks*; Hatje Cantz, Ostfildern-Ruit 2006

Geiser, Roger; Verband Schweizerische Grafiker VSG (eds.): *Schweizer Grafiker*; Käser, Zurich 1960

Gejko, Fjodor; Malsy, Victor; Teufel, Philipp (eds.): *Helmut Schmid – Gestaltung ist Haltung/Design is Attitude*; Birkhäuser Verlag, Basel 2013

Gerstner, Karl: *Programme entwerfen*; Niggli, Teufen 1963

Gerstner, Karl; Kutter, Markus: *Die neue Grafik*; Niggli, Teufen 1959

Gil, Emilio: *Pioneers of Spanish Graphic Design*; Mark Batty Publishers, New York 2009

Ginkel, Dirk van; Hefting, Paul: *Ben Bos – Design of a Lifetime*; BIS Publishers, Amsterdam 2000

Gluck, Felix; Mercer, Frank A.; Moody, Ella (eds.): *Modern Publicity – Issue of Art and Industry's International Annual of Advertising Art* (several volumes); Studio Vista, London 1930–86

Golden, Cipe Pineles; Strunsky, Robert; Weihs, Kurt (eds.): *The Visual Craft of William Golden*; George Braziller, New York 1962

Grignani, Manuela; Guerra, Leo; Quadrio Curzio, Cristina: *Franco Grignani – Alterazioni ottico mentali 1929–1999*; Allemandi, Turin 2014

Heller, Steven: *Paul Rand*; Phaidon, London 1999

Henrion, FHK: *Design Coordination and Corporate Image*; Studio Vista, London 1967

Henrion, FHK: *Top Graphic Design*; ABC Verlag, Zurich 1983

Herdeg, Walter (ed.): *Graphis* (several volumes); Graphis Press, Zurich 1944–86

Herdeg, Walter (ed.): *Graphis Annual* (several volumes); Graphis Press, Zurich 1952–86

Herdeg, Walter (ed.): *Schweizer Signete – Eine Auswahl der sinnfälligsten und schönsten modernen Schutzmarken, Signete, Drucker- und Verlegerzeichen*; Amstutz & Herdeg, Zurich 1948

Herman, Leonard: *Die Heraldik der Wirtschaft – Geschichte, Gestaltung und Wirkung moderner Warenzeichen*; Econ Verlag, Düsseldorf 1971

Hess, Dick; Muller, Marion: *Dorfsman & CBS*; American Showcase, New York 1987

Hillebrand, Henri (ed.): *Graphic Designers in Europe. Vol. 4 (Franco Grignani, Heinz Edelmann, Jacques Richez, Celestino Piatti)*; Universe Books, New York 1973

Hofmann, Armin: *Methodik der Form- und Bildgestaltung. Aufbau, Synthese, Anwendung*; Niggli, Teufen 1965

Hollis, Richard: *Graphic Design – A Concise History*; Thames & Hudson, London 1994

Hollis, Richard: *Swiss Graphic Design – The Origins and Growth of an International Style (1920–1965)*; Yale University Press, New Haven 2006

Hölscher, Eberhard (ed.): *Gebrauchsgraphik – International Advertising Art* (several volumes); Bruckmann, Munich 1950–90

Hölscher, Eberhard (ed.): *Deutsche Gebrauchsgrafik*; Bruckmann, Munich 1967

Ibou, Paul (ed.): *Logobook Paul Ibou – 200 Trademarks and Symbols*; Interecho Press, Zandhoven 1990

Ibou, Paul (ed.): *Banking Symbols Collection* (2 volumes); Interecho Press, Zandhoven 1990/91

Ibou, Paul (ed.): *Famous Animal Symbols* (2 volumes); Interecho Press, Zandhoven 1991/92

Ibou, Paul (ed.): *Logo World – Flanders Logo World Symbol Festival*; Interecho Press, Zandhoven 1995

ICTA Sektion Deutschland: *Report 65 – Jahresbericht des ICTA Sektion Deutschland*; Bad Homburg, 1966

Igarashi, Takenobu (ed.): *Idea Special Issue. European Trademarks & Logotypes*; Seibundo Shinkosha, Tokyo 1979

Ishihara, Yoshihisa (ed.): *Idea Special Issue. Who's Who of European Designers – Belgium, Spain, Czechoslovakia, Poland*; Seibundo Shinkosha, Tokyo 1972

Ishihara, Yoshihisa (ed.): *Idea Special Issue. American Trademarks & Logotypes*; Seibundo Shinkosha, Tokyo 1977

Ishihara, Yoshihisa (ed.): *Designers in Italy – Graphic, Photo, Illustration, Architecture, Product*; Seibundo Shinkosha, Tokyo 1981

Jaaks, Anke (ed.): *Wolfgang Schmidt, Worte und Bilder*; Verlag Hermann Schmidt, Mainz 1992

Jacobson, Egbert (ed.): *Seven Designers Look at Trademark Design*; P. Theobald, Chicago 1952

de Jong, Cees (ed.): *Corporate Identity Handbuch*; Edition Stemmle, Schaffhausen 1990

Jury, David: *Graphic Design Before Graphic Designers – The Printer as Designer and Craftsman 1700–1914*; Thames & Hudson, London 2012

Kamekura, Yusaku: *Trademarks of the World*; George Wittenborn, New York 1960

Kamekura, Yusaku: *Trademarks and Symbols of the World*; Reinhold, New York 1965

Kamekura, Yusaku: *Firmen- und Warenzeichen international*; Otto Maier Verlag, Ravensburg 1966

Kamekura, Yusaku: *The Graphic Design of Yusaku Kamekura*; Weatherhill, New York 1973

Kapitzki, Herbert W.: *Programmiertes Gestalten – Grundlagen für das Visualisieren mit Zeichen*; Gitzel, Karlsruhe 1980

Kapitzki, Herbert W.: *Design – Method and Consequence, A Biographical Report*; Menges, Stuttgart 1997

Klemp, Klaus; Koch, Julia; Wagner K, Matthias (eds.): *Alex Wollner Brasil – Design Visual*; Wasmuth, Tübingen 2013

Klemz, Willy: *Markante Firmen Zeichen*; Accidentia Buchdruck, Düsseldorf 1961

Koch, Rudolf: *Das Zeichenbuch*; W. Gerstung, Offenbach 1926

Kraft, K. Siegfried; Verband Bildender Künstler der DDR (ed.): *Die Schutzmarke*; Verlag Die Wirtschaft, Berlin 1970

Kuwayama, Yasaburo: *Trademarks & Symbols* (2 volumes); Van Nostrand Reinhold, New York 1973

Kuwayama, Yasaburo: *Zeichen, Marken und Signets – 3000 internationale Beispiele*; Callwey, Munich 1977

Kuwayama, Yasaburo: *Europäische Markenzeichen*; Nippan Verlag, Düsseldorf 1992

Lohrer, Hanns: *Hanns Lohrer – Ein visueller Lebenslauf*; Cantz, Stuttgart 1989

Maiwald, Heinrich; Wannemacher, Alois (eds.): *Graphik – Konjunktur, Werbung & Formgebung* (several volumes); Maiwald Verlag, Stuttgart 1948–1956

Märkte und Medien Verlagsgesellschaft: *Porträts Deutscher Grafik Designer* (4 volumes); Märkte und Medien, Hamburg 1972–75

Meggs, Philip B.; Purvis, Alston W.: *Meggs' History of Graphic Design* (5th edition); John Wiley & Sons, New York 2011

Meldau, Robert: *Zeichen, Warenzeichen, Marken – Kulturgeschichte und Werbewert graphischer Zeichen*; Verlag Gehlen, Bad Homburg 1967

Mendenhall, John: *Early Modernism. Swiss & Austrian Trademarks 1920–1950*; Chronicle Books, San Francisco 1997

Meshki, Saed; Sayfouri, Bijan (eds.): *The Book of Signs – Iranian Graphic Design*; Yassavoli Publications, Tehran 1996

Mollerup, Per: *Marks of Excellence – The History and Taxonomy of Trademarks*; Phaidon, London 1999

Müller, Jens (ed.): *A5/07. Rolf Müller – Stories, Systems, Marks*; Lars Müller Publishers, Zurich 2014

Müller, Jens; Weiland, Karen: *FilmKunstGrafik – Ein Buch zur neuen deutschen Filmgrafik*; Deutsches Filminstitut, Frankfurt am Main 2007

Müller, Jens; Weiland, Karen (eds.): *A5/05. Lufthansa + Graphic Design – Visual History of an Airline*; Lars Müller Publishers, Baden 2011

Müller, Lars (ed.): *Josef Müller-Brockmann – Gestalter*; Lars Müller Publishers, Baden 1994

Müller, Lars (ed.): *Neue Grafik. New Graphic Design. Graphisme actuel 1958–1965*; Lars Müller Publishers, Zurich 2015

Müller-Brockmann, Josef: *Geschichte der visuellen Kommunikation*; Gerd Hatje, Stuttgart 1971

Museo de Bellas Artes: *Gerd Leufert Diseñador*; Caracas 1976

Nakanishi, Motoo; Cocomas Committee (eds.): *Basic Design Elements and Their Systems – Design Systems for Corporations*; Institute of Business Administration & Management, Tokyo 1976/77

Nakanishi, Motoo; Cocomas Committee (eds.): *Corporate Design Systems 1*; Sanno, Tokyo 1979

Nakanishi, Motoo; Cocomas Committee (eds.): *Corporate Design Systems 2*; PBC International, New York 1985

van Nes, Irene (ed.): *Dynamic Identities – How to Create a Living Brand*; BIS Publishers, Amsterdam 2013

Neuburg, Hans: *Moderne Werbe- und Gebrauchs-Grafik*; Otto Maier Verlag, Ravensburg 1960

Ohta, Tetsuya: *Changes in Logos & Trademarks in Japan*; Rikuyo-sha, Tokyo 1989

Osterer, Heidrun; Stamm, Philipp: *Adrian Frutiger – Schriften. Das Gesamtwerk*; Birkhäuser Verlag, Basel 2008

Pedersen, B. Martin: *Graphis Corporate Identity 1: Visual Corporate Identities*; Graphis Press, Zurich 1989

Pentagram Partners (ed.): *Pentagram Marks*; Laurence King Publishing, London 2010

Pentagram Partners; Gorb, Peter (eds.): *Living by Design*; Lund Humphries, London 1978

Piazza, Mario (ed.): *La Grafica del Made in Italy – Comunicazione e aziende del design 1950–1980* (2nd edition); Aiap Edizioni, Milan 2012

Polano, Sergio; Vetta, Pierpaolo (eds.): *ABC of 20th-Century Graphics*; Electa Architecture, Milan 2002

Rand, Paul: *A Designer's Art*; Yale University Press, New Haven 1988

Rand, Paul: *From Lascaux to Brooklyn*; Yale University Press, New Haven 1996

Ray, Peter (ed.): *Designers in Britain*; Society of Industrial Artists, London 1947

Rechenauer, Ottmar; Stankowski, Anton: *Firmen-Image*; Econ, Düsseldorf 1969

Remington, R. Roger: *American Modernism – Graphic Design 1920–1960*; Yale University Press, New Haven 2003

Ricci, Franco Maria; Ferrari, Corinna (eds.): *Top Symbols and Trademarks of the World* (11 volumes); Deco Press, Milan 1973–83

Rouard-Snowman, Margo: *Jean Widmer – graphiste, un écologiste de l'image*; Editions du Centre Pompidou, Paris 1995

Schäfer, Detmar: *Pelikan – Die Marke. Wie das Küken ins Nest kam und wann wie viele*; Leuenhagen & Paris, Hannover 2013

Schmid, Helmut: *Typography Today*; Seibundo Shinkosha, Tokyo 1980

Schmidt, Klaus (ed.): *Corporate Identity in Europe*; Campus, Frankfurt am Main 1994

Schmittel, Wolfgang: *Design, Concept, Realisation*; ABC Verlag, Zurich 1975

Schmittel, Wolfgang: *Process Visual – Development of a Corporate Identity*; ABC Verlag, Zurich 1978

Schmittel, Wolfgang: *Corporate Design International – Definition and Benefit of a Consistent Corporate Appearance*; ABC Verlag, Zurich 1984

Sekiguchi, Yoshinobu (ed.): *Morton Goldsholl – A Review, 40 Years of Work*; Graphic-Sha Publishing, Tokyo 1987

Shaughnessy, Adrian; Brook, Tony (eds.): *Ken Garland – Structure and Substance*; Unit Editions, London 2012

Shaughnessy, Adrian; Brook, Tony (eds.): *FHK Henrion – The Complete Designer*; Unit Editions, London 2013

Shaughnessy, Adrian; Brook, Tony (eds.): *Manuals – Design & Identity Guidelines* (2 volumes); Unit Editions, London 2014

Sinclair, Mark: *TM – The Untold Stories Behind 29 Classic Logos*; Laurence King Publishing, London 2014

Sluiters, Tim (ed.): *Hans Karl Rodenkirchen – Eine grafische Reise ins Bergische Land*; labor visuell, Düsseldorf 2012

Stancheva, Magdalina: *Logo Book Stefan Kanchev*; Zhanet45, Sofia 2012

Stankowski Stiftung: *Der Kreis um Anton Stankowski – Ob Kunst oder Design ist egal – nur gut muss es sein*; avedition, Stuttgart 2010

Stigulinszky, Roland (ed.): *BDG 1919–1994 – Per aspera 75 Jahre Arbeit für einen künstlerischen freien Beruf*; Bund Deutscher Grafik-Designer, Düsseldorf 1994

Ströhl, Hugo Gerard: *Heraldischer Atlas*; J. Hoffmann, Stuttgart 1899

Teunissen van Manen, Teun: *Handboek voor het programmeren van de visuele uitingen van de ploeg*, Van Weverij de Ploeg, Bergeijk 1968

Thiemig, Karl (ed.): *Graphik – Werbung & Formgebung* (several volumes); Thiemig Verlag, Stuttgart 1957–71

Tippach-Schneider, Simone: *Das grosse Lexikon der DDR-Werbung*; Schwarzkopf & Schwarzkopf, Berlin 2002

Urban, Dieter: *Novum Press. Zeichen + Signets – Eine Sammlung internationaler Beispiele*; Bruckmann Verlag, Munich 1982

Urban, Dieter: *Novum Press. Markenzeichen + Firmensignets*; Bruckmann Verlag, Munich 1991

Verlag des deutschen Buchgewerbevereins: *Archiv für Buchgewerbe und Gebrauchsgraphik* (several volumes); Leipzig 1922–43

Verlag Die Wirtschaft: *Neue Werbung – Fachzeitschrift für Theorie und Praxis der sozialistischen Werbung*; Berlin 1954–91

Vignelli, Massimo: *The Vignelli Canon*; Lars Müller Publishers, Baden 2010

van der Vlugt, Ron: *Logo Life – Life Histories of 100 Famous Logos*; BIS Publishers, Amsterdam 2012

Vogt, Armin: *Eine Art Bilanz*; Chamaeleon Verlag, Basel 2006

Waser, Jack (ed.): *Siegfried Odermatt & Rosmarie Tissi – Graphic Design*; Waser, Zurich 1993

Webb, Brian: *FHK Henrion – Design*; Antique Collectors Club, London 2011

Weidemann, Kurt (ed.): *Der Druckspiegel – Ein Archiv für deutsches und internationales grafisches Schaffen* (several volumes); Blersch, Stuttgart 1950–70

Wendt, Hermann: *Warenzeichen-Fibel – Praktische Anwendung des Warenzeichen- und Ausstattungsschutzes*; Verlag Chemie, Weinheim/Bergstraße 1964

Wenzel, Erich (ed.): *Werbeform 2*; Scherpe, Krefeld 1958

Wiese, Bruno K.: *Bruno K. Wiese – Visual Design*; Fachhochschule Kiel, Kiel 1987

Wildbur, Peter: *Trademarks – A Handbook of International Designs*; Littlehampton Book Services, Faraday 1966

Wildbur, Peter: *International Trademark Design – A Handbook of Marks of Identity*; Barrie & Jenkins, London 1979

Willberg, Hans Peter (ed.): *Walter Breker – Marken und 'Marken'*; Gebrüder Mann Verlag, Berlin 1984

Wills, Franz Hermann: *Bildmarken, Wortmarken*; Econ, Düsseldorf 1968

Wlassikoff, Michel: *The Story of Graphic Design in France*; Gingko Press, Corte Madera 2005

Country Codes

Länderkürzel

Codes des pays

AR	Argentina
AT	Austria
AU	Australia
BE	Belgium
BG	Bulgaria
BR	Brazil
CA	Canada
CH	Switzerland
CN	China
CO	Colombia
CU	Cuba
CZ	Former Czechoslovakia
DE	Germany
DE-GDR	Former German Democratic Republic
DK	Denmark
ES	Spain
FI	Finland
FR	France
GR	Greece
HK	Hong Kong
HU	Hungary
IE	Ireland
IL	Israel
IN	India
IR	Iran
IS	Iceland
IT	Italy
JP	Japan
KR	South Korea
MX	Mexico
NL	Netherlands
NO	Norway
PL	Poland
PT	Portugal
RU	Russia
SE	Sweden
SI	Slovenia
TH	Thailand
TR	Turkey
TW	Taiwan
UK	United Kingdom
US	United States
YU	Former Republic of Yugoslavia
VE	Venezuela

Thanks
Danke
Merci

My warmest thanks go to all the designers whose work is represented in the book. My aim was to pay tribute to their splendid achievements in the field of logo design. I would like to thank those with whom I came into direct personal contact for giving me valuable insights into their working methods, for their expert advice and entertaining background stories, and for providing illustrations. My special thanks go to Brigitte Aust, Hanns Eckelkamp, Erich Frutiger, Fritz Gottschalk, Paul Ibou, Burton Kramer, Rolf Müller (†), Daisuke Nitta, Katharina Roller, Karol Śliwka, Tim Sluiters, Monika Solinas, Magdalina Stancheva, Marion Wesel-Henrion, Armin Vogt and Lance Wyman.

With regard to the publishers, I should like to offer Julius Wiedemann my heartfelt thanks for being so enthusiastic about my collection and my ideas for the book. I should also like to thank Daniel Siciliano Bretas and Nora Dohrmann for managing the project and for their creative input, and Stefan Klatte, who was in charge of its production.

My thanks also go to Marvin Hüttermann and Caroline Kryzecki, who worked on the layout and undertook the complex task of image processing; and to R. Roger Remington for contributing a superb essay on modernism. I should also like to thank Victor Malsy and Philipp Teufel, with whom I studied and who sparked my special interest in the history of design. My very personal thanks go to my partner Katharina Sussek for her professional advice and all-important support and patience throughout the project.

Mein herzlicher Dank gilt allen im Buch vertretenen Gestalterinnen und Gestaltern. Es war mir ein Anliegen ihre großartigen Leistungen auf dem Gebiet des Logoentwurfs zu würdigen. Denjenigen, mit denen ich persönlich im Kontakt war, danke ich für wertvolle Einblicke in ihre Arbeitsweise, fachlichen Rat, launige Hintergrundgeschichten sowie die Bereitstellung von Abbildungen. Besonders danke ich Brigitte Aust, Hanns Eckelkamp, Erich Frutiger, Fritz Gottschalk, Paul Ibou, Burton Kramer, Rolf Müller (†), Daisuke Nitta, Katharina Roller, Karol Śliwka, Tim Sluiters, Monika Solinas, Magdalina Stancheva, Marion Wesel-Henrion, Armin Vogt und Lance Wyman.

Auf Seiten des Verlags danke ich Julius Wiedemann, der sich von meiner Sammlung und der Idee für dieses Buch begeistern ließ. Außerdem danke ich Daniel Siciliano Bretas und Nora Dohrmann, die das Projekt mit kreativem Input gesteuert haben, sowie Stefan Klatte, der die Herstellung des Buches übernahm.

Weiter danke ich Marvin Hüttermann und Caroline Kryzecki für die Hilfe beim Layout sowie der aufwendigen Bildbearbeitung; R. Roger Remington für ein großartiges Essay zum Thema Modernismus; Victor Malsy und Philipp Teufel, die mich während meines Studiums für das Gebiet der Designgeschichte begeisterten. Mein ganz persönlicher Dank gilt meiner Freundin Katharina Sussek, die dieses Projekt mit professionellem Rat und mich mit unerlässlicher Geduld begleitet hat.

Mes remerciements s'adressent aux graphistes représentés dans ce livre. J'ai eu à cœur de rendre hommage à leurs extraordinaires réalisations dans le domaine de la création de logos. Je remercie tous ceux avec qui j'ai été personnellement en contact pour leurs précieuses explications concernant leur démarche, leurs conseils avisés, leurs anecdotes d'humeur et la mise à disposition des reproductions. Je tiens à remercier tout particulièrement Brigitte Aust, Hanns Eckelkamp, Erich Frutiger, Fritz Gottschalk, Paul Ibou, Burton Kramer, Rolf Müller (†), Daisuke Nitta, Katharina Roller, Karol Śliwka, Tim Sluiters, Monika Solinas, Magdalina Stancheva, Marion Wesel-Henrion, Armin Vogt et Lance Wyman.

Côté édition, je remercie chaleureusement Julius Wiedemann, qui s'est passionné pour ma collection et mes idées pour ce livre. Je remercie aussi Daniel Siciliano Bretas et Nora Dohrmann, qui ont dirigé le projet, ainsi que Stefan Klatte, qui s'est chargé de la fabrication.

Mes remerciements vont enfin à Marvin Hüttermann et Caroline Kryzecki, qui ont aidé au travail considérable réalisé sur les images, à R. Roger Remington essai sur la modernité, ainsi qu'à Victor Malsy et Philipp Teufel, qui ont su nourrir ma passion pour l'histoire du design pendant mes études. Pour finir, j'adresse des remerciements tout à fait personnels à mon amie Katharina Sussek, qui a accompagné ce projet de son professionnalisme et d'une patience sans faille.

Imprint

Mentions légales

Impressum

To stay informed about TASCHEN and our upcoming titles, please subscribe to our free magazine at www.taschen.com/magazine, follow us on Instagram and Facebook, or e-mail your questions to contact@taschen.com.

© 2020 TASCHEN GmbH
Hohenzollernring 53
D-50672 Köln
www.taschen.com

Picture Credits
p. 10: SLUB Dresden/
Deutsche Fotothek
pp. 18/19: Herzog Anton-Ulrich-Museum Braunschweig, photo: Claus Cordes

Design
Jens Müller/vista
www.studiovista.de

English Translation
Isabel Varea Riley for
Grapevine Publishing Services

German Translation
Ursula Wulfekamp for
Grapevine Publishing Services

French Translation
Wolf Fruhtrunk

Printed in Italy
ISBN 978-3-8365-4530-3